Privacy Rights

Privacy Rights

Cases Lost and Causes Won Before the Supreme Court

Alice Fleetwood Bartee

ROWMAN & LITTLEFIELD PUBLISHERS, INC.
Lanham • *Boulder* • *New York* • *Toronto* • *Oxford*

ROWMAN & LITTLEFIELD PUBLISHERS, INC.

Published in the United States of America
by Rowman & Littlefield Publishers, Inc.
A wholly owned subsidiary of The Rowman & Littlefield Publishing Group, Inc.
4501 Forbes Boulevard, Suite 200, Lanham, Maryland 20706
www.rowmanlittlefield.com

P.O. Box 317, Oxford OX2 9RU, UK

British Library Cataloguing in Publication Information Available

Library of Congress Cataloging-in-Publication Data

Bartee, Alice Fleetwood.
  Privacy rights : cases lost and causes won before the Supreme Court / Alice
Fleetwood Bartee.
    p.   cm.
  Includes bibliographical references and index.
  ISBN-13: 978-0-7425-5319-4 (cloth : alk. paper)
  ISBN-10: 0-7425-5319-1 (cloth : alk. paper)
  ISBN-13: 978-0-7425-5320-0 (pbk. : alk. paper)
  ISBN-10: 0-7425-5320-5 (pbk. : alk. paper)
    1. Civil rights—United States—Cases. 2. Privacy, Right of—United States—Cases.
3. United States. Supreme Court—Cases. 4. Judicial process—United States—Cases.
5. Political questions and judicial power—United States—Cases. I. Title.
KF4749.B337 2006
342.7308'58—dc22

                                                                    2005035908

Printed in the United States of America

⊗™ The paper used in this publication meets the minimum requirements of
American National Standard for Information Sciences—Permanence of Paper
for Printed Library Materials, ANSI/NISO Z39.48-1992.

For Wayne
Who Makes the Impossible, Possible

Contents

Acknowledgments

This book has been a long time in the making as I have waited for changes on the Supreme Court to produce decisions that would turn cases lost into causes won. Privacy issues will always be in flux, and, while at this moment many positive developments have occurred, the country is still divided. Those who oppose privacy rights are organized, vocal, and politically powerful.

As I waited for the most opportune moment when privacy rights seemed to be at the highest point, I found that the list of those who helped in making this book possible was growing enormously. While I can never name all who have assisted, I would like to mention a few. My graduate research assistants Steven A. Craig, Martha Morrison Clark, Amy Slavin, Kristen Straw, Donna Farr, Kimberly Balcos, Stephen Sporn, ND, and Gary Estensen have undertaken tasks from research to editorial production. I also want to thank my former student Kimberly Ross, who, as paralegal for attorney William Colby, gave me access to original documents in the *Cruzan* case. Willa Garrett was invaluable in her position as de facto law librarian in a university without a law school. Supreme Court librarian Brian Stiglmeier was gracious in making early materials from the 1940s available to me. I also appreciate the encouragement of Dr. Del Dickson concerning judicial conference decision making.

Attorney Richard Schnake, an expert on Missouri appellate practice, supplied historical data and kept me on track when dealing with Missouri law and practice. For medical advice and problem solving, I am indebted to Dr. Norman Knowlton III, Dr. Marion Wolf, and Christopher Crane, R.Ph., for their assistance.

Two major scholars who have influenced my work are Professor Walter Murphy and Professor Lee Epstein. Their models have inspired me and justified the approach I have used to study the judicial process.

I owe a profound intellectual debt of gratitude to Professor Alan F. Westin of Columbia University (New York City). As my mentor, he introduced me to issues centering on privacy and freedom. His seminal book bearing that title has remained a classic; it has impacted my research agenda tremendously as I attempted to relate privacy cases to the judicial process and to assess privacy and freedom in the area of morals.

Missouri State University has been generous with the award of released time, graduate assistants, and technicians. I am grateful for this support. My publishers have likewise provided enthusiastic support from the beginning. I am indebted to Mr. Chris Anzalone, Ms. Jennifer Knerr, Ms. Renee Legatt, and Ms. Jennifer Nemec, production editor, of Rowman & Littlefield, who improved both the form and style of the book. Finally, I would like to thank the anonymous reviewers hired by Rowman & Littlefield who made suggestions that have resulted in a much better book.

Preface

"We only win by losing" may not be a popular idea in an American culture addicted to success.[1] No one enjoys this prospect of being tagged as a "loser." However, the process of losing can be instructive for those committed to ideological causes and who are willing to "try and try again." Defeated leaders, a noted scholar tells us, provide models for analyzing causes for defeat as a beginning of renewed efforts.[2] Defeat itself may often carry with it the seeds of victory. This is true not only of the political process but also of the judicial process. Jurisprudence is uniquely suited for a study of losers and why they lost. Within the judicial process are a multitude of actors, conflicts, and levels of decision making. The courtroom setting offers a central stage for bringing to life litigants and their controversies. Attorneys, jurors, and judges become the actors. The play is acted out under the rules set by the Constitution and by laws. Each of these elements presents a doorway to analysis of defeat at particular stages of the process. The judicial process also opens a door to change: losers may ultimately become winners in the American legal system. In wartime, losing battles may be disastrous, but winning the war is what counts in the end. So it is in the legal field, where contentious issues trigger intense emotions and provoke critical battles that ultimately decide the nature of our democratic society. One of these issues—privacy rights—is today at the center of a "cultural war" that pits the rights of individuals against state regulatory power.[3] The issue is certainly an emotional one; it generates controversy, is ongoing, and evades compromise.

Privacy rights have always been vague and difficult to define. The word *privacy* does not appear in the Constitution, but it is nonetheless perceived as one of our most basic and coveted rights. Yet in the times of crisis, it is one right that Americans seem ready to curtail: security outweighs privacy. Wars have always been a catalyst for such limitations. World War I's Espionage Act gave government the authority to invade even the home, almost at will, and the infamous Palmer Raids under the direction of President Wilson's attorney general put privacy rights at risk. The American Civil Liberties Union was formed in response. World War II generated fears against racial groups and saboteurs at home. Governmental powers expanded to include wiretapping devices, which invaded not only offices and places of business but also the intimate recesses of the home. The Cold War period also generated attacks on privacy rights, as nationalism supplanted individual rights and the McCarthy hearings in Congress encouraged a "Big Brother" mind-set that rewarded spying on friends, business associates, and anyone perceived as being "different." The aftermath of the attacks on New York's Twin Towers and the Pentagon on September 11, 2001, brought the attacks on privacy rights to a new high. Fearing potential terrorist attacks, Americans rushed to embrace the Patriot Act. Government agencies armed with the provisions of this Act, executive orders, and other measures could now legally intrude on individual privacy in various ways, including collection and storage of health data, surreptitious wiretapping, inspection of library records and book sales, and secret detentions, searches, and seizures.[4]

Privacy rights today are at risk in many areas other than just those related to crises generated by wars, by terrorist attacks, and by threats to our cultural identity. Fear of a rising drug war has pitted privacy rights against that of law enforcement. Strip searches as well as investigations of school lockers and students' backpacks have become accepted norms to combat the sale and use of drugs. Big business has also found reasons to invade an individual's privacy. Claiming the need to "provide a safe and productive work environment, not to mention the right to make a profit," employers demand increased knowledge about their employees: their use of prescription and nonprescription medicine, their health records, their credit records, their lifestyle, and their psychological profile. Employers want to weed out employees who are a possible threat to their business interests. Creative technology, including the massive storage of minute data on the populace at large can make this possible, placing privacy rights at risk.[5]

The attacks on privacy rights in themselves give us a definition in action of the meaning of privacy. As governments sanction invasion into the life of the individual at many different levels, the individual loses the "right to be left alone."[6] This is the definition of privacy, according to Samuel Warren and Louis D. Brandeis in their influential article on the subject. The unclear right to privacy was recognized as the "right to be left alone," and it is today the standard Americans raise when they face official invasion of their environment. The Supreme Court has also recognized this "right to be left alone" as a valid defense against government's attempts to regulate home life, including marriage, child rearing, education, and religion.[7] In a series of cases, the

Court linked such rights to the "happiness" enshrined in the Declaration of Independence. Are these true privacy rights? Certainly they encompass areas where individuals claim the right to be left alone. Later Supreme Court decisions indeed used them in defining what came to be called a "privacy of the self."[8] In his classic treatise on *Privacy and Freedom* (1967), Alan F. Westin urged the Court to protect this "privacy of the self" as fundamental. This privacy right was vastly different from those that pitted privacy claims against law enforcement agencies, against the press, against the medical system, or against homeland security agencies. The Court's decisions on the "right to be left alone" in areas of "home life, marriage, child rearing, education, and religion" have set this type of privacy right apart from others.

The controversial and unusual nature of the "privacy of self" made headlines in the United States when, in 1965, the Supreme Court used it to block governmental regulation of sexual activity. An individual's right to possess and use birth control was legitimized by the Supreme Court under this concept of "privacy."[9] It soon expanded this privacy right to cover not only the prevention of pregnancy but also its termination.[10] From the birth arena, privacy rights expanded into yet another arena—that of death. Individuals claimed the right to be left alone during the dying process.[11] Between the beginning and the ending of one's human existence, privacy protection was invoked by those who found "happiness" in same-sex relationships. Thus they too claimed a right to be left alone.[12]

The differences among these types of privacy rights is that the privacy of the self involves issues that are moral and religious in nature. For this reason, they are not like issues connected with Fourth Amendment criminal law proceedings or issues that pit national security, terrorism, workplace, or business interests against claims of individual privacy. The issues of birth control, abortion, sodomy, and right to die are trigger issues at the heart of the culture war engulfing America. They are enduring issues. While defying rational analysis, they nevertheless require it. It is upon these issues of privacy that I have chosen to focus. I believe that we can learn about ourselves and our society as we analyze struggles over these privacy rights of self that have often resulted in a "paradise lost" for some Americans. We learn even more as we face the litigation process that has provided a "paradise regained" for some of these very losers. Moreover, as justices struggle with the choice of whether to give legitimacy to claims of privacy rights, the entire nature of the judicial process is exposed.

In this volume, I have completed a trilogy designed to encourage both academic and lay readers to open the door on the judicial process at work. David Easton's "Systems Theory" trilogy was the inspiration for my three-pronged study of the judicial process.[13] Easton linked a historical study of the political system's development with an analytical structure designed to explain decisions, and then provided in-depth applications. It was a unique approach. My trilogy follows this format but focuses only on the legal/judicial process. *Cases Lost, Causes Won: The Supreme Court and the Judicial Process* (1984) set up the analytical structure, the inputs into the judicial system, the interaction of justices, the judicial attitudes that produce decisions, the impact of the decision, and the beginning of a new case. *Litigating Morality: American Legal Thought and Its English Roots* (1993) explored the historical development of the legal/judicial process as it dealt with litigation of moral issues. This third and final volume seeks to apply the analytical structure to four aspects of privacy rights—birth control, gay rights, abortion, and the right to die. This approach follows logically from the previous two studies. All of these privacy issues were litigated before the Supreme Court. All lost at first. Why? Chapter 1 suggests a linkage between the attorneys and the birth control cases lost. Chapter 2 describes the state of confused judicial interaction that led to the initial failure to legitimize "gay rights." Chapter 3 focuses on the development of judicial attitudes sympathetic to the states' goal of excessive regulation of abortion so that the right seemed doomed. Chapter 4 explores the first "right to die" case and its controversial impact. Finally, chapter 5 describes victories snatched from the jaws of these earlier defeats as four new cases favor privacy rights in each area—from birth to death.

The case studies are all classics. They are dramatic and exciting. The cases selected afford insight into several aspects of the battles over privacy rights. Turning cases lost into causes won is central to our everyday life as we seek to persuade others to agree. Such is the goal of this book.

NOTES

1. Dr. Michael Fuhrman, "An Analysis of the Book of Revelation," address given at University Heights American Baptist Church, Springfield, MO, October 2003.

2. Rudolph Binion, *Defeated Leaders: The Political Fate of Caillaux, Jouvenel, and Tardieu* (Morningside Heights, NY: Columbia University Press, 1960).

3. Tom Sine, *Cease Fire: Searching for Sanity in America's Culture Wars* (Grand Rapids, MI: Eerdmans, 1995). Justice Scalia used the phrase "culture war" in *Lawrence v. Texas*.

4. Cynthia Brown, ed., *Lost Liberties: Ashcroft and the Assault on Personal Freedom* (New York: New Press, 2003).

5. Ellen Alderman and Caroline Kennedy, *The Right to Privacy* (New York: Vintage Press, 1997).

6. Samuel Warren and Louis D. Brandeis, "The Right to Privacy," *Harvard Law Review* 4, no. 193 (1890).

7. *Meyer v. Nebraska*, 262 U.S. 390 (1923); *Pierce v. Society of Sisters*, 268 U.S. 510 (1925).

8. Alderman and Kennedy, 55–159.

9. *Griswold v. Connecticut*, 381 U.S. 479 (1965).
10. *Roe v. Wade*, 410 U.S. 113 (1973).
11. *Cruzan v. Director, Missouri Department of Health*, 497 U.S. 261 (1990).
12. *Lawrence v. Texas*, 539 U.S. 588 (2003).
13. David Easton, *The Political System* (New York: Alfred A. Knopf, 1953); David Easton, *A Framework for Political Analysis* (Englewood Cliffs, NJ: Prentice-Hall, 1965); David Easton, *A Systems Analysis of Political Life* (New York: Wiley & Sons, 1965).

1

Incorrect Inputs

Attorneys' Mistakes in Birth Control Cases

The role of the attorney in court litigation is a central one. Attorneys have options and choices as they consider how to litigate a case, and clients are well aware that a lawyer's skill is central to winning or losing. Thus litigants look for advocates with winning records. All want to brag that they have secured the services of an outstanding litigator. Questions that involve federal constitutional rights require a special type of legal expertise. Whether or not the attorney has practiced before the U.S. Supreme Court becomes an important factor. Is the attorney familiar with the unique process of getting a case accepted by that court? Finally, clients look for experts in the subject matter to be litigated.

These requirements were not easily met by attorneys under consideration by birth control advocates in the early twentieth century. Selecting an attorney capable of arguing and winning cases involving reproductive privacy rights presented a unique problem. Women's right to vote had only recently been won in 1912 and many feared an emerging feminist movement that might upset the traditional family model. Freedom from childbirth was viewed as an attack on this very model. Advocates of reproductive choice became targets. For example, Margaret Sanger was prosecuted for promoting pornography as she wrote tracts and delivered speeches about birth control.

Training in this type of litigation was nonexistent. It was not a recognized field for legal practice. Lawyers were on their own to develop the questions, to find the constitutional rights to be presented, and to create the strategies for developing both the case and the argument for winning the right to possess and use birth control devices.

Legislators had no difficulty in producing numerous and detailed statutes outlawing birth control. Using the doctrine of "state police powers," legislators had written anticontraceptive statutes that pleased clergy and the medical profession, ignoring the protests of doctors and of women, even those of wealth and status.

Women had nevertheless organized and, with the aid of outstanding academics, sympathetic jurists, politicians, and medical specialists, had established birth control clinics in defiance of state prohibitions. The stage was set for legal challenges that would create new arguments and strategies and would ultimately lead to law school courses in right to privacy and gender discrimination. It was a long process. Beginning with the defense of Sanger in 1917, it shifted to litigation aimed at the anticontraception laws in states such as Massachusetts and Connecticut. Lawyers created the cases to challenge these laws, developed the questions to be raised before courts, designed the arguments to be used in challenging the legality of such laws, and finally took case after case to the U.S. Supreme Court in an attempt to create new law through the winning of judicial decisions.[1] Yet, they lost case after case.

CONNECTICUT LAWYERS AND THE DEVELOPMENT OF BIRTH CONTROL LITIGATION

Connecticut became the central focus of the ongoing conflict. The existence of Yale Law School and Yale Medical School provided the momentum and spearheaded the birth control movement. In addition, wealthy, socially prominent, educated women were drawn to work tirelessly in the movement. Planned Parenthood chapters began the search for attorneys who could win this new right of birth control. They recognized the difficulty of this task. Lawyers would be required to risk their status, prestige, and even their livelihoods if they embraced cases that involved birth control rights. Would the best and the brightest of the bar be attracted to such a practice? Some were. They were the unique ones, ready to challenge laws approved and defended by clergy, medical practitioners, and political leaders as directives from God Himself.

Connecticut's anti–birth control law had been enacted by its legislature in 1879. It had come into being as a result of the national antiobscenity campaign led by one Anthony Comstock. As passed by the Connecticut legislature, the law included some unique provisions. Obscene literature and materials concerning sex or reproduction were outlawed. The statute also forbade the use of drugs, medicine, and instruments for the purpose of preventing conception. This law had not been seriously challenged until 1923, following the successful conclusion of the suffragettes' campaign for the vote in 1920.[2] The problem facing women's groups in Connecticut was that of removing this restrictive law from the statute books.

There were two ways to do this: a legislative repeal or a judicial invalidation of the law. Beginning in 1923 and continuing through the 1950s, the Connecticut legislature refused again and again to repeal or modify the state statute. Birth control advocates in Connecticut were clearly in the minority. Election after election demonstrated the overwhelming political power of the Catholic Church in Connecticut politics. The influence of the Church over state legislators, whether Republican or Democrat, was pervasive. Birth control advocates increasingly accused the Church of imposing its religious views not only on legislators but also on Connecticut society. While polls showed approval of birth control as well as actual use of contraceptive devices, the majority of Connecticut voters routinely voted as Church leaders decreed.[3] Such results demonstrated that a referendum vote would fail. The right to possess knowledge about and to use anticontraceptive devices was not one that would be secured through the ballot box. The legislature would not repeal or alter the statutes.

Would the judicial forum offer a more favorable climate than the state legislature? In the 1950s, civil rights activists proved the wisdom of a judicial approach with their 1954 desegregation case win in *Brown v. Board of Education*. Could attorneys be found who could persuade Connecticut courts that Connecticut's statute violated the Constitution?

THE SEARCH FOR THE SUCCESSFUL ATTORNEY: UPSON, WIGGIN, ERNST, HARPER, AND THE CONNECTICUT BIRTH CONTROL CASES

As early as 1930, attorneys interested in securing the right to birth control had suggested that change would come only by the constant chipping away of the Connecticut law by judicial decisions. Some attorneys in Connecticut urged the opening of clinics to provide birth control services and to force state officials to arrest violators of Connecticut's law. This could then create standing for a court case. By 1937, there were four clinics in Connecticut. Success was short lived, however. Under attack, the clinics needed an attorney who would give inspired legal leadership. Connecticut attorneys of differing perspectives and personalities came forward to lead in what was to become one of the longest and most difficult of all legal battles ever fought in the courts. There were four attorneys who would play critical roles in this process: Warren Upson, Fritz Wiggin, Morris Ernst, and Fowler Harper. Cautious yet creative, Upson provided leadership in a state case known as *Commonwealth v. Nelson*.[4] Wiggin, a rather lackluster yet highly respected lawyer, was tapped to create and litigate the landmark case of *Tileston v. Ullman*.[5] Ernst, the most aggressive and charismatic of this group, would supplant Wiggin in a last-ditch effort to win the *Tileston* case on appeal. Finally, Harper, a Yale law professor and champion of lost causes, would resurrect the birth control battle in a new case—*Poe v. Ullman.*[6]

ATTORNEYS' STRATEGIC CHOICES
AND THE STRATEGIC CHOICE OF AN ATTORNEY

Attorneys play multifaceted roles in the litigation process, and in some cases they may be involved in the actual creation of the case. Attorneys know that litigants have to meet numerous standards in order to gain entry into the legal process. Standing to sue, elements of a true controversy, and the showing of actual harm or damage are but a few of the legal norms. Attorneys may find themselves actively engaged in locating litigants who possess these requisite characteristics. Moreover, attorneys may also find themselves in search of a case with a factual situation that is both specific enough to satisfy case and controversy elements and general enough to assure that the court's decision will not be limited to that one case's facts. Not only must attorneys predict correctly the appropriate parties for the case, as well as the merits raised by the case facts, but they will also be called upon to make strategic choices throughout the litigation process as the case proceeds upward from trial stage through various appellate stages. By 1938, the Connecticut Birth Control League believed they needed an energetic attorney, one who could be aggressive without being offensive, cautious without being cowardly, and charismatic rather than lackluster. They believed they had found their winner in the person of J. Warren Upson.

Upson was a young Yale Law School graduate and a junior partner in one of Waterbury, Connecticut's illustrious law firms. He had become a significant political figure as he led a fight against fiscal corruption in political machine politics. He was an activist who was always making headlines, mostly favorable ones, and had name and face recognition due to television appearances and newspaper reports covering his reformist activities to bring in good government. The words used to describe him said it all: "frank and honest," "brilliant of mind," and "bed-rock in character."[7] As a native of Connecticut, he was very familiar with state law. Upson seemed to be the ideal attorney to fight the legal battle for birth control activists in Connecticut.

Warren Upson agreed to take on the Connecticut battle for birth control. However, he found himself in a legal setting that could only be described as threatening. Massachusetts attorney Robert G. Dodge had come to grief in attempt to defend birth control advocates before the U.S. Supreme Court in the case of *Commonwealth v. Gardner.*[8] As he prepared to argue *Gardner*, Dodge, a cautious and careful attorney, had put together a large and impressive brief for the Court, but he had argued without the specific backup data needed to convince the justices of the U.S. Supreme Court. The use of specific data to quantify one's argument had been given the name "Brandeis brief."[9] Professor Felix Frankfurter of Harvard Law School had urged the use of such data, but Dodge had failed to provide the supporting information for Massachusetts' *Gardner* case. This case loss had been a disaster for birth control advocates. Would Upson be able to avoid such mistakes in Connecticut?

Upson's challenge began with a police attack on a birth control clinic. It was a beautiful June day in the summer of 1939. The birth control clinic in the town of Waterbury, Connecticut, was in full operation. Two doctors and a nurse were on duty to assist patients. Success had generated publicity about the clinic. Could this open violation of state law be tolerated? State's Attorney William B. Fitzgerald decided it was time to act and to enforce Connecticut's birth control law. The police descended on the Waterbury Birth Control Clinic, and Dr. Bill Goodrich, Dr. Roger Nelson, and Nurse Clara McTernan were placed under arrest. A case, *Commonwealth v. Nelson*, was under way.

Could Warren Upson rise to the challenge? Could he do in Connecticut what his colleague in Massachusetts had failed to do? Could he save the clinic from extinction and its personnel from imprisonment? The clinic had been part of a hospital, and Upson naturally turned to hospital administrators and doctors to come to the defense of the practitioners in the clinic. However, the hospital superintendent evaded interviews, the chief of gynecology asked to be "kept out of the matter," and witnesses to assert the need for the clinic refused to come forward.[10] Upson had to develop a new and winning strategy. His job was hampered because he was unsure about the actions the state's attorney was planning. What kind of arguments would Upson have to meet? What kind of judge would he have to persuade?

Upson developed a three-pronged strategy. First, he would challenge the constitutionality of the charges against the clinic's two doctors and nurse. Second, he would focus on the factual question, "Did the patients actually use the contraceptive devices?" This was a requirement for conviction of the three defendants. Finally, Upson would show that the clinic's clients had health reasons for seeking contraceptive devices and information. These points dominated Upson's brief for Connecticut Supreme Court of Errors judge Kenneth Wynne.

The impressive fifty-four-page brief used arguments that demonstrated Upson's skills as an attorney. He began with the federal precedents that gave meaning to state contraceptive statutes. These cases balanced an individual doctor's right to practice medicine with the state's right to use its police powers over morals. Upson asked, "What had state legislatures meant when they wrote such statutes?" The objectives behind the Connecticut 1879 statute had been clearly expressed. The legislatures wanted to suppress obscene materials and to prevent an immoral use of contraceptives. At this point, Upson appealed to the court with a "sociological contemporary morality" approach by agreeing that the state certainly had power to prevent high school students from having access to contraceptive information. The state's concern with preventing immoral behavior justified this control. However, the statute went much further into the life of married people.[11]

Upson knew that he needed arguments that went beyond the usual ones of statutory analysis and legislative intent. He found one in fundamental rights. This was an argument based on both common law and natural law. Common law had always embraced a right "not to be touched"—a right of bodily integrity—Upson argued. Natural law could be used to uphold the individual's rights over family: marriage, procreation, and education. Upson brilliantly articulated a phrase that would later become a stock item in the contraceptive-abortion vocabulary, "If people . . . have any rights whatsoever, one of them certainly is the right to decide whether or not they shall have children." Finally, Upson urged the court to ask and answer a very narrow question. His goal was to give the court a way to reach a compromise. Separate abortion from contraception, he told the court, regulate the latter under state police powers and leave contraception alone. He concluded that state regulation of abortion was clearly within the state's police powers.

Warren Upson's argument won in Judge Wynne's court, but in another state superior court, that of Judge McElvoy, where the seizure of contraceptive articles was the issue, the same argument lost. Connecticut legal procedure would complicate Upson's plans from then on and would tax his skills to the utmost. With superior court judges disagreeing on questions presented and reinterpreting each other's opinions, Upson began to feel pressure and a sense of exasperation. Was the larger constitutional argument being lost to procedural technicalities?

At last, the case was docketed with the Connecticut Supreme Court of Errors. Now came the challenge of finding the right argument and the right style—the legal and emotional appeal—to persuade the justices to declare the 1879 statute unconstitutional. The strategic choices for Upson came down to these: (1) a major amicus brief on behalf of doctors, (2) a new brief focusing on statutory interpretation and presumed legislative intent, or (3) a "distinguishing precedent" argument to overcome the negative *Gardner* decision from Massachusetts by contrasting "distribution" of birth control devices with "use." On its face, this seemed to be an impressive set of arguments. However, in the end the decision rested with the justices' own perception of law, with their view of their power, and with their own biases.

Upson, one of Connecticut's best lawyers, found that a hostile court could not be swayed. As he later tried to analyze his loss, it seemed certain that his arguments never had had a chance. The justices on the court were all drawn from the same environment. They all had attended law school at either Yale or Harvard; in religion, four were Congregationalists and the fifth a Baptist; they all belonged to the Republican Party; and most had had legislative experience. With such similar backgrounds, it was not surprising that these justices thought alike or that they shared the philosophy of judicial restraint. Courts and judges, they said, should not act like legislatures.

He had known that it would be difficult to persuade justices who deferred to the legislature and limited the court to a narrow role, but Upson's energy, his belief in himself, and the praise showered upon him had led to overconfidence. It was a painful loss for this highly successful young attorney. Yet the vote was actually very close (3–2), and if the two dissenters had written dissenting opinions, Upson might have reacted differently. As it was, he abandoned a plan for appeal to the U.S. Supreme Court and concentrated on extricating the doctors from further criminal prosecution. A glimmer of hope did persist, however. Could Upson somehow persuade Nurse Clara McTernan to stand trial in order to have the question clearly presented to the U.S. Supreme Court as a test case? In the end, this plan also collapsed; McTernan wanted out. Upson's legal advice to the Planned Parenthood League in Connecticut was harsh in the end: "Close down all the clinics." It would take twenty five years—with one hiatus—before Connecticut clinics reopened on a permanent basis.[12]

IF AT FIRST YOU DON'T SUCCEED . . .

Attorney Morris Ernst, unlike Warren Upson, was not downcast by the court defeat. Ernst was an aggressive attorney, and he was used to winning. Self-confident and sometimes arrogant, Ernst was a charismatic individual who generated adulation as well as great antagonism.[13] From his New York base, his practice extended into the birth control cases in both Massachusetts and Connecticut. The American Birth Control League, which had replaced the earlier National Birth Control League, had used Ernst's talents throughout the 1920s when he became personal attorney for the grande dame of birth control activists, Margaret Sanger.

State birth control activists were often divided over Morris Ernst's strategy and tactics. Some viewed him as idealistic and impractical, while others called him bold and creative. Ernst preferred federal case decisions over state decisions because the impact was greater. He also preferred judicial change to legislative battles, believing the former to be more lasting. "Birth control statutes," Ernst argued, "will not be repealed [by legislatures] until they have already been nullified [by courts]." To emphasize this point, he continued, "Nullification [of state anti–birth control laws] will take place by the constant whittling away of the law by judicial decisions."[14] Ernst saw himself as both a trial lawyer and an appellate attorney, excelling equally in both areas. But was he? Arguments before judges alone usually differ from those made before a jury, and judicial personality makes each appellate action as unique as a court's members.

The unpredictability of the judicial process was well known to Ernst. He understood the incremental approach so characteristic of judicial change. "Courts which are too cowardly to declare laws in conflict with our basic Constitution wheedle out of dilemmas by casting new interpretations on old statutes, eventually destroying the word of the law given," he said.[15] Judicial lawmaking, according to Ernst, was a very good thing. He was never ready to give up on the judicial process.

Ernst's fighting spirit bubbled up following Upson's defeat in *Nelson*, and he concocted a bold plan of action. It was a two-part plan based upon a detailed analysis of the court's opinion and coupled with a direct action proposal. He suggested a public press conference to put a different spin on the court's decision. As an attorney, he could show the public what the opinion said and what it had not said. The court had not held that birth control was illegal—it had said only that a generalized health interest was insufficient reason to void the statute. Ernst proposed that the Planned Parenthood League announce (through him) that all the Connecticut clinics would be reopened at once, along with new ones attached to churches. They would assure the court that informational birth control devices would be strictly limited to cases where a women's very *life*—not her general health—was threatened. Privately, Ernst reassured the birth control advocates stating, "Jeopardy to life does not mean jeopardy of death."[16] There would be a loophole for future cases.

Ernst could see himself in his most judicious posture, making these statements in a majestic and dignified setting calculated to show the greatest respect for the court, while at the same time moving forward boldly. He believed it would be a masterful performance. However, the Connecticut attorneys did not agree with his plan. Warren Upson led the way in raising objections that medical careers would be at risk and that money for defense was limited. Upson spoke from experience. In response, Ernst reconfigured his plan and waited. It took a year before the Connecticut lawyers would even listen to Ernst's newest strategy—to create a test case involving a birth control publication; then hearing it, they rejected it. Ernst was marginalized as just another attorney with another plan trying to take center stage in the birth control battle.[17]

THE BEST-LAID PLANS . . .

In January 1941, Connecticut's pro–birth control attorneys carefully weighed the pros and cons for a new judicial battle. Could they create a case where no one would be in danger, yet the statute could be nullified? The idea seemed to carry the seeds of its own destruction under the U.S. Supreme Court's rule on "case and controversy."[18] How could a case without "danger" be one of real "harm and injury"?

The legal device of a declaratory judgment was chosen as the vehicle most likely to survive this judicial test while endangering no one. In a declaratory judgment action, a doctor could initiate a civil suit on behalf of women patients needing birth control. The difficulty lay in finding a well-respected physician willing to be party to such a suit, patients needing birth control advice, and a lawyer shrewd enough to create a legal question the court could answer in the affirmative. It is a well-known fact in legal circles that getting a court to use one attorney's question over that of his opponent will determine the winner and the loser. The attorney's clever questions thus become the sine qua non of the judicial process. It would take an attorney of unusual capability to perform this feat in the case of the Connecticut birth control statute. The description was exacting: only a "senior lawyer with the highest reputation in the bar" need apply. There were three potential candidates who seemed to meet this standard; two declined to apply, however, and the job fell to one Frederick H. Wiggin. "Fritz" Wiggin was a former state bar association president and a partner in New Haven's most prominent and prestigious law firm. He would not prove to be the best choice.[19]

Fritz Wiggin was more like attorney Robert Dodge of Massachusetts than he was like Warren Upson; he was decidedly no Morris Ernst. Although he had helped to prepare an amicus curiae brief in the *Nelson* case, he had never been optimistic about its chances for success. Wiggin, although creative, could also catalogue all the reasons why a case might be lost. At one time he had even stated that no case could ever succeed in persuading Connecticut's judges, much less the members of the U.S. Supreme Court. That, however, was before he personally had been approached to undertake this challenging task. It was clear that he was both flattered and excited by the challenge.

Wiggin's strategy, like that of Dodge and Upson, was to put together the right parties in the right setting with the right questions. For the parties involved, Wiggin decided that he needed at least one married woman who would be likely to lose her life in pregnancy if refused birth control, and he needed a respected doctor willing to act as plaintiff. The setting should be that of a private practice to which hospitals referred cases. The question should be both a state and federal constitutional issue that could be raised in the form of a declaratory judgment suit. Thus, Fritz Wiggin began to assemble the elements for the case *Tileston v. Ullman.*

In Dr. Wilder Tileston, Wiggin had the right physician with the right credentials. Tileston was a sixty five-year-old Yale Medical School professor who was also in private practice. He had a high standing in the medical community and a reputation for conservative medical diagnostic advice. Moreover, he was regarded as extremely knowledgeable, a skilled practitioner, and an excellent teacher. To Wiggin's delight, Dr. Tileston had three patients who would be "right" for the declaratory judgment suit. Tileston outlined his patients' problems for Wiggin, using fictitious names to protect their privacy. "Jane Roe" was the first possible candidate. High blood pressure made pregnancy life threatening for her. "Mary Doe," a young bride suffering from severe lung problems that would be aggravated by pregnancy, was the second candidate. Finally, there was "Sarah Hoe." Hers was an economic problem—three children and no money. She needed to postpone having any more children until she could provide for them. With two of his requirements satisfied—plaintiffs and setting—Wiggin needed only to relate them to each other through a compelling question to persuade a court to give him a "yes" answer. Connecticut's birth control statute could become a thing of the past.

Under Connecticut law, could Dr. Tileston provide the birth control information needed to prevent possible death or serious, permanent injury to the health of his patients? Wiggin asserted that the 1879 statute prohibited Dr. Tileston from this action. Did this kind of prohibition violate state or federal constitutional protections for individuals? Wiggin believed that it did and that the Fourteenth Amendment's guarantee against deprivation of life without due process could apply. He also reasoned that Dr. Tileston was being deprived of property rights guaranteed by the Fourteenth Amendment because the 1879 statute stopped him from practicing his profession as a doctor qualified to offer birth control. Wiggin contemplated these arguments, as documented in notes, letters, and memoranda, and they were included in the formal complaint that Wiggin filed in the Connecticut Superior Court on March 20, 1941.[20]

Connecticut birth control activists and other attorneys hailed it as an excellent job. Nevertheless, the months passed, and Wiggin grew impatient with the delay caused by crowded court dockets. Why not abandon the idea of an actual trial and simply proceed through a "stipulation"? A voluntary agreement of opposing counsel to limit the number of issues in the case would simplify Wiggin's task. The state's attorney, Abraham S. Ullman, agreed, and on December 2, 1941 (five days before the Pearl Harbor attack), Wiggin and Ullman filed the *Tileston* stipulation in New Haven County Superior Court, with oral argument scheduled for February 1942.

The case could now move forward quickly, but looking back, Wiggin would discover that he had made a fatal mistake. He had lost sight of the very elements he initially documented for inclusion in the question to be presented to the court. The stipulation stated only that prosecutors "claim or may claim" that medical prescription of birth control violated the 1879 statute. Furthermore, Wiggin had not included Dr. Tileston's *personal* constitutional rights in the stipulation—only those of the three women patients who were not actual plaintiffs in the case. Wiggin had not included the patients as plaintiffs in the stipulation. He had failed to assert Dr. Tileston's Fourteenth Amendment property rights. The desire for speed had caused this attorney to forget his own third critical ingredient for a successful case: the perfectly constructed constitutional question. Already handicapped by the declaratory judgment action and its inherent difficulty in creating an actual controversy, the case's stipulation contained a more deadly flaw in the absence of the "right" question.

By the time Wiggin prepared a brief for the Connecticut Supreme Court, he had decided to focus on three major points. The first dealt with the question of statutory construction of the 1879 law and the intent of those who had framed it. Wiggin told the court that the statute had been designed to combat obscenity and thus should not be interpreted as applying to medically approved contraception for the serious health cases. His second point focused on "distinguishing" the facts in *Tileston* from earlier case precedents that could be used negatively. In Massachusetts, the state court had already retreated from the hard-line approach it had used in *Gardner* to a more lenient attitude. In the case of *Commonwealth v. Corbett* (1942), the Massachusetts court had approved selling condoms that could be used for protection against disease as well as for contraception. Since the Connecticut Supreme Court had relied on the *Gardner* ruling when deciding the *Nelson* case, it stood to reason that *Corbett*'s modifications should now undermine that precedent. Wiggin also suggested that the *Nelson* opinion itself had left a loophole. The state court in that case had not ruled on the doctor's right to prescribe birth control in life-threatening cases. Expanding on this, Wiggin's final point raised the federal constitutional question. Suppose, he suggested, the court were to find the 1879 statute did prohibit birth control in such serious cases. Then, surely, it would have to be struck down as unconstitutional. It would be a violation of the Fourteenth Amendment protection of the "life and liberty" of the doctor and of the patients involved. The "fundamental rights" argument here was similar to Warren Upson's earlier one of "inherent right to protect one's life and health," an "inalienable right."

Fritz Wiggin also demonstrated his public relations skills at this moment. He knew he would be arguing his points before a hostile court. He did not want to do or say anything that might alienate the justices still further, so he proposed a low-key approach. He told Planned Parenthood members there should be no press releases, no meetings to whip up support, no marches, and no turnout of members for the oral argument. Nevertheless, he soon found that Connecticut's chief justice was not to be appeased under any conditions. The chief justice was "frosty," asking questions in oral argument that clearly showed his bias. Wiggin retained his calm, and his answers to the court were "dignified." Birth control advocates wondered later if passion might have served Wiggin better. Wiggin himself, however, was beginning to see the major obstacle he faced. The Connecticut court was not just hostile to birth control—it also had a philosophical view on which it operated. The "role of the court," said Connecticut justices, was to stay within its proper boundaries. Courts should not try to be "super legislatures." They should act only when the political process itself was "clogged." And in Connecticut the elected legislative representatives had refused to amend the 1879 statute in any way. The legislature had refused not once but many times to permit a doctor to authorize birth control. If the legislature so interpreted a legislative statute, how could Wiggin suggest that the judiciary find a loophole? The Connecticut Supreme Court refused to do so.[21]

A LAST DITCH ATTEMPT: "ON APPEAL"

The court was divided, 3–2, but the case of *Tileston v. Ullman* nevertheless was lost. Was it Wiggin's fault? No one said so openly, but actions taken by the Connecticut Birth Control League indicated its members thought so. Was it, at last, Morris Ernst's golden opportunity? Could he enter the case, salvage it, and win it on appeal to the U.S. Supreme Court? Ernst naturally thought so, and Connecticut leaders were personally ready to let him try. Ernst, a high-powered, wealthy attorney, promised to do it for free! His name, status, and success record made him the logical candidate to argue the appeal should the U.S. Supreme Court agree to hear *Tileston*. That would be Ernst's first challenge. His appeal was successful, and in November 1942, the Supreme Court agreed to hear the case. But it would have been better for birth control advocates if the court had refused the appeal, for Morris Ernst would find that Fritz Wiggin had left him with a flawed case.

The U.S. Supreme Court has many different ways that it can approach a case. For instance, it can begin with the most basic question: jurisdiction. Here, the Court asks, "Do we have power under the Article III requirement of 'case and controversy' to hear the case?" In essence, the Court is asking whether the case record as presented to them actually has the elements to make it a "real case"—an "actual controversy." The Supreme Court has developed for itself the list of elements that will meet this standard. To be a "case and controversy," the parties must have *standing*, acquired by personally suffering real harm or damage. The parties must be truly *adverse*, almost in a "fight" mode, and must be *directly involved*. Plaintiffs must present distinct injuries, show that the injuries were caused by the defendants, and prove that the injuries could be made right if the court were to decide in their favor. The issue cannot be a hypothetical or "what if?" question; the Court will not decide imaginary scenarios. Moreover, the case-and-controversy standard means that the question has come to the Court at the right time, having exhausted all other remedies possible; it is then "ripe" for the Court to hear it. This implies too that what the Court decides will make a difference: that the case is a "concrete" one, not "moot." Standing is really a jurisdictional issue and has little to do with the facts or merits of a plaintiff's claim.[22]

The Supreme Court had agreed to hear *Tileston* under its "on appeal" jurisdiction. Since 1942, this was the usual way a case would come from a state supreme court. Morris Ernst assumed this meant that the case would be decided "on merits." He did not prepare for a jurisdictional battle, yet that was exactly the issue on which the case would be won or lost.[23]

Two other lawyers understood this. The first was State's Attorney Abraham S. Ullman. Ullman had come to the birth control battle not as a matter of choice, but because of his job. He had only been in office as state's attorney for a few months when Fritz Wiggin had filed *Tileston*'s original complaint. Ullman represented the state's interest during the negotiations with Wiggin, agreeing to void a trial and to proceed with the case by stipulation. Ullman had won before the Connecticut Supreme Court with a threefold argument, citing precedent, legislative intent, and the duty of courts to exercise judicial restraint by not usurping the role of elected representative bodies. Ullman himself was not an opponent of birth control, and both Wiggin and Ernst saw him as a "friendly, professional adversary who was conscientious in his duty." He was "calm" in his style of oral argument and "straightforward" in his written briefs.

By the time Morris Ernst inherited *Tileston* and filed his initial appeal papers with the U.S. Supreme Court, Abe Ullman had uncovered the jurisdictional flaw. "Who had standing-to-sue?" Ullman's new brief asked. The patients were the real parties in the case. It was their liberty and life interests that were at risk, yet they were not on the record as actual parties. Instead, only Dr. Tileston was listed. Could such a case be decided "on the merits"? Ullman said no. He urged the Court to dismiss the case on jurisdictional grounds because Dr. Tileston did not have standing to raise the issue.[24]

Another attorney who almost immediately spotted the jurisdictional flaw on which the Supreme Court could dismiss the case without deciding it was a young law clerk, Vern Countryman, who clerked for Justice William O. Douglas. Countryman was an advocate of birth control, and he was known as a liberal. However, a flawed case was a flawed case, as he told his justice. In a memo to Justice Douglas, Countryman analyzed the *Tileston* appeal. He noted that there was no "present controversy" and "the claim was a hypothetical one." Criminal charges had not been filed against Dr. Tileston since he had not broken the law. Even more important, Countryman argued that Dr. Tileston did not have that essential "standing" status. Dr. Tileston had claimed violations of the constitutional rights of his patients, but what about his own life or liberty?

Countryman could see a way around all of the other obstacles in the case. He found a valid basis to distinguish *Tileston's* facts from the earlier anti–birth control precedents.[25] The problem of standing remained. The Supreme Court could choose to ignore this. The Court was the one that interpreted the Article III jurisdictional phrases, "to all cases . . . to controversies," and the Court was the one that said these phrases meant "standing." It was also the one that defined "standing to sue" to mean actual, personal damage. In *Tileston* the Supreme Court had agreed to take the case "on appeal." Should the Court now say that it could not decide the case on its merits because of a flaw in the record and because the patients suffering personal damage were not parties to the case? For those not trained in the law, it seems strange that the Court might take a case, hear arguments, and then decide that it lacked power to decide the case. Such is, however, the nature of the judicial process. It had happened many times previously. Morris Ernst began to understand that it could happen again in *Tileston*. It was less than two months before he would face the issue in oral argument; could he satisfy the court's standard?

For all of his own self-confidence, Ernst knew that he was not an expert in every type of suit. *Tileston* was a declaratory judgment suit, and he needed help from an expert in that type of law. Yale Law School provided that assistance in the person of Professor Edwin Borchard. Borchard analyzed the situation and advised Ernst to secure some amicus curiae briefs designed to support the argument that doctors' rights were under attack in Connecticut. However, Borchard, like Ernst, did not zero in on what would become the fatal flaw: the omission of the three women patients as plaintiffs.[26] Thus Ernst was not prepared for this question from the Supreme Court justices when oral argument in *Tileston* began.

It was late in the afternoon of January 13, 1943, before the case was called. Experts disagree about the best time for oral argument. Is morning better than afternoon? Is early afternoon better than late afternoon? Is it helpful or harmful to have argument carried over to the following day? Arguing before the Supreme Court in the late 1960s in the case of *Walker v. Birmingham*, Jack Greenberg, lawyer extraordinaire and counsel for beleaguered civil rights activists including the Reverend Martin Luther King Jr., found late afternoon to be a disastrous time.[27] However, Morris Ernst, arguing in *Tileston*, was grateful for a late afternoon argument that spilled over into the following day: it gave him an evening to try to salvage his case.

Ernst had barely begun his opening argument that afternoon when the first blow fell. Chief Justice Harlan Fiske Stone, ignoring Ernst's impassioned presentation of the merits of the case, interrupted him with a technical question. Stone asked, "In light of . . . [Wiggin's] initial complaint, . . . is the issue limited to whether the Connecticut statute deprives someone of 'life' without 'due process of law'?"[28]

Realizing the pitfall in this reference to Wiggin's appeal, Ernst responded, "In my initial appeal papers to this [the U.S. Supreme] Court, I . . . [cited] the Fourteenth Amendment's rights of 'life, liberty, or property.'" Of course Ernst knew, as Stone was subtly pointing out, the real issue was the initial record as presented to the Connecticut Supreme Court. Ernst himself had cited "life, liberty, or property"; Wiggin had not.

The chief justice left no doubt about this as he responded, "This court is . . . limited to [what] the Connecticut Supreme Court . . . [passed upon]." Ernst, unsure of the precise focus of the "life, liberty, or property" phrase, pointed to Dr. Tileston's loss of liberty to practice medicine as he saw fit, and the corresponding loss of property. The chief justice countered, "Is Dr. Tileston's 'life' at issue here?" Ernst had to admit that it was not and that it was the life of the patient he referred to.

Flustered by this exchange, Ernst welcomed some different questions from justices Douglas and Jackson. His respite was short lived. Once again the chief justice took control of the questioning. Focusing on the original complaint, Stone noted that it said nothing about any prosecution of Dr. Tileston. The chief justice inquired, "Is there any actual controversy here?" He then answered his own question by stating, "There does not seem to be any real threat of prosecution."

Not wanting to agree that Dr. Tileston personally had not been warned or threatened by officials, Morris Ernst resorted to a linkage argument. Ernst said that the Connecticut birth control statute by its very existence threatened doctors and that the threat of prosecution was very real. He reminded the court that in *State of Connecticut v. Nelson* two doctors and a nurse had been charged. Stone's response was quick and devastating: "The original complaint . . . did not cite *Nelson.*"

Acting as an appellate court in *Tileston,* the U.S. Supreme Court would look only at the record of a case that clearly was flawed. At this point, what could Morris Ernst do to salvage his case? He was grateful that adjournment time had come and he had the evening to ponder his next move. But he found no solution.

Assisted by none other than attorney Warren Upson of *Nelson* fame and his staff, the birth control advocates spent the evening researching precedents. It was to no avail. As argument opened the following morning, Morris Ernst acknowledged the problems he was facing and suggested the possibility of a continuance to ask the lower court whether "liberty" and "property" had been part of the issue they decided. All of his attempts to argue on the real merits of the case had been overwhelmed by the technical and procedural questions.

Sensing at the conclusion of the oral argument that he had lost, Ernst resorted to an unusual tactic. He prepared a "post argument" letter for Chief Justice Stone. Sometimes referred to as a "supplemental and reply brief,"

Ernst's letter urged the Court to use the *Nelson* precedent even though he had not cited it. He pointed out that *Nelson* demonstrated a "more than adequate threat of criminal prosecution for . . . Dr. Tileston should he prescribe contraception for Jane Doe or Mary Roe."[29] Chief Justice Stone ignored the letter because *Tileston* had already been voted on in the conference and it was a fatally flawed case. During the conference discussion, all of the justices agreed with the chief justice that the case should be dismissed on procedural grounds. Justice William O. Douglas's memo of that discussion listed the major flaw: Attorney Fritz Wiggin had cited only the Fourteenth Amendment issue of "life." Wiggin could easily have included the "liberty" and "property" elements, but he had not. It was a mistake that could not be corrected. Ernst should have realized this from the beginning and refused to take this case to the Supreme Court.[30]

WHEN EVEN THE BEST ATTORNEY IS NOT
GOOD ENOUGH: LOSING *TILESTON V. ULLMAN*

The U.S. Supreme Court dismissed *Tileston*'s appeal in a short, unsigned per curiam opinion. It almost seemed as if the Court were saying, "This is not worthy of our attention and time. Don't bother us if this is the best you can do!" Because a per curiam opinion cannot be traced to its particular author and because such an opinion is usually brief, it can be an embarrassment to an attorney—and Morris Ernst was embarrassed. In fact, the Court had not even referred to his points. The Court did not mention the legal reasoning elements from his brief, and the supporting amicus briefs were ignored. It was as though Ernst had not even argued the case. *Tileston* was flawed because Fritz Wiggin's original complaint had not claimed a constitutional violation of the doctor's federal constitutional rights. That was the end of the argument.

Why had Ernst failed to anticipate this inherent problem when Wiggin was constructing the case in Connecticut? Ernst certainly had had opportunities for input throughout the entire process. When Warren Upson had lost the *Nelson* case, Ernst had named the problems: Upson's case lacked patients with life-threatening pregnancies and he did not show the need for actual dissemination of birth control information by a clinic doctor to such patients. State prosecution of the clinic and its staff was lacking in *Nelson*. Yet, knowing this, Ernst had remained idle while Wiggin constructed the *Tileston* case scenario.

Ernst should have seen from the beginning that the *Tileston* record was not one to be appealed to the Court. Why then did he take such a record forward? Possible answers include the psychological makeup of this aggressive attorney and the unpredictability of the judicial process itself. More than any other attorney of that period, Morris Ernst personally believed in a woman's right of reproductive choice, but his personal involvement in the cause worked to blind him. Ernst believed not only in the cause, though, but also supremely in himself. His extensive experience and his knowledge of the inner workings of the Court were well known. Experience and knowledge usually create a cautious attorney, but in Ernst's case it created an arrogant one.

Tileston's failure brought about an end to Ernst's participation in the battle for birth control. That is not to say that Ernst quietly left the field. He continued to try unusual tactics. For example, he urged Wiggin to petition the Connecticut Supreme Court to reopen *Tileston* so that "the initial defects can be corrected and the case resubmitted to the U.S. Supreme Court." Ernst suggested that a new, perfectly constructed case scenario could be created. Both proposals fell flat; Fritz Wiggin categorically refused to act. By this time, Morris Ernst was being regarded as a "has been" and an embarrassment to the birth control movement. The media portrayed him in unflattering terms. *Life* magazine described him as "preoccup[ied] with sex" and "a middle-aged Lothario" given to "bottom pinching."[31] He was characterized as a name-dropper who relished association with important people. Commentators wondered if this might be a sign of his personal insecurity? His tenacious belief in the ultimate victory for birth control rights was billed as inability to accept the reality of his own mistakes. The birth control battle needed a new champion and a new case.

Yale Law School had provided a number of attorneys who had assisted birth control activists over the years. Once again the school offered a solution to the attorney problem. The search for the unique advocate whose skills and personality could create a winning case culminated in the person of law professor Fowler V. Harper, who shared many of Ernst's characteristics. He was known for his outspoken opinions, flamboyant style, aggressiveness, and championship of controversial causes. During the 1940s, Harper had forsaken his Midwestern roots for Washington, DC, and was soon described as a New Deal liberal. When he joined the Yale Law School faculty in 1947, he was already known for his attacks on the House Un-American Activities Committee. Defending communists and communist sympathizers during the 1950s resulted in charges of subversion against Harper himself. His reputation as a popular teacher, brilliant lecturer, and creative author of legal treatises is what saved him from the repercussions such attacks often generate. Furthermore, Fowler Harper's sound legal scholarship raised him above an attorney like Morris Ernst. His respected position at Yale protected him, and it also provided him with a forum where he could debate controversial issues and litigate unpopular cases, which were varied and numerous.

Unlike Ernst, Harper was popular even with colleagues who disagreed with his political views. While Ernst was viewed as a self-aggrandizing attorney, Harper was seen as altruistic and compassionate. Fowler Harper's generous nature made friends for him even among his enemies. Some said it was because he was never mean or hateful. Yet, like Ernst, Harper's approach to his causes was often unorthodox. He did not like to compromise, and he relished violent controversy. Harper and Ernst shared the love of a good fight. Admirers said that both men were "tremendous fighters of enormous courage." Critics said that Harper, like Ernst, was a "soggy thinker, a sleazy character, a left-winger, and an exaggerated liberal who delighted in shocking people."[32] However, both men shared a commitment to eradicate injustice, and it was this commitment that helped bring Harper into the birth control battle that Morris Ernst had struggled so long to win. Would Harper's positives make a difference in a new case, or would his Ernst-like characteristics condemn him to failure?

Harper's interest in the right of birth control began in a rather routine and ordinary way—he was invited to take part in a public forum discussion in the winter of 1956. The invitation came because his wife Miriam worked at Yale's marriage consultation service, which was subsidized by Connecticut's Planned Parenthood League. It was during this meeting that Fowler Harper met Dr. Charles Lee Buxton, the chairman of Yale's Gynecological Department and a committed birth control advocate. Buxton had patients who, because of chronic illness, were threatened by pregnancy. Harper, for his part, had an irate student for whom the difficulty of securing birth control advice in Connecticut had become more than just an irritant. The Connecticut statute had become a challenge for Marvin and Jean Durning. Thus, a case in the making came into conjunction with a birth control attorney in the making. Dr. Buxton and Professor Harper began an association that would end in the landmark case of *Poe v. Ullman.*[33]

As Buxton and Harper talked during the year that followed, Harper began to put together the type of case scenario he would need in order to successfully challenge Connecticut's birth control law. However, there was an initial problem: Harper was not licensed to practice law in Connecticut. He could and would help put together the case script, and he was ready and eager to prepare and argue an appeal to the U.S. Supreme Court. But another attorney was needed to guide the case through the Connecticut system. It is interesting to note that even at this early stage Harper assumed that the case, no matter how carefully constructed, would be lost in all of the state courts. He stated this in no uncertain terms. "There is no realistic expectation that the . . . statute will be reinterpreted or struck down by the Connecticut courts," he said.

Could he find a Connecticut lawyer who would knowingly argue a losing case before the hostile state courts? Fowler Harper called a woman. Catherine G. Roraback—daughter of a Congregationalist minister, granddaughter of a Connecticut Superior Court judge, and graduate of Yale Law School—was the one Harper needed for this job. She understood the challenges that she would be facing, and she had long known Harper's reputation as a dangerous liberal. Her own expertise was in labor law, not in birth control, which was an unpopular issue in Connecticut; she could count on losing. Yet, without hesitation, Roraback accepted the challenge Harper offered her. Her only requirement was delivered succinctly: "No Morris Ernst in this case!" Everyone agreed.[34]

Harper immediately turned his attention to a careful analysis of the legal elements in the cases that Dr. Buxton was offering him. Dr. Buxton himself asserted his personal rights of property and liberty—the right and freedom to practice his profession. One of his cases involved a patient who had already suffered a stroke as a result of pregnancy. She would be called the "Jane Doe" plaintiff. A second case involved a couple that had lost every baby they had conceived, creating an intense emotional burden for the wife. These would be called the "Poe" plaintiffs. Their federal constitutional claims focused on both the "life" and "liberty" guarantees of the Fourteenth Amendment. The third case combined elements of the first two. The blood incompatibility of the "Hoes" had led to four late term miscarriages. The couple felt traumatized and they wanted freedom from the fears of another pregnancy. Finally, Fowler Harper's student couple joined the suit, citing career reasons as their basis for needing birth control. They were not ready to have children. This couple would be known as the "Roe" plaintiffs and would cite the most basic right—that of liberty. Surely, among all of these, Harper reasoned, there would be at least one plaintiff who could satisfy all of the Supreme Court's requirements: the right party, the right issue, and the right time.

BARRIERS TO NEW LITIGATION: IT TAKES TWO TO FIGHT

Why should the judicial process respond once again to the same issue? How often can the same law be tested? When Harper and Roraback filed their cases on May 22, 1958, they expected the judicial process to begin to operate. These attorneys believed that a democratic system had to have an "open" judicial process into which individuals and groups could enter with relative ease. They expected courts to hear such suits, render decisions, and allow appeals in an open and continuing process of litigation. All systems, however, have rules that assert specific requirements and procedures. The judicial process in particular has many such rules. For instance, there must be two sides for a case to enter the system. In addition, they must truly be adversaries, and one side must be able to show that personal damages have been inflicted by the other side. Other such rules stress the necessity of timing and remedy. The 1958 birth control cases encountered a judicial process that was clogged—not open. The very first rule of entry was the major obstacle: Connecticut did not want to litigate another birth control case. Connecticut officials and courts believed that they had been open to birth control litigation long enough. State's Attorney Abe Ullman was not at all happy to see the new cases that Catherine Roraback filed. While he was unable to prevent their filing, he could and did ignore them; the system, in a sense, shut down.[35]

Americans are accustomed to complaining about the delay encountered in judicial proceedings. Sometimes such a delay is caused by a court's heavy load of cases. It may be due to "judicial pen paralysis," as some justices find it difficult to write up their decisions.[36] Delay might be due to staffing problems, which can occur if judicial positions are not filled in a timely fashion. Attorneys themselves often contribute to delay in the system; mistakes made in drafting motions and failure to meet filing deadlines are only two among the numerous examples of attorneys' errors. Even clients themselves can create blockages within the process. It is a sign of the democratic nature of the American judicial process that devices have been created for dealing with such obstacles, and Roraback and Harper were clearly in need of some of these.

What could the attorneys do to force a fight if the state of Connecticut refused to do battle, since it takes two sides to fight? There are methods to either compel a fight or to maneuver around the lack of one. One device for accomplishing this is called an *in re* proceeding, where one side makes an application alone. Sometimes called an *ex parte* proceeding, this method allows a case to move forward even though one side resists involvement. Another procedure to force a fight is known as a "motion for default judgment." This motion asks a court to render a verdict favoring the aggrieved party. Catherine Roraback chose this second device to maneuver Connecticut into a birth control fight once again.

Roraback had hoped that the state would respond to her case filing in a timely fashion. As spring gave way to summer and then to fall, however, it became clear that State's Attorney Ullman and the state attorney general's office were ignoring the suits. So, in late October 1958, she filed her motion for default judgment, claiming, "If the state won't fight, then we should win!" On November 7, 1958, the state attorney general's office belatedly responded, and the birth control fight began once again.[37]

The setting in which Catherine Roraback would test Fowler Harper's strategy and case choices was not an auspicious one. The court was the Connecticut Superior Court of New Haven County. Attorney Ray Cannon of the state attorney general's office represented Connecticut. The judge, Frank T. Healey, was a veteran of the birth control battles. Roraback's job was first to convince the judge that the 1958 cases were completely different from the early birth control cases. She noted that the parties, their damages, and their constitutional rights combined to create truly new cases. If Judge Healey would not "distinguish" the new cases from the old precedents, Roraback's second job was to build a record at this initial hearing that contained judicial flaws and errors that could be appealed to the next level of courts.

The oral argument was the first step. Judge Healey's questions revealed his bias as he accepted Ray Cannon's arguments and challenged Catherine Roraback to refute them. "Is there really a justifiable issue here?" he asked Roraback. "[Didn't] *Nelson* and *Tileston* authoritatively determine that the judiciary has no power to create any exception in . . . the statute?"

Roraback's factual distinctions of her client's constitutional claims fell on deaf ears. Her focus on the rights of "normal marital relations" without the state's interference was dismissed. In addition, another issue surfaced to derail the proceedings: the anonymity of the litigants. Attorney Roraback had filed motions in four of the five cases seeking judicial approval to use fictitious names. She had done this on May 28, 1958, only six days after filing the initial complaints, and Superior Court Judge James Shannon had pronounced the Doe, Poe, Hoe, and Roe usages acceptable. However, he was not the judge before whom the cases were argued, and Judge Healey saw anonymity as a "serious and perhaps fatal procedural problem."

The oral interchange between the attorneys and the judge demonstrated favoritism and bias. Attorney Cannon and Judge Healey were both Roman Catholic graduates of Holy Cross College and Yale Law School. Judge Healey's inclination, not surprisingly, was to follow Cannon's arguments. Nonetheless, the judge's handling of the case during the arguments was procedurally correct. Where could Roraback find flaws that would help bolster her appeal? The answer came on January 5, 1959, when Judge Healey issued a sloppy and carelessly written two-page decision upholding Cannon's objections. The flaws in the written opinion were quickly noted by Roraback. Judge Healey had not mentioned the U.S. Supreme Court ruling in *Tileston*, the major precedent, and his discussion of *Nelson* was factually incorrect. An appeal could certainly be filed. Harper and Roraback were relieved and optimistic.[38]

HINDRANCES TO SUCCESSFUL LITIGATION: TOO MANY ATTORNEYS CONFUSE THE ISSUE, TOO FEW LITIGANTS DISTORT THE MERITS

New problems appeared, however. Fowler Harper and Catherine Roraback faced pressures from within their own camp. Birth control advocates and attorneys eager to get into the action wanted yet another case added to the five already filed. They particularly wanted a case that focused on religious freedom. Three ministers—C. Lawson Willard, George Teague, and Luther Livingston—agreed to file suit. They claimed that Connecticut's 1879 statute was an "unconstitutional infringement of their religious liberty and pastoral counseling rights as protected by the free exercise clause of the First Amendment." Harper did not really need the distraction of yet another set of litigants, particularly those making a very different sort of claim. Nevertheless, he agreed to the addition and to the entry of another attorney, Louise Evans Farr, to handle it. Since this was filed after the initial group of plaintiffs had already entered the process, the attorneys could only hope that it would catch up to the others in the U.S. Supreme Court.

Still, birth control advocates were not happy with the litigation strategy. Attorneys Morris Ernst and Harriet Pilpel from New York urged Harper to drop the Doe case as inappropriate. They pointed out that Jane Doe needed surgery, not birth control. "We need new attorneys, more attorneys, expert advice . . . ," said birth control leaders from New York. Some suggested appealing to prestigious attorneys like Whitney North Seymour and judges like Learned Hand for advice. Would the old axiom "Too many cooks spoil the broth" prove true in the Connecticut birth control cases? Would too many attorneys confuse the litigation strategy?

Another problem also arose involving the litigants themselves. Two of the four patient-plaintiffs suddenly dropped out. It became clear that Harper had not been as careful or as methodical as he should have been when putting together the claims of Dr. Buxton's patients. He should not have been surprised when the problems arose. "Jane Doe" (Ruth Oldendorf), whose severe condition required radical surgery, was never really a good candidate for a birth control device (Morris Ernst had even pointed this out to Harper). She had had little to do with Harper, and although she had agreed for Harper to represent her, there was no signed letter to this effect. Jane Doe had been paralyzed following a miscarriage. Unable to use her right leg or arm, and barely able to speak, she had turned over the legal arrangements to Dr. Buxton. Buxton had actively recruited the Does (Ruth and her husband Bob Oldendorf) to challenge a Connecticut law. He got their consent by promising them anonymity, and although they did not "really understand" what this would lead to, they had agreed because of Buxton's kindness.[39] With such a reluctant litigant, it is not surprising that Harper hesitated to press for an actual signature giving consent for litigation, and Jane Doe never gave it.

The Hoes (Anne and Hector Kinloch) had not met with Fowler Harper, either. They too had not signed a formal document authorizing Harper to act as their attorney or file a case on their behalf. The Hoes' experiences were entirely confined to their medical relation with Dr. Buxton as he struggled with Anne's Rh-negative-induced miscarriages. They were not reluctant litigants, but they too would create a problem for Harper. In January 1960, the Hoes told Buxton and Harper the bad news. They were moving to Australia that June. Harper had no choice but to drop their case from the litigation. It was a loss. The Hoes' particular constitutional claim had been valuable because it was broader than that of the Does. Jane Doe claimed a narrow Fifth and Fourteenth Amendment right to life that the Connecticut statute jeopardized, whereas the Hoes asserted a broader health and welfare issue. The Hoes wanted to "be free of the searing and tragic experiences of repeated miscarriages that create stress, trauma, and despair."[40] Could this claim be covered in the companion case of the Poes?

The Poe couple (Elizabeth and David Odegard) preferred anonymity, as did the Does, but their claim closely resembled the Hoes'. Three children had been born to the Poes: all three had died soon after birth. Surely this claim was sufficient as a health and welfare issue. Unfortunately, once again Fowler Harper had not done his homework. The Poes were not Connecticut residents. Even when the case was filed, the Poes were not considered to be residents of the state. Harper did not know this—but fortunately for him, the State Attorney General's Office did not know it, either. Without Connecticut residency, the Poes had no standing to challenge Connecticut's law.

The Roes (Jean and Marvin Durning) presented the final problem for Harper. This couple asserted an important claim among the original set of cases. Connecticut's statute, they said, was "governmental intrusion into marital privacy." The Roes were young professionals who wanted to postpone having children for economic and career reasons. Fowler Harper regarded this claim as a critical one. He knew this couple personally, and he had their full cooperation in the case. The problem arose when, like the Hoes, the Roes needed to leave Connecticut. Marvin Durning had a job offer in the state of Washington.

Harper and Durning began the search for another young married couple that would assert the claim of marital privacy. They found Louise and David Trubek, both law students at Yale. The Trubeks met with Harper. They agreed to become the new plaintiffs, taking the Roes' place and asserting a Fourteenth Amendment right of liberty to use contraceptives. They did not want anonymity like the other couples. Their case, however, became a new case entirely. Attorney Catherine Roraback filed *Trubek v. Ullman* in May 1960, and it could not catch up with the original set of cases. Fowler Harper's test case, designed for the U.S. Supreme Court, had lost both the Roe and the Hoe plaintiffs;[41] Doe and Poe were left, but both had internal flaws. Were there too few litigants left to properly present the real issues?

THE WRONG WAY TO LOSE: A UNANIMOUS "NO"

Fowler Harper did not expect to win the appeals lodged in the Connecticut Supreme Court. He had told Catherine Roraback to expect to lose in all of the Connecticut courts. Yet, as he well knew, there is a right way and a wrong way to lose a case. For a superior appellate court to accept a case, attorneys must be able to document procedural and substantive flaws. Moreover, it is always helpful if there is a dissent in the lower court ruling. Attorneys can use dissents in their briefs and arguments as they file motions for appeals. Sometimes a dissenting judge's opinion will give an attorney the clues needed to formulate a better argument. Additional points of law and case citations may be mentioned, and attorneys can make use of this advice. It is always helpful if an attorney can show that the case was lost on a closely divided vote. No attorney wants a unanimous verdict against his or her client.

Harper and Roraback wanted to lose "successfully." They did not expect all three judges of the Connecticut Supreme Court to be swayed by this new set of birth control cases, but they did not anticipate a total loss. The chief justice, Raymond E. Baldwin, originally had supported birth control liberalization. True, he had switched sides as his political career changed, but he was expected to be sympathetic. Hope for a divided court did not seem unrealistic.

Oral argument opened October 7, 1959. Roraback and Harper felt prepared; however, justices are often unpredictable and their questions surprising. The chief justice and Justice John H. King together dominated the hearing, and their questions focused on everything but the actual merits of the cases. Harper had hoped for questions about the constitutional claims of life, health, and welfare presented by the individual claimants under the Fifth and Fourteenth Amendments. Those questions were never asked. Instead, the justices of the Connecticut Supreme Court questioned the attorneys about the anonymous patient plaintiffs.

The opposing counsel, Ray Cannon, argued that the plaintiffs were fictitious persons and the questions they presented were not real. Cannon argued they were only "academic" issues: no one was actually suffering personal pain, damages, or injury. While the justices had read the original complaints that had described the medical problems of the plaintiffs (Roe, Doe, Hoe, and Poe), they nevertheless focused on the use of fictitious names. Question after question soon made this issue the dominant one. The birth control attorneys found no opening to argue constitutional liberty claims or those of individual rights. Thus the case closed in the State Supreme Court.

Two months later, the expected defeat was announced: the Connecticut Supreme Court upheld Connecticut's 1879 law criminalizing the use or counseling of birth control. The vote was unanimous. The opinion, written by Chief Justice Baldwin, highlighted a very different issue from that which had dominated the oral argument. It was a study in judicial restraint and judicial deference to legislative power. Using a legislative history approach, Chief Justice Baldwin argued that the state legislature had repeatedly affirmed the birth control statute. All of the legislative attempts to remove or alter the original statute had failed. Turning to a semantics argument, the chief justice noted that the language of the statute was unambiguous; the words were clear and simple. Baldwin concluded that the legislature had the power to pass such a law. A textual analysis of the state constitution detailed the power of the legislative branch under its police powers to pass a statute promoting public, health, safety, and morals. The court's own judicial test was satisfied in this case: the state statute was "rational or reasonably related to its objective." Finally, two precedents, *Nelson* and *Tileston* were controlling. Both of the cases had upheld the birth control statute. Thus, the justices refused to distinguish these precedents even though the individual constitutional claims here had been made clearly. The opinion also pointedly refused to take into account the medical evidence concerning the health benefits of contraceptives. The Brandeis brief–style evidence Harper had submitted was unpersuasive.[42]

It was a stunning defeat for Fowler Harper. Expecting to lose, he nevertheless had not expected to lose by such a margin. His strategy had failed to sway even one justice. Fritz Wiggin had lost *Tileston* before the Connecticut Supreme Court by a 3–2 vote, but *Poe* would have to be appealed against a unanimous state supreme court rejection. It was not an auspicious beginning.

BRIDGING THE BARRIER: *POE ET AL. V. ULLMAN* IN THE SUPREME COURT

Fowler Harper was an optimist. His was not a shallow optimism based on a superficial view of reality; Harper focused on specific actions he could take to reposition his case to win where it ultimately counted: the U.S. Supreme Court. He personally was now in charge, and his first challenge was to persuade the high court to accept *Poe v. Ullman* for oral argument. Clearly, *Poe* was not the case scenario Harper had envisioned in 1957 when he had first met Dr. Lee Buxton. But Harper realistically accepted the fact that the case itself had changed. He had lost his *Roe* and *Hoe* plaintiffs, *Trubek* had not caught up,[43] and the religious freedom case, *Teague, Livingston, and Willard v. Ullman*, was stalled in the New Haven (Connecticut) Superior Court.[44] Nevertheless, Harper was not overly worried as he commenced his appeal.

Writing a brief for the Supreme Court requires skill—and Fowler Harper had this skill. In addition, he had friends like attorney Eugene Gressman, an expert on Supreme Court procedure, to help him. Harper himself could easily have lectured his Yale Law School classes on the various elements to include in an appeal. Able to dissect a Supreme Court opinion, Harper was equally at home in putting these elements together. He could anticipate that justices would ask "Where do we get power to hear this case?" He knew that justices would want proof that the case had no other forum in which to be heard, that the high court's decision would be the final one, and that the decision would actually make a difference. Moreover, justices expected attorneys to provide for them an anatomy of the constitutional provisions and state statutes or actions. What did the words of the law say? What might the words mean? The history of the laws, the constitutional provision involved and the intent of the framers who wrote those laws were certainly appropriate material. This traditional or historical approach often dominates an attorney's submissions to the high court. By the late 1950s, the Supreme Court justices also welcomed arguments based on sociological or economic findings. Technical data arranged into a Brandeis brief might even include polls documenting the contemporary morality standard. Naturally, for Supreme Court review, all arguments and submissions have to be linked to rights and privileges guaranteed by the federal constitution. Finally, the high court expects attorneys to cite the precedents of earlier court decisions and the "tests" the judiciary itself has created for analyzing and balancing claims. A plaintiff's case could have real constitutional merit, but if a litigant so much as stubbed a toe on the "threshold" barrier, the case would be lost. Gaining and preserving an "entry" right was essential.

With all of these barriers in mind, including the history of *Tileston's* defeat in the high court, Harper constructed his initial submission: the jurisdictional statement. He vividly described Roe's and Poe's medical problems. The high court needed to see the litigants as real people with real problems. Harper hoped thus to avoid the issue of fictitious patients with hypothetical grievances. Harper linked these to a constitutional argument based on the Court's precedents. Harper reminded the Court that the "right to marry and [have] children" had been established in 1923 in *Meyer v. Nebraska*. In *Skinner v. Oklahoma* (1942), the Court had provided protection against forced sterilization, thus recognizing a right to "procreate or not procreate." Surely the Court had protected procreation as a "fundamental" right satisfying a judicial test designed by the justices themselves to determine constitutional priorities. In addition, Harper invited the justices to use yet another of their tests, that of "rationality." Could the 1879 Connecticut statute pass this test? Did the very words of the statute violate the constitutional right of privacy in the home? Citing Fourth and Fourteenth Amendment protection, Harper appealed to the history and tradition surrounding protection for one's home. Precedent suggested the argument that privacy of the home was superior to that of a public place. Concluding his use of these various elements of legal reasoning, Fowler Harper offered data from sociological and contemporary morality findings. His Brandeis brief statements cited medical information on birth control, as well as public opinion polls showing its popularity. Harper's arguments were calculated to include as many as possible of the legal elements involved in decisions. He was convinced, as he had always been, that the Court would accept *Poe v. Ullman* for oral argument.

That barrier had to be bridged first: the judicial conference had to vote on Harper's jurisdictional statement.[45] The Supreme Court's "Rule of Four" requirement had to be satisfied for a case to be accepted. It took the vote of four of the nine justices to docket the case for oral argument. Harper got five votes.

An analysis of this *certiorari* voting offers insight into judicial strategies and choices. It helps predict the ultimate votes of the justices. Understanding a justice's vote to "grant *cert*" involves a number of factors that call out for study by those interested in Supreme Court decision making.[46] Do justices "aggressively" vote to grant certiorari to hear cases that they want to reverse? Fowler Harper certainly hoped so. He was dealing with nine highly intelligent men, each possessing his own unique set of values. Chief Justice Earl Warren was regarded as rather "prudish" and might seek to avoid a sexual issue like birth control. Justice William O. Douglas had no such reservations. The wife of Justice John M. Harlan's former law partner had been on the board of Planned Parenthood League of Connecticut, and Harlan was thought to be sympathetic. Justice Felix Frankfurter, as a law professor during the 1930s, had advised the league about attorneys best qualified to win cases before the Supreme Court. Harper knew some of this. He also knew that before the justices ever looked at his appeal, their clerks would have already evaluated it. A clerk in each of the nine offices would have written a memo that would meet the justices' eyes first. How would these law clerks respond? What sort of memos would they write? The attorneys could only guess.

In fact, the justices' law clerks had a wide variety of reactions. Justice Douglas's clerk, Steven Duke, wrote a cautiously worded memo to the effect that the patients had a stronger claim under "life" and "health" than did the physician.[47] Justice Tom Clark's clerk, Cecil Wray, described Harper's use of precedents as "strong and persuasive." Murray Bring, law clerk to Chief Justice Warren, urged the chief justice to view Harper's submissions favorably. He suggested a focus on the "liberty" provision of the Fourteenth Amendment in order to overturn the Connecticut statute. Bring also complimented Harper's brief, calling it "very persuasive" with clearly stated facts. Harper, according to this law clerk, was a counsel of extreme competence.[48]

Justice Harlan's clerk, Howard Lesnick, reacted negatively. Lesnick described Harper's brief as "poor" in quality. He appeared to doubt Harper's concern for the patients, suggesting that the desire for attorney fame motivated the case. Lesnick suggested that the high court dodge the issue. Could deciding such a "ticklish" question as birth control help the Court as an institution? It was a "hot potato" issue. Moreover, Lesnick claimed, the Connecticut statute had not been evoked against the litigants; was the case a "sufficiently ripe controversy"?

As the conference vote on hearing *Poe* was taken, the chief justice and justices Douglas, Harlan, William Brennan, and Potter Stewart lined up in favor of accepting the appeal. Justices Clark, Hugo Black, and Charles Whittaker voted to dismiss the appeal. Only Justice Frankfurter declined to vote. Clark had ignored his clerk's advice to hear the case, while Harlan had conversely ignored his clerk's advice to dismiss the case; Warren and Douglas voted as their clerks had suggested.[49]

BUILDING JUDICIAL BRIDGES:
ATTORNEYS' AND JUSTICES' ATTITUDES

The U.S. Supreme Court accepted *Poe et al.* and *Buxton v. Ullman* for oral argument following the conference vote which took place on Friday, May 20, 1960. The cases were to have been heard that fall. Fowler Harper had at least five to six months to prepare his oral argument. He had time to study the makeup of the court. Attorneys know that justices are only human beings; assuming a judicial role does not turn a justice into an impersonal robot. It is a wise and prudent attorney who studies judicial voting patterns and ideological attitudes.

Harper could have put together such a profile of each of the justices composing the Warren Court of 1960. The Court had taken a stand on racial integration in 1954. Harper also knew these justices were inclined to protect political suspects. He had successfully defended Yale Medical School's Dr. John Peters against allegations of Communist Party affiliation. By 1960 the court was described as a liberal one, and analysts identified the 1956–1957 term of the Court as a high point in the protection of civil rights and liberties. However, it was a Court reluctant to deal with state laws involving marriage and sex. It had refused to deal with Virginia's criminalization of interracial marriage (*Naim v. Naim,* 1956, 1957). Harper's knowledge of this could have easily put together judicial voting profiles based on such material— information that he could use to create a winning coalition. But he seemed to have forgotten that a vote to hear a case did not necessarily mean a vote to reverse the lower court. Unfortunately, Fowler Harper lost his focus.

It was July 1960. *Poe's* argument was to be scheduled for October, November, or December. However, the Department of State altered this when they offered Harper a once-in-a-lifetime opportunity as visiting legal scholar/consultant to Africa. It would be a four-month job of considerable significance for several emerging African nations. Harper was flattered. He accepted the offer and asked for postponement of *Poe.* It was not a wise move. Could any attorney adequately prepare for oral argument before the Supreme Court while occupied with advising foreign leaders? Harper, forgetting the strategy of meticulous and careful planning he had always advocated, assured birth control activists that he could play two roles at the same time.

The Court granted a postponement, and the oral argument was scheduled for February 27, 1961.[50] In the interval from June to February, new law clerks entered the justices' chambers. These clerks wrote new memos and had new ideas. In the chambers of Justice Brennan, the arrival of Richard S. Arnold, Harvard Law class of 1960, made a difference. An Arkansas native who attended Yale as an undergraduate, Arnold should have had sympathy for the Connecticut litigants in the birth control cases. He had actually known the Hoes, but was unaware that Professor Kinlock, his favorite history instructor, was none other than "Harold Hoe." By 1961, the Hoes had dropped out of the litigation, and law clerk Arnold was not impressed with the Poes' argument. A brilliant, thoughtful young man, Arnold had an analytical mind that comprehended elements ignored by others. In later years Senator Dale Bumpers of Arkansas would employ Richard Arnold, recommend his appointment to the Eighth Circuit Court of Appeals, and even urge his nomination to the U.S. Supreme Court following the 1992 election of a pro-choice president, Bill Clinton. In 1988 Judge Arnold would vote against Missouri's antiabortion restriction in the case of *Webster v. Reproductive Health Services.* In 1961, however, a very different Richard Arnold worked to persuade Justice William Brennan to dismiss the *Poe* case and leave Connecticut's law intact. Arnold found in *Poe* a unique procedural flaw that Fowler Harper had totally overlooked. It would give Justice Brennan a prudential basis for evading *Poe's* merits.

Justice Harlan's new clerk, Charles Fried of Columbia Law School, like Arnold, attacked Harper's jurisdictional statements, although he supported the constitutional issue of privacy. Fried cited as the major barrier a lack of enforcement of the Connecticut statute.

Arnold, increasing his attack on *Poe*, stressed his own newly discovered barrier: ripeness. The *Poe* case, Arnold maintained, was not ripe for Supreme Court review. His argument came in layers. If the Supreme Court reversed the Connecticut court, litigation would still continue. Connecticut's rules of procedure would require a trial in the state court and appeals. No trial had taken place earlier, so a decision on *Poe* would be premature. The Supreme Court's prudentially developed barriers required that all legal avenues must be exhausted before it takes a case—a Supreme Court decision must be the final one. Only cases that met these standards would be ripe for Supreme Court review. Richard Arnold concluded that *Poe* was not "ripe," its record was "skimpy" and not "properly constructed."[51]

Fowler Harper knew nothing about Richard Arnold; he also seemed to have forgotten that Justice William Brennan was the Court's only Catholic justice. Would individual rights and liberties be more important in Brennan's hierarchy of values than his religious views? Harper assumed so. He also assumed, without study or evaluation, that justices John M. Harlan and Felix Frankfurter would be favorable to *Poe's* claims. Both had earlier ties to Connecticut's Planned Parenthood League. Harper took their votes for granted even though Justice Frankfurter had refused to vote on whether to accept

Poe. Harper seemed unconcerned that his own testimony against Tom C. Clark's nomination to the Supreme Court might be remembered negatively by that justice.

Nor did Harper develop strategy or tactics for persuading the remaining five justices on the high court. He ignored the views and voting patterns of Hugo L. Black, William O. Douglas, Charles E. Whittaker, and Potter Stewart. He made no plans to cope with Chief Justice Earl Warren's well-known prudish attitude toward cases dealing with sex. Harper was so focused on his constitutional arguments that, like Morris Ernst, he forgot that procedural barriers could block constitutional issues. Fowler Harper had not learned from Fritz Wiggin's failure to build a complete record in *Tileston.* He himself had not created a case scenario that could survive jurisdictional barriers and present the constitutional merits. As *Poe* waited for its day in court, the list of procedural barriers—constitutionally mandated and prudentially developed[52]— grew, and the record could not be changed at this stage.

TILESTON REDUX: ORAL ARGUMENT IN *POE*

Oral argument in *Poe* opened on March 1, 1961. It was a repeat of that in *Tileston* eighteen years earlier. Then, Chief Justice Harlan Stone had interrupted Morris Ernst with a question about the record of the case. "Was there a showing of real harm, injury, or damage, suffered by the patient plaintiffs?" Stone had asked. Stone's query in 1943 was repeated in 1961 by Justice Potter Stewart, who interrupted Fowler Harper with the first question: "Does any Connecticut statute, aside from . . . [this] accessory one . . . prohibit the sale or prescription of contraceptive articles?" Stewart continued, "Is the 'use' of contraceptives statute being challenged only in the context of women facing serious health threats?" Once again, the status of the plaintiffs and the actual enforcement of the statute occupied center stage as they had in *Tileston.*

Harper should have expected these questions. He should have anticipated that some justice might ask, "How many people are prosecuted . . . [each] year . . . under this statute?" It was Justice John M. Harlan who voiced that query, and Harper had to utter the fateful words dreaded by every attorney: "I don't know." When Justice Stewart then pounced with the question "Is the law really enforced?"[53] Harper's case was lost. Harper did not have the data he needed.

Yet the argument in *Poe* had hardly begun. It would last three interminable hours. With questions concerning Dr. Lee Buxton's claims as well as those concerning the patient plaintiffs, each side had been allocated an hour and a half for oral argument. Harper found himself fielding questions from "Why haven't you made a First Amendment free speech argument on behalf of Dr. Buxton?" to "Is freedom to practice one's religion involved here?" However, question after question returned to the issue "Isn't this just an abstract attack on a law . . . [which itself] has no impact?" As the three hours finally ended, Justice Brennan also signaled a lost case when he observed, "I take it that the Poes and the Does can get what they need almost any place in Connecticut."[54]

Fowler Harper, like Morris Ernst, spent the days following oral argument searching for evidence of prosecution under the statute. Looking back over the birth control litigation from 1939–1940, Harper found the *Nelson* case. Doctors Roger B. Nelson and William A. Goodrich, along with Nurse Clara L. McTernan, had been prosecuted under the Connecticut statute. Attorney J. Warren Upson had left a complete record of this prosecution. Harper turned to Upson for help, and Upson did his best. He located a three-page copy of the court reporter's transcripts of State's Attorney William Fitzgerald's remarks during the *Nelson* litigation. Upson noted that in 1939 Fitzgerald had prosecuted those who broke the law. As state's attorney in 1960, he could be expected to do likewise. Harper sent these documents to Chief Justice Earl Warren.[55] In 1943, Ernst, who had also forgotten *Nelson*, sent Chief Justice Stone a post-argument letter to cite the significant *Nelson* precedent. Stone had ignored Ernst's letter; Chief Justice Warren, though he shared it with Justice Frankfurter, likewise ignored Harper's letter.

Nevertheless, hope remained. It was a divided Supreme Court that dismissed *Poe v. Ullman* on a 5–4 vote. The justices were not united as they had been in *Tileston*. Justice Frankfurter's opinion represented only a plurality of the court; Justice Harlan's dissent was a powerful one. Fowler Harper had succeeded in persuading four justices; he was only "one vote shy."

What would it have taken to gain that vote? The justices' law clerks, knowledgeable of judicial interactions and attitudes, provided answers, as did the written opinions in *Poe*. Three justices—Warren, Frankfurter, and Brennan—wanted a better "record." To be precise, they wanted a trial record containing evidence of either prosecution under the law or data demonstrating the law's "chilling effect" on birth control providers and users. Declaratory judgment type actions would never work.[56] Harper should have understood this from *Tileston*. "Timeliness" was another essential. Case precedents such as *Nelson* should have been included in the record from the very beginning of litigation and preserved throughout. It was not the job of the justices to correct the mistakes of the attorney. For example, the justices knew that New Haven's state attorney, William Fitzgerald, would enforce the Connecticut law in the 1960s as he had in the 1940s. He had not changed, yet Justice Frankfurter omitted it from his opinion. As he noted, the information came too late.[57]

Fowler Harper's tardiness and carelessness offered the justices a procedural escape hatch. In fact, Connecticut's law not only had been enforced in the past, it was being enforced even as Justice Frankfurter penned the opposite conclusion in the court's decision. A pharmaceutical salesman in Connecticut was arrested, charged, and convicted for supplying condoms for sale at a gas station. Current events in Connecticut could be ignored by the justices, however, if the attorney did not present them to the Court.

Would Harper have improved his oral argument by anticipating a hostile judicial attitude from an expected supporter? Had the attorney alienated Justice Frankfurter by assuming his support? There was evidence from the beginning of the *Poe* appeal that should have raised questions about Justice Frankfurter. First, he recused himself from the certiorari vote to accept or refuse the *Poe* appeal. Why did he refuse to vote or discuss the case at this stage? In fact, Harper did wonder about it, and he asked birth control advocates for information. There was no evidence that the justice or his wife had ever given money to Planned Parenthood. It was, however, a well-known fact that, as a law professor at Harvard, Frankfurter had acted as an informal adviser of Planned Parenthood of Connecticut. He had urged the substitution of Morris Ernst for Fritz Wiggin in the *Tileston* litigation. Fowler Harper had this information. He assumed that Justice Frankfurter would be sympathetic to *Poe*'s claim. However, a second event involving the justice should have warned Harper to exercise caution. Harper thought that since Frankfurter had recused himself from the appeal's vote, he would do likewise at the time of oral argument. Harper's guess was incorrect. In fact, Justice Frankfurter expressed himself as "most anxious" to participate in *Poe*'s oral argument and discussion. *Poe* was even delayed for two days while Frankfurter recovered from laryngitis. His dominance of the oral argument disconcerted Harper.[58]

Felix Frankfurter's unpredictable nature was well known within the legal community. He was known to be argumentative, and some described him as having an irascible and perverse disposition. Frankfurter's legal brilliance caused others to regard him with awe. Did this create expectations or impose burdens that the justice himself then felt obliged to meet? At any rate, Frankfurter often seized center stage both during oral arguments and the judicial conferences. He did so in *Poe*. Harper could have hypothesized that Frankfurter did not like to be taken for granted. He was known to dislike classifications or labels and took delight in defying pundits who tried to predict his votes. He enjoyed uncovering arguments overlooked by others and testing the creative intellect of both friend and foe. Law was his game.

The oral argument in *Poe* and the assignment of the opinion to Justice Frankfurter showed that he was perhaps the key player in the loss of a case he had been expected to support. The merits of marital privacy as a constitutional right fell before Frankfurter's gamesmanship approach. Yet privacy had been one of Frankfurter's cherished "fundamental rights." He often quoted from Justice Louis D. Brandeis's seminal article on the right of privacy.[59] In 1949, Frankfurter cited that concept when he condemned a police "search" via a stomach pump. If the law could not countenance invasion of bodily privacy, could it countenance invasion of the marital bedroom in search of contraceptives? These very arguments, linking Justice Frankfurter's opinion in the "stomach pump" case—*Wolf v. Colorado*—to *Poe*, had been made in the amicus curiae brief submitted by the American Civil Liberties Union's Ruth Emerson. Harper's brief had developed this right of privacy argument even further, yet Frankfurter refused to apply it in *Poe*.[60]

Nevertheless, it would be this argument that would survive *Poe*'s demise. "Security of one's privacy against arbitrary intrusion . . . is implicit in the concept of ordered liberty," Frankfurter had written in 1949, and Justice Harlan's dissent in *Poe* highlighted Frankfurter's inconsistency. Harper's characterization of privacy rights found their way into Harlan's dissent. Harlan and his law clerk, Charles Fried, both felt passionately about the right to privacy. In a memo to his justice, Fried enthusiastically supported Harper's basic position: "The right to privacy is one which enjoys specific constitutional sanction . . . [and] the right to privacy of the home [is] the purpose behind the Fourth Amendment."

Although Brennan voted to dismiss *Poe* on procedural grounds, he was not happy with his vote. On the constitutional merits of a right to privacy, Justice Brennan was ready to void the Connecticut birth control statute. He made this clear to his law clerks. He even said so openly in an address to English barristers in London.[61]

Fowler Harper had lost *Poe v. Ullman* by the narrowest of margins, but indeed he had lost it. Surely he could learn from his own mistakes, if not from those of his predecessor, Morris Ernst. Unlike Ernst, who never got a second chance with *Tileston*, Harper would get another chance. It would take four years and still another case, but, in the end, Harper would have the opportunity with the right case, and at the right time.

NOTES

1. Christine A. Lunardini, *From Equal Suffrage to Equal Rights* (New York: New York University Press, 1986), 6–7, 19, 138.

2. The Connecticut Birth Control law, passed by the legislature in 1879, was the most restrictive in the country because it forbade the use of contraceptives. Anthony Comstock, a New York moralist, had led in the creation of the 1873 federal antiobscenity and anticontraceptive statutes known as the "Comstock laws" on which the Connecticut statute was based.

3. Thomas S. Dugan, *The Catholic Church in Connecticut* (New York: States History, 1930), 375–400.

4. *State of Connecticut v. Nelson*, 11 A.2d. 856 (1940).

5. *Tileston v. Ullman*, 318 U.S. 44 (1943).

6. *Poe v. Ullman*, 376 U.S. 497 (1961).

7. "Warren Upson," *Waterbury Republican*, 5 April 1960. Upson was described in these words in an article about his selection for the American College of Trial Lawyers.

8. *Commonwealth v. Gardner*, 300 Mass. 372, 15 N.E. 2d. (1938).

9. T. R. van Geel, *Understanding Supreme Court Opinions*, 3rd ed. (New York: Longman, 2002), 57. A "Brandeis brief" is a form of appellate brief that supplements legal arguments and focuses on economic, social, and psychological surveys, using statistical data.

10. David J. Garrow, *Liberty and Sexuality: The Right to Privacy and the Making of* Roe v. Wade, rev. ed. (Berkeley: University of California Press, 1998), 63.

11. Ibid., 69–70, 74–78. A "sociological contemporary morality" justification is created through the use of social data surveys and polls designed to show the changing nature of moral views. It is predicated on the idea that the Constitution was designed to be a living, evolving document.

12. Ibid., 81. Warren Upson's chief concern was protecting the interests of his clients. Their livelihoods, possible imprisonment, and the loss of rights to practice medicine were at stake. See Harriet Pollack, "An Uncommonly Silly Law: The Connecticut Birth Control Cases in the U.S. Supreme Court" (Ph.D. diss., Columbia University, 1967), 81.

13. Fred Rodell, "Morris Ernest, New York's Unlawyerlike Liberal Lawyer: Is the Censor's Enemy the President's Friend?" *Life*, 21 February 1944.

14. Morris Ernst, "How We Nullify," *Nation* 134 (27 January 1932): 113–114.

15. Ibid.

16. Garrow, *Liberty and Sexuality*, 84.

17. Ibid., 92.

18. Van Geel, *Understanding Supreme Court Opinions*, 9. The cases-and-controversy standard requires a definite, concrete legal issue between two parties having adverse interests. Such an issue cannot be hypothetical; it must be "justiciable," in that a court decision can be effective.

19. Garrow, *Liberty and Sexuality*, 92.

20. Brief for Plaintiff, *Tileston v. Ullman*, 129 Conn. 84. 26 A.2d., 582 (1942).

21. The Superior Court reserved (certified) three questions to the Connecticut Supreme Court of Errors. This strategy meant that the judges of the lower court believed that these questions were of a nature that only the state Supreme Court was competent to address. *Tileston v. Ullman*, 129 Conn. 84, 29 A.2d., 582 (1942).

22. Van Geel, *Understanding Supreme Court Opinions*, 9n2. The Supreme Court interprets the constitutional requirement of "cases and controversy" so as to create barriers that weed out cases. Parties must show that they have "standing to sue"; the requirement of concrete issues with actual harm or damage suffered must be met. "Ripeness" implies that every other option has been explored and exhausted; a case must not be "moot." A dead issue or one where the Court's decision can be of no effect is a formidable barrier. All of these are judicially created and are ignored at will by the justices themselves.

23. A case decided on its "merits" involves a focus on the strict legal rights of parties, as distinguished from considerations depending on practices or jurisdiction. The legal significances or the intrinsic right and wrong of a case stand in stark contrast to matters of form and procedure. Abraham Ullman's brief and arguments before the Connecticut court sought to avoid the merits of the case. Procedural standards pro-

vided a technical way to avoid a highly emotional issue. See Garrow, *Liberty and Sexuality*, 103.

24. Pollack, "An Uncommonly Silly Law."

25. Vern Countryman, "*Tileston v. Ullman*," Douglas Paper Box 78, Manuscript Division, Library of Congress, Washington, DC, cited in Garrow, *Liberty and Sexuality*, 102, 781.

26. Morris L. Ernst and Edwin Borchard, "Appendices to Appellant's Brief," *Tileston v. Ullman*, 318 U.S. 44 (1943).

27. Alice Fleetwood Bartee, *Cases Lost, Causes Won: The Supreme Court and the Judicial Process* (New York: St. Martin's, 1984), 83.

28. The exchange before the Supreme Court described here is taken from Charles E. Scribner, "The Argument of *Tileston v. Ullman* in the U.S. Supreme Court," 15 January 1943, 9 pgs., Planned Parenthood of America, Box 39.

29. Garrow, *Liberty and Sexuality*, 104.

30. Del Dickson, ed., *The Supreme Court in Conference, 1940–1985: The Private Discussions behind Nearly 300 Supreme Court Decisions* (New York: Oxford University Press, 2001), 795–797.

31. Rodell, "Morris Ernest."

32. Garrow, *Liberty and Sexuality*, 114.

33. Mary Dudziak, "Just Say No: Birth Control in the Connecticut Supreme Court before *Griswold v. Connecticut*," *Iowa Law Review* 75 (May 1990): 915–939.

34. Garrow, *Liberty and Sexuality*, 151.

35. Dudziak, "Just Say No," 932–933.

36. Merlo J. Pursey, *Charles Evans Hughes* (New York: Macmillan, 1951), 2:667–668.

37. Garrow, *Liberty and Sexuality*, 156.

38. Pollack, "An Uncommonly Silly Law," 101–104.

39. Garrow, *Liberty and Sexuality*, 143–147, 154.

40. Ibid., 144.

41. Pollack, "An Uncommonly Silly Law," 102.

42. C. Roraback, "Briefs of Plaintiffs-Appellants," and R. Carson, "Brief of Defendant-Appellee," *Poe v. Ullman* #4796, *Hoe* #4797, *Doe* #4798, *Buxton* #4794; Connecticut Supreme Court, *Record and Briefs*, March Term, 1959. Supplemental and reply briefs were also filed.

43. *Trubeck v. Ullman*, 367 U.S. 907 (1961).

44. Pollack, "An Uncommonly Silly Law," 100–101.

45. Garrow, *Liberty and Sexuality*, 168–169.

46. Lee Epstein and Jack Knight, *The Choices Justices Make* (Washington, DC: CQ Press, 1998), 80, 122.

47. Garrow, *Liberty and Sexuality*, 174–176.

48. Ibid., 170.

49. Ibid., 169.

50. Ibid., 170.

51. Richard Arnold, "A Remembrance of Mr. Justice Brennan, October Term 1960," *Journal of Supreme Court History* (1991): 5–8.

52. "Constitutionally mandated" is a phrase used by justices to give credence to the belief that "case and controversy" is a standard of clear constitutional directive.

53. See *Poe v. Ullman* for the oral argument. 367 U.S. 497 (1961) www.justia .us/us/367/497/case.html.

54. Ibid.

55. Dickson, *Supreme Court in Conference*, 797–799.

56. Bernard Schwartz, *Super Chief: Earl Warren and His Supreme Court* (New York: New York University Press, 1983), 378–380. David Garrow uses the phrase "one vote shy" for the title of chapter 3 in *Liberty and Sexuality*.

57. Dickson, *Supreme Court in Conference*, 799.

58. Garrow, *Liberty and Sexuality*, 170.

59. Samuel Warren and Louis D. Brandeis, "The Right to Privacy," *Harvard Law Review* 4 (1890): 193.

60. Dickson, *Supreme Court in Conference*, 797–798.

61. William J. Brennan, speech to the Law Society in London, 10 July 1961.

2

Confusion in the Conference

While many cases are lost at the very first stage of the judicial decision-making process, many others are stopped due to mistakes at the second stage. Birth control advocates had struggled to survive that first level when the mistakes of attorneys so tied up the privacy cases that the merits of the issues were never debated. The actual case facts, the sad stories of the litigants, and the data to prove the need for birth control had not gotten into the record. Their absence proved a major hurdle and birth control advocates found themselves unable to overcome the mistakes made at the beginning. Other privacy issues, however, found their greatest challenge at another stage of the process, the deliberations among the justices based on individual perceptions of case litigations. This stage often proved to be the Waterloo for privacy rights advocates. Such was the story of gay rights litigation as it unfolded at the Supreme Court decision-making level known as the conference.

Decision making at the conference level has always been shrouded in mystery. Its mystique intensified due to the *Bowers v. Hardwick* gay rights case. Court analysts, legal experts, reporters, and law clerks all sought to bring together the pieces of that confused conference, which ended so disastrously for gay rights advocates.[1] Laurence Tribe, the attorney for Michael Hardwick, had won his case when the Supreme Court's conference discussion of the nation's first gay rights case concluded in March 1986. Justice Harry Blackmun certainly thought he had the votes of four other justices who had been persuaded by Tribe's articulate presentation of the privacy rights of gay people within their home. The conference discussion had placed justices Brennan, Marshall, Stevens, and Powell in agreement with Blackmun. With Chief Justice Warren Burger in the minority, Justice William

Brennan was the senior associate for the majority and could assign the opinion to Blackmun. However, Justice Powell changed his mind. The conference vote shifted and the dissenting justices—White, Rehnquist, O'Connor,
and Burger—suddenly became the majority. A case won became a case lost,
and the pivotal role of the Supreme Court's conference came under intense
scrutiny.

THE CONFERENCE SETTING: A SEARCH FOR POWER POSITIONS

The Supreme Court's private ceremonial conference rooms are precisely
that: ceremonial. The blue-motif West Conference Room is often used for informal receptions. The rose-motif East Conference Room, with its portrait of
the legendary Chief Justice John Marshall above the fireplace, is frequently
the site of small discussion seminars. Neither of these rooms is the real conference room. That chamber is located across the corridor from the courtroom proper. Its main door opens onto the central corridor that runs the
length of the building. Inside, this conference room is connected with the office of the chief justice. The room itself is not unique and has been little
changed since Chief Justice Charles Evans Hughes held the first conference
here in 1935. The rectangular room's spaciousness is emphasized by its high
ceiling. It is lighted by a magnificent crystal chandelier and enhanced by
three large floor-to-ceiling windows. The heavy red rug, elaborate drapes,
book-lined walls, oak paneling, and massive furniture combine to reduce the
impression of size of the room and to make it more conducive to small-
group discussion. In addition, the black marble fireplace with matching
clock, brass fireplace accessories, and imposing portrait of Chief Justice Marshall add to the overall sense of dignity and tradition imparted by the room.
The focal point of attention is the massive twelve-foot-long Honduran mahogany conference table directly in front of the fireplace. Around the table
are nine high-backed green leather swivel chairs, each with the brass name-
plate of a justice. Built into the table are shallow drawers, one for each justice, fitted with lock and key.[2]

From the beginning of the Court's history, the justices have conferred together, and the conference itself has been shaped by historical forces.
Among these forces, there are at least three that can shed light on the "private court" and its behavior. First, the location of the conference discussion
is central for understanding the judicial decision-making process. Second,
the size of any Court, the justices, and the issues the different Courts have
confronted over time have molded the conference. Third, the personality of
the chief justice and his management style also have shaped the development of the conference.[3]

At first, there was no official location for the conference. The justices on the Court followed the pattern established by the Inns of Court in London, where English legal training took place. The English system was "communal." Barristers and law students lived and dined together near the court. Students read law reports and records and "mooted" or argued cases. Occasionally lectures by senior members provided additional instruction.[4]

John Marshall encouraged this system during his tenure as chief justice. The six justices on the Court had lodgings at the same boardinghouse. The justices' families did not move to Washington, which most regarded as a "grim" place. The justices were thus isolated from families and friends and were grateful for a comfortable rooming house. Here they dined together, met informally, and ultimately developed a sense of group loyalty. There were few distractions from the Court's workload. Discussing cases and gossiping dominated the life of these early justices during each term of Court. Marshall also used his position as chief justice to mold the conference's procedure. Stressing the need for consensus, Marshall worked to produce decisions that all justices would sign. He was willing to compromise in the interest of unity, believing that this enhanced the power and prestige of the Court. When the justices adjourned into a private meeting room following dinner at the boardinghouse, Marshall urged them to employ negotiation, bargaining, and compromise with each other in order to secure unanimity. When such interaction occurred in these private meetings, Marshall insisted upon great secrecy: No one outside the justices themselves should ever know how a decision had been reached. The conference as a secret institution was thus born.

Under Marshall, the justices "conferenced" six days a week when the Court was in session. Marshall, as chief justice, also claimed the right to begin each discussion with his own "statement of a case"—the facts, issues, and law. That allowed him to shape and control the discussion that followed.[5] For nearly twenty-nine years, Marshall prevailed, but by 1832, some justices began insisting on separate accommodations and others brought their families to Washington. Some decisions of the pre–Civil War period would change the tenor and outcome of the conference.

Partisan politics dominated the chief justiceship of Roger Brooke Taney, Marshall's successor. The communal lifestyle that had softened "regional, ideological, and doctrinal" differences was gone. Tension increased in the daily conference discussions, which now took place in a library conference room rented by Congress for the justices. Congress finally allotted a basement room at the Capitol for this purpose. However, it was seldom used, and it was not until 1860 that the justices finally moved into better quarters. The Old Senate Chamber became the new Courtroom, and the vice president's office became the conference room. This pre–Civil War Court was also larger than its predecessors. Nine justices now sat on the bench. Both size and environment worked against Chief Justice Taney's efforts to "marshall" his court.[6] It was a Court of "many men of many minds." Long and tedious hours of acrimonious conference debate resulted. Dissents became the norm, and the chief justice no longer attempted to assign to himself the majority of the cases. Nevertheless, Taney, like Marshall, presided at these conferences and stated the issues as he saw them. Following discussion, voting took place, with the most junior justices voting first. Taney then made the opinion assignment.[7]

The Court's prestige and power eroded significantly at this time, and the post–Civil War years continued this trend. The close judicial associations of boardinghouse days were now only a memory. Justices lived with their families and worked alone at home. The daily conference gave way to weekly meetings, usually held on Saturdays. The conferences were short. There was little attempt at judicial persuasion—no negotiation, no bargaining, no compromise. Ideological voting was the norm, and partisan politics ruled. From this situation developed a major procedural practice: the "rule of four." This allowed a minority of four justices, if they so chose, to force their colleagues to take a case for oral argument and decision. A minority could thus affect the Court's agenda. However, this effort to appease the minority did not stop the increasing number of dissents that accompanied each case decision. The conference meetings reflected this. Discussion, voting, and opinion assignment all occurred on the same day, and opinions were written within a very short period of time. As the twentieth century approached, those types of conferences still characterized the Court.[8]

The personality and management style of each chief justice certainly impacted the conference at this time, as it still does today. However, even the most skillful chiefs have found it impossible to prevent intracourt bickering and fighting. Chief Justice Melville Fuller's strategy was designed to restore conference civility. Described as a superb "social" leader, Fuller employed tactics that included "courting" his colleagues. He provided dinner and scheduled conferences in the relaxed atmosphere of his home. He often catered to one or another justice's ego through flattery. Fuller's personality helped him. He was a warm, kind, and congenial person, with a charming manner. Some said he was "lovable." His idea of opening each conference discussion with formal handshakes, however, did not reduce the intracourt wrangling. Antilabor, anti–government regulation, and anti–civil rights positions taken by the justices affected the public's perception of this Court period. However, lobbying Congress to expand the Court's power to refuse cases succeeded. Ultimately the "*certiorari* conference" would emerge from this as the Court expanded its discretionary jurisdiction.[9]

While social leadership skills were valuable to chiefs who wanted to control conference discussions and votes, they were not enough. Could a chief justice who was also an intellectual leader do what social leaders could not do? "Task" or intellectual leadership did not characterize most chief justices.[10] Fuller, Edward Douglass White, and former president turned chief justice William Howard Taft were not intellectual giants. Nevertheless, Taft, like Fuller, was a superb social leader and was successful in lobbying Congress to increase judicial power. His control of the conference was due to his ability to charm his colleagues. Using all the tactics earlier developed by Fuller—courtesy, deference, flattery, persuasion—Taft won allies. "He is so nice that it is hard to disagree with him," Justice Oliver Wendell Holmes once remarked. Since Taft lacked the intellectual skills to be a successful "task" leader and to "persuade on the merits," he delegated this job to his good friend Willis Van Devanter. Thus, he was able to hold down the number of dissents in spite of the ideological divisions that were rooted in controversial economic and social problems. Nevertheless, these differences ultimately undermined Taft's control of the conference. Leadership skills were simply not enough. A united, efficient, and powerful Court was desired by most chief justices. However, it was difficult to achieve.

With the exception of John Marshall, Charles Evans Hughes is credited with being the most successful chief justice in achieving his goals. Hughes, like Fuller and Taft, was a superb social leader, but he was also a legal genius who could dominate his court as the intellectual or "task" leader. He generally was able to manipulate and control the conferences. The new Supreme Court building, the "Marble Temple," brought the Hughes's Court to today's conference room. It was luxurious and comfortable, and it provided a stage for Hughes.[11]

Hughes had precise ideas about the way in which discussions should take place. He liked order, and he understood power. He always opened the conference discussion by reviewing the facts of the case, the lower court decision, and the constitutional law questions that were raised. By his choice of the several questions which a case might present, Hughes was able to focus the proceeding discussion. Through his personality, Hughes dominated that discussion. Surrounded by legal volumes, each carefully and visibly marked with white paper markers, Hughes cited precedents without having to open the volumes in front of him. His photographic memory and intellectual powers were legendary even in his own time, and few of his associates relished a disagreement with him. However, Hughes was not a dictator; he was never devious in his handling of the conference discussion. It is true that his opening statements and focus questions were designed to persuade, but his strategy was a "persuasion on the merits."[12] He hoped through his mastery of the details of a case and the marshalling of legal justification, including precedents, to persuade the other justices to accept his view.

Discussion in Hughes's conference room, as in earlier ones, proceeded according to seniority. However, Hughes insisted that while discussion should proceed according to seniority, with the senior justices speaking first, voting would take place in reverse order; the most junior justice was asked to vote first. Hughes may have had an ulterior motive in the practice. By not voting while the discussion was proceeding, each justice would be given time to change his mind. By voting last, Hughes could break any ties, determine the winning side, and then assign the opinion. This method increased the power of the chief justice. The "Hughberts Game" demonstrates this. Hughes often found himself agreeing with three liberal justices. His vote alone would not create a majority; he needed the vote of another moderate conservative: Justice Owen J. Roberts. When Roberts voted with the four conservatives, then Hughes would vote against his own policy goal, join the majority of five, and assign the opinion. Often he would choose Roberts to write the opinion, which undermined the "ultraconservatives" plans.[13]

The personalities, strategies, and management skills of the three chief justices who followed Hughes—Harlan Fiske Stone, Frederick Moore Vinson, and Earl Warren—were well known to Warren E. Burger when he became chief justice in 1969, but he did not want to emulate any of these. John Marshall, and Marshall alone, was the role model for Warren Burger. There were reasons for rejecting the Stone, Vinson, and Warren conference procedures. The "free-wheeling conference debates" under Chief Justice Stone did not build consensus nor increase the power and prestige of the Court.[14] Individual policy predilections separated justice from justice, and compromise was forgotten as individual beliefs and agendas dominated voting. The Constitution's meaning hinged on the vote of five justices: any coalition of five would make law. Stone was academic, interested in debate, and "combative and sarcastic." Conferences under Stone were too long, too unstructured, and too acrimonious. His poor management style, combined with ever-increasing discord concerning an "evolving" Constitution, set the stage for even greater problems. Judicial battles became public ones; feuds and quarrels between the justices were reported in newspapers across the country.[15]

This was the situation that Fred Vinson inherited when Stone died on the bench on April 22, 1946. Vinson could not look to Stone's record for help in conference management. The Court was "leaderless and bitterly divided."[16] Vinson, like Burger, dismissed Stone as a model; as chief justice, he proved equally unable to provide leadership for the Court or to bring unity. He was not an intellectual leader like Hughes. Seen as a legal lightweight, Vinson could not earn the respect of his colleagues. Divisive issues escalated the Court's problems—civil rights, civil liberties, and economic regulation among them. Religious issues also focused intense scrutiny on the justices' deliberations. Dissents increased.

Vinson's death after only seven years as chief brought another style of leader to the Court in 1953. Earl Warren's personality, ideology, and management style were naturally reflected in his conferences. Warren possessed social leadership skills, while Justice William Brennan acted as his intellectual lieutenant. Together, this team functioned to increase the Court's power.[17] The conference procedures Warren found useful included the seniority system for discussion and reverse order for voting. All of the elements associated with secrecy were pursued under Warren. Even so, stories of judicial rivalries and divisions were reported regularly. The Court divided as Warren and Brennan pushed forward with a pro–civil rights and liberties agenda. Warren Burger would seek to reverse all of this when he assumed the role of chief justice in 1969.

During the chief justiceships of Hughes, Stone, Vinson, and Warren, little was written about the conference room. However, with the appointment of Burger as chief justice in 1969, the furnishings in the conference room became the source of much speculation. It was reported that Chief Justice Burger had had the table sawed into three pieces and fitted together into an inverted "U" shape, an alternative designed deliberately to eliminate the second "end" and "along with it . . . the possibility of legitimizing by special position the role of leadership" of the senior associate justice who traditionally sat at the front of the table facing the chief justice. Apparently, the chief justice did want to make some changes that would increase his influence over the Court; however, he did not "saw" the conference table into three pieces: the table is still intact.

What Burger did was to move an antique desk into the room, placing it some distance from the conference table. Some speculated that he had hoped to link his own office more closely with the conference room because Burger had never liked the chief justice's chamber, which he told clerks was smaller than his old one at the Court of Appeals. He particularly wanted a workroom to expand his office space. As Burger had contemplated his new office space on becoming chief justice, he envisioned the Court's conference room as the perfect place for the chief justice to welcome visitors and entertain. Thus, he toyed with the idea of removing the conference meetings to either the East or West Conference Room, although they were on the other side of the building from the justices' offices. Only the stubborn opposition of the other justices stopped Burger from this scheme. Having already moved his antique desk into the conference room, though, Burger determined to leave it. His new approach was to move the conference table to one side of the room, with his desk on the other side. Although the other justices were irritated, Burger won on that point: his desk remained in the conference room.[18]

Chief Justice Burger did not follow Hughes's model. Burger insisted that each justice announce his voting position when his turn came to speak. This system did not work well for Burger, however, especially when positions he espoused began to lose support as the conference proceeded. Thus Burger developed an additional strategy—an "as I see it" summation. At the conclusion of the vote and discussion period, Burger would announce his tally of the re-sults. There were occasions when his tally would disagree with that of other justices, but his power as chief gave him opportunity to manipulate the vote, and with it, the opinion assignments.

Some justices believed that Burger would deliberately change his own po-sition and vote in order to gain assignment power over the cases. Before his retirement from the Court in 1975, Justice William O. Douglas, the most lib-eral member of the court, claimed that Burger had done this four times in one term. As senior associate, Douglas insisted in each instance that he should have had the assignment power. Douglas particularly believed that this had occurred in the abortion cases, where he claimed that Burger had mistallied the vote. Burger's response to Douglas's charge showed how he operated the conference. The voting in the abortion cases was "too compli-cated," Burger wrote to Douglas. "There were literally not enough columns to mark up an accurate reflection of the voting," he continued. As a result, Burger explained, "I [did not] mark down votes; I said this was a case that would have to stand or fall on the writing, when it was done." Concluding his defense of the assignment of *Roe v. Wade* and *Doe v. Bolton* to Justice Harry Blackmun, Burger added, "[This was] my view of how to handle these two sensitive cases which . . . are quite probable candidates for re-argument." Douglas naturally believed that Burger was deliberately manipulating the process to insure reargument, which he himself found unnecessary.[19]

In 1986 when *Bowers v. Hardwick* was discussed in this room, Warren Burger had been chief justice for seventeen years; he would resign that very year. He had not been able during that time to significantly change the con-ference room or its procedures. The justices still were positioned around the table according to seniority: Chief Justice Burger sat at one end of the table with senior associate justice William Brennan at the opposite end. However, the conference to decide *Bowers*, like all other argued cases, represents only part of the total conference proceedings. The powers of the chief justice are tested by two different types of decisions the Court must make at conference. The Court, even before it can decide a case, must first decide to hear it.

THE CONFERENCE: PURPOSES AND PROCEDURES

Justices sitting around the twelve-foot mahogany table in the conference room do indeed vote on who will win and who will lose in a case argued be-fore them. While that particular conference vote is not "binding" and a jus-tice may later shift his position, it is nevertheless a dramatic scene in the un-folding drama that is the judicial process. The other type of decision that also is made during a conference discussion has drawn less attention. Its signifi-cance in the development of constitutional law is as critical to the decision-making process as the vote that decides a case: Justices can choose which cases to hear and which cases to discard. They cast these votes during a conference discussion. This "process of choice" determines the scope and limits of major social and political questions the court will address during a term. The mystery that surrounds this process must be investigated in order to understand the full purpose of the conference itself.[20]

How does the Supreme Court decide which cases to hear? Cases that are filed with the Court have their roots in the political, economic, and social forces that are moving in the country. The questions generated by claims of privacy—reproductive choice, sexual partners, and death and dying freedoms—all have been translated into legal questions and presented to the Court. As lawyers and groups take such cases to the Court, there are a number of rules they must follow, procedures that must be used, and forms that must be employed. A case must be appropriately "dressed" so that a Court will decide to open the door and admit it for consideration.

The first place a case is noted is on the Court's dockets. Until 1970 there were three dockets. The first was reserved for the few cases that come under the Court's Article III "original jurisdiction." Not many cases both begin and end in the Supreme Court, so this docket has always been very small. The second docket, the appellate docket, contained petitions for certiorari or jurisdictional statement (for appeals). These petitions and statements must fit a certain format: printed, bound, and covered. Such a format can be expensive, so Courts developed a "miscellaneous docket," where unpaid appeals, often in shabby format, could be received and processed. Today the appellate and miscellaneous dockets have been merged with only a numbering system to distinguish "paid" from unpaid ones. Thousands of cases are filed each year and the justices in their conference accept a few while rejecting many. During the years when Warren Burger was chief justice, the Court accepted and decided some 150 cases each year out of approximately 4,500 cases filed.

Why do the justices vote to hear some cases but not others? How do they make this entry-level decision? How do they decide that one applicant should be deemed worthy of an interview, but not another? What rules govern this part of the decision-making process?[21] The Court requires that cases raise a constitutional question involving statutory interpretation, criminal procedure, equal protection, due process, or the equivalent. The Court looks carefully at cases that raise questions about the separation of powers between the legislative, executive, and judicial branches of government. Issues of federalism—state government power versus national government powers—also receive careful scrutiny from the justices.

Using its "discretionary power" granted by Congress in the 1925 Judges Bill, the Court can weed out cases. The central test lawyers must pass in their initial petitions asks the question, "Why should the Supreme Court take the case?" Does it really present a "substantial federal question"? If four justices vote yes, the case will be accepted. This grant of a *writ of certiorari* is the means by which a large number of the Court's cases will be processed. It is a procedure based on nine individual decisions. In earlier times, every case was discussed; later, the chief justice claimed power to circulate a "dead list," containing cases he personally found inappropriate. Justices could challenge this list and seek to remove a particular case from it. The list of cases to discuss, also compiled by the chief justice, gave Chief Justice Warren E. Burger significant power. The "dead list" and the "discuss list" were impacted by Burger's own ideology, as they were by earlier chief justices. No justice is completely neutral in questions involving public policy. Some cases may lie in a justice's "zone of indifference," while others trigger challenges to the chief's initial listing of cases.[22] Justices' interests can be intensified by the presence of a large number of amicus curiae briefs. The Court's attention is also captured by those cases where the government is involved. Finally, cases where lower courts have rendered conflicting opinions will likely make the "discuss" list.

The conference vote on whether or not to hear a case often reveals the policy predilection of the justice. When justices like the decision of the lower court, they are often ready and eager to grant certiorari. However, even if four justices can be found for this purpose, there remains the problem of the fifth vote in order to win on merits of the case. At that point, a voting bloc of four justices, sharing a common ideology and having power to force a review of a case, must nevertheless consider whether or not to do so. They must analyze the probability of attracting at least one more vote to their bloc. It may be to their advantage not to bring the case up only to lose it, thus establishing an undesired Supreme Court precedent. The calculations which drive each justice in this process differ according to the policy issue raised by the case. Justices know one another's attitudes, voting patterns, and maneuvers. In addition, justices might worry that the politically elected branches of government, Congress and the president, might oppose them. A case win for five or more justices could be turned into a cause lost if Congress or the president should mount an attack on the Court or ignore the decision. Courts lose power when decisions are not enforced and apparently make no difference.[23]

Justices have been found to behave somewhat like fortune tellers, as the conference voting on certiorari reveals. Two terms have been coined to describe this voting behavior: *aggressive grants* and *defensive denials* of certiorari.[24] Justices vote "aggressively" when they think they have a case that would further their own ideology and have the added bonus of winning on the facts of the case alone. However, those same justices might deny certiorari to a case they would otherwise like to hear because they think they will not be able to win at the merits stage. This would be a "defensive denial" of certiorari.

One other type of decision is made during a conference: *issue suppression*.[25] This decision deals with the question of the focus within a case. Could the Court decide the case on a "procedural technicality"? The issue of abortion rights often has been evaded due to the birth of the fetus—the mother no longer had "standing" and the question was "moot." Or the justices might decide to evade the question presented by the parties to the case and focus on another issue. What goes on during the various conferences is clearly central to the judicial process. During the conference, cases are selected, justices vote, and opinion writing begins. Documenting the workings of a conference dealing with a particular case exposes the complex nature of a decision. The complexity is enhanced when a conference ends in confusion and a case won becomes a case lost, even if not necessarily a cause lost. Such a conference occurred in the gay rights case of *Bowers v. Hardwick*.

THE FIRST "GAY RIGHTS" CASE: *BOWERS V. HARDWICK*

Michael Hardwick was a complex individual. College educated, he had trained to be a landscape architect. The search for a "life's meaning" led him from Catholicism into Buddhism and then into "New Age" theology. Sensitive, creative, and talented, Hardwick was constantly seeking to find focus for his life. At twenty-one, he had recognized his homosexual orientation. His talents and lifestyle drew him into a number of different vocations: bartender, health food store owner, sculptor, and entrepreneur. He had opened a business in Miami called Growth Concept Environment Design and done well at first. However, a move to Atlanta changed the course of his life.[26]

Like many cities, Atlanta maintained an "uneasy truce" with its gay population. This was especially true of the city's Piedmont Park area and Virginia Highland district. Here gays congregated and lived openly homosexual lives. They formed softball teams with uniforms and cheerleaders and competed with each other. However, they were always under surveillance. They knew that at any moment the police might appear and make a series of arrests. Georgia law authorized arrest for sodomy as a felony, but the Atlanta police in these areas usually avoided using this charge. They generally opted for a "public indecency" charge—a misdemeanor—when they happened to catch gays engaging in acts of sodomy.

Michael Hardwick lived in the Virginia Highland neighborhood and worked at a gay bar. A beer bottle was the beginning of his conflict with the Atlanta police. Georgia law prohibited drinking on a public street. Hardwick, coming out of a gay bar one morning, had thrown a beer bottle into a trash can by the front door. His timing was bad. At that very moment, a police car drove by and Officer K. R. Torich saw him with the open beer bottle. He gave Hardwick a ticket for drinking in public, and Hardwick was ordered to appear in court to pay a fine. Due to confusion over the appointed date for the hearing, Hardwick missed his court date. However, he immediately sought to rectify this and presented himself to the county clerk and the judge, who then fined him fifty dollars. Hardwick paid the fine.

Three weeks elapsed and a new chapter opened. It was 8:30 A.M. on August 3, 1982, when Officer K. R. Torich reappeared in Michael Hardwick's life. As he knocked on the door that morning, Torich had in his a hand the old warrant for Hardwick's arrest on the charge of failing to appear in court for drinking in public. He had not checked to see if the warrant was still valid. The front door of Hardwick's house was open, and Officer Torich entered. In the living room, he found one of Hardwick's friends asleep on the couch. Torich later described the exchange. "[Hardwick's] roommate opened the door. He told me he didn't know if Hardwick was home but said I could come in to look for him. While walking down the hallway inside the house, I saw a bedroom door partially open." Inside that bedroom, Officer Torich found Michael Hardwick and a male friend engaged in oral sex. Although the warrant Torich carried had indeed expired, Torich now had a new charge, and he arrested Hardwick and his friend for violation of Georgia's sodomy law.

It would take twelve hours to get Hardwick out of the jail on bail. After an initial municipal court hearing, the sodomy case was docketed before the Fulton County (Georgia) Superior Court. Hardwick and his attorneys from the American Civil Liberties Union (ACLU) decided to challenge Georgia's sodomy law. They hoped to reach the U.S. Supreme Court with the case. However, before they could proceed, the door was shut: District Attorney Lewis Slaton decided not to go forward with the charges and pulled the case from the court's docket.[27]

Refusing to give up, Hardwick's attorneys turned to the federal courts. They cited Hardwick's continued fear of prosecution under a four-year statute of limitation and attacked the Georgia sodomy statute, which dated from 1816, as deprivation of "privacy, due process, and freedom of expression and association." Under the leadership of attorney Kathleen Wilde, the ACLU recruited additional plaintiffs. "John and Mary Doe," a heterosexual, married couple joined the case. Their sexual practice also violated the Georgia law, and they, like Hardwick and his friend, were equally targets of that law.[28]

District Judge Robert H. Hall ruled against Hardwick in the first encounter. He based his ruling on a 1975 decision of a federal judicial panel, which in *Doe v. Commonwealth's Attorney for the City of Richmond* had upheld a Virginia sodomy law similar to that of Georgia. The panel had denied that homosexuals were protected by the earlier privacy decision involving marriage, home, and family life.[29] The U.S. Supreme Court had refused to hear an appeal of that case, and while a denial of certiorari means only that four votes could not be found to hear the case, lawyers and judicial experts often interpret such refusals as support for the lower court's decision. Judge Hall interpreted *Doe* this way, noting that "all the constitutional arguments made by Hardwick were rejected in *Doe*." The married couple, John and Mary Doe, was denied "standing" because the two had not been threatened with prosecution and had not suffered a direct injury as a result of the statute's enforcement.[30]

The case then moved to the federal appellate court in Atlanta, where two years later Hardwick won his first victory. Judge Frank M. Johnson's opinion interpreted privacy rights precedents to extend to "private consensual sexual behavior among adults." Georgia officials immediately filed a petition of certiorari asking the Supreme Court to reverse this decision. Michael Hardwick and his ACLU attorneys seemed to have achieved their goal of reaching the Supreme Court, but they were soon disappointed to learn that the Court had voted not to take the case. However, a changed certiorari vote finally brought the case before the justices for oral argument on March 31, 1986.[31]

BOWERS'S CERTIORARI CONFERENCE

When *Bowers v. Hardwick* came to the docket of the Supreme Court in 1985, the Court's membership consisted of Chief Justice Warren E. Burger and justices William Brennan, Byron White, Thurgood Marshall, Harry Blackmun, Lewis Powell, William Rehnquist, John Paul Stevens, and Sandra Day O'Connor. Their initial response to the petition for certiorari was a negative one. On its face, *Bowers* presented the Court with several problems. Michael Hardwick, the plaintiff, had no real standing. Even before the first trial of Hardwick's case, the local district attorney in Georgia had pulled the case by refusing to present the charges to a grand jury for indictment. It had been Hardwick and his attorney who had decided to test the Georgia sodomy law by pursuing the matter in federal district court. The basis for Hardwick's case rested on the fact that under the four-year statute of limitations he might be charged at any moment, yet the legal and procedural flaws surrounding Hardwick's arrest on charges of sodomy had deterred Georgia officials. Because of these flaws, the Supreme Court could certainly ask, "Is Hardwick in any real danger of arrest?"—and a "no" answer was a reasonable response. The Supreme Court also could have dismissed the petition for "want of jurisdiction." However, the state of Georgia had petitioned the Court, and a federal district court and a federal court of appeals had decided the case differently. The federal appellate court decision had been based on a claim of "privacy rights" and seemed to be in conflict with the U.S. Supreme Court's attitude toward *Doe v. Commonwealth's Attorney*.[32]

It appeared at first that four votes to grant certiorari would not be found among the nine justices of the Supreme Court. By 1985–1986 justices Brennan, Marshall, Blackmun, and Stevens were already coming together as a voting bloc in defense of individual rights, and they might have pushed to hear the case. The federal court of appeals decision, however, was one with which they agreed; it did not need to be reversed, and there was always the concern that this favorable policy decision might be reversed if the four could not pick up a fifth vote. Chief Justice Burger did not seem eager to hear the case. Justice Rehnquist voted to reverse the lower court's decision summarily—without hearing argument.

Justice Byron White, however, wanted to grant certiorari, and at that moment he took center stage in the certiorari conference. Seeing a negative configuration of seven justices—Burger, Brennan, Marshall, Blackmun, Stevens, Powell, and O'Connor—arrayed against him, White resorted to "threats"—a judicial strategy designed to persuade, if possible.[33] His argument was pointed. Noting that there were conflicting precedents in the lower federal circuit courts—Georgia and the District of Columbia—White wrote, "Given this lack of consistency among the circuits on this important constitutional question, I would grant the petition."[34] His view was that the Court was "obligated" to hear a case where there were conflicting federal precedents. Should the Supreme Court refuse to grant certiorari, White told his colleagues, he would go public with his "dissent from the denial of certiorari" and publish it for the record. His "threat" worked: three justices reversed their initial votes, and certiorari was granted.[35]

Confusion and misperception explain the changed vote in the *Bowers* certiorari conference. The central players at this point in the "certiorari game" were White, Rehnquist, Brennan, Marshall, and Burger.[36] The first move was made by Brennan and Marshall, two liberal justices who supported the lower court's decision in *Bowers*. It represented a policy goal they wanted to pursue, but they had feared that their position would attract only two other votes—those of Blackmun and Stevens. Powell seemed ambivalent toward the issue, and Brennan and Marshall had decided to pursue a strategy of "prudence."[37] It was better for the liberal justices to refuse to hear *Bowers* than to risk having the lower court ruling overturned. White's vote to grant certiorari was a surprise to these justices. Could it be that he was signaling a favorable attitude toward individual privacy rights? White had a mixed record on this issue. While he had dissented with Rehnquist against the recognition of abortion rights in *Roe v. Wade* (1973), he had upheld the right of birth control as a privacy right in *Griswold v. Connecticut* (1965). At first, Rehnquist and White appeared to be divided in their attitude toward *Bowers v. Hardwick*. White had not joined Rehnquist's vote to summarily reverse the lower court's ruling. Instead, White insisted that his brethren hear the case on its merits. Did this mean that White would be the fifth vote to affirm privacy rights for homosexuals?

As Justice Brennan analyzed White's vote, he employed a strategy known as "forward thinking."[38] In essence, he was forming hypotheses about

White's motives and plans. Brennan hypothesized that White was pursuing an "aggressive grant" certiorari strategy.[39] If so, that could mean that White wanted to reach out and take *Bowers* in order to affirm it. White's threat of a public dissent from the denial to grant certiorari might mean that he would provide the fifth vote the liberal bloc needed to affirm *Bowers*. Brennan was delighted; so was Marshall. These two justices moved to change their "defensive denial" of certiorari to a vote to grant certiorari.[40] This provided a vote of three for granting certiorari: justices White, Brennan, and Marshall. A fourth vote was needed, and it did not come from the liberal bloc.

To Brennan's surprise and consternation, Justice Rehnquist stepped forward to provide the fourth vote required under the "rule of four" for granting certiorari. Brennan then realized he had made a mistake. His theory that White and Rehnquist had split on the sodomy case was clearly flawed, and he recognized this. When Rehnquist moved to join White, he told White that he now felt so strongly about hearing the case that he was considering "writing a little something."[41] His decision to reverse the lower court might yet be secured in a full-dress hearing of the case. Rehnquist understood White's real motive and strategy. It was Rehnquist's changed vote and his support for White's demand for a grant of certiorari that signaled Brennan concerning White's maneuvers. White wanted to reverse, not affirm, the lower court decision. Brennan immediately withdrew his vote to grant certiorari and returned to his original "defensive denial" position. Before Marshall acted to do likewise, the chief justice moved to take Brennan's place, maintaining the four votes (White, Marshall, Rehnquist, and Burger) necessary to bring *Bowers v. Hardwick* back from the graveyard of "dead listed" petitions for certiorari. It had taken one week in a confused certiorari conference that exposed the scope and limits of the elements of judicial strategy available to the justices.[42]

ORAL ARGUMENT: A PRELUDE TO CONFERENCE DISCUSSION

By the time the justices meet in conference to cast votes deciding winners and losers in cases, they have already been through several stages of decision making. From the perusal of petitions for certiorari through the analysis of written briefs and culminating in oral argument, the justices have had time to formulate their responses. As they move into final conference discussion, the most recent event in their minds is the oral argument. The Court usually hears arguments Monday through Wednesday during the session, listening to approximately twelve cases each week. Thursday is designated as a "study day" for the justices to prepare for the Friday conference.

Does the oral argument play a role in the conference discussion? Does it impact judicial positions? Does it persuade or change a justice's vote? The role and influence of oral argument is debatable. Certainly oral argument helps to highlight points attorneys have previously made in their written briefs. In addition, the attorneys have an opportunity to focus on the question they deem essential for their side. However, the time allotted for oral argument is extremely brief. During the 1800s, attorneys could argue for two hours each; by the early 1900s, this was reduced to one and one-half hours each. Under Chief Justice William Howard Taft, a limit of one hour per side was imposed. Finally, it was during the chief justiceship of Warren E. Burger that the present time limit of thirty minutes per side became the norm. Naturally the Court can add additional time if needed; highly significant or exceptional cases may be deemed worthy of more time. Different justices evaluate the role and significance of the oral argument differently.[43]

During the chief justiceship of Earl Warren, a number of the justices went on record to assert the value of oral argument, and some insisted that it had changed their votes in numerous cases. Justice John Marshall Harlan II insisted that oral argument, during which the justices question the attorneys, helped him to "get at the heart of an issue and find out where the truth lies."[44] Justice William Brennan noted that there had been "numerous occasions" when his "judgment of a decision ha[d] turned on what happened" during the oral argument.[45] For both of these justices, the interaction of Court members with attorneys and with each other during this time was a key factor in decision making.

Their comments draw attention to the way oral argument works. While each attorney is usually granted a few minutes to begin the presentation, the justices very quickly begin to pose questions. From that time on, the attorney faces the difficult task of answering these questions while maintaining a central focus. It is not easy. One ACLU attorney complained, "I sometimes feel like a postman with justices using me to communicate their views to their colleagues."[46]

Professor Burt Neuborne of the New York University School of Law noted that an attorney addressing the Court might prefer not to answer a time-consuming question because it detracts from the central issue. While the justice who asked the question might find it "intellectually stimulating," the attorney might need that time to persuade some other justice. As an example, he explained: "I might like to say to Justice Scalia, 'Let me put you "on hold" while I answer Justice O'Connor.'"[47] Naturally, an attorney would do this only at grave peril to his or her case.

The fact that Justice Antonin Scalia was cited in Neuborne's example stresses another problem attorneys face. What if one justice dominates the questioning? Some justices ask more questions than others; sometimes justices focus on one side more than the other. Justice Scalia is a frequent questioner. In fact, he so often dominates the oral argument that his colleagues have attempted to stop him. In this they have been unsuccessful; justices

Lewis Powell and Byron White criticized Scalia openly, to no avail. He simply responded, "The devil made me do it." Scalia's purpose seems to be that of debating his associates through the attorneys. By "hammering" on some difficult point, Scalia lets the other justices know that they will have to resolve his point in conference. He also makes his own position clear and nonnegotiable.[48]

Evidence of the significance of the oral argument can be documented from several sources. Written opinions may repeat arguments which the attorneys made, and conference discussions may focus on these very issues. In the case of *Bowers v. Hardwick*, the oral argument seemed, at first, to persuade Justice Powell to join with the liberal bloc on the Court and to rule in favor of privacy rights. The question-and-answer exchanges of the justices and attorneys had an impact on him. What points had the attorneys raised to achieve this result?

ORAL ARGUMENT AND *BOWERS V. HARDWICK*

Oral argument in the first gay rights case took place on Wednesday, March 31, 1986. It would be very current in the minds of the justices at that Friday's conference. Georgia's position was argued by an assistant attorney general for the state, Michael E. Hobbs. The ACLU's legal team was headed by Professor Laurence H. Tribe of Harvard Law School, who presented the case for Michael Hardwick and gay rights activists. The type, number, and the tone of the questions all provided clues to Court watchers trying to predict the outcome of the case.

Hobbs faced a barrage of questions immediately. Some dealt with procedural technicalities, such as, "Why didn't the Atlanta district attorney indict Michael Hardwick?" Some questions were factual ones: "Has any married couple ever been prosecuted for sodomy in Georgia?" Some dealt with interpretation of the Georgia sodomy statute: "Would prosecution of a married [heterosexual] couple be lawful under Georgia's statute?" In all, Georgia's attorney had to respond to some twenty-seven questions from the justices in the thirty minutes allotted him. The questions fell primarily into two groups. Fourteen questions centered on the administration and enforcement of Georgia's statute; ten questions tied into these by focusing on the state's interest, the "public interest" in the case, and its handling of the issue.

For Assistant Attorney General Hobbs, this was not the line of argument he had wanted to pursue. His written brief had already signaled his desire to narrow the case to one central question: "Is there a fundamental right under the Constitution of the United States to engage in consensual private homosexual sodomy?" Ultimately, Hobbs was able to make the points that would support a "no" answer to this question. He turned questions about the state's

interest into a presentation of a "family values" standard. For example, he reminded the justices that the state had always possessed "police power" to
condemn "irresponsible liaisons outside the bonds of marriage." He urged a
narrow reading of the Court's precedents dealing with privacy rights and
linked protection of such rights to the historical, traditional values associated
with marriage and with the bearing, rearing, and educating of children. In
conjunction with this line of reasoning, Hobbs was also able to make his
point that the gay rights case was not a general Fourth Amendment "unreasonable search and seizure" issue; it was not a question of an unreasonable
intrusion into the privacy of the home.[49]

The line of questioning which Hobbs would have liked to avoid, however,
dominated his time before the Court. Fourteen questions centered on Georgia's enforcement of its statute. Hobbs had to name earlier prosecutions,
dates, and individuals prosecuted. The justices wanted to know what judicial
test was operating in Georgia to balance individual freedom and state order.
Hobbs at last admitted that for Georgia the compelling interest test asserted
that "there is [no] fundamental right to engage in sexual relationships outside
of the bonds of marriage."

Michael Hobbs was allowed to conclude his oral presentation to the Court
uninterrupted by further questions. He defended Georgia law by stressing
points he believed would appeal to the justices. Social and moral issues
needed to be decided by voters, he maintained. Hobbs described a "parade
of horribles"—legalized prostitution, permissive attitudes toward fornication
and adultery, consensual incest, polygamy, and same-sex marriage.[50] Were
such practices to be given federal constitutional protection? Would not these
violate the very test for fundamental rights? That test, articulated by Justice
Benjamin Cardozo in *Palko v. Connecticut,* had described fundamental
rights as those that were "rooted and grounded in the history and traditions
of the nation and essential to an 'ordered liberty' for society."[51]

These elements of legal reasoning—justifications for judicial decisions—
certainly impacted Chief Justice Warren Burger and justices White, Rehnquist, and O'Connor. They were ineffective arguments for justices Brennan,
Marshall, Blackmun, and Stevens, however, leaving only Justice Powell open
to persuasion as Professor Tribe took the podium to ask an entirely different
question from that posed by Georgia's attorney: "[Does] Georgia [have]
power to dictate how every adult, married or unmarried, in every bedroom
in Georgia will *behave* in the closest and most intimate personal association
with another adult?"[52] The ultimate outcome of *Bowers v. Hardwick* would
depend on whether Powell would ask and answer Tribe's question or would
focus on the one asked by Georgia's attorney.

Laurence Tribe was no stranger to the justices of the Supreme Court. He
had argued—and won—an impressive number of cases, presenting some of
the most difficult issues that the Court had confronted. The justices expected

him to answer hypothetical questions, to defend his position creatively, and to discuss the right of privacy with them as though they were in a law school seminar. It was no easy task.

A transcript of the oral argument in *Bowers* documents the thirty-two questions specifically directed to Tribe. They can be grouped into some five categories and were quite different from those addressed to Hobbs. They were questions concerning substantive rights rather than procedural ones.[53] The questions focused on historical examples and practice, on judicial precedents and judicial philosophies dealing with other privacy issues, on the judicial tests created and used over time, on constitutional foundations, and on the proper role for the Court in this type of decision making. These elements of legal reasoning and judicial justification were couched in hypothetical scenarios as the various justices articulated them.[54]

Not all justices participated. Justices Brennan, Marshall, and Blackmun remained noticeably quiet, and Chief Justice Burger and Justice O'Connor raised only a few questions. Justices White and Stevens were more vocal and posed several issues for Tribe to debate with them. However, the greatest number of questions came from justices Rehnquist and Powell. It was Powell who asked the very first question and then continued in what became a one-on-one dialogue with Tribe. Tribe had already identified Powell's vote as critical and Powell's first question alerted Tribe to the damage done by Hobbs's "parade of horribles" with which he had closed the state of Georgia's case.

Powell was disturbed. He wanted to know how far Tribe was going to push privacy rights, and he expressed his concern. "Professor Tribe," he asked, "is there a limiting principle to your argument [about privacy]? What are the limiting principles when places like a motel room or the back of an automobile or toilet are involved?" Powell also raised questions about *practices* such as bigamy, adultery, incest, prostitution, and so forth, versus the *places* where the acts occurred. In other words, he was concerned about the extent to which acts long considered illegal by state governments could be protected in the privacy of the home.[55]

As Professor Tribe responded to Justice Powell's concern for retaining state power to punish these practices, he understood what Powell was really asking him to do. Powell wanted to know what test the justices could articulate to retain a balance between state power over morals and an individual's right to engage in consensual sexual relationships within the privacy of one's home. Tribe was prepared. "The private home does not shield anything that one might do there," he said. However, he suggested, state powers should be limited so that there would be protection for "all physical, sexual intimacies of a kind that are consensual and non commercial in the privacy of the home." He continued, "When a state asserts the power to dictate the details of intimacies in what it calls 'irresponsible liaisons' even in the privacy of the home, it has a burden to justify its law through some form of [a] heightened scrutiny [test]." Tribe concluded by pointing out that states could find other methods of restricting behavior that society deemed unacceptable. For instance, adultery could be prosecuted as a "breach of contract" issue rather than as a moral one.[56]

It was Justice White who bluntly posed the basic questions of constitutional law. White asked, "What constitutional provision do you rely on to strike down that statute?" Tribe answered by citing the Fourteenth, Third, Fourth, and Ninth Amendments. When asked, "What precedents support your position?" Tribe countered with more than twenty cases, stressing the birth control precedents. Was there a fundamental right at stake in Hardwick's case? For Tribe, the answer was yes, and this fundamental right was quite different from that discussed by Hobbs. Tribe explained, "We are saying that there is a fundamental right to restrain government's intimate regulation of the privacies of associations like in the home." "We champion," he continued, "the principle of limited government [as a fundamental right] . . . it is not a principle of a specific catalogue of rights."[57]

When Justice Rehnquist suggested that fundamental rights should be identified by a majority vote in the state legislatures, not by courts, Tribe disagreed. "Surely this Court would never say as to individual rights that the ability of an individual to possibly persuade a legislature to protect them is enough."[58] The proper role for the Court, according to these arguments, was to identify and set beyond majority control those special rights that protect even the most unpopular actions.

As Tribe concluded his argument, he had every reason to feel hopeful. His associates were elated. Michael Hardwick, who was in the courtroom, described this sense of success, noting that "everyone thought that . . . we had won."[59] They were right—but they were also wrong. The conference vote would ultimately shift and a case won would become a case lost for gay rights supporters.

CONFUSION IN THE CONFERENCE

Two days later, on Friday, April 2, 1986, the nine Supreme Court justices met in their conference room to debate, persuade, and decide the status of gay rights under the U.S. Constitution. There are several ways in which this secret discussion can be revealed. First, although the justices are totally alone and follow an antiquated procedure designed to emphasize the privacy of this process, law clerks may be able to piece together the scenario from remarks made by their justices. They may know ahead of time the position their justice intended to take as well as the arguments. What they do not know and cannot predict is the impact of the interaction that takes place during the discussion. Second, the justices themselves leave notes—some are extensive, while others may be sketchy. The notes may reflect the personal reaction of the justice, indicated by the doodlings in the margin.[60] Third, on rare occasions, a justice may offer a public explanation. Finally, subsequent biographies and interviews may give insight into the decision-making process.

Over the years, increased interest in the conference has resulted in an expansion of the information justices usually want concealed. The information age has begun to open up the secret conference. The conference procedure itself is known to Court watchers. It has changed in some aspects over time, as noted earlier when various chief justices have experimented with methods to increase their personal power. The *Bowers* conference, under the aging Chief Justice Burger, followed the procedure he had adopted seventeen years before. In this case however, it was a conference marked by confusion. A confused conference is ideal for demonstrating how justices react to each other and shows how a case won may suddenly become a case lost as justices change their votes. *Bowers* was such a case.

"NINE SCORPIONS IN A BOTTLE"

Chief Justice Warren Burger, having followed the expected protocol of the ceremonial handshake, proceeded to take his place at the head of the table to begin the conference. At the foot sat his rival, Justice William Brennan. The other seven justices were grouped on either side: three to Burger's left (White, Marshall, and Blackmun) and four to his right (Powell, Rehnquist, Stevens, and O'Connor). As chief, Burger spoke first. The conference notes left by Brennan document in detail the discussion that ensued.

Burger, according to Brennan, opened the conference discussion with his own definition of the question. It was designed to eliminate the issue of privacy rights. Adopting Assistant Attorney General Michael Bowers's question—Is there a fundamental right under the Constitution to engage in a consensual private homosexual relationship?—Burger's answer was no. He then proceeded to offer his rationale. First, he distinguished precedents set in cases of marital privacy (*Griswold v. Connecticut*) and those based on the protected privacy of the home (*Stanley v. Georgia*). Unlike these precedents, he concluded, "this [case] does not infringe on privacy rights." Second, he advanced a sociological or contemporary morality argument. "Our society has values that should be protected," he explained. Finally, he used a traditional, historical rationale. "The teaching of history and custom frown on this, and sanction its prohibition," he stated.[61]

As Burger concluded and Justice Brennan began his remarks, the style of the Burger conference once again reflected the impersonal level, lack of discipline, and closed mindedness of the justices. Under Burger, the justices did not really try to persuade each other; they simply stated their own position and rationales, and then voted immediately after speaking.[62] Brennan knew that most of the justices had already taken a position. Only one justice had seemed ambivalent and open to persuasion during the oral argument: Justice Lewis Powell. Thus, Brennan put forward in detail his best argument in his most persuasive style primarily for Powell's benefit.

First, Brennan appealed to judicial precedent and cited two cases stressed by Professor Tribe in oral argument—*Griswold v. Connecticut* and *Stanley v. Georgia.* The privacy issues had been central in these cases involving both issues of sexual relationships and the home. Second, Brennan turned to the question of the proper judicial test to be used: rational basis or strict scrutiny.[63] He suggested remanding the case to the lower court and asking the state to show a compelling reason for its statute. "Does it advance a substantial state interest?" Brennan asked. If so, Georgia needed to prove it.

Then Brennan made his move to secure Powell's vote. Referring to Powell's request for "limiting principles," Brennan suggested that "this case should be restricted to a consideration of conduct that takes place within the home, and that is (1) non-commercial, (2) consensual, and (3) that involves the most private forms of sexual intimacy."[64] Brennan understood Powell's fear that states would not be able to prosecute moral crimes such as adultery and incest. He addressed this concern directly: "I have no doubt but that a state would be able to show sufficient interest to defend these statutes."[65] However, Brennan insisted that states must articulate reasons "beyond saying merely that they do not like oral sex, or sodomy, or homosexuals." To add weight to this point, Brennan cleverly quoted Justice Byron White's statement in *City of Cleburne v. Cleburne Living Center,* in which White had stated that "a state—even under a rational basis test—must advance reasons beyond naked preference to support legislation."[66]

Brennan concluded by restating Professor Tribe's response concerning the central question the Court should be asking. It was *not* a question about a fundamental right to be a homosexual; it was a question about "sexual privacy in the home between consenting adults."[67]

Brennan's tip of the hat to White fell on deaf ears with White himself. Speaking next, White made that clear with six words: "I agree with the Chief Justice."[68] Tribe's argument and Brennan's persuasive tactics were deemed unworthy of a response.

On the heels of White's terse answer, Justice Thurgood Marshall's response came quick and blunt: "I agree with Bill Brennan."[69] Justice Blackmun, stepping into the tense atmosphere, tried to elevate the conference proceeding by offering justifications for finding in favor of gay rights. He focused on Hardwick's very real fear of prosecution, a threat that was sufficient to give him "standing to sue." He compared the Georgia statute to the ugly miscegenation laws struck down in 1976 by the Court on the grounds that individuals had a fundamental liberty to marry a person of another race and states could not prohibit this. Finally, Blackmun linked Georgia's sodomy statute to religion, suggesting that such "religious underpinnings" violated the First Amendment.[70]

Justice Oliver Wendell Holmes's famous description of the justices' behavior as "nine scorpions in a bottle" aptly fits this verbal maneuvering.[71]

JUSTICE POWELL: CONFUSION COMPOUNDED

Five votes had been cast when it became Justice Lewis Powell's turn to speak. Three justices—Brennan, Marshall, and Blackmun—were in favor of striking down the Georgia sodomy statute on privacy grounds and extending the right of privacy to include homosexual activities within the home. They were opposed to state laws criminalizing such behavior. Two justices—Burger and White—wanted to uphold Georgia's law and to refuse to extend privacy rights to cover homosexual activity. Powell was the sixth justice in order of seniority. He would be followed by justices Rehnquist, Stevens, and O'Connor. His vote, however, was the critical one because no one knew for certain where he stood. His law clerks did not know; even Powell himself did not know.

Powell's indecisiveness and confusion affected his colleagues in the conference.[72] Justice Brennan's records demonstrated this. On the one hand, Brennan could note that Powell strongly supported decriminalizing homosexual conduct. He recorded Powell as saying, "I would hold that in the context of the home this conduct [sodomy] is not criminally punishable."[73] Powell had apparently been upset by the fact that Georgia law criminalized Hardwick's conduct and could inflict a substantial prison term on him. "We ought to decriminalize this 'conduct,'" he stated. Powell had been particularly impressed with Professor Tribe's emotional arguments centered on the home and the privacy rights protected there.

However, Powell's other statements on privacy and fundamental rights left Brennan and the other justices in some confusion. Powell's legal justification for striking down the Georgia law was very different from that advanced by Brennan, Marshall, and Blackmun. Powell introduced an unexpected and unique constitutional argument to uphold his position: the Eighth Amendment's "no cruel and unusual punishment" and no excessive penalties clauses. This argument, the basis of Powell's position and vote in conference, had not been raised during the *Bowers* proceedings. It had not been mentioned in the written briefs and had not been addressed in oral argument. At no time prior to the conference had the Eighth Amendment issue been discussed.[74]

Nevertheless, Justice Powell had a record for supporting Eighth Amendment challenges to state power. In 1983 in the case of *Solem v. Helm*, Powell had written an opinion declaring that life imprisonment without parole was an excessive penalty for a six-time offender.[75] In that case, Jerry Helm's seventh felony offense, like his other six, was for a nonviolent crime. His criminal record subjected him to South Dakota's habitual offender law and the judge had sentenced him to life imprisonment without parole. Powell, disturbed by the severity of the penalty, had launched an extensive inquiry into the historical background of the Eighth Amendment. His clerks had uncovered ancient English cases from 1316, 1615, and 1689, and using these and others, Powell had argued that criminal penalties must be proportional to the severity of the crime committed.

The Georgia law at stake in *Bowers* set a penalty of a prison term of twenty years for the crime of sodomy. Although Georgia had not gone forward with its prosecution of Michael Hardwick, it retained the power to do so. With a four-year statute of limitation, Georgia could have prosecuted, convicted, and sentenced Hardwick to a maximum of twenty years at any time during those four years. As Powell raised his Eighth Amendment argument in the *Bowers* conference, he did not refer to his decision in the *Helm* case, even though it had occurred only three years earlier. Instead he focused on another Eighth Amendment precedent from 1962, *Robinson v. California*. This case had held that "while individuals could be held criminally responsible for their acts, no one could be punished criminally for their status."[76] Robinson had been a drug addict and had been convicted for his addiction to narcotics. Powell decided to compare the homosexual status to that of drug addicts, reasoning that Georgia law thus could not criminalize a person for being a homosexual.

Powell had developed this argument in the days before the April 2 conference. He had searched actively for a constitutional reason to justify a vote against the Georgia law, specifically asking his law clerks to find material to support him. His clerks responded with this Eighth Amendment argument based on *Robinson v. California*. They did not mention *Solem v. Helm*.

Powell had four law clerks in 1986: two of these would play significant roles in Powell's struggle over *Bowers*. Powell's personal dilemma had become apparent to his clerks from the moment the Court received the certiorari petition. Powell had not wanted to hear the case and had voted against granting certiorari on October 11, 1985. When a vote of four forced consideration, Powell was "deeply troubled" according to his clerks.[77] He did not like the arguments of either side, regarding both positions as too extreme. Powell's judicial temperament inclined him toward a middle ground. Unfortunately, there *was* no middle ground in *Bowers*. Powell looked to the attorneys arguing the case for solutions; he sought help from his colleagues on the Court; he demanded creative arguments from his clerks. None of them helped him out of his dilemma.

Wanting to uphold the sanctity of the home, Powell nevertheless could not extend constitutional protection to acts society should be able to prohibit—acts of incest, bigamy, or adultery, for example. He did not accept the argument that Michael Hardwick had any "fundamental constitutional right to engage in homosexual sodomy." He opposed criminalizing it as the Georgia statute did, however. Powell's clerks described his attitude as "waffling . . . vacillating between the extremes presented," consumed by "doubt," "querulous," "emotional," and "repulsed" by homosexual behavior.[78] His confusion grew out of his inability to understand sexual attraction between males and how this attraction could be translated into sexual activity. Acknowledging his "unpreparedness," Powell confessed that *Bowers* presented "deeply troubling" questions. He "recoiled" emotionally from "arguments that seemed to place homosexual sodomy on a par with the sexual intimacy between man and wife."[79]

Thus Powell needed help, and his habit was to set his law clerks to debate troublesome issues and present him with options. For Bowers, Powell's one ultraconservative clerk, Mike Mosman, and the most liberal of the other three clerks undertook this job. Each prepared arguments designed to convince their justice and settle his doubts. Mosman, described as a "Mormon by faith and a moralist by disposition,"[80] prepared his bench memo for Powell utilizing legal and emotional arguments designed to overturn any privacy right claims for homosexuals. Two days before oral argument, he presented Powell with a comprehensive and carefully constructed case against sodomy.

Knowing Powell's predilection for using the historical, traditional approach to legal reasoning, Mosman began his memo with this focus. Sodomy, he noted, had never been accepted in American society. Next, he argued that the existing judicial precedents establishing sexual rights could all be distinguished from homosexual sodomy. Mosman linked the Court's privacy decision to those "fundamental rights of marital and family privacy . . . to marriage, family, and procreation . . . [all] traditions."[81] A third approach Mosman employed involved an appeal to long-respected judicial philosophies, particularly those articulated by the second Justice John Marshall Harlan. Powell's respect for Harlan was well known by his clerks, and Harlan, writing in dicta in an earlier case, had exempted "adultery, homosexuality, fornication, and incest" from protected privacy rights.[82] In an earlier case, Powell had limited privacy rights to family and to historical and traditional practices. Finally, Mosman demonstrated his understanding of his justice's attitudes. Powell believed that courts should practice judicial self-restraint. Judicial activism, whether liberal or conservative, did not fit with Powell's conception of the role of the Court under the Constitution.

However, Powell's other clerks had very different views. One, identified later as Powell's "gay clerk," would have the opportunity to educate his justice about what it meant to be gay. Powell did not know of his clerk's lifestyle, and he would have been shocked if his clerk had so identified himself. Powell did know that this particular clerk was the most liberal of his four, however, and it was therefore natural to ask him for arguments to rebut Mosman's views. Powell was searching for more than legal arguments and precedents. The questions he put to his clerk revealed a desire to understand homosexual behavior. Were gay men not sexually attracted to women? How could two men be sexually attracted to each other? These were the type of questions Powell posed, and his clerk answered without ever identifying himself as gay.[83] The legal arguments and precedents he put forward would succeed at first in persuading Powell to vote to strike down the Georgia sodomy statute on Eighth Amendment grounds, though they were not, in the end, sufficient to overcome Powell's personal attitude toward a lifestyle he did not understand. Would it have made a difference to Powell had his clerk identified himself as gay? Would it have made homosexuality seem "less bizarre and threatening"? Powell insisted that he had never met a homosexual, yet one sat in his presence, unrecognized but liked and respected by the justice.[84]

Powell's statements in the conference were confusing to the other justices. His approach was novel. No justice was prepared to discuss gay rights under a "cruel and unusual" punishment framework. A full and open exchange among the justices did *not* occur: the Burger conferences did not function that way. Would a more searching verbal exchange have made a difference at this point? Could either Justice Brennan or Justice Blackmun have advanced arguments to cement Powell into the gay rights bloc of justices? Brennan and Blackmun were unprepared. Powell's vote was recorded: to strike down Georgia's sodomy law. The constitutional basis was the Eighth Amendment.[85]

THE JUNIOR JUSTICES WEIGH IN

Three justices had not yet spoken as Powell finished. Justice William Rehnquist's remarks were predictable and unexceptional. Short and to the point, Rehnquist said, "I agree with the Chief Justice and Byron [Justice White]."[86] Focusing on the Fourth Amendment and issues of substantive due process, Rehnquist dismissed the attack on the Georgia sodomy statute. The conference vote at that point was 4–3 in favor of overturning Georgia's law. The vote of Justice John Paul Stevens would provide the needed fifth vote for those espousing gay rights, and Stevens provided it.

However, Stevens, like Powell, had made his decision based on very different points from those raised by the other justices. Laurence Tribe's attack on majority power to limit minority protection granted in the Bill of Rights had impressed Stevens. "It is not enough that a moral condemnation is made by the majority," he noted.[87] Georgia had to show a compelling reason for limiting privacy rights. In addition, Stevens expressed concern that the Georgia law had never been applied against heterosexual sodomy. There were married couples who engaged in acts of oral and anal sex, Stevens noted, and *Griswold v. Connecticut* certainly would protect them from an intrusive law like Georgia's. Stevens was not out of step with Brennan, Marshall, and Blackmun. The points that he made reinforced the arguments of the liberal bloc. Unlike Powell's unexpected position, Stevens's views were well known and predictable.[88]

For Justice Sandra Day O'Connor, the last justice to speak, liberties were *not* "absolutes." There were limits on all of the personal freedoms guaranteed by the Bill of Rights, and courts had always set these boundaries. As she explained, "The Fourth Amendment guarantee of personal liberty . . . [is] not absolute and [does] not extend to private, consensual homosexuality." O'Connor, a states' rights advocate, believed Georgia had acted constitutionally in passing and enforcing its law.[89]

With these comments, voting ceased. The position of each justice had been stated, and gay rights appeared to have won. Since Chief Justice Burger was on the losing side with justices White, Rehnquist, and O'Connor, Justice Brennan, the senior justice with the majority, assumed that it would be his right to assign the majority opinion. This was clearly going to be a difficult task given Justice Powell's vote, and Justice Brennan worried that the conference decision was "bizarre." "The result," he wrote, "was distressingly narrow." With conservatives "baffled" and liberals "unhappy,"[90] the conference ended as it had begun—in confusion.

A CONFERENCE DECISION REVISED: POWELL CHANGES HIS VOTE

The *Bowers* conference ended that April 2 with what could be described as a 4–4–1 vote. Brennan, Marshall, and Blackmun were in a bloc that stressed rights of privacy as the justification for striking down the Georgia sodomy law. Justice Stevens, while not convinced by the privacy argument or the focus on the sanctity of the home, had joined this bloc because he had reached the same result as his three liberal colleagues. These four justices united to strike down the Georgia sodomy statute and protect homosexuals. On the opposite side were Chief Justice Burger and justices White, Rehnquist, and O'Connor. Their holding centered on the question of fundamental rights protected by the Constitution. Homosexual sodomy, they insisted, was not one of these. Justice Powell found himself alone. To vote with Brennan, Marshall, Blackmun, and Stevens meant giving recognition to a new fundamental right under privacy, and Powell did not want to do this. However, that is exactly what he had done by his conference vote. Powell had left the conference with his vote on record to strike down the Georgia law but not to recognize sodomy as a constitutional right. The gay rights privacy issue was clearly not settled by this vote.

Conference votes are not "binding."[91] A justice may be persuaded to change a recorded conference vote even after the formal discussion and voting have been concluded. This is exactly what happened in *Bowers*. Between April 2 and April 8, Powell found himself under intense pressure to change his vote. Chief Justice Burger acted immediately. The day after the conference concluded, Burger wrote a private letter to Powell. While Burger did not try to disguise his intense personal feeling about the decision, he did try to organize his arguments so as to appeal to Powell.

Burger used several well-known legal tactics to do this: "persuasion on the merits," "an appeal to oughtness," and "institutional loyalty."[92] The first of these focused on the actual facts of the case, and here Burger's argument was effective. Michael Hardwick had *not* been subjected to cruel and unusual punishment, Burger argued. Georgia's law had *not* been applied to place Hardwick in jail. Hardwick's "status" as a homosexual had not resulted in a punishment. It was Hardwick, Burger argued, who wanted active constitutional support for his own form of "gratification." Burger contended that the merits of the case did not support Powell's ruling.[93]

The "appeal to oughtness" also carried weight with Powell. Here history and tradition were on the side of the state. Powell himself was repelled by acts of sodomy, and Burger's question cut through rhetoric to ask Powell if he really wanted to turn his back on the tradition of centuries of Western Civilization that had defined sodomy as a "willful, reprehensible act." Powell would be uncomfortable in "leading this sort of revolution," and the chief justice knew this very well. Defining homosexuality as a personal choice robbed it of the character of an immutable trait that deserved protection.[94]

The judicial strategy known as "institutional loyalty" concluded Burger's appeal. This did not work well, however. Powell did not like Burger's personal appeal, which he found "excessive." Burger's reminder of his upcoming retirement, his personification of himself as the Court itself, deserving of loyalty, and his argument that Powell's expansion of the Court role would damage that institution did not impress Powell. Powell noted on the top of Burger's letter, "There's both sense and nonsense in this letter—mostly the latter."[95]

Although Burger's appeal was for the most unsuccessful, Michael Mosman's was quite effective. After the conference, Mosman sent a memo to his justice urging a vote change. This memo demonstrated that the *question* and the *phrasing* of that question were the critical variables in determining who won and lost in a case. Mosman asked, "*Is* the question about the Eighth Amendment's limits on criminal penalties for consensual sodomy [actually] before the Court?" Powell knew very well that he alone had introduced that issue. It had *not* been mentioned in the lower courts or in any of the legal proceeding before the Supreme Court until Powell brought it up at the April 2 conference.

Ultimately, Powell reconsidered. A week following the conference, he wrote a memo to the other justices: "Upon further study as to exactly what is before us," he declared, "I have to uphold Georgia's law,"[96] and he changed his vote. The reaction of the other justices was dramatic: the conservatives were "jubilant," the liberals "bitter." Chief Justice Burger now controlled the assignment of the majority opinion, and the liberals' opinion now became a dissent. The depth of the resentment felt by Brennan, Marshall, Blackmun, and Stevens was expressed in a note from the latter: "[Your] change of heart remind[s] [me] of a case . . . in which the Court, with all nine justices participating, refused to resolve an issue on the ground that it was equally divided."[97]

Powell, reading Stevens's comment, noted that this would have been a 4?–4? vote—an accurate description of Powell himself in *Bowers*. Powell had clearly lost the respect of his liberal colleagues. What had he gained from his switch? Would he be able to influence Justice Byron White, to whom the chief justice had assigned the opinion?

White's first draft distressed Powell. It was "abrupt, superficial, peremptory, and insensitive" in tone, according to many analysts. Powell appeared shaken by it. He wrote Justice White a note to the effect that he would "not join the opinion" and would "write separately." Then, one month later, Powell backed down again. Not only did he "abandon his plan for a full scale opinion of his own," but his short, two-paragraph concurrence added nothing and was ignored by press, public, and legal scholars.[98] It gave no hint of Powell's intense personal and legal struggle, nor did it indicate the degree of ambivalence and restraint that actually surrounded his vote with the majority.

A CASE LOST

The decision in *Bowers v. Hardwick* was announced by the Court on June 30, 1986. Justice Byron White read his majority opinion, and Justice Harry Blackmun responded with the dissent. This was unusual. In earlier days, justices regularly read their opinions, but that practice had fallen into disuse.[99] *Bowers* had generated an inordinate amount of hostility and bitterness within the Court due to Justice Powell's vote change. This division became public as White and Blackmun read from their opinions. Journalists, sensing a major story, pressed for answers. Liberal newspapers attacked the Court's decision, and their reporters targeted Powell as the critical vote. They wanted a full story about the decision.

By July 13, the *Washington Post* had the complete story and the inner workings of the *Bowers* conference were laid open to public scrutiny.[100] It was not the most flattering picture of the judicial process at work. It did not increase public respect for the judiciary, nor did it put to rest the issue of gay rights. Powell himself would soon place the decision in jeopardy and give encouragement to the Michael Hardwicks of the future when he openly stated, "When I reread the opinions [in *Bowers*] a few months later, I thought the dissent had the better of the Arguments." He concluded, "I think I probably made a mistake in that one [*Bowers*]."[101]

Was *Bowers v. Hardwick* lost in the conference stage? Perhaps in one sense it was. Had the conferences functioned to encourage a free exchange of ideas and to explore in detail the various opinions and theories of the justices, Powell's concerns might have been addressed. A conference characterized by simply voting and then defending one's vote is ineffective to a resolution of difficult and divisive issues of public policy. Ultimately, the issue of the *Bowers* case would have to be settled in still other cases. The judicial process itself would continue to work until the gay rights cause could ultimately be won.

NOTES

1. Del Dickson, ed., *The Supreme Court in Conference, 1940–1985: The Private Discussions behind Nearly 300 Supreme Court Decisions* (New York: Oxford University Press, 2001), 824.

2. Alice Fleetwood Bartee, *Cases Lost, Causes Won: The Supreme Court and Judicial Process* (New York: St. Martin's, 1984), 44–45, 70n9. See also Dickson, *Supreme Court in Conference*, 3–4.

3. Dickson, *Supreme Court in Conference*, 3–4.

4. Ibid., 31.

5. Ibid.

6. Walter F. Murphy, *Elements of Judicial Strategy* (Chicago: University of Chicago Press, 1964), 37–40.

7. Dickson, *Supreme Court in Conference*, 47.

8. Lewis F. Powell Jr., remarks to the Southwestern Legal Foundation, Dallas, Texas, 1 May 1980, reprinted as "What Really Goes On at the Supreme Court," 52 *New York State Bar Journal*, 454 (6), October 1980.

9. James W. Ely Jr., *The Chief Justiceship of Melville W. Fuller, 1888–1910* (Columbia: University of South Carolina Press, 1995), 30–39.

10. Murphy, *Elements of Judicial Strategy*, 83.

11. Edwin McElwain, "The Business of the Supreme Court as Conducted by Chief Justice Hughes," *Harvard Law Review* 63 (1949): 5. See also David Danelski, "The Influence of the Chief Justice in the Decisional Process," in *Courts, Judges, and Politics: An Introduction to the Judicial Process*, ed. Walter F. Murphy and C. Herman Pritchett (New York: Random House, 1961), 497–508.

12. Murphy, *Elements of Judicial Strategy*, 43–44.

13. Glendon Schubert, *Constitutional Politics: The Political Behavior of Supreme Court Justices and the Constitutional Policies They Make* (New York: Holt, Rinehart, & Winston, 1960), 161–165.

14. Alpheus T. Mason, *Harlan Fiske Stone: Pillar of the Law* (New York: Viking Press, 1956), 605.

15. Ibid.

16. Dickson, *Supreme Court in Conference*, 98–105.

17. Stephan J. Markman and Alfred S. Regnery, "The Mind of Justice Brennan: A 25-Year Tribute," *National Review*, 18 May 1984, 31.

18. Bartee, *Cases Lost, Causes Won*, 43–45, 70n6, 70n9.

19. William O. Douglas, *The Court Years, 1939–1975: The Autobiography of William O. Douglas* (New York: Random House, 1980), 232–233.

20. Lee Epstein and Jack Knight, *The Choices Justices Make* (Washington, DC: CQ Press, 1998), 232–233.

21. Stephen L. Wasby, *The Supreme Court in the Federal Judicial System*, 4th ed. (Chicago: Nelson-Hall, 1993), 191, 203–205, 280.

22. Ibid., 211, 377.

23. Epstein and Knight, *The Choices Justices Make*, 9–17, 142–157.

24. Ibid., 80, 122.

25. Ibid., 88.

26. Peter Irons, *The Courage of Their Convictions* (New York: Free Press, 1988), 392–403.

27. Ibid.

28. Ibid., 383–384.

29. *Doe v. Commonwealth's Attorney*, 425 U.S. 901 (1976).

30. Ibid.

31. Epstein and Knight, *The Choices Justices Make*, 61–62, 80, 122.

32. Donald A. Dripps, "*Bowers v. Hardwick* and the Law of Standing: Non Cases Make Bad Law," *Emory Law Journal* 44 (Fall 1995): 1417.

33. Murphy, *Elements of Judicial Strategy*, 54–55.

34. Epstein and Knight, *The Choices Justices Make*, 61, 122.

35. Ibid.

36. Schubert, *Constitutional Politics*, 161–165.

37. Murphy, *Elements of Judicial Strategy*, 208.

38. Epstein and Knight, *The Choices Justices Make*, 79.

39. Ibid., 80.

40. Ibid.

41. Ibid., 61, 107n10.

42. Ibid.

43. John M. Harlan, "The Role of Oral Argument," in *The Supreme Court: Views from Inside*, ed. Alan F. Westin (New York: W. W. Norton, 1961), 57–61.

44. Wasby, *Supreme Court*, 287.

45. Justice William J. Brennan Jr., interview by David Frost, "Inside the Marble Temple," program 2 of *This Honorable Court*, video, 58 min. (Alexandria, VA: PBS Video, 1988).

46. Ibid.

47. Ibid.

48. Ibid.

49. Gerald Gunther and Gerhard Casper, eds., *Landmark Briefs and Arguments of the Supreme Court of the United States: Constitutional Law*, vol. 68: *Bowers v. Hardwick*, ([Washington, DC]: University Publications of America, 1975), 631–657.

50. Ibid., 641.

51. *Palko v. Connecticut*, 302 U.S. 319 (1937).

52. Gunther and Casper, *Landmark Briefs and Arguments*, 642.

53. *Black's Law Dictionary*, 7th ed. (1999), s.v. "substantive due process," states: "The essence of substantive due process is protection from arbitrary and unreasonable denials of 5th and 14th Amendment rights. The focus is on the 'content' of the legislation—on what the law is, as opposed to how it is administered. It establishes the right to equal enjoyment of fundamental rights, privileges, and immunities. Substantive due process gives/defines rights. Procedural due process focuses on the methods used to deprive a person of his 5th and 14th Amendment guarantees. Procedural due process prescribes the manner in which rights may be exercised and enforced. Simply stated, substantive due process creates and defines rights while procedural due process prescribes methods of enforcing the rights or obtaining redress for their invasion."

54. Gunther and Casper, *Landmark Briefs and Arguments*, 642–656.

55. Ibid., 642–644, 646–647.

56. Ibid.

57. Ibid.

58. Ibid., 653.

59. Irons, *Courage of Their Convictions*, 399–400.

60. J. Woodford Howard, *Mr. Justice Murphy: A Political Biography* (Princeton, NJ: Princeton University Press, 1968), 250–255.

61. Dickson, *Supreme Court in Conference*, 822.

62. Wasby, *Supreme Court*, 230. See also William H. Rehnquist, *The Supreme Court: How It Was, How It Is* (New York: Morrow, 1987), 288–303.

63. T. R. van Geel, *Understanding Supreme Court Opinions*, 3rd ed. (New York: Longman, 1991), 78–80, 117–118. The "rational basis" test places the burden of proof on the party challenging the law or regulation. The test also requires proof that the law or policy serves a "legitimate purpose" and is "rationally related" to that purpose. It is a lenient standard, and the government usually wins when it is used. The "strict scrutiny" test places the burden of proof on the government and requires proof that the law is necessary. The government must assert and prove a "compelling" interest in having the regulation. It must also show that the means chosen to achieve this purpose does not "sweep unnecessarily broadly." This test makes it more difficult for government regulations to survive.

64. Dickson, *Supreme Court in Conference*, 822–823.

65. Ibid.

66. *City of Cleburne v. Cleburne Living Center*, 473 U.S. 432 (1985).

67. Dickson, *Supreme Court in Conference*, 822–823.

68. Ibid., 823.

69. Ibid.

70. Ibid., 824.

71. Max Lerner, *Nine Scorpions in a Bottle: Great Justices and Cases of the Supreme Court*, ed. Richard Cummings (New York: Arcade, 1994).

72. Dickson, *Supreme Court in Conference*, 824.

73. John C. Jefferies Jr., *Justice Lewis F. Powell, Jr.* (New York: C. Scribner's Sons, 1994), 520–527.

74. Ibid.

75. *Solem v. Helm*, 463 U.S. 277 (1983). See also Wayne C. Bartee and Alice Fleetwood Bartee, *Litigating Morality: American Legal Thought and Its English Roots* (New York: Praeger, 1993), 129–131.

76. *Robinson v. California*, 370 U.S. 660 (1962).

77. Jefferies, *Justice Lewis F. Powell, Jr.*, 514.

78. Ibid., 511.

79. Ibid., 521.

80. Ibid., 516.

81. Ibid., 516–518, 524.

82. *Griswold v. Connecticut*, 381 U.S. 479, 499 (1965); see Harlan's concurrence in the judgment.

83. Jefferies, *Justice Lewis F. Powell, Jr.*, 521.

84. Ibid.

85. Ibid., 22.

86. Dickson, *Supreme Court in Conference*, 824. See also David J. Garrow, *Liberty and Sexuality: The Right to Privacy and the Making of Roe v. Wade*, rev. ed. (Berkeley: University of California Press, 1998), 656, 658–661, 663–667.

87. Ibid., 824.

88. Ibid.

89. Ibid.

90. Jefferies, *Justice Lewis F. Powell, Jr.*, 522.

91. Wasby, *Supreme Court*, 230.

92. Murphy, *Elements of Judicial Strategy*, 39, 43, 46.

93. Jefferies, *Justice Lewis F. Powell, Jr.*, 523.

94. Ibid.

95. Ibid., 524.

96. Ibid.

97. Ibid., 524–525.

98. Ibid., 525.

99. Ibid.

100. Ibid., 529.

101. Al Kamen, "Powell Changed Vote in Sodomy Case; Different Outcome Seen Likely If Homosexual Had Been Prosecuted," *Washington Post*, 13 July 1986.

3

To Decide and How to Decide

Judicial Attitudes and Abortion Decisions

The privacy rights battle over birth control demonstrated that the initial stage involving the choice of the attorney, the assembling of the litigants with their complaints, and the building of a case record was of critical importance in explaining early losses. The second stage in the judicial decision-making process came to the forefront when gay rights issues arose in the landmark *Bowers v. Hardwick* case. The judicial conference, a proceeding little known to the general public, held the key to understanding the major case loss for gay rights supporters. The interaction of the nine Supreme Court justices as they debate an issue is not visible to the public, yet it may be the very stage in the process where a case is won or lost.

However, the most visible of all of the parts of the judicial decision-making process is the third stage: the written opinion. Abortion decisions have overshadowed almost every privacy rights issue, and when it seemed that a pro-life focus might succeed in persuading the Supreme Court to rescind that right, the public eagerly has awaited the announcement of the decision. In 1989, the crucial case was *Webster v. Reproductive Health Services*. Would this case reverse the grant of the privacy right to abortion in *Roe v. Wade?* If so, why? How could pro-life forces succeed in such an endeavor? The answer would be given in the written judicial case decision.

The Supreme Court's case decisions, as reported in the *United States Reports* and other publications, are a clear statement of choices the justices have made between conflicting claims. Citing the case's names, numbers, origin, record, and facts, the justices explain why they have decided for one party and against another. Their written opinion or opinions are published to say to all who would read them: "This is our decision."

It would appear on the surface that examining such decisions would be relatively simple. Yet behind the written words that constitute the decision are significant factors that must be analyzed and evaluated before the decision can be meaningful. The view that judges simply find the law and then announce it in their decision has been shown to be a myth. Although couched in legal phrases and peppered with earlier case precedents and examples, as well as appeals to history and tradition, judicial decisions are nevertheless "functions of attitudinal variables."[1] Stated simply, these decisions reflect the personal values, beliefs, and attitudes of the justices involved in the case decision. Understanding a decision thus requires knowledge of judicial preferences and ideologies. Nowhere is this clearer than in cases involving abortion. This issue has triggered intense emotion among justices, and their attitudes have become critical variables in decision making. Thus a third stage in the judicial decision-making process becomes the focus in a study of why and how cases are won or lost.

JUDICIAL ATTITUDES AND JUDICIAL DECISIONS

Justices bring to a case their own individual attributes and attitudes, developed during their formative years and out of unique background experiences and pre-Court career experiences. Each justice also has a personal perception of the proper role to play individually as a justice and for the Supreme Court as a body. These role perceptions contribute to the reactions engendered by each case and its facts, issues, and litigants, and these reactions intermesh and contribute to the development of a justice's decision. Background and pre-Court experiences, professional socialization within the Court itself, and the particular case inputs combine to trigger a set of attitudes and values that affect decision making.[2]

Any analysis of judicial decision making must attempt to answer the question, Why do justices decide the way they do? Such an analysis must include, among other things, an attitudinal profile of each member of the Court, a study of the voting record of each of the justices, and an appraisal of the written record in the particular case in order to determine the degree of coincidence between private attitudes and the public decision making.

To know how and why justices decide as they do is to know the very essence of the judicial process. If one scrutinizes a case in which the justices were sharply divided, an even clearer and more detailed picture of decision making can be drawn. When justices resort to separate concurrences or dissents as they vote to decide who wins or loses in a case, they raise the curtain shrouding the mystery of judicial decision making and give the spectator an opportunity for gaining a better understanding of the total process. One such case was *Webster v. Reproductive Health Services,* a case loss for abortion right advocates.[3] The justices split into blocs and a 5–4 decision resulted. Four separate opinions were written (two were separate concurrences), demonstrating the intensity of the conflicting attitudes of the justices. Thus an analysis of *Webster* is appropriate for understanding a case loss by focusing on one set of critical factors in the decision-making stage of the judicial process: the attitudes of the nine justices who made the decision.

THE ROAD TO *WEBSTER: DANFORTH* AND *ASHCROFT*

The *Webster* case was Missouri's third challenge to the U.S. Supreme Court's 1973 landmark abortion decision, *Roe v. Wade.*[4] The state's 1969 statute outlawing all abortions except those to save the physical life of the mother had fallen before the *Roe* standard within three months after that decision. Thus an annoyed state legislature had to search for new ways to outlaw abortion. It decided on restrictive regulations: the plan was to regulate abortion to death. Statutes were enacted in 1974 and 1979, each with a different set of restrictions. Both of these statutes generated Supreme Court challenges, and both were partially struck down by the ensuing decisions. Attesting to the tenacity of Missouri's attorneys general and governors, as well as the antiabortion lobbyists who dogged the paths of the legislators, a new antiabortion law was passed in 1986, leading to the challenge of *Webster.*

The first post-*Roe* antiabortion statute, passed by the Missouri legislature in 1974, was called the Fetal Protection Statute. With five major restrictions on abortion, it generated a court challenge immediately. *Planned Parenthood of Central Missouri v. Danforth* placed each of the provisions before the Court for an answer.[5] Could Missouri require women to sign consent forms and, if married, have written permission from their husbands in order to have an abortion? Could Missouri require minors to have the consent of both parents? Could doctors be required to file detailed reports or to use only procedures designed to save the life of the aborted fetus?

State Attorney General John Danforth won and lost in this first Missouri challenge to *Roe.* The Court answered yes only to the physicians' record-keeping and reporting duties; to everything else, the Court said no.

The Missouri legislature was undeterred; by 1979 a new statute had been devised and passed. Limitations on minors were restored, with parental consent modified by a judicial bypass. Hospital abortions were required for women more than twelve weeks pregnant. Second-trimester abortions required the presence of two doctors, and a pathology report on every abortion was mandatory. Once again a challenge was docketed before the U.S. Supreme Court. John Danforth, later Senator Danforth, had been replaced as state attorney general by his protégé, John D. Ashcroft, soon to be Governor and then Senator Ashcroft and eventually U.S. attorney general. Ashcroft was encouraged in his fight to uphold the Missouri law by the return of the governorship to a strong antiabortion politician, Christopher Bond, who would also later become a senator. The state's top leadership was thus openly and unanimously opposed to all abortions, and John Ashcroft was unapologetically defiant as he argued *Planned Parenthood of Kansas City v. Ashcroft.*[6]

Ashcroft would claim later that he had successfully defended Missouri's 1979 limitations. In part, he did succeed: the Supreme Court upheld Missouri's second-physician requirement, pathological reporting, and parent or judicial consent requirements for minors. Some analysts suggested that the justices might have even allowed the hospital requirement had Ashcroft's attitude not alienated them. However, his assertion of absolute state power to force women to deliver their children in hospitals was answered by a resounding no from the Court. Claiming victory nevertheless, Ashcroft, in the role of governor of Missouri from 1984 to 1992, encouraged the state legislature to pass still more abortion restrictions. In 1986 the legislature responded with its most complex and ingenious statute.

SETTING THE STAGE FOR *WEBSTER*

Missouri's strictest abortion law was conceived during a six-mile jog around St. Louis's Forest Park. It was a dreary fall day in 1983 when Andrew F. Puzder began his thrice-weekly jog. Puzder, then thirty-eight years old, was a lawyer with a large firm in downtown St. Louis. His career had been devoted to complex civil litigation involving breach of contract. As a college student in the late 1960s and early 1970s, Puzder had been an antiabortion activist. Entering Washington University's School of Law in 1973, he was just in time to encounter the Supreme Court's decision in *Roe v. Wade.* Law professors are notorious for dissecting judicial opinions, focusing on perceived flaws of legal reasoning, lack of precedent, analogies, and power, and Puzder took all the criticism of *Roe* as an open invitation to seek its demise. Thus, in the years following his graduation, Puzder thought continually about ways to do this, while dedicating his pro bono work to the defense of antiabortion activists in criminal proceedings. In addition, he provided free legal services to Missouri's pro-life movement. Puzder used a unique defense for abortion protestors. Known as the "necessity defense," Puzder's argument declared that it was necessary for protestors to break the law in order to save the lives of unborn children.

Legal defense, however, was not enough, Puzder reasoned. What was needed was a law containing a philosophical underpinning for a reversal of *Roe v. Wade.* Jogging around Forest Park that November day in 1983 Puzder experienced a revelation. "I was thinking about the fact that law, common law, had addressed the rights of unborn children in the areas other than abortion," Puzder recounted. "I thought, wait a minute. Why not have a law that explicitly states that life begins at conception for purposes of tort, property and criminal law with a specific exemption for abortion?" He continued, "I reasoned that if I could set up an incredible dichotomy in law, it would cause people to wonder why, if the law stated that human life begins at conception and the unborn child has legal rights with regard to property and crimes, would the Supreme Court permit the mother to kill it?"[7] For Puzder, this became the relevant focus question for forcing the Court to do what it had evaded in *Roe*: to confront the question of when life begins. His goal was to move the abortion debate from the privacy issue to the taking of human life.

Entering his home in Clayton, a St. Louis suburb, still in his sweats, Puzder grabbed an envelope and jotted down his thoughts. The Missouri law that was ultimately enacted in 1986 was essentially what Puzder wrote on his envelope. Antiabortion activist Ann O'Donnell was the first to study Puzder's idea. She encouraged him to draft it into bill form and sought the assistance of state representative Judy O'Connor, a Catholic Democrat from Bridgeton. O'Connor introduced Puzder's bill in the Missouri legislature in 1985. It was not introduced as an abortion statute for strategic reasons. Indeed, this first version included the provision that "nothing in this section shall be interpreted to interfere with lawful abortion."[8] The committee to which it was referred was unimpressed by this sophistry, and the bill died in the committee.

In the meantime, a lobbyist by the name of Samuel F. Lee had been engaged in similar activities. As executive director for Missouri Citizens for Life, Sam Lee had become acquainted with Andrew Puzder in 1983 when Lee was in jail for his part in an antiabortion protest. Arrest was a regular event for Lee; he had been apprehended more than fifty times for participating in antiabortion sit-ins. He had also served time in jail for contempt of court. In 1983, however, he would find a defender in the person of Puzder, and the two began a close friendship.

At first, Lee wanted to address the viability issue instead of Puzder's more philosophical question, When does life begin? Lee, by age thirty-one, had developed his own theories for ending abortion. A college dropout, he had moved to St. Louis in 1978 to prepare for the priesthood. Although he later abandoned this, he was captivated by his studies of Mahatma Gandhi's theory of nonviolence. Lee was convinced that activities modeled on Gandhi's would bring about an end to abortion services. As the unpaid chairman of Missouri Citizens for Life, a nonprofit organization that he founded for that purpose, Lee proposed abortion restrictions that would chip away at legal abortions. Thus Lee had designed a major legislative initiative in 1985 to outlaw abortion for reasons of race or sex selection. It, like Puzder's bill, died in the state legislature during state senator J. B. Banks's filibuster on the final night of the 1985 session.[9]

The summer of 1985, therefore, found the two activists frustrated, and Lee, impressed with Puzder's "necessity" defense, decided to adopt Puzder's "life begins at conception" strategy if it could be joined to specific restrictions around which antiabortion groups could rally with some guarantee of success. He proposed four elements for inclusion in a bill: (1) allowing antiabortion protestors to argue in their defense that they had a "necessity" to defend life; (2) a modification of the informed consent and parental consent requirements for abortions; (3) a requirement that abortions be performed in a hospital after the fetus reached sixteen weeks; and (4) protection for any workers who refused to service abortion clinics. With this "kitchen sink" bill, Lee sought to win over those in the Citizens for Life Movement who were concerned about supporting Puzder's bill, which appeared to exempt abortion from its application. The president of Missouri Citizens for Life, Kathy Edwards, urged Lee to make the sex selection provision the group's major focus. Lee ultimately overcame the internal dissension, and his proposal to join with Puzder's bill was accepted.

In early 1986 still another antiabortion bill was making its way through the Missouri House. It too had been written by a lobbyist and then handed to legislators. Louis C. de Feo had been executive director of the Missouri Catholic Conference since 1981 and its general counsel since 1969. Even before *Roe v. Wade* was decided in 1973, de Feo had been writing and lobbying for antiabortion legislation. De Feo's bill called for the banning of state funding for abortion, prohibiting public hospitals from giving information about abortion, and prohibiting those hospitals from performing abortions except where the woman's life was threatened. Sam Lee called de Feo's bill "brilliant in its simplicity."[10] Moreover, the bill built upon the 1977 U.S. Supreme Court decision *Poelker v. Doe*,[11] which had come out of St. Louis. In that case the Court had held that cities did not have to subsidize abortions. According to de Feo, he "basically took that decision and later ones along the same line and built on them."[12] By barring public money for performing, assisting, or encouraging abortion, he hoped to effectively overturn *Roe*. De Feo insisted that his approach could win the support of a majority of Supreme Court justices, since it did not break new ground. He believed that this method would be more successful than that of Puzder and Lee, who he thought were deliberately creating conflict and tension before the Court.

Lee, however, believed that the bills would have a better chance of passage if they were combined. He lobbied de Feo to this end and ultimately Puzder, Lee, and de Feo proposed a comprehensive statute that included the provisions of all three earlier bills. With this draft in hand, the three collaborators were ready for legislative participation. The legislator they chose to shepherd their bill through the legislative process was state senator John D. Schneider. A Democrat from Florissant, a St. Louis suburb, Schneider was the chairman of the Judiciary Committee and a trial lawyer in private life. He had been elected to the Senate in 1970, and although a Democrat, he was pro-life like many of his Catholic Democrat constituents. Schneider, however, un-like Puzder, Lee, and de Feo, accepted *Roe v. Wade* as law and did not want to try to overturn it. Sam Lee explained his choice of Schneider this way: "I didn't know Schneider well at the time, but I had studied the Missouri legis-lature very carefully, and I knew who the main players were."[13]

Schneider took the drafted bill from Puzder, Lee, and de Feo and, after studying it, decided to make it his own. In general, his input was editorial in nature, although he did eliminate some provisions he thought might be un-constitutional. He added in his own pet theory—that a woman could exer-cise her free choice to abortion even though all public institutions and assis-tance were denied to her. Schneider also added a section to the bill requiring doctors to determine whether the fetus was viable before proceeding with a second-trimester abortion. It was this composite bill—the product of a pri-vate citizen, two lobbyists, and a legislator—that, with only a few amend-ments added on the floor of the General Assembly, passed both chambers and was signed into law in April 1986. Planned Parenthood's Missouri Chap-ter had fought its passage unsuccessfully. The final vote was 119–36 in the House and 23–5 in the Senate. As Governor John D. Ashcroft signed the bill into law, he called it the stiffest law limiting abortion in the nation. Ashcroft also declared that the law gave the state an important statement of moral principle. Samuel Lee agreed. "It's beyond what any other state has ever done," he noted, as he and Puzder both waited eagerly for the law to be chal-lenged in court.[14]

ATTORNEY GENERAL WILLIAM WEBSTER'S FAST TRACK TO THE GOVERNOR'S MANSION

When John Danforth decided the time had come for Republicans to seize control of state leadership, he looked for protégés. In Christopher Bond, John D. Ashcroft, and William Webster, he found three picture-perfect can-didates. Bond, although wealthy and well educated, was so personable that he could attract many segments of Missouri society. Looking like Li'l Abner, Bond could appeal to big and small business interests as well as Missouri farmers. Ashcroft, the straight-as-an-arrow son of an Assemblies of God preacher and college president (Evangel College), was the all-American boy. Closely cropped hair, tanned skin, and muscles combined to give Ashcroft the look of a football hero. His life was centered on religion, and he ap-pealed to Christian fundamentalists of all denominations. Ashcroft's Ivy League education at Yale and his law degree from the University of Chicago combined to attest to his intellectual abilities. His conservative Christian cru-sade for change, however, demonstrated the power of family tradition over education. His daily acts of piety attracted many in Missouri's Bible Belt. A gifted soloist, Ashcroft was in demand in churches across the state.[15] Danforth would live to see both Bond and Ashcroft in high state offices of state auditor and attorney general as well as the office of governor. He himself would be joined in the U.S. Senate by Bond and would then retire from the Senate to make a seat for Ashcroft.

William Webster was part of this trio. Endowed with movie-star good looks, he was the 1980s version of the 1990s Tom Cruise—black hair, roguish eyes, and the complexion of an angelic choirboy. Articulate and personable, William Webster was known as a charmer. A graduate of the University of Missouri at Kansas City Law School, he had been born into a politically active family. His father, Richard M. Webster of Carthage, Missouri, was a state senator and wealthy landowner who knew everyone worth knowing politically in the state. It was not surprising therefore that this son would enter politics and experience a meteoric rise to power. In addition, William Webster's early experiences as a radio announcer had given him insight into the power of the media to sway voters, and he understood advertising. Webster entered the political-legal world of Missouri politics while still in law school. Between classes he worked as a legal intern in the prosecutor's office in Jackson County, Missouri.

By age thirty-five, Webster had become one of the nation's youngest state attorneys general. Before his election as attorney general in 1984, he served two terms in the Missouri General Assembly, where he was remembered as a conservative, ambitious lawmaker. As state attorney general, Webster was named one of the nation's "ten most feared attorneys general" by *Ad-week* magazine.[16] He received awards from numerous law enforcement agencies, and by the late 1980s he gained national attention because he had persuaded the Supreme Court to take up seven Missouri cases, including four of the most controversial on the Court's docket. Among these were a teenage death-penalty case, a right-to-die case, and the abortion rights case.

DUELING IN LOWER FEDERAL COURT:
STATE LOSSES AND PRIVACY GAINS

Like Danforth, Bond, and Ashcroft, Webster was personally committed to an antiabortion agenda. Agreeing with the governor's assertion that Missouri's new law was an "important statement of moral principle,"[17] Webster was prepared to defend it in court. Webster understood Puzder and Lee's plan to use the law to force the Supreme Court to confront the question of when life begins. However, his main goal was to secure Supreme Court acceptance of Missouri's right to regulate. Whether *Roe* stood or fell was of secondary importance to William Webster: winning cases was his first priority.

The challenge to the new law came quickly. Five public health providers in a class-action suit docketed in the Eighth Circuit District Court joined the Planned Parenthood Federation of America and Reproductive Health Services, a nonprofit clinic in St. Louis, in seeking a declaratory judgment striking down the law as unconstitutional and an injunction against enforcement of the law. On August 2, 1986, Chief U.S. District Judge Scott O. Wright of Kansas City, Missouri, temporarily set aside the law that was scheduled to take effect twelve days later. Both sides agreed to the temporary stay, and preparation began for the hearing.

In December 1986, a parade of witnesses was called to testify in Wright's courtroom. Judith Widdicombe, the chairman of the board of St. Louis's Reproductive Health Services, testified regarding the 1,500 second-trimester abortions performed at the clinic in 1985. She produced statistical data to confirm that Reproductive Health Services was both safe and cost-effective. Dr. Warren Hern, head of a Boulder, Colorado, abortion clinic, supported Widdicombe's statistics. Both argued that access to abortion would be severely restricted if Missouri required all second-trimester abortions to be performed in hospitals. Stanley K. Henshaw, deputy director for research at the Guttmacher Institute in New York, also testified that an in-hospital requirement was a curb on abortion and was unwarranted as a health measure.

Arguing for the state's right to set restrictions, Webster assembled most of the major points of argument he would later use as the case moved through the legal system. At the district court level, he was unsuccessful in persuading Judge Wright. On April 30, 1987, Wright overturned the principal provision of the Missouri law. Although Webster disingenuously argued that its preamble's declaration—that life begins at conception—had not been intended to apply to abortion but only to give to unborn children the rights permitted by the Constitution and court decisions, the judge still found it unconstitutional. Wright also struck down the hospitalization requirement for post-fifteen-week abortions, the viability testing, and the ban on the use of state facilities and funds for abortion counseling and services. Judge Wright held that the state had failed to show a compelling interest in maternal health.[18]

Attorney General Webster's appeal was immediately lodged before a three-judge panel of the Eighth U.S. Circuit Court of Appeals in St. Louis, but once again Webster was rebuffed. Chief Judge Donald Lay, Judge Theodore McMillan, and Judge Richard S. Arnold affirmed in general Judge Wright's rulings. The court's decision held that Missouri could not require tests of lung maturity: the state lacked the power to tell a doctor what he must do to determine viability. The Eighth Circuit Court panel also agreed with the district court ruling that the language of Missouri's statute did "exactly what the Supreme Court has declared it may not do: espouse a theory of when life begins as the foundation of the state's regulation of abortion."[19]

As Webster contemplated that panel's decision, he had open before him two options: he could either seek a full-court review by the Eighth Circuit sitting *en banc* or bypass this stage and appeal directly to the U.S. Supreme Court. Webster opted for the latter course of action. His decision was influenced in part by Puzder and Lee, who feared that the full Court of Appeals would rule in favor of the state. As Puzder explained, "We actually didn't want [a favorable ruling] because then we would have to depend on the pro-choice side to appeal to the Supreme Court, and we didn't think we could count on it."[20] Samuel Lee reminded Webster that the state law had been drafted specifically to provide a "broad challenge" to *Roe v. Wade*. All three men believed that Supreme Court personnel changes had eroded the *Roe* majority. Lee explained, "When the [Missouri antiabortion] bill passed in April, 1986, there was still a 6–3 majority for abortion on the court . . . but we knew some of those guys were getting old, that Ronald Reagan was president, and that we only need two more justices on our side. We also knew that it could take three years for the law to get to the Supreme Court which by then would be due for another big abortion case."[21]

William Webster, addressing the Clergy for Life antiabortion group, explained his strategy. First, he noted, recent Court decisions on abortion had revealed a fractured Supreme Court. "Our greatest hope," Webster told the clergy, "is that with the change in direction of the Court, there will be a return to the states of the right to determine what kind of conduct will and will not be allowed."[22] Webster's focus centered on justices Sandra Day O'Connor, Antonin Scalia, Anthony Kennedy, and William Rehnquist. Rehnquist, one of the two dissenters in *Roe*, had replaced Warren Burger as chief justice, and Byron White, the other *Roe* dissenter, remained on the Court. Kennedy had taken the place of Lewis Powell, a *Roe* supporter, while O'Connor had replaced the pro-choice Potter Stewart. Scalia, moving into the vacancy created by Rehnquist's elevation to chief, was known to oppose abortion. Although Webster cautioned his audience, "It is very difficult to predict what a judge is going to do,"[23] he nonetheless pointed out that the voting record of all these justices in abortion cases supported his position. Webster was optimistic that Missouri would win its case before the Supreme Court.

Those challenging Missouri's 1986 statute were represented by a veteran pro-choice attorney, Frank Susman of St. Louis, who had bested Ashcroft in oral argument in *Planned Parenthood of Kansas City v. Ashcroft*. They recognized that the Supreme Court had become less firm in its support of abortion rights. Nevertheless, the Missouri statutes had to be tested. To allow the statutes to go unchallenged, Susman explained, would threaten the availability of low-dose birth control pills, intrauterine devices, and in-vitro fertilization because "all those devices lead to the destruction of fertilized eggs, which the Missouri law defined as human beings with protectable interests."[24] Thus Planned Parenthood of America and the Reproductive Health

Services clinic had no choice but to go to court just as their opponents desired. They had the assistance of an American Civil Liberties Union attorney, Kathryn Kolbert, to coordinate the amicus briefs from an awakening pro-choice constituency.

PERSUADING JUSTICES: *WEBSTER* BEFORE THE U.S. SUPREME COURT

The U.S. Supreme Court that agreed to hear Missouri's *Webster* case was a very different Court from the 1973 *Roe* Court. A 7–2 voting bloc in favor of privacy rights had shrunk to 5–4 by 1989. The appointments to the Court made by President Reagan appeared to consolidate a bloc of antiabortion justices as Lee and Puzder had expected. Pro-choice groups dreaded taking the case to court: the fear of losing had become very real. For those opposed to reproductive choice, success seemed imminent.

When the Supreme Court accepted *Webster* on appeal on January 6, 1989, and scheduled oral argument for April 26, 1989, the national debate over abortion intensified. Pro-choice groups had ignored warning signs, believing that *Roe* was settled law. However, when the Republican Party leadership under presidents Reagan and George H. W. Bush embraced the pro-life position, it became clear that abortion rights were truly in jeopardy. *Webster* galvanized pro-choice groups to mobilize to protect *Roe*. They began to flood the Court with amicus curiae briefs: more than three hundred organizations and individuals ultimately filed some seventy-eight briefs. The Court found itself submerged under a mountain of data and arguments.[25]

Webster received help from the most powerful legal player in the judicial process, the outgoing solicitor general, Charles Fried. President Bush gave Fried a special assignment: to file an anti-*Roe* brief in *Webster*. Fried would also assist Webster in oral argument. An additional forty-six briefs attacked *Roe*. Diverse religious groups banded together to advance the pro-life agenda, including both Catholics and evangelical fundamentalist Protestants. Pro-life physicians and nurses filed briefs supporting Missouri's law. Still other briefs came from state attorneys general, state legislatures, and members of Congress, all urging the Court to overrule *Roe v. Wade*. Some argued that medical science had already nullified *Roe*'s thesis. The trimester standard with its definition of viability surely could not survive the advances of medical science, they insisted. To reinforce this argument, some groups produced briefs asserting the primacy of natural law over constitutional law. Other groups used federalism and separation-of-powers arguments, urging the Court to restrain itself and to restore power to the states. Traditionalists tried to argue that *Roe*'s use of historical data about abortion practices in English and American common law was flawed.[26]

Pro-choice groups banded together to protect *Roe*. Briefs were organized to debate point by point the charges leveled against *Roe*. The American Medical Association's brief, submitted by prominent doctors and noted scientists, refuted the claim that life began at conception. In particular, they cited scientific proof that viability had not been—and could not be—pushed back to the point of conception: lungs did not develop before twenty-four weeks. This medical brief urged the Court to uphold *Roe*'s trimester standard for regulating abortions by allowing women more control before viability and states more control after viability. Thus, the AMA's brief supported *Roe* and affirmed the Court's ruling that abortion should be a private medical decision made by a woman and her doctor.[27]

Roe was also defended by a group of American historians. Prominent among these academics was Professor James Mohr, author of the leading historical treatise on abortion. Historians documented the wide acceptance of abortion in colonial America and throughout the Civil War period. They argued that later restrictions were enacted because of social and economic fears that were no longer relevant. Professor Mohr specifically repudiated the solicitor general's use of historical data.[28] Women's groups joined the historians and doctors, submitting briefs that urged the Court to uphold *Roe*. They focused on the small number of late-term abortions. Women had used their freedom responsibly under *Roe*, these groups asserted, and the viability standard had balanced interests well. There were also religious groups who banded together to submit amicus briefs supporting *Roe* and urging the Court to strike down Missouri's law. Those Baptists who were committed to the belief in "separation of church and state" joined forces with like-minded groups to urge the Court to keep religion and secular law separate. "Law," they told the Court, "should not be based on a particular religious belief."[29] Finally, pro-choice briefs were submitted on behalf of 145 members of Congress.

JUDICIAL VOTING BEHAVIOR IN PRE-*WEBSTER* ABORTION CASES

A state's rights mentality has never been confined to Southern states alone nor to their inhabitants. Rooted in the very origin of the Constitution itself, this doctrine has been asserted continually throughout American political history. No state wants to be told no. Beginning with the landmark birth control case of *Griswold v. Connecticut* (1965),[30] the U.S. Supreme Court had said no to state bans on contraceptives for married couples. Seven years later in the New York case *Eisenstadt v. Baird* (1972),[31] the Court said no to state bans on contraceptives for single individuals. It was only a short step to the 1973 abortion rights decision in *Roe v. Wade*. Once again the Court said no to a state, striking down its laws criminalizing abortion.

States were locked in a power struggle with the federal government. They did not, however, respond with absolute refusals to abide by the Supreme Court decisions: instead, they responded by deliberately creating as many restrictions on abortion as they could conceive. Many states were unabashed concerning their intent: to regulate abortion out of existence. Cloaked under the guise of "protecting the mother" arguments, statute after statute poured out of the hands of state legislators, anxious to recover the power that they had lost. These statutes would ultimately be tested before the justices of the U.S. Supreme Court. Some would fall, but others would stand.

Thirteen major abortion cases involving such statutes were litigated before the Court between *Roe* (1973) and *Webster* (1989). These precedents served as the backdrop against which *Webster* was played out. Each of these thirteen cases involved different states and different regulations. They were decided by different coalitions of justices as the Court personnel changed from 1973 to 1989. What did these decisions actually say? What types of state regulations did they uphold? What impact did judicial attitudes toward abortion itself and toward states' rights have on each decision?[32]

Roe's companion case from Georgia, *Doe v. Bolton* (1973),[33] struck down that state's requirements that abortions be performed in licensed hospitals, approved beforehand by a hospital committee, and supported by two physicians. Two years later the Court rebuffed the state of Virginia, holding that a state may not prevent newspaper advertisements for abortion services.[34] In 1976, Massachusetts secured both a yes and a no from the Court: a state may require a minor to obtain parental consent, but a "judicial bypass" must be offered.[35]

As described earlier, Missouri also received both a yes and no from the Court in 1976. In *Planned Parenthood of Central Missouri v. Danforth*, the Court allowed the state to require a woman's written, informed consent to an abortion; she was required to assert in writing that all dangers associated with abortion had been fully explained to her by her doctor. Missouri could not, however, require a married woman to secure spousal consent, nor could the state require doctors to use all means possible to save the life of the aborted fetus.[36]

The next year, in 1977, the Court dealt with contraceptive advertisements once again, this time from New York. Could a state prohibit the sale and advertisement of contraceptives for minors? The Court said no.[37] That same year, however, a trio of cases—*Poelker v. Doe, Beal v. Doe*, and *Maher v. Roe*—allowed Missouri and Connecticut, as well as any other state, to refuse to fund abortions that were not essential to save a woman's life.[38] Indigent pregnant women did not have a right to state-funded abortion, and state public hospitals did not have to provide for them.

Pennsylvania appeared before the Court in *Colautti v. Franklin* in 1979 to defend its version of Missouri's fetal protection statute.[39] The Court said no

to Pennsylvania as it had to Missouri: legislatures could not define the time
of fetal viability nor require doctors to attempt to save aborted fetuses. This
Pennsylvania law so closely mirrored that of Missouri that many wondered
how often the Court would be asked to address the same issue.

When Utah passed a parental notification law for minors, it too seemed an
old question, for the Court had upheld a parental consent requirement in
1976. In the 1981 case, the Court agreed that a state could require a doctor
to tell (notify) the minor's parents of her impending abortion plans, in addition to the consent requirement.[40] However, when Ohio attempted a series
of detailed restrictions, the Court once again said no.[41] A state could not require hospitalization for second-trimester abortions, could not require a
twenty-four-hour waiting period, could not detail the elements of "informed
consent," and could not tell clinics how to dispose of fetal remains.

In 1983, Missouri was once again before the high court. The state's law set
forth requirements similar to those the Court had struck down in the Ohio
case. However, in *Planned Parenthood Association of Kansas City v.
Ashcroft*, the Supreme Court said both no and yes to Missouri. Missouri could
require pathological reports on each abortion and could require the presence of two doctors for post-viability abortions, but it could not have a
second-trimester hospitalization requirement. However, a Virginia law mandating hospitalization requirements for second-trimester abortions was upheld that year in *Simopoulos v. Virginia*.[42]

The last major abortion case decided by the Court before the *Webster* appeal was from Pennsylvania. The issues presented in the Pennsylvania case
could not convince the Court to require doctors to use "scare tactics" to talk
women out of abortions, to require doctors to try to preserve the life of
aborted fetuses, or to rule that two doctors were necessary at *all* abortions—
only post-viability ones.[43]

Taken together, these thirteen major abortion decisions demonstrated the
determination of state legislatures to assert control. Their strategies had embraced a number of devices: consent and notification laws; licensing and reporting laws; viability, post-viability, and fetal protection laws; advertisement
and promotion bans; and prohibitions on public funding and use of public
facilities. The high court for the most part had held fast to its central doctrine
of a woman's right to reproductive choice. However, by the mid-1980s the
judicial makeup of the Supreme Court had changed.

Knowing the voting habits of the justices is essential for any attorney who
seeks a case win before the high court. The thirteen abortion cases that preceded *Webster* revealed the various blocs and voting alignments that had
emerged over time. These major abortion cases that the Court decided in the
years between *Roe* and *Webster* provided data on these judicial blocs and
alignments. While facts differed in these cases and created varied coalitions
of justices, a pattern did develop. It could be documented, traced, and eval-

uated for each justice and combination of justices. The *Roe* Court's personnel had experienced its first change in 1975: Justice John Paul Stevens replaced the totally predictable liberal justice William O. Douglas. No other personnel change occurred until 1981 when the first female justice, Sandra Day O'Connor, replaced Justice Potter Stewart. Another five years passed before the next change in the Court's makeup. Following the 1984 presidential election and the retirement of Chief Justice Warren E. Burger, President Ronald Reagan elevated one of *Roe*'s two dissenters, Justice William H. Rehnquist, to chief justice. His position on the Court was then filled by Justice Antonin E. Scalia. In 1988, on the eve of the *Webster* litigation, Justice Lewis F. Powell resigned. Justice Anthony M. Kennedy, his replacement, would hear and vote on *Webster* in 1989. These four personnel changes impacted the decision of the Court.

The split votes in the thirteen major abortion cases between 1974 and 1988 demonstrated where the justices were likely to come down when deciding a case of this nature.[44] *Roe*'s seven-strong majority had written three separate concurrences: Douglas's, Stewart's, and Burger's. Douglas expanded on the right of privacy. Linking it to the Fourteenth Amendment's "liberty" term, he agreed with the majority in defining abortion choices as a "limited" fundamental right. Stewart, like Douglas, tied *Roe* to the liberty protected by the Fourteenth Amendment and also cited "due process." Chief Justice Burger's concurrence, however, placed him closer to the dissenting duo of Rehnquist and White. These nuances within the 7–2 official categorization of *Roe*'s voting blocs demonstrated that numbers did not tell everything about the decision.

The nine-man *Roe* Court encountered only one major abortion decision before personnel change brought Justice Stevens to replace Douglas in 1975. That case, *Bigelow v. Virginia*, was decided by the same 7–2 vote that characterized *Roe*. Justices Rehnquist and White dissented in favor of state power over abortion advertisements, while the majority of seven held the opposite view. However, time, different issues, and personnel changes soon created different voting blocs.

The new state regulations that did this made their way to the Court in 1976 in two cases: *Belotti v. Baird* (*Baird I*) from Massachusetts and *Planned Parenthood of Central Missouri v. Danforth*. Restrictions on physicians, previable fetal protection, spousal consent, and parental consent were the major issues that created different voting blocs in these two cases. A bloc of six said no to spousal consent. Newcomer Stevens joined justices Blackmun, Brennan, Marshall, Powell, and Stewart; Chief Justice Burger shifted to join Rehnquist and White in dissent. The majority bloc was reduced still further when the issue became one of parental consent. Stevens shifted to approve this restriction, and a 5–4 vote demonstrated the volatility of the issue. A bloc of six upheld Missouri's regulation of doctors, but only five were willing to

strike down pre-viable fetal protection requirements and legislative definitions of viability.

Other state laws soon presented the Court with additional divisive regulations. The year 1977 found the Court accepting four significant cases. Three
were almost identical: money was the central issue. Could states refuse to
provide funds for "nontherapeutic" abortions? Could a state deny indigent
women access to nontherapeutic abortions in public hospitals? *Beal v. Doe*
from Pennsylvania, *Maher v. Roe* from Connecticut, and *Poelker v. Doe* from
Missouri were all decided by 6–3 votes. *Roe's* dissenters moved into a majority position when Chief Justice Burger and justices Powell, Stewart, and
Stevens joined them to uphold the antifunding laws. Only justices Blackmun,
Brennan, and Marshall saw these laws as economically discriminatory, targeting a class: indigent women. The fourth case of 1977 created different voting blocs, triggered by questions of minors' rights to contraceptives. New
York's law, litigated in *Carey v. Population Services International*, brought
Justice White to join the liberal bloc, while Chief Justice Burger dissented
along with Justice Rehnquist. Separate concurrences by Justices Stevens and
Powell highlighted the internal divisions within the ostensible 7–2 official
vote recorded by *Carey.*

The 1979 case from Pennsylvania, *Colautti v. Franklin* reaffirmed physicians' power over viability, and a 6–3 vote demonstrated the division. Voting against the state's vague regulation were justices Blackmun, Brennan,
Marshall, Stewart, Powell, and Stevens. Justices Rehnquist and White and
Chief Justice Burger made up the minority. While the Court considered
other abortion cases in 1979, they were repeats of earlier decisions. *Bellotti
v. Baird* (*Baird II*), dealing with parental consent, and *Harris v. McRae* and
Williams v. Zbaraz, dealing with funding, raised no new issues.[45] *Stare decisis* reigned. These cases did demonstrate, however, that states had developed a useful strategy: targeting groups such as minors and indigents—
these groups were least likely to attract judicial support. It was a successful
ploy in many cases.

A 1981 Utah case demonstrated this for minors in a 6–3 decision in *H. L.
v. Matheson*.[46] It allowed parental notification so long as it did not mandate
parental consent. Only justices Blackmun, Brennan, and Marshall still voiced
dissent. The significance of the Utah case was that it clearly showed the impact of a presidential election on the Court. At the end of 1980, Justice Marshall had had a majority bloc ready to strike down the Utah criminal statute
that required doctors to give prior notification for minors' abortion. However, the first Monday following the presidential election of 1980 saw Marshall's majority crumble: Stewart and Powell withdrew their support. A new
majority emerged, and Utah's statute was upheld.

H. L. v. Matheson demonstrated the chilling effect that the 1980 election
had on the Court, even before the personnel changes commenced. Never-

theless, the cases of 1983 continued to send mixed and confusing signals. Justice Stewart's replacement on the Court was less inclined to support reproductive choice. The Court's first female justice, Sandra Day O'Connor, understood the goals of the Reagan administration that had nominated her. In the abortion cases that were decided in 1983, O'Connor, who had been on the Court for fourteen months, began to play a pivotal role. *City of Akron v. Akron Center for Reproductive Health* and *Planned Parenthood Association of Kansas City v. Ashcroft* were the two leading cases in 1983.[47] Issues of hospitalization, parental consent, and waiting periods divided the justices in these cases, but one clear trend emerged. O'Connor, along with Rehnquist and White, would uphold all the regulations that states like Ohio and Missouri could design.

Justice O'Connor moved into alignment with the duo of Rehnquist and White. The chief justice usually joined this group to create a pro–state regulation bloc of four. The bloc composed of Blackmun, Brennan, and Marshall most often attracted the vote of Stevens. Justice Powell was the lone "swing" vote between the two camps as the 1983 term ended. Most notable had been O'Connor's articulation of an earlier but little noticed Blackmun phrase, "undue burden." This phrase, used seven years earlier in the first *Bellotti v. Baird*, was elevated by Justice O'Connor into her own special test. Only those state restrictions that unduly burdened a woman's choice should be voided, O'Connor asserted, and, as 1983 ended, she launched her attack on *Roe v. Wade*.

The last major constitutional attack on that precedent before *Webster* came in 1986 in *Thornburgh v. American College of Obstetricians and Gynecologists*.[48] Its 5–4 vote showed the precarious status of reproductive choice in constitutional law. Pennsylvania's set of five enhanced restrictions once again attempted to deter physicians from performing abortions. Four justices voted to uphold all of these. Justices Rehnquist, White, and O'Connor and Chief Justice Burger continued to affirm states' power to enact deterrent regulations over abortion. Only the vote of Justice Lewis Powell stood in the way.

By 1989, when *Webster* took center stage, this barrier was gone. Justice Anthony Kennedy now sat in Justice Powell's seat.

THE BACKGROUNDS AND PRE-COURT CAREERS OF THE SUPREME COURT JUSTICES OF *WEBSTER*

As Missouri Attorney General William Webster and his counterpart, Frank Susman, contemplated their chances for success, they focused on each of the nine justices. Who were these justices? What could cause them to vote in a certain way? Were there background factors that could be triggered so as to create a favorable response? Biographical data to document the life experiences of each justice became crucial in discovering and predicting judicial attitudes. Susman and Webster studied this information carefully. The judicial profiles that emerged were highly encouraging for William Webster; Frank Susman had every reason to worry.

Chief Justice William H. Rehnquist

William H. Rehnquist had been chief justice for three years when the *Webster* case was argued in 1989. Appointed by President Richard Nixon in 1971 and elevated to chief justice by President Ronald Reagan in 1986, Rehnquist was a veteran in abortion debate. Ascending to the Court at the very moment *Roe v. Wade* was being considered for reargument, Rehnquist had begun his career as an opponent of reproductive choice. Could this attitude be linked to his formative years and background experienced in Milwaukee, Wisconsin, during the 1930s?

Eight years old in 1932 when Franklin D. Roosevelt assumed the presidency, Rehnquist had already experienced the devastation of the Great Depression. The reaction of his family had been at sharp odds to that of the New Dealers who had sought to ameliorate that disaster through governmental intervention in the economy. Instead, the Rehnquist family defended Herbert Hoover, and by the late 1930s they were embracing the philosophy of Father Charles E. Coughlin, the conservative "radio priest."[49]

Coughlin's political sermons evolved into diatribes against Roosevelt and his New Deal policies. Sometimes appearing to be anti-Semitic and sometimes labeled "pro-fascist," Coughlin's main themes stressed a return to community decision making and individual citizen power. Coughlin could uphold state governmental restrictions on birth control information yet oppose governmental restrictions on consumption of alcohol: he saw no contradictions in his philosophy and neither did his supporters. It was, however, Coughlin's appeal to cultural conservatism that spoke most powerfully to the troubled middle class of which the Rehnquist family was a part.

The vitriolic attacks made by Coughlin permeated and colored William Rehnquist's formative years in the white middle-class suburban community of Milwaukee known as Shorewood. The Rehnquist family had little sympathy for the problems of cities, of the poor, or of racial minorities. They sought a return to the traditional world of local community control and a revitalization of the self-sufficient individual within that community. Their Swedish ethnicity and conservative Lutheran theology reinforced this view.

By the time William Rehnquist entered high school, he was already demonstrating a political attitude that reflected this background. He advanced goals of an almost reactionary conservatism that exceeded even that of his friends. Opposition to the social and economic programs of FDR's

New Deal so dominated Rehnquist's formative years that not even the educational benefits he would be given under World War II's G.I. Bill would soften his antagonism to big government. While governmental largesse made possible Rehnquist's graduation with both bachelor's and master's degrees from Stanford University, his opposition to government was only intensified by this education. Encounters with Harvard "liberals" while he was seeking a second master's degree in political science only added fuel to his uncompromising political conservatism.

Having once announced to his elementary school class that one day he would "change the government,"[50] the adult Rehnquist reasoned that a legal career could help him eradicate the ideas of the New Deal. Rehnquist certainly possessed in abundance the talents that made for a successful attorney: aggressive but not only openly antagonistic, clever but not overtly critical. He graduated from Stanford Law School at the top of his class and was recommended by a professor for a clerkship with Supreme Court justice Robert Jackson. No hint of Rehnquist's agenda and ideology emerged during his interview with Jackson. Instead, Jackson—much to Rehnquist's surprise—focused on his unusual name and his ethnicity.[51]

Rehnquist, however, soon was pushing his conservative views on Justice Jackson, particularly in the area of race. Two cases would demonstrate Rehnquist's ideology at work: *Terry v. Adams* and *Brown v. Board of Education*.[52] Rehnquist, stressing freedom of association and majority rule in memos to Justice Jackson, argued that white Southerners should be allowed to exclude blacks from political associations that nominated candidates for public office. In *Brown*, Rehnquist urged maintaining segregation. Once again he stressed majoritarianism and coupled this argument with that of commitment to stare decisis. This approach did not win Rehnquist friends among the Roosevelt appointees to the Supreme Court nor among the other clerks. Rehnquist was particularly at odds with justices Black and Douglas and accused them of trampling on state's rights and coddling criminals.[53]

When Rehnquist went into private practice following his clerkship, his very choice of location and of political association demonstrated his ideology. Moving to Phoenix at the moment the ultraconservative wing of the Arizona Republican Party seized power, Rehnquist at once began to establish himself as a spokesman for this group. During his sixteen years in Phoenix, Rehnquist regularly spoke against members of the Warren Court, labeling them "socialist" and "communist." He attacked local ordinances aimed at ending racial discrimination in private restaurants. Rehnquist, as a poll watcher in elections, also appeared to condone efforts to turn away Hispanic voters. His insensitivity to restrictive racial covenants in the property he purchased would later surface to lend credence to charges of racial prejudice. The mature Rehnquist appeared to retain the unchanging philosophy of the young elementary school student; neither education nor early job experience changed him.

Political party affiliation was important in Rehnquist's development: friendships with powerful Arizona conservative Republicans opened doors to national positions. Rehnquist worked diligently for Barry Goldwater's presidential campaign in 1964 as well as Richard Nixon's in 1968. His reward was an appointment to President Nixon's Office of Legal Counsel. Here, Rehnquist used his position as assistant attorney general to defend the president's war powers, his expanded use of executive powers, and his attack on the Fourth Amendment limitations on police. By 1971, Rehnquist had become a lightning rod for Democrats. In the process, he demonstrated that he could be the judicial conservative President Nixon was seeking for the Supreme Court. When justices Hugo L. Black and John Marshall Harlan retired, Nixon had the opportunity to nominate justices "in his own image." Rehnquist fit that job description. He was forty-seven years old when, after stringent questioning by the Senate, he was confirmed. He had successfully deflected questions about his controversial views on civil rights and civil liberties. Only time would confirm how very narrow his approach to those issues was.

The Burger Court, which Rehnquist joined on January 7, 1972, was facing one of its toughest issues, abortion, in the cases of *Roe v. Wade* and *Doe v. Bolton*. These cases had been argued on December 13, 1971, before a Court of only seven justices, in spite of attempts to postpone argument until the Court reached its full strength of nine members. However, after hearing argument and attempting to produce an acceptable draft of the opinion, the Court decided to reconsider its approach. Rehnquist and Justice Lewis Powell had taken their seats on the Court by this time, and both justices were urging the Court to hold the abortion cases over for reargument so that they could take part in the decision. Justice Harry A. Blackmun, the designated opinion writer, came to agree that reargument "would perhaps be desirable," and on June 26, 1972, the Court announced that *Roe* and *Doe* would be reargued that fall. Thus, Rehnquist would vote in the first major case of abortion rights. His questions to counsel arguing those cases indicated the line of argument he would quickly develop to oppose reproductive choice: arguments centered on the Court's jurisdiction and on history's treatment of abortion.

Conference discussions of *Roe* and *Doe* misled analysis concerning Rehnquist's attitude. He had appeared at first to be ready to vote differently in *Doe* and *Roe* and had signaled he would "probably concur in part and dissent in part" to the Court's opinion upholding reproductive choice rights.[54] He ended up, however, in a "tart" dissent, declaring that abortion was not a right of privacy, it lacked historical justification, and the cases failed to meet judicial standards for case and controversy.[55]

From 1973 to 1989 Rehnquist dealt with a large number of abortion cases. His opposition took different forms depending on the question presented, but his focus on limiting and ultimately reversing *Roe* never wavered in any of the major thirteen cases decided during the sixteen years that separated *Roe* from *Webster*. Rehnquist approved every state restriction on abortion. He upheld restrictions couched in health terms, upheld bans on advertising of abortion services, and approved all state viability and post-viability regulations as well as spousal and parental consent laws. He also supported states' denial of public facilities and funds for abortion services.

By 1989, Rehnquist finally was in position to enact his policy preference. The *Roe* majority of seven had become six in 1983 and dropped to five in 1986. The election of Ronald Reagan to the presidency in 1980 and 1984 and his appointment of pro-life justices made a difference. Justice Sandra Day O'Connor was the first of these. When Chief Justice Warren Burger retired and President Reagan tapped Rehnquist to be chief justice, he also added another sympathetic vote in Antonin Scalia. Rehnquist thus appeared to command a Court majority of five justices who were ready to use *Webster* to overturn *Roe v. Wade*.

Justice William J. Brennan Jr.

Justice William Brennan had been on the Supreme Court for thirty-three years when the *Webster* case reached the high court. Appointed by President Dwight Eisenhower in 1956, Brennan, the senior associate justice in 1989, was, like Rehnquist, a veteran of the abortion debate. His support for the right of privacy was triggered by the birth control case of *Poe v. Ullman* and emerged in *Griswold v. Connecticut*.[56] Was his an unusual position? He was Irish Catholic, appointed by a staunch social conservative Republican.[57] William Brennan, however, put the value of freedom over the values of religion and culture. Brennan's Catholic religious views did not shape his ideology. Because of persecution by government in Ireland, his ancestors had sought freedom in the United States. It was a freedom he felt "obliged to defend."[58] If being a Roman Catholic conflicted with what the Constitution meant or required, Brennan said, then his "religious beliefs have to give way."[59]

On the high court, Brennan soon became a liberal voice. Brennan's early environment in a working-class neighborhood in Newark, New Jersey, may have been the critical variable in explaining this ideology. Growing up surrounded by suffering people, Brennan was sensitized to individual needs. He believed government should address these needs. Being the son of an Irish immigrant coal stoker linked Brennan to the real life of the blue-collar manual laborer. When his father became an American Federation of Labor organizer, Brennan found friends among the attorneys who supported labor.[60]

Merit scholarships provided for his education at the University of Pennsylvania and at Harvard Law School, where he specialized in labor law. When World War II called him into service, his job was to resolve labor–management disputes dealing with war production. After the war, corporations pursued him to represent them in labor disputes. He made friends with powerful Republican businessmen and politicians, but his sympathy remained with labor. Personally charming and witty, Brennan faced few questions about his ideology. Instead, Republican friends gladly recommended him for prominent judicial posts, and he was appointed to the New Jersey Supreme Court. Few knew that he held many views of a liberal Democrat.

His early experience on the New Jersey Supreme Court did not define him as a liberal who would support laws creating social and economic reform while opposing those laws that interfered with individual rights. Indeed, Brennan was perceived as a "conservative" by Attorney General Herbert Brownell, who heard him deliver a speech, not knowing that Brennan was only reading a message from his chief justice, who was ill. So it was that Brennan's nomination to a vacancy on the U.S. Supreme Court came to hinge on a misconception of his judicial philosophy. Brownell knew that Eisenhower wanted a "conservative, northeastern, Catholic Democrat with judicial experience" to fill a vacancy on the Supreme Court, and he thought he had his man in Bill Brennan. Few would have expected the profound impact Brennan would have in the field of privacy rights.[61]

The test came on May 20, 1960, when Brennan joined four other justices to vote in favor of hearing the appeal in *Poe v. Ullman*. A veteran of four years when this birth control case was argued before the Court, Brennan at that time ruled on procedural technicalities rather than on the merits of the case. Along with Chief Justice Earl Warren, who had become his close friend, Brennan joined justices Felix Frankfurter, Tom C. Clark, and Charles Evans Whittaker in dismissing *Poe*. However, Brennan was the shaky fifth vote. In the end he concurred separately, telling his clerk that were he "actually to reach the merits in *Poe*, I definitely would vote to void the Connecticut [birth control] statute as applied!"[62] Brennan got this chance five years later when *Griswold v. Connecticut* was placed on the Court's docket. He made his new position clear when his turn came to speak in the conference following *Griswold*'s oral argument. Connecticut's statute infringed upon the "realm of privacy,"[63] Brennan stated. He voted to void the statute and reverse the convictions of those involved. Ultimately, Brennan's ideas were incorporated into the Court's majority opinion and a right to privacy was established. Thus began his protection for the right of reproductive choice.

Brennan's "sense of mission to the underdog" had grown out of his economic and social background experiences. His father had often lamented the lack of a champion of the people—"someone to stand up for [the underdog]."[64] Brennan assumed that role, and women fit the category of "underdogs." Brennan believed passionately in individual freedom and thought women should have a "right to be free from unwarranted governmental intrusion" into their bedrooms.[65] Brennan went even further, however; he believed that the government needed to assume a positive, proactive role to help achieve the fulfillment of the privacy right of reproductive choice. Brennan's experiences during the 1930s Depression affirmed his belief in a government that helped provide jobs, social security, and medical care. Shouldn't government also both promote privacy while keeping "hands off"? Shouldn't government help women exercise their privacy rights through funding? He believed that the Court could be the vehicle through which government could achieve this goal.[66]

Brennan nevertheless remained a true legal scholar as he approached cases. Pragmatism and compromise were also essential elements in this approach. He carefully tested cases involving the right to birth control and the developing claim to abortion rights. Did each case satisfy the exacting jurisdictional standards set by Court precedents? This was as important to Brennan as the setting of new precedents. He might support a lower court's decision extending privacy rights yet at the same time refuse Supreme Court review on procedural and jurisdictional grounds.[67]

As Brennan approached the *Webster* decision, however, he would perceive no barriers to Court review. Frank Susman, attorney for St. Louis's Reproductive Health Services, could feel optimistic, even certain, as to Brennan's support. In 1986 Brennan had responded to the question about the constitutional right to abortion by saying:

> In this society, nobody can dictate for everyone else what must be done with respect to the most intimate choices, private choices, family decisions, that individuals face. . . . The right to privacy that is protected by the Bill of Rights . . . [is] part of a fundamental charter of civilized society.[68]

Justice Byron R. White

Justice Byron White was second in seniority on the Supreme Court when the *Webster* case arrived: only Justice Brennan had dealt with more cases of reproductive privacy. Appointed to the Court in 1962 by President John F. Kennedy, White had participated in *Griswold v. Connecticut* and had appeared, in that case, to support the right of contraception. However, time would quickly show the narrow view that he would adopt toward privacy.

The choice of Byron White for the position of associate justice had raised a few questions. Some observers had pointed out that he had no judicial experience. Others noted that he had never been considered a legal scholar. Yet he was confirmed quickly and without controversy. He was a football hero, a Rhodes scholar at Oxford, and a graduate of Yale Law School. President Kennedy admired mental and physical prowess, and White seemed to be a Renaissance man who excelled at both.[69] He was also a Republican who had become a Democrat. A personal friend of Kennedy's, they shared World

War II naval experience. More to the point, White had actively campaigned for Kennedy in 1960 and became friends with Robert Kennedy, who, following the election, tapped him as the second-in-command in the U.S. Department of Justice.

White's background offered few clues to his future behavior as a justice. His formative years had been spent in Colorado, where his father was a lumber dealer and a staunch Republican. His older brother had become a doctor and directed medical research for a large foundation. With college and law school expenses funded by academic scholarships and football awards, Byron White had little experience with economic or social deprivations. His only contact with issues of civil rights was brief: as deputy attorney general, he became involved with the demonstrations that shook Montgomery, Alabama, in 1961. During his initial clerkship with Chief Justice Fred Vinson in 1946–1947, White encountered no cases that would impact either his views of civil rights or of privacy, the two elements underlying issues of reproductive rights. Finally, White's private practice in Denver concentrated on civil law, and his own focus had been on corporate cases. How would a justice with this background perceive the role of the Court as it encountered questions about the civil rights of women and, in particularly, the right to the privacy of reproductive choice?[70]

The answer emerged quickly. There were only a few weeks remaining in the 1961–1962 term of Court when White took his seat, yet he ended up writing three opinions and one major dissent. That dissent, delivered June 25, 1962, the last day of the term, defined the approach White would use in decision making. Simply stated, White held that the Court should limit the Constitution to the context in which it was written. Thus a term such as "cruel and unusual punishment" could not be used to strike down a California law that made narcotics addiction a crime. The majority view that it was cruel and unusual punishment to make an illness a crime, according to White, was driven by the justices' own "philosophical predilections."[71] Such a dissent was an unusual step for a freshman justice, and it demonstrated White's belief in a very limited, narrow role for the Court. This early move to strict construction of the Constitution and judicial restraint would only intensify with time.

In 1965, White first faced the issue of privacy as it encompassed birth control devices used by married couples. In *Griswold v. Connecticut*, White voiced one major question during oral argument, one that would later assume a critical dimension for him: "Is there a difference between contraceptive devices and abortion?" White asked defense counsel Tom Emerson.[72] In the judicial conference that followed oral argument, White said little but did vote to overturn Connecticut's ban on birth control practices of married couples. However, his reticence was deceptive. In memos to Justice William O. Douglas, who was drafting the opinion, White demonstrated the "off-color" humor he was known for,[73] suggesting that Douglas base the decision either on a "4th amendment search and seizure for the inter-uterine coil"[74] or the use of a "cruel and unusual punishment argument that targeted sex as an 'addiction.'"[75] When Douglas, in consultation with justices Brennan and Arthur J. Goldberg, chose "privacy" as the basis for the *Griswold v. Connecticut* opinion, White distributed a six-page concurrence. He argued that privacy was not a constitutional right.

As Justice White focused on the cases involving issues of reproductive choice, his style of decision making and his hierarchy of values began to emerge. His would be a narrow focus always, one that began with a careful identification of the factual record of each case and a word-by-word analysis of state statutes. Issues of federalism were central to White's analysis. For example, when faced with the question of state power to regulate the distribution of contraceptive devices, White queried whether it was the proper role of the Court to question legislative "wisdom."[76] While White would void state actions that drew lines between married persons, unmarried ones, and minors, he limited his holdings to the specific facts and thus crafted narrow rulings. He never invoked privacy rights as a basis for his rulings, referring instead to due process liberty.

White's antagonism to the concept of privacy rights grew. For example, he voted against garbage "privacy," holding that trash bags, with their revealing contents on sexual practices, could be searched at will.[77] Prisoners in their prison cells likewise had no right of privacy. As White moved through the cases that followed *Griswold*'s decision, his approach made him appear almost pedantic. In one instance, he chose to concentrate on the meaning of "health" as it applied in an early abortion law case. Was a District of Columbia statute that criminalized abortion unless the life or health of the woman was at risk void for vagueness? This case, *U.S. v. Vuitch*, also raised in White's mind a question about *Griswold*.[78] Did the "right of a woman to decide whether to bear a child" apply only before conception?[79] If not, at what stage? For White, contraception and abortion were different, and the state's power to protect a fetus became central to his thought.

By the time *Roe v. Wade* reached the Court, White's attitude had taken shape: abortion was not contraception. Nevertheless, as he dissented in *Roe*, his legal argument made no mention of this attitude, invoking instead the traditional argument of judicial restraint. He accused the *Roe* majority of "judicial legislation," which he did not consider a proper role for the Court.[80]

In all of the major abortion cases that followed *Roe*, White would vote to sustain restrictions. His would not be a likely vote to overturn the Missouri regulations in *Webster*. With his focus centered on a contraception–abortion distinction, any argument that tried to demonstrate the absence of this "bright line" would fall on deaf ears.[81] For attorney Frank Susman, Justice White was a no-win vote in *Webster*.

Justice Thurgood Marshall

Thurgood Marshall came to the Supreme Court two years after the first privacy rights cases had been decided. *Griswold v. Connecticut* (1965) had identified a personal right of privacy for the first time. When Marshall was in the confirmation process in 1967, privacy rights did not play a significant role in his bitter battle to overcome the opposition of Southern senators. The battle over confirmation focused on civil rights and states' rights. Privacy rights would appear on the Court agenda in a very few years, however.

The cases of *United States v. Vuitch* in 1971 and *Eisenstadt v. Baird* in 1972 brought Marshall face to face with the scope and limits of a right to privacy as it involved issues of individual freedom versus state control. From the beginning, Marshall voted on the side of privacy rights. By the time *Roe v. Wade* reached the Court in 1973, it was very clear that Marshall was passionately committed to privacy rights. A statement in the 1969 majority opinion in *Stanley v. Georgia* had made Marshall's policy predilections well known.[82] Holding that the private possession of pornography could not be subject to prosecution, Marshall wrote that "a state has no business in telling a man sitting alone in his own house what books he may read or what films he may watch."[83] This was a mind-set that balked at arguments in favor of state control over reproductive rights.

In 1973 when Justice Harry Blackmun was putting together the majority opinion for *Roe v. Wade*, it was Marshall who contributed the most significant passage. In a memo to Blackmun, Marshall outlined the trimester division that would balance state control and women's choices. The three-part test had been suggested to Marshall by his law clerk Mark Tushnet, and it satisfied Marshall's concern for women who did not recognize their pregnancy immediately. Tushnet's draft of the trimester approach appealed to Marshall and was ultimately accepted by Blackmun as well. It became the centerpiece of *Roe v. Wade* and committed Thurgood Marshall to the right of reproductive privacy as articulated in *Roe*.[84]

Nevertheless it is a well-known fact that judicial voting behavior can alter in cases where conflicting values vie for attention. Justices are forced to balance their own priorities and "hierarchy of values" as case facts change.[85] Such conditions can only be understood and evaluated in the context of a justice's own development. What in Marshall's background experiences gave hope to attorneys arguing against the restrictive Missouri statute under litigation in *Webster*?

The first African American appointed to the Court, Thurgood Marshall had experienced hardships and difficulties never encountered by any of his colleagues on the Court. Born and educated in Baltimore, Marshall could trace his lineage to a slave from "the toughest part of the Congo" region of Africa.[86] His great-grandfather had won his freedom and passed his own indomitable spirit to his son, grandson, and great-grandson. When Thurgood Marshall was born on July 2, 1908, his family had finally achieved a middle-class level of economic stability. His mother was an elementary school teacher in a segregated school; his father, a waiter on a Pullman railway car, also held a job as a steward at an all-white yacht club. Marshall's mother pushed her son to secure a college education, and she pawned her wedding and engagement rings to pay his fees. Marshall's father, however, was the one who taught Marshall how to argue and thus encouraged a legal career. "My father turned me into a lawyer," Marshall insisted. "He was the most insidious of my family rebels."[87]

Marshall's education was impacted by his work experience, much of which would relate to issues he later confronted as a justice. During high school he worked as a delivery boy for a women's clothing store; dealing with gender issues thus came into his experiences in a unique way. His knowledge of medical issues came by way of his initial pre-med curriculum in college; his mother had hoped he would become either a dentist or a physician, and Marshall explored these areas. He also worked as a file clerk in a Baltimore clinic and enrolled in the biology classes necessary for a medical career. The love of argument, however, ended his pre-med career. As Marshall himself later explained, "a run-in with my biology professor" was the turning point.[88]

His education at Lincoln University in Oxford, Pennsylvania, and then at Howard Law School in Washington, D.C., set Marshall apart from his colleagues on the Court. He alone had to attend all-black schools. Segregated institutions were Marshall's forums for learning about discrimination and "losing causes."[89] As he entered into a small private law practice following graduation from Howard, Marshall could not rid himself of the burning desire to see law used to change society. The challenge of working for the National Association for the Advancement of Colored People called to him, and he began a career that involved him in litigation designed to change the status of African Americans.

Marshall's litigation strategy, developed during those years, involved the type of judicial legal reasoning that would later characterize his decision making in Supreme Court cases. As a trial lawyer, Marshall wanted facts and details about a case. He also wanted to know the psychological effects of policies on individuals: people of different races, different religions, different economic status, and different gender. "I want 20th century arguments to defend 20th century positions," Marshall asserted.[90] Should sociological arguments be given greater weight than historical ones? For Thurgood Marshall, like John Marshall, the Constitution was a living document, growing with the times and encouraging the expansion of rights. As one of his law clerks later explained, "Marshall tended to be opposed to things that, in his view, kept human beings from being all that they could be."[91]

This attitude, growing out of his formative years and pre-Court careers was conducive to a vote in favor of reproductive privacy rights. His voting record on the Court was, from the very beginning, an affirmation of this right. Marshall insisted that states provide minors with a judicial bypass option when an abortion decision needed to be made, and he voted against regulations designed to constrain doctors and frighten women. Expensive hospitalization requirements and denial of public funding for abortion sought by indigent women triggered Marshall's greatest ire. He understood the plight of young, poor girls, and he saw most state regulations as both economically and socially discriminating. He was thus, for attorney Frank Susman, a sure vote in *Webster.*

Justice Harry A. Blackmun

Justice Harry Blackmun's name was synonymous with the law of reproductive privacy when *Webster v. Reproductive Health Services* reached the Court. Given the task of researching and ultimately writing the opinion in the first abortion rights case, *Roe v. Wade,* Blackmun had made himself an expert in the history and medical practice of abortion. His commitment to reproductive privacy can be linked to factors in his background: his formative years in Minnesota, his education, and the judicial temperament rooted in his personality. The product of a lower middle-class environment, Blackmun understood economic and social problems. Education was the solution, and Blackmun's scholastic achievements culminated in merit and work-study scholarships to Harvard University.

Blackmun had taken as his guide the Puritan ethic of hard work and personal piety. He neither smoked nor drank. In religion he was a committed Methodist who understood a "dissenter's" tradition. Politically, he was a "nominal" Republican who was not averse to helping Minnesota Democratic candidates, such as Hubert Humphrey. Moderation and balance were the two main elements that characterized all that he did. His mathematics major at Harvard prepared him for either a medical or legal profession, instilling in him a scientific and logical approach to problem solving. In the end, he chose law over medicine and graduated with highest honors. Math and medicine both later affected his specialties within law: he was a tax law expert in a prestigious Minnesota firm before becoming the resident counsel at the Mayo Clinic.[92]

It was his early judicial clerkship with Judge John A. Sandborne that ultimately led to his nomination to the Supreme Court. Judge Sandborne had been impressed by Blackmun's style of reasoning, his meticulous research habits, and his "think tank" approach to decision making.[93] When Sandborne retired, he recommended Blackmun for appointment to his seat on the Eighth Circuit Court of Appeals. President Eisenhower placed him on the bench in 1959. By the time President Nixon nominated him for the highest court, Blackmun had ten years of judicial experience. He was Nixon's third choice: the Senate had already refused to confirm Judge Clement Haynsworth and Judge Harold Carswell. Judge Blackmun appeared, on the basis of his appellate rulings, to meet the president's litmus test: He had expressed a conservative, limited view of the role of the judiciary, and he appeared to be hard on criminals and unwilling to expand minority rights—two basic attitudes emerging in the new Republican majority party of the 1960s. However, a more careful reading of his opinions would have revealed that in those very decisions approved by President Nixon, Blackmun had opened doors and provided loopholes. For example, he had invited both the Supreme Court and Congress to alter one of his appellate court decisions and had recommended the grounds for doing so.[94]

It was this particular ability that had so impressed Judge Sandborne as he had read law clerk Blackmun's legal memos on cases; this was an "open mind" which "weighed every reasonable argument."[95] Blackmun's assessment of himself should have alerted conservative Republicans to the fact that his would not be an automatic vote for a narrow interpretation of the Constitution. "The Constitution is a document of specific words and construction," he told the Senate Judiciary Committee. However, he added, "The meaning of these words is often obscure." His view of the Supreme Court was that it should be a "bastion of freedom and liberty."[96]

During his first two years on the Court, Blackmun had demonstrated a "freshman" attitude: he had followed the lead of Chief Justice Warren Burger.[97] When *Roe v. Wade* came before the Court in 1971, Blackmun was the junior justice of a seven-man Court. Conference notes confirm the ambivalence Blackmun felt when first confronting the issue of reproductive privacy. He saw the question as one of balance between a pregnant women's Ninth Amendment rights and the right of states to regulate health and protect future life.[98] Because of this stand, the chief justice assigned Blackmun the task of writing a "memorandum" to clarify this issue, and Blackmun began the long months of research that would ultimately culminate in the Court opinion of *Roe v. Wade*.

Historical and medical research at the library of the Mayo Clinic led Blackmun to his definition that "the right of privacy . . . is broad enough to cover the abortion decision."[99] Blackmun viewed his *Roe v. Wade* decision as a compromise: it balanced individual rights with society's powers. States could regulate abortion, but not forbid it. Women would have a choice, yet not an "absolute" one, and the physician would play a primary role. The states' powers to regulate would increase as the fetus grew. The decision represented a number of influential factors. Blackmun's "open mind" was persuaded to this course in large part because of his own independent medical research.[100] He became impressed also by historical briefs, which were submitted during the reargument of *Roe* and drafted by Professor Cyril Means of New York University School of Law. Means's argument, based on English common law tradition, was highly persuasive, and Blackmun incorporated it into his opinion.[101] Blackmun was also sensitive to the views on privacy held by justices Douglas, Brennan, and Goldberg in *Griswold v. Connecticut*. Justice Thurgood Marshall's concern for women who might fail to recognize their pregnancy in a timely fashion also impacted Blackmun. His attempt to divide personal and state powers throughout the pregnancy period, with viability being the critical point, was designed to address Marshall's concern.

Blackmun's own religious tradition and sense of personal piety led him to prefer individual freedom to state coercion.[102] The approval of his wife and daughters supported him. Blackmun had never been a part of the ultraconservative wing of the Republican Party and always perceived himself as a centrist. His own orderly and logical mind had been persuaded by the aforementioned factors, and he hoped to persuade others. Although his opinion invited states to regulate—but not prohibit—abortion, he did not anticipate the type and extent of the regulation that would be enacted. Thus, in the years between *Roe* and *Webster*, Justice Blackmun voted against a large number of state regulations. In case after case, Blackmun argued against state policy to proscribe newspaper advertisements for contraception and abortion services, to allow unqualified parental veto over a minor's decision to have an abortion, to define viability, to allow spousal veto, to enact fetal protection statutes for pre-viable fetuses, to refuse funding of nontherapeutic abortion, to deny indigent women abortion services, to require hospitalization for second-trimester abortions and the presence of two doctors, and to require pathological reports on every abortion. He also opposed state-mandated directives to doctors on how to advise and counsel abortion recipients.

Blackmun saw most of these regulations as designed to prevent reproductive choice by regulating it out of existence and making *Roe v. Wade* a nullity. He therefore approached *Webster* with suspicion. Charles Fried and William Webster did not expect to influence him.

Justice John Paul Stevens

No one expected John Paul Stevens, once described as an "unspectacular" judge,[103] to emulate his predecessor on the bench, Justice William O. Douglas. Douglas had been the Court's left-liberal voice for years; his retirement was expected to change the Court significantly. Yet Douglas's "maverick" mantra would descend on Stevens, and he would surprise the conservatives that pushed his candidacy.

It was 1975. President Gerald R. Ford had picked up the reins of the presidency in the wake of the Watergate scandal after Richard Nixon had succeeded in appointing four justices: Burger, Blackmun, Rehnquist, and Powell. Nixon had, however, suffered defeat at the hands of the Senate with two of his nominees. Ford wanted a noncontroversial nominee to fill Douglas's vacancy, one who would not evoke intense opposition. John Paul Stevens seemed to be this kind of candidate. Stevens's name had come to the top of the presidential selection list for several reasons: he knew the right people, he was from the correct party yet was not partisan, and his ideology of judicial restraint seemed solid. It was said that he was the right person, at the right time, at the right place. How did this come about? What were these elements that combined to elevate Stevens to the high court? Would these factors actually produce the type of justice the Republican Party sought?[104]

As a young man growing up in Chicago, Stevens was influenced by his university-centered community, his family's social and economic standing, the religious environment of his home life, and his education. The Stevens family was prominent in Chicago. They operated major hotels including a Chicago landmark, the Stevens (now Conrad Hilton) Hotel. Economic losses during the Depression did not make the family bitter; they retained their high economic status. The Stevens residence where John Paul grew up was located in the campus area of the University of Chicago, and these academic surroundings were significant in his early life. After attending the University of Chicago High School, he pursued his undergraduate education at the University of Chicago. At that time the university was a liberal institution and quite different from the conservative center it would become later. Stevens's contacts during these years would also play an important role in securing his political and judicial career. Charles H. Percy, who would become a Republican U.S. senator, was a classmate and good friend. It was Senator Percy who would help Stevens win a Nixon appointment to the federal bench in Chicago (Seventh Circuit Court of Appeals).[105]

Stevens studied law in Chicago as well. His choice of a legal career came naturally. His father and two brothers all trained for the legal profession, although his father did not practice law. Legal knowledge was valuable in the hotel business, and Stevens himself would focus on antitrust law during his years at Northwestern School of Law. Graduating at the top of his class in 1947, he was chosen as a law clerk by Supreme Court justice Wiley Rutledge. Rutledge, at that time, was known as a liberal justice who, along with Justice Frank Murphy, emphasized individual rights even during wartime.[106]

These formative and pre-Court years offer clues concerning Stevens's ideology. His was not the same sort of community-centered life that characterized justices Rehnquist, O'Connor, Scalia, and Kennedy. Stevens's community was that of the academic world, where ideas were debated and interaction within a scholarly context created an inquiring and open environment for both social and intellectual learning. It was a very cosmopolitan community.

As an American Northern Baptist, Stevens was influenced by a religious tradition that extolled individualism. Baptists in Chicago were a significant factor: the University of Chicago itself had a Baptist affiliation at its inception. This religious group held to a doctrine of separation of church and state.[107] It had grown out of a dissenting tradition that had been persecuted by the Church of England. In addition, this Baptist tradition stressed ideas such as "soul competency," which promoted individual accountability in religious decision making. As a Baptist, Stevens's attention was immediately triggered when religious ideas were connected to Court cases. Would this affect his view of the Missouri law's preamble, which stated that "life begins at conception"?[108] Would Stevens see this as a theological question with which religion, not government, should deal? Would his focus on individual accountability and individual rights, a product of his own religious tradition, impact his judicial ideology?

Few people thought about these variables when Stevens was being selected and confirmed as a Supreme Court justice. Instead, his academic and political connections would provide the major impetus that gave him his new role. As an expert in antitrust law, Stevens had established a preeminent reputation as a partner in a major law firm in Chicago. He was described by his partners as a kind and generous attorney who treated poor clients with as great respect as his wealthy ones. He, like Justice Wiley Rutledge, cared about the "little man."[109] Stevens also won fame as a professor of antitrust law at both the Northwestern and University of Chicago law schools. His teaching skill impressed Chicago's dean, Edward H. Levi, and it would be Levi, as attorney general to President Ford, who would sell the president on Stevens's candidacy. Levi understood the type of justice Ford needed. Stevens, he would tell the president, was the right man.

Stevens was well respected by the bar, and he was a moderate Republican. Moreover, Stevens had built a good record during his five years as a federal court of appeals judge. His written opinions were for the most part noncontroversial. During oral arguments, Stevens listened with patience and asked pointed questions. He drafted decisions that were well written and showed a practical approach and were not bound by the conventional wisdom.[110]

His idea of judicial restraint was not quite the same as that of other justices, however. For Stevens, judicial restraint meant respect for precedent (stare decisis); it meant deciding cases on narrow grounds and avoiding constitutional questions when other grounds could settle issues. Stevens also focused on each case's facts and decided issues on a case-by-case basis. He was deeply committed to the safeguards for procedural due process as it applied in criminal cases. One such case raised a privacy issue and should have alerted conservative Republicans. "A man's privacy in his home is more important than the government's interest in catching him with drugs," Stevens wrote, as he decided a warrantless search case.[111] A moral community would best be achieved under a doctrine of "adherence to established and respected procedures."[112]

For some groups, however, Stevens's nomination to the Court was very controversial. In particular, women's groups were alarmed. Stevens had expressed doubt that an Equal Rights Amendment was necessary to do anything not already possible under the Fourteenth Amendment. He appeared to some to be callous in his attitude toward women, saying, "Women should have exactly the same rights as men, but I do not think they should win every case they file."[113] Moreover, he had distinguished between rules based on sex and those based on marital status: he believed airlines could have a singles-only rule for stewardesses.[114] These rulings, however, were open to interpretation, and Stevens's ideology as it embraced rights of privacy and women's rights was not clear.

Contraceptive rights for singles as well as married women had been established before Stevens took his seat on the Supreme Court bench; by 1976, *Roe v. Wade* was already a three-year-old precedent. During the years that would precede the *Webster* case, Stevens established a mixed voting record as he dealt with women's rights. While he insisted that he was receptive to allegations of discrimination based on sex, he nevertheless voted to uphold the all-male draft (1981) and also denied the theory of "comparable worth."[115] Yet in case after case dealing with state regulations of abortion, Stevens voted to protect reproductive privacy. Like Justice Thurgood Marshall, Stevens wanted minor girls to have freedom to make choices and funds with which to make such choices. He voted to overturn state regulations requiring consent of both parents for a minor's abortion, declaring this to be excessive. He also thought that a law requiring a minor to notify parents of her upcoming abortion was unconstitutional. As Stevens voted to uphold federal funding of abortions for indigent women, his concern for the poor, the uneducated, and the powerless of society became evident. He opposed state requirements involving waiting periods and spousal notification.

Stevens, more than any other justice, was concerned about the relationship of religious views and antiabortion restraints. He accepted *Roe's* holding that denied legal personhood to a fetus. The equating of personhood with conception was, for Stevens, a theological or religious definition, not a legal or medical one. Would a law that wrote a religious doctrine into policy be constitutional? Would it not violate the First Amendment's religion clauses? A firm believer in separation of church and state, Stevens feared laws based on one group's definition of morality.[116] A firm believer in stare decisis, Stevens also saw *Roe's* trimester standard as a precedent that provided a legal, not a religious, standard, and he supported this. It would be this focus on the First Amendment's "no establishment of religion" and "free exercise of religion" clauses that would alarm Attorney General William Webster and also Charles Fried as they presented the Missouri law, with its controversial "life begins at conception" preamble. Justice John Paul Stevens was not likely to be receptive to their arguments.

Justice Sandra Day O'Connor

In 1981 when President Ronald Reagan nominated Sandra Day O'Connor to the U.S. Supreme Court, reproductive privacy rights dating from *Griswold v. Connecticut* had been settled law for sixteen years. Yet throughout that period, constant attacks had attempted to limit the use of birth control devices, abortion procedures, and abortion counseling so that in reality the concept of reproductive privacy rights was far from being "settled law."

Assuring President Reagan that she found abortion "personally repugnant,"[117] O'Connor seemed to fit both the image and role Reagan envisioned for the Court. Her background, formative years, and pre-Court career contained few elements that would link her to support for reproductive privacy.

Born in Texas and raised on a large ranch in Arizona, O'Connor embraced the philosophy of "rugged individualism." Her father wanted her to be self-sufficient—she learned to shoot a gun by age six, to ride any horse, to brand cattle. It was her father who wanted her to go to Stanford University and to become a lawyer, thus fulfilling an ambition he had once held for himself. Moreover, he also instilled in his young daughter a deep distrust for the economic and social policies that had grown out of the New Deal. Like William Rehnquist, Sandra Day, as a very young child, wanted to overturn "FDR's New Deal."[118]

The isolation experience of ranch life was intensified when, at age five, she was sent to El Paso, Texas, to be educated at an elite private girl's school. She remained there for nine years. She entered Stanford University as an undergraduate at age sixteen, married at age twenty, and graduated from law school at age twenty-two. Her husband, John O'Connor, was a fellow law student. The high economic status of Sandra Day's family, its social prominence, and its Republican political ideology dominated her life throughout this early period. Although she sought a legal position following graduation, there was no monetary need for her to work.

She would later recount her surprise when no prestigious firms offered to hire her as an attorney, but she quickly embraced community service on various private and public boards and commissions. Here she demonstrated a concern for "discrete and insular"[119] minority groups such as aliens, but she did not consider herself, or women in general, to be part of a minority group needing private, much less public, assistance. Although birth control had been illegal under state and federal laws throughout her teenage and young adult years, O'Connor showed no interest in this issue. She had three sons and settled into family and community life in Phoenix, where her husband's law practice was located.

Arizona's Republican Party organization became the critical variable in O'Connor's life throughout the 1960s. Within the party, she formed her friendships, socialized, and gained access to various state jobs. She became assistant attorney general for Arizona, a member of the Arizona State Personnel Commission, and an Arizona state senator. Politics had become her life, and she found, as history has repeatedly demonstrated, that law is the stepping-stone into politics. O'Connor's record in the Arizona Senate demonstrated her Republican Party loyalty: she supported the death penalty, deregulation and privatization of flood control policies, and downsizing of governmental services.[120]

When abortion issues reached the Arizona Senate, O'Connor opposed funding abortions for indigent women, and she supported the right of public hospitals' personnel to refuse to assist in abortions. She did, however, favor contraceptive educational incentives. Her belief in the self-sufficiency of a woman as an individual moved her to support "right to work" laws that abolished maximum hour limits for working women. She had no interest in protective laws of this nature.[121]

O'Connor's judicial experiences, like her legislative ones, were limited to the state scene: she won election to a county superior court in 1974. Throughout this period, she worked diligently within the state Republican Party as it related to the national scene. She served as cochair of Arizona's Committee to Re-Elect the President supporting Richard Nixon, and she backed Ronald Reagan against President Gerald R. Ford in 1976. O'Connor considered running for governor of Arizona, but instead accepted Democratic governor Bruce Babbitt's nomination to the Arizona Court of Appeals. She was not highly rated by the Arizona Bar Association—her scores both as a trial judge and as an appellate judge were deemed "undistinguished."[122] Nevertheless, she won elevation to the court of appeals, where the cases she dealt with involved mostly workman's compensation, divorces, bankruptcies, and tenant–landlord disputes. None of these could be described as issues of constitutional law, the constant diet of the U.S. Supreme Court. O'Connor disliked the intervention of federal courts into state court proceedings. Federal courts, she wrote, should "defer to the state courts [even] on federal constitutional questions when a full and fair adjudication has been given in the state court."[123] She went on to insist that state judges were "equally competent" to federal judges. It was this political ideological stance on "decreasing the caseload of federal courts and reducing intervention of federal courts in state and local matters"[124] that would endear her to President Reagan in 1981.

O'Connor immediately moved into the social circle of Washington, D.C., following her confirmation by the Senate on September 22, 1981. Some referred to her as an "enthusiastic party goer,"[125] which should not have been a surprise given her earlier Junior League activism in Arizona. She played tennis and golf with Barbara Bush, wife of Vice President George Bush. However, as issues that involved women coalesced into concrete cases that the Supreme Court had to face, O'Connor found herself in a different milieu, under a public microscope. Was she, Justice Sandra Day O'Connor, sensitive to the problem of working women? What about poor, uneducated women? What about women with their unique health problems? Equal pay issues, a nonhostile working environment, funding for child care, facilities for exercising rights of reproductive choice—all of these became cases, and O'Connor's voting record was a mixed one. She showed little interest in remedying claims of gender discrimination. She did not see women as a "group" or as "outsiders": hers was a "community majority" approach,[126] as opposed to taking an individual rights focus. What would this attitude mean for reproductive privacy rights?

Between 1981 and 1989 when *Webster* reached the Court, O'Connor had voted in four major abortion cases. She had been on the Court for fourteen months at the beginning of the 1983 session, when the Supreme Court heard argument in *Simopoulos v. Virginia*, *City of Akron v. Akron Center for Reproductive Health*, and *Planned Parenthood Association of Kansas City v. Ashcroft*. O'Connor voted with Rehnquist and White to uphold all of the state restrictions on abortion involved in these cases, including requirements for parental consent, waiting periods, two doctors for late-term abortions, and pathology reports.

For *Akron*, O'Connor penned an important dissent, which Justice Powell declared would "uphold virtually any abortion regulation [and overturn] *Roe v. Wade*."[127] In her opinion, O'Connor used an earlier phrase of Justice Blackmun's but gave it an entirely different meaning. The "undue burden" standard in O'Connor's hand became a useful tool to support, not strike down, every type of state restriction. O'Connor also openly attacked the trimester framework for balancing individual and state interests and noted that fetal viability, due to advances in science, might soon be within the first twelve weeks of pregnancy or even at conception. One pithy sentence, suggested by her law clerk, summed up her stance: "The *Roe* framework, then, is clearly on a collision course with itself."[128] She ended her dissent by casting doubt upon whether there was any "fundamental right to terminate pregnancy in some situations."[129]

Thus, by 1986 when *Thornburgh v. American College of Obstetricians and Gynecologists* reached the Court, O'Connor had established a voting record that placed in jeopardy any right of reproductive privacy. Dissenting in *Thornburgh*, O'Connor voted to uphold all of Pennsylvania's abortion restrictions, concluding, "I dispute not only the wisdom but the legitimacy of the Court's attempt to discredit and preempt state abortion regulation[s]."[130]

There was little in O'Connor's background, formative years, pre-Court career, or voting record on the Court to offer any hope to attorney Frank Susman as he prepared to urge the overturning of Missouri's restrictive regulations. Yet he continued to be optimistic. Would O'Connor want to go down in history as the vote that overturned reproductive privacy? Her approach of "aggressive majoritarianism" fostered a community of sameness, not of diversity.[131] She was a woman, but her voting record put her squarely in the political conservative camp on the Court. She could insist that women were certainly not unified on the question of reproductive privacy. Would O'Connor be open to solid medical evidence that her belief in possible fetal viability at the moment of conception was unrealistic?

For attorneys Webster and Fried, O'Connor seemed a certain vote to affirm Missouri restrictions. Surely that would accomplish the purpose of regulating *Roe*'s abortion rights out of existence.

Justice Antonin Scalia

When *Webster v. Reproductive Health Services* reached the Supreme Court for decision in 1989, Antonin Scalia had been there only three years. Nevertheless, even during that short period, he had gained an unusual degree of notoriety: words like "passionate," "arrogant," "showoff," "sarcastic," "melodramatic," and "self-righteous" were already being used by critics to describe him. He, like Chief Justice Rehnquist, had become a lightning rod that attracted either intense criticism or fervent praise.[132] He was also known to be an inveterate opponent of *Roe v. Wade* and its progeny. What, in Scalia's background, had given rise to this attitude? Why was he so opposed to the very concept of a right of privacy?

Did factors such as ethnic roots, religious fervor, and educational experiences play a part in creating Justice Scalia's policy predilections? Did politics and political ideology impact his attitude as a justice? Fifty years old when appointed to the Supreme Court in 1986 by President Reagan, Antonin Scalia was the first Italian American to occupy such a position. Born in an "Italian enclave" in Trenton, New Jersey,[133] the only child of Sicilian immigrant parents, his ethnic roots were deep and he would admit later that he harbored an "ethnic resentment of WASP justices."[134] In particular, he resented justices like "White and Powell . . . whose ancestors oppressed blacks and who now try to rectify the error through affirmative action programs at the expense of more recent immigrants."[135] Praising his immigrant father, who had become a literary scholar and a college professor of Romance languages at Brooklyn College, and his mother, who had become a school teacher, Scalia believed that "rugged individualism" would open doors to success without government assistance.

Religion was central in the life of the Scalia family. Antonin was described by friends as an "arch conservative Catholic."[136] By the time he was a teenager at Xavier High School, Catholic religious tradition so dominated his life that he seemed ready to be a "member of the Curia" advising the pope.[137] Scalia, coming from the tradition of an "established" church, reinforced his own "Catholicism and [his view of] Christianity" with his choice of educational experiences.[138] The Jesuit academy Scalia attended produced religious scholars. The concepts of order, obedience to higher law, respect for authority, and discipline permeated Scalia's educational background. Once on the bench it would be easy to see why one of his clerks would observe that this justice was "fundamentally Catholic and Christian."[139] His jurisprudence would show the impact of this early training.

Scalia also chose a Jesuit college, Georgetown University, which strengthened his religious high school experiences. His goal was to do what he believed to be "true and good."[140] Majoring in history, he took few science courses. Arguments based on history later appealed to Scalia more than those grounded in science. In lectures and opinions, he would refer to racial differences as "blood" differences. During one of the Court's oral arguments, he interrupted the defense of the Federal Communications Commission's set-aside program to benefit black broadcasters with the exclamation, "Blood, blood! [It's not a black person's] background and environment. Isn't that right? It's blood!"[141] Since this type of argument was often heard in the fascist Italy of his father's day, it was not surprising that Scalia himself would be affected. He often referred to his own "blood line" and once remarked, "I owe no man anything, nor he me, because of the blood that flows in our veins."[142] Biology and chemistry courses contradicted such a view, but Scalia ignored their evidence. A career in medical science would never appeal to Antonin Scalia.

Instead, politics attracted Scalia, and his love of debate made law the appropriate career choice. He graduated from Harvard Law School, but went into practice with an Ohio-based corporate law firm. He defended big business interests for seven years and then left the firm before becoming a partner. Embarking on a teaching career at the University of Virginia, Scalia abandoned corporate law for the field of administrative law. From this position, he began to develop political ties with the Republican administration of President Richard Nixon, and by 1971 he had succeeded in a series of jobs within the executive branch. He was a part-time general counsel and then an assistant attorney general. Within the Department of Justice, he became part of the Office of Legal Counsel, offering advice to a beleaguered president facing possible impeachment proceedings in the wake of the Watergate scandal. When Gerald Ford replaced Nixon as president, Antonin Scalia remained. He would urge presidential, not governmental, ownership of the Watergate tapes and documents and defend executive branch powers throughout the remainder of the Ford presidency.

When his political ambitions were derailed by the advent of the Democratic Carter administration in 1977, Scalia retreated to two bastions of conservative Republican ideology—the American Enterprise Institute and the University of Chicago Law School—where he wrote and taught. His focus was law and economics, and he advocated deregulation and privatization of the marketplace.[143] In lectures and speeches, Scalia pushed for majority rights over individual rights. This viewpoint can be linked to his experiences of community life during his formative years. The Italian Catholic neighborhood of Trenton, New Jersey, had provided, as Scalia saw it, the "good life." It was a life where a "community majority" could set and define the "moral rules" that produced "virtuous activity."[144] The local community thus was always to be preferred to big government. People in communities would learn the "virtues of labor and thrift"; there should be no governmental "largesse" in the form of grants and subsidies.[145]

Scalia's elevation of community rights paralleled that of Chief Justice Rehnquist, whose formative years were spent in a Swedish Lutheran community. Both of these justices would deplore the individual exercise of rights, which might threaten the order, stability, and sense of moral virtues of the community. This was also the view of Justice O'Connor, coming from her experiences of a western ranch community. This dominance of community over individual rights was at odds with a doctrine of individual reproductive privacy rights. Antonin Scalia would also carry this viewpoint into his discussion about affirmative action programs for women and for racial minorities. Such programs would, for Scalia, violate the primacy that should be accorded community majoritarian rule.

Scalia's writing style and lectures expanded these theories and were filled with satire. His bitter "witty put-downs" and tongue-in-check remarks suggested contempt for courts and lawyers of opposing views.[146] They also attracted attention. These writings, expressing Scalia's views on law and economics, coupled with his support of the Nixon administration, appealed to President Reagan's advisers, who urged the president to appoint Scalia to the U.S. Court of Appeals for the District of Columbia. It was 1982 when he took his seat on this federal tribunal, second only to the Supreme Court in power and influence.[147] In the four years that followed, Judge Scalia rendered two decisions—one involving homosexuality in the Navy and the other involving sexual harassment—that made clear his attitude toward a right of privacy and showed his ideology at work. In both cases Judge Scalia rejected the "broad interpretation of the Constitutional right of privacy that underpinned *Roe v. Wade*."[148] The rulings confirmed the Reagan administration's growing belief that Scalia was the right man for the Supreme Court.

With Justice Rehnquist's elevation to the chief justiceship in 1986, Judge Scalia was chosen to fill the vacancy. The Senate, ignoring the protests of civil rights and feminist organizations, accepted his refusal to comment on controversial social issues such as reproductive privacy. Did his ethnicity as the first Italian-American nominee trigger an affirmative action response

from the Senate? Did the very affirmative action programs he opposed work
to elevate him to the position of associate justice on the U.S. Supreme Court?

In his first three years, Antonin Scalia did not have to confront privacy issues as a Supreme Court justice. *Webster v. Reproductive Health Services*
would be the first such case in which he would vote. His views were well
known, however, by this time. Attorney Frank Susman did not expect to win
Scalia's vote in behalf of reproductive privacy rights.

Justice Anthony Kennedy

The *Webster* case presented Anthony Kennedy with his first opportunity to
demonstrate what he had meant by his Senate confirmation statements about
reproductive choice. Kennedy had been chosen in late 1987 to replace the
retiring Justice Lewis Powell. He had actually been President Reagan's third
choice for this vacancy; the Senate's defeat of Judge Robert Bork's nomination had emphasized the president's loss of party dominance in that body.
The core issue on which Judge Bork had been defeated was the right to privacy as articulated in *Griswold v. Connecticut.* He had stated that *Griswold*
had been wrongly decided; Judge Kennedy would not make that mistake.[149]
However, the question of reproductive privacy rights as they extended to
abortion remained. Attorney Frank Susman believed that he could persuade
Kennedy that the two rights could not be separated, that medical science had
coalesced them into one right. As Susman and his team evaluated Justice Anthony Kennedy, they should have focused on at least four background variables that could have helped predict his vote: the community where he spent
his formative years, his religion, his pre-Court career, and his political party
affiliation.

The Sacramento, California, suburb of Land Park played a significant role
in the life of Anthony Kennedy. The Kennedy home was a center for community interaction. Community leaders from priests to grocers regularly
gathered around the breakfast room table for social and political discussions.
Kennedy's father had chosen that house's colonial architecture, an architecture rooted in a historical period. It seemed to model the very image of
Kennedy's parents: "pillars of the community."[150] As a lawyer-lobbyist, the
elder Kennedy spent time in the halls of the California state legislature, and
politics was central to his success. Anthony's mother combined a teaching
career and volunteer work with numerous civic organizations: she was at the
very center of the civic life of this community.

Anthony Kennedy thus spent his formative years experiencing the significance of the local community in charge of its own decision making. He
would later assert that community must be allowed to "express its collective
outrage at the transgression of the criminal" by enacting stringent criminal
laws.[151] The very purpose of the criminal justice system was, he noted, "to

provide a catharsis" for "community outrage."[152] Community values clearly outweighed individual rights.

Politics were pervasive; the Republican Party's program became Kennedy's program. At age 9, Kennedy began work as a page in the California Senate, and his fascination with law and politics grew. Interludes of home schooling, coupled with regular public school, allowed him time to spend in the state senate listening to debates or attending legal trials. He began building contacts and friendships that would mold his future.[153] Religion clearly played a role in Anthony Kennedy's life. "My father," he remarked, "was a regular churchgoer."[154] Kennedy himself was an altar boy in the Roman Catholic Church in Land Park. The church's opposition to reproductive privacy rights had a long tradition: would it impact Kennedy?

Kennedy's educational experiences also contributed to his worldview. Entering Stanford University in 1954, he majored in history and political science and spent a year studying at the London School of Economics. There was never any question about his career: he would be a lawyer. At Harvard Law School he specialized in tax and constitutional law, the first for its practicality, the second for its history. The practical tax law focus secured his first job in San Francisco, but he returned to his father's law office after two years and became a legal lobbyist. His two major lobbying clients were the liquor distilling company Schenley Industries and the California Association of Dispensing Opticians. He also taught constitutional law in the night school of McGeorge School of Law (University of the Pacific). Kennedy's political activities in the state legislature, combined with his expertise in tax law, brought him into contact with California governor Ronald Reagan. Committed to tax limitation, Reagan gave Kennedy the job of drafting a bill which, although defeated at first, would eventually succeed and cut property taxes by 57 percent. It was a highly controversial bill, creating bitterness among those who needed governmental services but generating praise from wealthy homeowners. Kennedy had performed as Governor Reagan desired, and his reward was a seat on the U.S. Court of Appeals for the Ninth Circuit.[155]

Thus began Anthony Kennedy's judicial career, moving closer to the U.S. Supreme Court. During the period from 1975 to 1987, Kennedy participated in 1,400 decisions and personally wrote more than 400 opinions. The range of issues involved questions of federalism, separation of powers, and individual rights. He was for states' rights, for greater executive power, and against individual rights. It was this last area that would provide clues to Kennedy's probable approach to reproductive privacy. He had ruled in *Beller v. Middendorf* that the Navy could dismiss homosexuals from the service, although he noted in dicta that "homosexuality might be [a] constitutionally protected activity in some other contexts."[156] Kennedy had also ruled against the concept of "comparable worth," the idea that women and men

should receive equal pay when performing similar jobs.[157] Kennedy himself
had memberships in three clubs that discriminated against women and minorities. He believed in an economic approach to laws, the view that per-
vaded the conservative University of Chicago School of Law. For Kennedy,
the "fundamental economic principle such as the law of supply and demand" overrode civil rights laws.[158] The state, he noted, was not "obligat[ed]
to eliminate an economic inequality, which it did not create."[159] Such decisions worried women, blacks, and gay rights supporters. These early decisions would also concern Attorney Frank Susman as he sought to win
Kennedy's vote in the *Webster* case.

Throughout Kennedy's confirmation hearings, he had successfully side-
stepped questions about reproductive privacy rights. His speeches, writings,
and opinion had left him "wriggle room." In one breath, he denied that there
was any "broadly defined categor[y] of unenumerated rights," and in another
he stated that "[the Court] should not announce in a categorical way that
there are no unenumerated rights."[160] Which view would Justice Anthony
Kennedy espouse once on the Supreme Court? What did his stated belief in
a "zone of liberty . . . where the individual can tell the government: Beyond
this line, you may not go" mean?[161] What did his commitment to judicial restraint really indicate? Was it, in actuality, judicial activism to reverse gains in
reproductive privacy rights?

PERSUADING JUSTICES: ORAL ARGUMENT IN *WEBSTER*

Crowds stood in line and filled the Supreme Court chamber when oral argument for *Webster* opened on April 26, 1989.[162] Missouri attorney general
William Webster was the first to address the Court. By 1989 Webster was a
veteran of Supreme Court litigation: he had already argued six cases during
his tenure as attorney general. His presentation was clear and organized.
There were, he told the Court, four issues or questions the Court needed to
answer: What, if any, were the constitutional boundaries for public funding
of abortions? Can a law that declares "life begins at conception" be constitutional on its face? Can a state require physician testing and reporting on fetal
viability? Would the Court consider adopting the "rationality" standard to review state abortion regulations?

These questions quickly brought Webster into dialogue with individual
justices. It was Justice Sandra Day O'Connor who first interrupted his presentation with a technical question.[163] "What point are you appealing, Attorney General Webster?" she asked. "Isn't your first question really about limiting doctors' freedom of speech in a publicly funded hospital?" Her question
was repeated by Justice John Paul Stevens, who asked, "What is the conse-
quence of a violation of . . . abortion counseling by physicians in a public fa-

cility? If the doctor should go ahead and offer advice is he committing any kind of a misdemeanor or crime?"

William Webster understood the unpopularity of limitations on doctors' ability to advise their patients, so he evaded O'Connor's and Stevens's questions. However, no attorney can permanently avoid answering questions that the justices want answered. When Justice Anthony Kennedy repeated the question again, Webster admitted, "If a doctor in a public hospital counseled . . . an abortion, he would be . . . dismissed."

The second issue Webster presented to the Court had been very carefully planned, and he became more relaxed and confident as he prepared to defend the preamble of the Missouri statute. As Webster quoted the law's "life begins at conception" thesis, he ignored the intent of its framers. Andrew Puzder and Samuel Lee had drafted this preamble to unravel *Roe*, but Webster denied this intent.

Writing in the *St. Louis Post-Dispatch* the day before oral argument, Puzder had stated the intent clearly: Missouri's "simple, factual statement that the life of each human being begins at conception extends essential legal rights to unborn children. Thus personal injury law and criminal law can be used against those who deprive the unborn of these legal rights."[164] Puzder had continued, "The conflict the court *must* resolve is how it [the Court] can allow a state to recognize that human life begins at conception and at the same time preclude that state from enacting statutes to protect such unborn human life from abortion."[165]

Did Attorney General William Webster, in his oral argument, place this claim squarely before the Court as Puzder believed he must? Absolutely not. "This declaration [that life begins at conception] . . . does not affect anyone," Webster insisted in response to a question from Justice Antonin Scalia. "[It] is a philosophical statement, not a substantive right . . . and does not impose any substantive responsibility." In fact, Webster continued, "The statute does not in any way affect a woman's constitutional right to choose abortion over childbirth."

Puzder's critical "dilemma," so carefully constructed to demolish *Roe*, had been gutted by the advocate defending it. The Supreme Court justices chose to take the attorney general's explanation at face value, although Justice Kennedy, seeking reassurance, inquired, "You . . . contend there is no case or controversy on that [preamble as meaningless philosophy] point?" Puzder's "incredible dichotomy," the essence of his labor, fell victim to its own cleverness and the political fears of Attorney General William Webster. The Supreme Court in *Webster* would not confront the question of when human life begins.

Did states have power to require physical testing and reporting on viability? Webster quickly moved to this third point of his argument. Missouri wanted to define the medical tests for viability, and the attorney general insisted that state legislatures had this power. As Justice Stevens pressed for examples, the attorney general once again played down the real intent of the law. "Only tests that are 'necessary' are required," Webster told Stevens.

"Suppose a doctor says a test is unnecessary," Stevens asked. "Can he refuse to perform [it]?"

Webster's replies were once again disingenuous. "If a test would not be dispositive, it cannot be necessary," he answered. "I don't believe that [the statute] requires an unnecessary test." Stevens, however, pushing for a semantic analysis of the statute, ultimately got the attorney general to admit that the statute required doctors to perform all three types of medical tests: gestational age, weight, and fetal lung maturity.[166]

Charles Fried, in his role as special assistant to the U.S. attorney general, made the final point in the argument on behalf of Missouri's regulation. Fried had changed during the years following his clerkship with Justice John Marshall Harlan in 1961. Then he had been fresh out of Columbia University's law school—and liberal on the issue of sexual rights of privacy. It was Fried who wrote Harlan's great dissent in the Connecticut birth control case *Poe v. Ullman.* As noted by the other law clerks, its tone and language was "all Charlie."[167]

Perhaps Fried had written only to please his justice; Harlan had been passionate about rights of marital privacy. Yet, Fried had also originally applauded *Roe v. Wade*'s ruling and defended it. Why then, in the 1980s, would Charles Fried aggressively work to overturn *Roe?* As a law professor at Harvard, Fried had adopted a theory of "judicial retrenchment" that went far beyond mere judicial restraint by supporting the overturning of precedents.[168] He adopted the "original intent" doctrine, seeing the Constitution through the lens of the eighteenth century. Was this a response to the new winds of political change? Was Fried motivated by political ambition? At Harvard, he was constantly challenged by Professor Laurence Tribe, a dynamic liberal and a spectacular lecturer and litigator. Holding the only constitutional law chair at Harvard, and winning case after case before the Court, Tribe had seemingly overshadowed his colleague Fried.[169]

Then, in 1985, the Reagan administration tapped Charles Fried for solicitor general. His job was to turn the office into an advocate for the administration's policies, at the heart of which was the reversal of *Roe v. Wade.* Only a change of Court personnel could accomplish this, and finally at the end of the Reagan era, Fried had the opportunity to succeed where so many others had failed. The Bush administration asked him to persuade the justices to replace *Roe* with *Webster,* creating a new landmark decision—one ending abortion rights. The stage was well set: the two dissenters from the 1973 *Roe* decision remained on the Court, one as the chief justice. Three sympathetic justices had joined them: Scalia, O'Connor, and the newly appointed Kennedy. Fried, backed by the prestige and authority of both the Reagan and

Bush administrations, had an advantageous position. As both outgoing solicitor general and special assistant to the new attorney general, he indeed occupied a very unique position.[170]

The Supreme Court justices traditionally give great weight and deference to the arguments made on behalf of the government, and this intrinsic advantage is well understood by all parties. Fried's job was to address the question, Should the Court reconsider its standard of review for judging state abortion regulations?[171] His approach was direct and personally aimed at particular justices, especially Justice Kennedy. Fried's goal was to assure Kennedy that overturning *Roe* and abortion rights would not impact the *Griswold* decision supporting contraceptive rights. Having seen Judge Robert Bork denied a seat on the Court—the seat Kennedy occupied—for his refusal to uphold *Griswold*, Fried worked to separate abortion from contraception. In so doing, he raised unexpected questions from both Kennedy and O'Connor.

"What is the right involved in *Griswold*?" asked Kennedy. When Fried answered, "The right not to have the state intrude in a violent way into the details of marital intimacy," O'Connor was moved to action. "Do you say there is no fundamental right to decide whether to have a child or not? A right to procreate? Do you deny that the Constitution protects that right?"[172]

The solicitor general's answer was clear: "I would [not] formulate the right in such abstract terms." Fried believed the Court should prevent only those state regulations that ignored the life of the mother. He urged the justices to adopt a different standard of review, one the Court itself had developed over time, namely, a "due process rational basis" test. If the Court used it, then states could pass any laws regulating abortion so long as they were reasonable ones. That should not affect contraception, Fried maintained. Thus, Charles Fried defended his *Poe v. Ullman* position. He urged the Court to see abortion rights as uniquely different from those of birth control. He appealed to the "ghost of Harlan" and cloaked his conclusion with the mantle of authority. His thesis: "We are asking the court to pull this one thread"—that of abortion.

Frank Susman, the attorney for Reproductive Health Services, refused to separate contraception from abortion. Susman, like Fried and Webster, was no stranger to the justices. A veteran abortion rights attorney from St. Louis, Susman was making his fifth appearance before the Court in the *Webster* case. He had been Missouri attorney general John Ashcroft's opponent in the 1983 case *Planned Parenthood of Kansas City v. Ashcroft*, which had succeeded in striking down earlier Missouri abortion regulations.

Most attorneys go into the Court with prepared speeches outlining the points they consider most relevant. As Susman took the podium, he had several options open: he could follow his plan to attack the provisions of the Missouri statute or he could attack Webster's defense of those provisions, point by point. On the other hand, he could seize the more general issues raised by Fried and hope to attack the statute collaterally. This latter option emerged only during Fried's argument, allowing no time for a planned attack and requiring a split-second decision. Susman took the gamble, and his opening remarks would make headlines and become sound bites for future debates.

"The Solicitor General's submission is somewhat disingenuous," Susman asserted. "He asserts that he does not seek to unravel the whole cloth of pro-creational rights, but merely a thread. It has always been my personal experience that when I pull a thread, my sleeve falls off."[173] Insisting that Fried was attacking birth control rights in *Griswold* as well as *Roe*'s abortion rights, Susman challenged the justices to define a difference between the two. "There no longer exists any bright line between the fundamental right that was established in *Griswold* and the fundamental right of abortion that was established in *Roe*," Susman asserted. "These two rights, because of advances in medicine and science now overlap. They coalesce and merge and they are not distinct."

With this bold declaration, the battle was on. Justice Scalia interrupted to ask why doctors could not draw such a line. Susman's response would bring into the oral argument some of the carefully prepared data submitted to the Court in amicus briefs written for the American Medical Association. Susman named the modern types of birth control—pills and IUDs—and then defined them as "abortifacients." "They are . . . [so] labeled," he noted.

Then Susman moved to connect his argument to the Missouri statute he was attacking. "Under this statute, which defines fertilization as the point of beginning, these forms of contraception are also abortifacients."[174] Thus, Susman insisted, Missouri's definition of life beginning at conception was a direct attack on *Griswold*'s protection for birth control devices.

Questions from Justice Kennedy, who was most anxious not to upset the *Griswold* ruling, led Susman into a second major point. When could a state, through legislation, limit or prohibit reproductive choice? Was the attorney for Reproductive Health Services saying that states lacked any power in this area? Susman's position was very clear: at viability, states could regulate and even prohibit reproductive choice unless the life or health of the mother was endangered. He linked his defense of this line of attack to Missouri's declaration that life would be defined as beginning at conception. Arguing from the amicus brief submitted by American historians, including the preeminent authority Dr. James Mohr, Susman detailed the history of abortion rights. In the final analysis, he argued that the definition of when life begins differs according to one's religious faith and was not answered by science with a non-debatable standard. Historically, many had accepted that at quickening—when the mother could feel movement or viability—the fetus, if born, could live on its own. That point remained very close to *Roe*'s twenty-four weeks and would not change because lungs needed that long to develop.

Susman's judicial target at this point was Justice O'Connor. In earlier abortion cases, O'Connor had implied that science and medical technology might ultimately allow viability and the "moment of conception" to coincide. Susman's reference to the American Medical Association's amicus brief, citing medical and biological facts, would persuade Justice O'Connor to abandon her assumption. Her questions to Susman, and her acceptance of his responses, signaled this change.[175]

Justice Scalia, however, was undeterred. He pointed to arguments advanced by other medical and historical groups. Susman simply invited the justice to examine the credentials of each group and weigh the status, longevity, and respectability of each. Susman urged the Court not to be deceived by the state attorney general's argument that the Missouri statute did not really penalize doctors for giving medical advice nor limit only legal abortions. Referring to another Missouri case argued the preceding day by one of Webster's associates, Susman cautioned the Court, "This is not the first time in the last 24 hours that we have heard persons from the Missouri Attorney General's office suggest interpretations of statutory or constitutional language that are not there on the clear face with the literal meaning of the English words used."[176]

Could the Supreme Court return the case to Missouri courts to determine what the law really said? Justice O'Connor proposed this as a possible way out for the Court. However, Susman reminded her that two lower federal courts had already interpreted the statute as unconstitutionally limiting doctors' free speech and had thrown out the attorney general's assurance that the preamble was "unenforceable" and that a doctor's evasion of the testing requirements would produce "no penalty." When Justice Stevens urged Susman to accept the attorney general's assurances, Susman refused: "The Missouri Department of Health and Truman Medical Center . . . interpret[ed] this [statute], 'no more discussion about abortion, period.'" So ended Reproductive Health Services' oral argument in *Webster*.

Attorney General William Webster had the final word. It was not, however, the note on which he would have preferred to end the case. Pressed by Justice Stevens to demonstrate that the Missouri statute did not touch contraception, Webster was unable to provide an example. He left unanswered Justice Stevens's penetrating question, "[Isn't] the concept of what an abortion *is* affected by [the statute's] preamble?"

OPINION DAY: THE SUPREME COURT
ANNOUNCES THE *WEBSTER* DECISION

It came down with the fireworks of the Fourth of July. The Court usually completes its case load before the end of June, but it was July 3, 1989, before the justices announced the decision in *Webster v. Reproductive Health Services*, which resounded in the Independence Day headlines of every newspaper across the country. The decision upheld all of Missouri's abortion restrictions, but it did not overrule *Roe v. Wade*'s holding that a woman had a fundamental right to abortion. Instant analysis with conflicting claims of victory raised more questions than before. Was *Roe* dead? Partially dead? Had *Webster*'s decision dismantled the privacy rights won in *Roe*? Or, would yet another case be necessary to deliver the coup de grâce?

The Court's decision in *Webster* was a surprise even to the justices themselves; it was no wonder that the country would be confused by the decision. Accounts of the judicial conference of April 28 following oral argument in *Webster* demonstrate that Chief Justice William Rehnquist had every reason to believe that there was a five- or even six-vote majority to uphold all of the Missouri abortion restrictions. When Rehnquist opened the conference discussion, he stated that he "disagree[d] with *Roe v. Wade*." He pointed his colleagues to his "1973 dissent which [governed his] thinking."[177] As the other justices voiced their opinions, only justices Harry Blackmun, William Brennan, and Thurgood Marshall appeared to totally support *Roe*. So why didn't the Court publish a 6–3 or at least a 5–4 decision overturning *Roe*? How did *Roe* survive? What did *Webster* really decide?

WEBSTER: ANALYSIS OF A JUDICIAL DECISION

The Court decision in *Webster* is recorded as a 5–4 decision. In fact, the judicial splits show one group of 3+1+1 and a minority group of 3+1. The record of the opinion acknowledged the splits among the justices. Chief Justice William Rehnquist announced the judgment of the Court and delivered the opinion of the Court "with respect to Parts I, II-A, II-B, and II-C." He also delivered "an opinion" with respect to parts II-D and III, speaking only for himself and two other justices—Byron White and Anthony Kennedy.[178]

Twenty-three pages later Justice Sandra Day O'Connor penned a "concurring in part and concurring in the judgment." She wrote, "I concur in Parts I, II-A, II-B, and II-C of the Court's opinion." However, she did not join in part II-D or III. Instead, O'Connor limited her argument to the "judgment announced in Part II-D."[179]

Following O'Connor's eleven-page explanation, Justice Antonin Scalia penned his own remarks, "concurring in part and concurring in the judgment." "I join in Parts I, II-A, II-B, and II-C of the opinion of the Chief Justice," he wrote. "As to Part II-D, I think that [it] should . . . explicitly overrule *Roe v. Wade*."[180] It took Justice Scalia just seven pages to explain his position.

Justice Harry Blackmun, joined by justices William Brennan and Thurgood Marshall, concurred in part and dissented in part in a dissent of twenty-three pages.[181] Finally, Justice John Paul Stevens, also concurring in part and dissenting in part, explained that while he "joined Part II-C of the Court's opinion," he dissented from the rest of the chief justice's decision.[182] His explanation covered thirteen pages.

What truly constituted "the majority" decision in *Webster*? Labeled parts I, II-A, II-B, and II-C, the majority opinion spelled out what five justices agreed to and what they rejected. For example, the five justices in the majority refused to decide the constitutionality of the Missouri statute's questionable preamble. "We will wait until the state courts apply the preamble to restrict . . . [abortion] activities in some concrete way," the opinion stated. They also agreed to refuse to revisit their earlier precedents denying the use of public facilities or public employees to assist nontherapeutic abortions. The state's ban did not burden procreational choice, the majority declared.

The five justices in the majority—Rehnquist, White, Kennedy, Scalia, and O'Connor—also agreed that they did not have to decide whether the statute's ban on "encourag[ing] or counsel[ing] a woman to have an abortion violated the physician's right to care for the patient." Instead, the Court majority accepted Attorney General William Webster's assurance that the statement applied to the state's "fiscal officers." So defined, that portion of the statute became a nullity.

The parts of the decision labeled II-D and III represented the views of only Chief Justice Rehnquist and justices White and Kennedy. These three justices argued that doctors did not have to read the viability-testing provision to require all of the tests named in the statute. Thus, the statute's provisions did not violate the doctor's duties to his patient. The chief justice and the two associate justices also agreed that the "trimester analysis" that the Court had designed in *Roe v. Wade* "should be abandoned." *Roe*'s system had placed the abortion choice in the hands of the woman and her doctor up to the end of the first three months of pregnancy. During the second three-month period, control began to pass increasingly into the hands of the state until the final trimester, during which the state could forbid abortion unless the mother's life or health was at risk. This trimester standard had been based on the "point of viability" doctrine, which identified the time at which the fetus could live on its own. Rehnquist, White, and Kennedy also sought to "distinguish" abortion and birth control, while suggesting that the decisions on these issues should be decided by majority vote in state legislatures. Finally, the three claimed that their decision did not "disturb *Roe*'s holding."[183]

One section of *Webster* carried a unanimous vote: part II-C. This was the section the Court decided was moot because Reproductive Health Services had withdrawn its claims in light of Missouri's stated interpretation of the section of the law dealing with doctors' right to advise their patients about abortion. The state had assured the Court that the three sections of its statute that related to "encouraging or counseling a woman to have an abortion not necessary to save her life" were "not directed at the conduct of any physician or

health care provider, private, nor public . . . [but] solely . . . those persons responsible for expending public funds."[184]

Two separate concurrences, written by justices O'Connor and Scalia, reduced Chief Justice Rehnquist's majority to only a plurality. Each was written
for a very different reason, and they represented diametrically opposing
views. Such "concurrences" clarify a decision as complex as *Webster.* They
offer insight into the judicial decision-making process. Judicial attitudes are
often exposed as justices write to explain their votes and, in the process, suggest the "strategic choices" they have made.[185] An analysis of O'Connor's and
Scalia's concurrences also reveals why the chief justice failed to secure his
"personal policy" goal, the reversal of *Roe v. Wade.*

Justice O'Connor's concurrence was narrowly confined to the provisions
of the Missouri statute. Her question was different from that asked by her colleagues, and the test she used also separated her from the other justices. She
did not support Rehnquist's attack on *Roe v. Wade.* Thus only four justices—
a minority—voted for the demise of *Roe.* For O'Connor, the question was, Do
the Missouri restrictions constitute an undue burden? Justice O'Connor
claimed that the restrictions designed by the state legislature were not prohibitions: a woman could still find a way to exercise a right of choice. For example, if Missouri's requirement for viability tests after twenty weeks was interpreted to mean that a state could employ useful tests to determine when
viability was possible, then it would not impose an "undue burden" on a
woman's abortion decision. It would still be consistent with the basic protection offered by *Roe v. Wade.*

O'Connor's approach was not a novel one. Justice Louis D. Brandeis had articulated it in his own famous concurrence in a 1936 case known as *Ashwander v. TVA.* The Court, Brandeis had written, should not "anticipate a question
of constitutional law in advance of the necessity of deciding it."[186] Neither
should the Court "formulate a rule of constitutional law broader than is required by the precise facts to which it is to be applied."[187] Using this approach,
Justice O'Connor concluded that the *Webster* case could be decided without
answering the question of *Roe's* constitutionality. If the Missouri restrictions
were seen as valid under *Roe,* the justices should not reach out to decide an issue not before them. Specifically, she wrote, "when the constitutional invalidity of a state's abortion statute actually turns on the constitutional validity of
Roe v. Wade, there will be enough time to reexamine *Roe.* And to do so carefully."[188] Justifying this approach as one of judicial restraint, O'Connor demonstrated her knowledge of the legal reasoning employed by Supreme Court justices from the very beginning. Citing goals of "prudence," the Court often has
refused to decide an issue and thus limited its own jurisdiction.

Justice O'Connor's concurrence also demonstrated the narrow focus that
numerous justices have employed when dealing with explosive issues. First,

she insisted that only the record actually before the Court could be considered. This eliminated speculation about how the Missouri restriction might be applied by Missouri courts. Second, O'Connor undertook a careful word-by-word analysis of the statute. In so doing, she attempted to confine the law itself to a narrow meaning. This semantic focus sent a clear signal to Missouri: the restrictions would be under careful scrutiny. Justice O'Connor's use of precedent to justify her concurrence was designed to demonstrate that *Webster* was not to be interpreted as overturning the Court's prior decisions.

The most significant element of legal justification that O'Connor employed came at the end of her concurrence. Medical data submitted by the American Medical Association in their amicus curiae brief had had a profound impact on her. In an earlier opinion,[189] she had implied that medical advances might allow a fetus of perhaps a month to be viable. The AMA's brief flatly contradicted this, and O'Connor corrected herself as she wrote, "It is well known that fetal lungs do not mature until 33–34 weeks gestation."[190] Without lung development, fetal viability was nonexistent. The use of this type of data comprised a "Brandeis brief" approach, and Justice O'Connor employed it as she defended her new position. Her concurrence therefore placed her on a collision course with her former allies, justices White, Kennedy, and Scalia and Chief Justice Rehnquist.

Justice Scalia's concurrence demonstrated this collision. He had hoped to be part of a five-person majority that would overturn *Roe*. It was Justice O'Connor who prevented this. Scalia penned his opinion specifically to debate O'Connor's justifications. His attack involved the "self-denying" ordinance that O'Connor had cited: in particular, "the principle that we [the Court] will not formulate a rule of constitutional law broader than is required by the precise facts to which it is to be applied." Covering three pages, Scalia's refutation of this principle became a personal attack on Justice O'Connor. Her argument that judicial restraint required the Court to avoid reconsidering *Roe*, he maintained, "cannot be taken seriously." In addition, he asserted that she had answered more than one question "incorrectly" and that her new test for viability was "irrational."[191]

Justice Scalia's concurrence had the earmarks of a judicial strategy known as "massive retaliation."[192] This occurs when one justice decides to "go public" with personal disagreements. It demonstrates that the justice has decided that future negotiation, compromise, or bargaining is impossible. In effect, this strategy is no strategy at all: it is a tactic of destruction. Scalia's attack was directed toward Justice O'Connor's professional competence. Some experts would describe it as "sexist," others as "mean-spirited," and, as with every massive retaliation response, a deep gulf would separate the two justices in future cases on this issue.[193]

THE MINORITY IN *WEBSTER*

In the months that preceded the announcement of the *Webster* decision, Justice Harry Blackmun struggled with his dissent. At first he was designing it to address a firm majority of five, but Justice O'Connor's defection reduced Chief Justice Rehnquist's opinion to that of a plurality. Blackmun could strike "*Roe* no longer survives" from his draft.[194] In *Webster* the votes did not exist to overturn *Roe v. Wade*. Nevertheless *Roe* was in jeopardy, and Justice Blackmun, writing for himself and justices William Brennan and Thurgood Marshall, designed his dissent to make his point. In all, he employed six major elements of legal reasoning designed to defend *Roe*, attack the plurality opinion, create an alliance with Justice O'Connor, and appeal to public opinion.

Using the doctrine of stare decisis and precedent, Justice Blackmun attacked in detail the plurality's refusal to accept a fifteen-year-old decision. The two dissenters in *Roe* had finally become a majority, he noted, and were now ready to overturn precedent. He charged them also with a deliberate misapplication of precedent in the *Webster* decision. Should *Maher* and *Poelker*—cases that banned public funding—decide *Webster*? Blackmun said no. The Missouri law had targeted hospitals that were only marginally public and had proceeded to forbid abortion there even though the facility and its doctors were private actors. Since *Maher* and *Poelker* dealt with public facilities, they should not govern those that were essentially private. The plurality was applying precedent incorrectly in *Webster*, as Blackmun presented it.

A second legal justification that Blackmun invoked in his dissent centered on the concept called "the role of the court."[195] Many justices had accepted their role as "the least dangerous branch"[196] and translated that into a doctrine of "judicial restraint."[197] They cited constitutional limits on their powers; they also urged prudential ones, self-imposed in order to protect the Court. Justice Louis D. Brandeis in *Ashwander v. TVA* had summarized many of these self-imposed "ordinances,"[198] and Justice O'Connor had centered her concurrence in *Webster* on two of them. Building on her decision, Justice Blackmun highlighted the plurality's "attempt to precipitate a constitutional crisis." The plurality had "reach[ed] out to address constitutional questions that [were] not actually presented."[199] This particular "self-denying ordinance" was at the heart of the doctrine of judicial restraint that the plurality professed to honor. Had the plurality in this case adopted a role of "judicial activism"?[200] In seeking to overturn precedent and abandon stare decisis, had they themselves become activists? It was an argument designed to appeal to Justice O'Connor.

As Justice Blackmun moved to a defense of "judicial tests,"[201] he resorted once again to this strategy of alliance building, and once again Justice O'Connor was the target. Blackmun's defense of judicial tests was both historical and practical. The test in *Roe*, he declared, was a historical one. Based on viability as the balancing point, it allowed the Court to give power both to the woman and to the state. Reproductive choice, according to the test, was at its maximum before viability. States' rights to restrict, or even prohibit, abortion increased after viability. Defining this balance, Blackmun asserted, was the role judges historically had undertaken. Courts over time had developed and used many such tests. Sometimes they asked whether there was a "rational relationship" between a law and its goal. Could and should a goal be achieved by a certain method? It was a means-versus-ends type of test. The ghost of the great Chief Justice John Marshall hovers over this test, yet no words in the Constitution name it. If it could still be used, why not a viability test? As Blackmun reminded his audience, judges had decided issues of speech (obscenity), religion, education, and criminal culpability though such judge-made tests.

At this point in his dissent, Justice Blackmun cited yet another test—one he had actually created, but which Justice O'Connor had appropriated and taken for herself. It was the "unduly burdensome" test. O'Connor had queried, "Is a state restriction unduly burdensome on a woman's right to reproductive choice?"[202] For Blackmun, the use of such tests defined the very job courts were asked to do. For the plurality to argue that courts should not do this was, in essence, to deny that they should exist at all.

Justice Blackmun also called attention to the legal justification known as "statutory analysis."[203] Since the plurality had carefully examined Missouri's statute, the dissenters did so, too. They asked, "What is the plain meaning of this law? What are the actual words used?" Their focus centered on the word "shall" in the law requiring physicians to carry out certain tests. The section stated that "the physician shall perform . . . tests necessary to make a finding of gestational age, weight, and lung maturity." Was this word *shall* chosen by the legislature with the intent of making it a command? Semantic usage would answer yes. Yet the Court's plurality had refused to read it that way. Combining the legal justification elements of statutory analysis, legislative intent, and semantics, Justice Blackmun accused the Court of deliberately misreading the Missouri law in order to find it constitutional.[204]

Another of Justice Blackmun's points of legal justification focused on the concept known as "framers' intent."[205] In using this principle of legal reasoning, Blackmun highlighted Justice Scalia's call for majority vote rather than judicial line drawing to decide issues like reproductive choice. Did the framers of the Constitution and the Bill of Rights intend this? Blackmun answered succinctly, quoting Justice Robert Jackson: "The very purpose of a Bill of Rights was to withdraw certain subjects from the vicissitudes of political controversy, to place them beyond the reach of majorities and officials and to establish them as legal principles to be applied by the courts. One's right to life, liberty, and property . . . may not be submitted to vote; they depend on the outcome of no election."[206] The "intent of the framers," original intent, would be destroyed by the very justice, Scalia, who prized it as the cornerstone of his own philosophy, if his view prevailed.

In concluding his dissent, Justice Blackmun applied one of the more modern forms of legal justification. Identified as a sociological or contemporary morality type of reasoning,[207] it too was linked historically to Justice Brandeis. In the days before becoming a Supreme Court justice, attorney Brandeis had developed a type of brief that came to bear his name, the "Brandeis brief." Combining economic data, statistical analysis, and psychological and sociological findings, the Brandeis brief, over time, made an impact on American law. Its greatest impact was noted in the famous segregation decision of the Warren Court, *Brown v. Board of Education*,[208] in 1954. Even before that, however, the justices of the Supreme Court had incorporated into their decisions findings presented from these briefs. Although scorned by some justices, such data could not remain ignored.

Justice Blackmun closed with the sociological argument appropriate to the *Roe-Webster* debate. What would happen if women lost their fundamental right to reproductive choice—their right to privacy? Blackmun's data provided the answer. He concluded that "every year hundreds of thousands of women, in desperation, would defy the law, and place their health and safety in the unclean and unsympathetic hands of back-alley abortionists, or they would attempt to perform abortions upon themselves, with disastrous results."[209] Appealing to the medical brief submitted by the American Medical Association, he contrasted these medical findings with Justice O'Connor's pre-*Webster* criticism of *Roe*. *Roe's* framework, Justice Blackmun noted, was not on a "collision course with itself." The point of viability was not going to "recede with advances in medical technology." Instead, as the medical data from the AMA amicus brief confirmed, "no technology exists to bridge the development gap between the three-day embryo culture and the 24th week of gestation." The medical community's report on fetal survivability saw no possibility of the "development of such technology in the foreseeable future" and added, "Predictions to the contrary are pure science fiction."[210]

This Brandeis brief argument had an impact on Justice O'Connor, and Justice Blackmun knew it. In her concurrence in *Webster*, she had admitted, "It is well known that fetal lungs do not mature until 33–34 weeks gestation," documenting her source as the AMA's brief with its data.[211] Justice Blackmun sought to cement the new alliance he hoped to build with a cautious O'Connor, using the technique of "persuasion on the merits."[212] Facts showed, Blackmun wrote, that "the threshold of fetal viability [remains] . . . what it was at the time *Roe* was decided."[213]

The concluding dissent written by Justice Stevens showed his agreement with his three colleagues, Justices Blackmun, Brennan, and Marshall. Why then did Justice Stevens feel compelled to write some nine pages? The answer centered upon the religious argument that he wanted to make. Justice

Stevens had earlier shown himself as a proponent of the doctrine of separation of church and state. Prompted perhaps by his background experience with historic Baptist values, Stevens wanted to uphold the balance of a "free church in a free state."[214] He abhorred the idea that a civic religion might arise in the country. "I am persuaded," he wrote in *Webster*, "that the absence of any secular purpose for the [Missouri] legislative declaration that life begins at conception . . . makes the [Missouri law's] preamble invalid under the Establishment Clause of the First Amendment to the Federal Constitution." Stevens called the "Missouri preamble," which Andrew Puzder and Samuel Lee had so carefully devised, an "unequivocal endorsement of a religious tenet." He turned to a historical argument to make this point and spent two pages examining in detail the view of St. Thomas Aquinas. Stevens concluded that there was no justification for a "state legislature's official endorsement of the theological tenet embodied in [Missouri's preamble]." It was perhaps the fitting conclusion to this case. Stevens's dissent returned the case to its origins, namely, the religious alliance between Missouri's Catholic leaders and Fundamentalist Protestant activists, which had created the law litigated in *Webster*.[215]

WEBSTER V. REPRODUCTIVE HEALTH SERVICES:
EXCERPTS FROM THE OFFICIAL TEXT

Chief Justice Rehnquist announced the judgment of the Court and delivered the opinion of the Court with respect to Parts I, II-A, II-B, and II-C, and an opinion with respect to Parts II-D and III, in which Justice White and Justice Kennedy join.

> This appeal concerns the constitutionality of a [1986] Missouri statute regulating the performance of abortions. The [Court of Appeals] struck down several provisions of the statute on the ground that they violated [*Roe v. Wade* and its progeny. We reverse.]

> I. [The 1986 law consists] of 20 provisions, 5 of which are now before the Court. The first provision, or preamble, contains "findings" by the state legislature that "(t)he life of each human being begins at conception," and that "unborn children have protectable interests in life, health, and well-being." The Act further requires that all Missouri laws be interpreted to provide unborn children with the same rights enjoyed by other [persons]. Among its other provisions, the Act requires that, prior to performing an abortion on any woman whom a physician has reason to believe is twenty or more weeks pregnant, the physician ascertain whether the fetus is viable by performing "such medical examinations and tests

as are necessary to make a finding of gestational age, weight, and lung maturity of the unborn child." The Act also prohibits the use of public employees and facilities to perform or assist abortions not necessary to save the mother's life, and it prohibits the use of public funds, employees, or facilities for the purpose of "encouraging or counseling" a woman to have an abortion not necessary to save her [life].

II. Decision of this case requires us to address four sections of the Missouri Act: (a) the preamble; (b) the prohibition on the use of public facilities or employees to perform abortions; (c) the prohibition on public funding of abortion counseling; and (d) the requirement that physicians conduct viability tests prior to performing abortions. We address these seriatim.

A. [In] invalidating the preamble, the Court of Appeals relied on this Court's dictum that "'a State may not adopt one theory of when life begins to justify its regulation of abortions,'" quoting [*Akron*], in turn citing *Roe v. Wade*. It rejected Missouri's claim that the preamble was "abortion-neutral" and "merely determine(d) when life begins in a nonabortion context, a traditional state prerogative." The Court thought that "(t)he only plausible inference" from the fact that "every remaining section of the bill save one regulates the performance of abortions" was that "the state intended its abortion regulations to be understood against the backdrop of its theory of life." The State contends that the preamble itself is precatory and imposes no substantive restrictions on abortions, and that appellees therefore do not have standing to challenge it. Appellees, on the other hand, insist that the preamble is an operative part of the Act intended to guide the interpretation of other provisions of the Act.

[In] our view, the Court of Appeals misconceived the meaning of the Akron dictum, which was only that a Sate could not "justify" an abortion regulation otherwise invalid under *Roe v. Wade* on the ground that it embodied the State's view about when life begins. [The] Court has emphasized that *Roe v. Wade* "implies no limitation on the authority of a State to make a value judgment favoring childbirth over abortion." *Maher v. Roe*. The preamble can be read simply to express that sort of value judgment. We think the extent to which the preamble's language might be used to interpret other state statutes or regulations is something that only the courts of Missouri can definitively decide. [It] will be time enough for federal courts to address the meaning of the preamble should it be applied to restrict the activities of appellees in some concrete way. [We] therefore need not pass on the constitutionality of the Act's preamble.

B. § 188.10 provides that "(i)t shall be unlawful for any public employee within the scope of his employment to perform or assist an abortion, not necessary to save the life of the mother," while section 188.215 makes it "unlawful for any public facility to be used for the purpose of performing or assisting an abortion not necessary to save the life of the mother."

[As] we said earlier this Term in [*DeShaney* (1989)], "our cases have recognized that the Due Process Clauses generally confer no affirmative right to governmental aid, even where such aid may be necessary to secure life, liberty, or property interests of which the government itself may not deprive the individual." [See also *Maher v. Roe*, *Harris v. McRae*, and *Poelker v. Doe*, all abortion-funding cases noted above.] The Court of Appeals distinguished these cases on the ground that "(t)o prevent access to a public facility does more than demonstrate a political choice in favor of childbirth; it clearly narrows and in some cases forecloses the availability of abortion to women." The Court reasoned that the ban on the use of public facilities "could prevent a woman's chosen doctor from performing an [abortion]" [and] thought that "(s)uch a rule could increase the cost of obtaining an abortion and delay the timing of it as well."

We think that this analysis is much like that which we rejected in *Maher*, *Poelker*, and *McRae*. [Just] as Congress' refusal to fund abortions in *McRae* left "an indigent woman with at least the same range of choice in deciding whether to obtain a medically necessary abortion as she would have had if Congress had chosen to subsidize no health care costs at all," Missouri's refusal to allow public employees to perform abortions in public hospitals leaves a pregnant woman with the same choices as if the State had chosen not to operate any public hospitals at all. The challenged provisions only restrict a woman's ability to obtain an abortion to the extent that she chooses to use a physician affiliated with a public hospital. This circum stance is more easily remedied, and thus considerably less burdensome, than indigency, which "may make it difficult—and in some cases, perhaps, impossible—for some women to have abortions" without public funding. *Maher*. Having held that the State's refusal to fund abortions does not violate [*Roe*], it strains logic to reach a contrary result for the use of public facilities and employees. If the State may "make a value judgment favoring childbirth over abortion [and] implement that judgment by the allocation of public funds," *Maher*, surely it may do so through the allocation of other public resources such as hospitals and medical staff.

"[Constitutional] concerns are greatest," we said in *Maher*, "When the State attempts to impose its will by the force of law; the State's power to encourage actions deemed to be in the public interest is necessarily far broader." Nothing in the Constitution requires States to enter or remain in the business of performing abortions. Nor, as appellees suggest, do private physicians and their patients have some kind of constitutional right of access to public facilities for the performance of abortions. [*Maher*, *Poelker*, and *McRae*] all support the view that the State need not commit any resources to facilitating abortions, even if it can turn a profit by doing so. [Thus] we uphold the Act's restrictions on the use of public employees and facilities for the performance or assistance of nontherapeutic abortions.

[C. The Court dismissed as moot the issue of the constitutionality of the provisions barring the use of public funds to encourage or counsel abortion not necessary to save a woman's life. The Court emphasized that the appellees were no longer "adversely" affected by the provisions, in view of the State's claim that the provision was "not directed at the conduct of any physician or health care provider," but "solely at those persons responsible for expending public funds."]

D. § 188.029 of the Missouri Act provides:

"Before a physician performs an abortion on a woman he has reason to believe is carrying an unborn child of twenty or more weeks gestational age, the physician shall first determine if the unborn child is viable by using and exercising that degree of care, skill, and proficiency commonly exercised by the ordinarily skillful, careful, and prudent physician engaged in similar practice under the same or similar conditions. In making this determination of viability, the physician shall perform or cause to be performed such medical examinations and tests as are necessary to make a finding of the gestational age, weight, and lung maturity of the unborn child and shall enter such findings and determination of viability in the medical record of the mother."

[The] parties disagree over the meaning of this [provision]. The State emphasizes the language of the first sentence, which speaks in terms of the physician's determination of viability being made by the standards of ordinary skill in the medical profession. [Appellees] stress the language of the second sentence, which prescribes such "tests as are necessary" to make a finding of gestational age, fetal weight, and lung maturity. [We] think the viability-testing provision makes sense only if the second sentence is read to require only those tests that are useful to making subsidiary findings as to viability. If we construe this provision to require a physician to perform those tests needed to make the three specified findings *in all circumstances*, including when the physician's reasonable professional judgment indicates that the tests would be irrelevant to determining viability or even dangerous to the mother and the fetus, the second sentence [would] conflict with the first sentence's *requirement* that a physician apply his reasonable professional skill and [judgment].

The viability-testing provision of the Missouri Act is concerned with promoting the State's interest in potential human life rather than in maternal health. § 188.029 creates what is essentially a presumption of viability at 20 weeks, which the physician must rebut with tests indicating that the fetus is not viable prior to performing an abortion. It also directs the physician's determination as to viability by specifying consideration, if feasible, of gestational age, fetal weight, and lung capacity. The District

Court found that "the medical evidence is uncontradicted that a twenty-week fetus in not viable," and that "23 to 24 weeks gestation is the earliest point in pregnancy where a reasonable possibility of viability exists." But it also found that there may be a four-week error in estimating gestational age, which supports testing at 20 weeks.

[We] think that the doubt cast upon the Missouri statute by [our earlier] cases is not so much a flaw in the statute as it is a reflection of the fact that the rigid trimester analysis of the course of a pregnancy enunciated in *Roe* has resulted in subsequent cases like Colautti and Akron making constitutional law in this area a virtual Procrustean bed. Statutes specifying elements of informed consent to be provided abortion patients, for example, were invalidated if they were thought to "structur(e) [the] dialogue between the woman and her physician." [*Thornburgh*.] As the dissenters in *Thornburgh* pointed out, such a statute would have been sustained under any traditional standard of judicial review, or for any other surgical procedure except abortion.

Stare decisis is a cornerstone of our legal system, but it has less power in constitutional cases, where, save for constitutional amendments, this Court is the only body able to make needed changes. We have not refrained from reconsideration of a prior construction of the Constitution that has proved "unsound in principle and unworkable in practice." [*Garcia*, chap. 3 above.] We think that the *Roe* trimester framework falls into that category.

In the first place, the rigid *Roe* framework is hardly consistent with the notion of a Constitution cast in general terms, as ours is, and usually speaking in general principles, as ours does. The key elements of the *Roe* framework—trimesters and viability—are not found in the text of the Constitution or in any place else one would expect to find a constitutional principle. Since the bounds of the inquiry are essentially indeterminate, the result has been a web of legal rules that have become increasingly intricate, resembling a code of regulations rather than a body of constitutional doctrine.[1]

---

[1] For example, the Court has held that a State may require certain information be given to a woman by a physician of his assistant [*Akron*], but that it may not require that such information be furnished to her only by the physician himself. [Ibid.]. Likewise, a State may require that abortions in the second trimester be performed in clinics [*Simopoulos*], but it may not require that abortions in the second trimester be performed only in hospitals. [*Akron*]. We do not think these distinctions are of any constitutional import in view of our abandonment of the trimester framework. The dissent's claim that the State goes too far, even under [*Maher, Poelker,* and *McRae*], by refusing to permit the use of public facilities[for] the performance of abortions is another example of the fine distinctions endemic in the *Roe* framework. [Footnote by Chief Justice Rehnquist.]

[In] the second place, we do not see why the State's interest in protecting potential human life should come into existence only at the point of viability, and that there should therefore be a rigid line allowing state regulation after viability but prohibiting it before viability. [The] tests that § 188.029 requires the physician to perform are designed to determine viability. The State here has chosen viability as the point at which its interest in potential human life must be safeguarded. [It] is true that the tests in question increase the expense of abortion, and regulate the discretion of the physician in determining the viability of the fetus. Since the tests will undoubtedly show in many cases that the fetus is not viable, the tests will have been performed for what were in fact second-trimester abortions. But we are satisfied that the requirement of these tests permissibly furthers the State's interest in protecting potential human life, and we therefore believe § 188.029 to be constitutional.

The dissent takes us to task for our failure to join in a "great issues" debate as to whether the Constitution includes an "unenumerated" general right to privacy as recognized in cases such as [*Griswold*] and *Roe*. But *Griswold*, unlike *Roe*, did not purport to adopt a whole framework, complete with detailed rules and distinctions, to govern the cases in which the asserted liberty interest would apply. As such, it was far different from the opinion, if not the holding, of *Roe*, which sought to establish a constitutional framework for judging state regulation of abortion during the entire term of pregnancy. That framework sought to deal with areas of medical practice traditionally subject to state regulation, and it sought to balance once and for all by reference only to the calendar the claims of the State to protect the fetus as a form of human life against the claims of a woman to decide for herself whether or not to abort a fetus she was carrying. The experience of the Court in applying *Roe v. Wade* in later cases suggests to us that there is wisdom in not unnecessarily attempting to elaborate the abstract differences between a "fundamental right" to abortion, as the Court described it in [*Akron*], a "limited fundamental constitutional right," which Justice Blackmun's dissent today treats *Roe* as having established, or a liberty interest protected by the Due Process Clause, which we believe it to be. The Missouri testing requirement here is reasonably designed to ensure that abortions are not performed where the fetus is viable—an end which all concede is legitimate—and that is sufficient to sustain its constitutionality.

The dissent also accuses us, inter alia, of cowardice and illegitimacy in dealing with "the most politically divisive domestic legal issue of our time." There is no doubt that our holding today will allow some governmental regulation of abortion that would have been prohibited under the language of cases such as *Colautti* and *Akron*. But the goal of constitutional adjudication is surely not to remove inexorably "political divisive" issues from the ambit of the legislative process, whereby the people through their elected representatives deal with matters of concern to them. The goal of constitutional adjudication is to hold true the balance between that which the Constitution puts beyond the reach of the democratic process and that which it does not. We think we have done that today. The dissent's suggestion that legislative bodies, in a Nation where more than half of our population is women, will treat our decision today as an invitation to enact abortion regulation reminiscent of the dark ages not only misreads our views but does not scant justice to those who serve in such bodies and the people who elect them.

III. Both appellants and the Unites States as Amicus Curiae have urged that we overrule our decision in *Roe v. Wade*. The facts of the present case, however, differ from those at issue in *Roe*. Here, Missouri has determined that viability is the point at which its interest in potential human life must be safeguarded. In *Roe*, on the other hand, the Texas statute criminalized the performance of all abortions, except when the mother's life was at stake. This case therefore affords us no occasion to revisit the holding of [*Roe*] and we leave it undisturbed. To the extent indicated in our opinion, we would modify and narrow *Roe* and succeeding cases.
[Reversed.]

Justice O'Connor, concurring in part and concurring in the judgment.

I concur in Parts I, II-A, II-B, and II-C of the Court's opinion.

I. Nothing in the record before us or the opinions below indicates that [the] preamble to Missouri's abortion regulation statute will affect a woman's decision to have an abortion. [I] agree with the Court, therefore, that all of [the] intimations of unconstitutionality are simply too hypothetical to support the use of declaratory judgment procedures and injunctive remedies in this case. Similarly, it seems to me to follow directly from our previous decisions concerning state or federal funding of abortions that appellees' facial challenge to the constitutionality of Missouri's ban on the utilization of public facilities and the participation of public employees in the performance of abortions not necessary to save the life of the mother cannot succeed. [I] also agree with the Court that [there] is no longer a case or controversy before us over the constitutionality of [the abortion counseling provision].

II. In its interpretation of Missouri's "determination of viability" provision, the plurality has proceeded in a manner unnecessary to deciding the question at hand. I agree with the plurality [that] "the viability-testing provision makes sense only if the second sentence is read to require only those tests that are useful to making subsidiary findings as to viability," and, I would add, only those [tests] that it would not be imprudent or careless to perform in the particular medical [situation]. Unlike the plurality, I do not understand these viability testing requirements to conflict with any of the Court's past decisions concerning state regulation of abortion. Therefore, there is no necessity to accept the State's invitation to reexamine the constitutional validity of *Roe v. Wade*. Where there is no need to decide a constitutional question, it is a venerable principle of this Court's adjudicatory processes not to do so. [When] the constitutional invalidity of a State's abortion statute actually turns on the constitutional validity of *Roe v. Wade*, there will be time enough to reexamine *Roe*. And to do so carefully.

In assessing § 188.029 it is especially important to recognize that appellees did not appeal the District Court's ruling that the first sentence of § 188.029 is constitutional. There is, accordingly, no dispute between the parties before us over the constitutionality of the "presumption of viability at 20 weeks" created by the first sentence of § 188.029. [I] do not think the second sentence of § 188.029, as interpreted by the Court, imposes a degree of state regulation on the medical determination of viability that in any way conflicts with prior decisions of this Court. As the plurality recognizes, the requirement that, where not imprudent, physicians perform examinations and tests useful to making subsidiary findings to determine viability "promot(es) the State's interest in potential human life rather than in maternal health." No decision of this Court has held that the State may not directly promote its interest in potential human life when viability is possible. Quite the contrary. [Thus,] all nine Members of the *Thornburgh* Court appear to have agreed that it is not constitutionally impermissible for the State to enact regulations designed to protect the State's interest in potential life when viability is possible. That is exactly what Missouri has done in § 188.029. There are a number of different methods in standard medical practice to determine fetal lung maturity at twenty or more weeks gestation. The most simple and most obvious is by inference. It is well known that fetal lungs do not mature until 33–34 weeks gestation. If an assessment of the gestational age indicates that the child is less than thirty-three weeks, a general finding can be made that the fetal lungs are not mature. This finding can then be used by the physician in making his determination of viability under § 188.029; cf. Brief of the American Medical Association et al. as *Amici Curiae* 42.

[Finally,] and rather half-heartedly, the plurality suggests that the marginal increase in the cost of an abortion created by Missouri's viability testing provision may make § 188.029, even as interpreted, suspect under this Court's decision in *Akron*, striking down a second-trimester hospitalization requirement. I dissented [in] *Akron* because it was my view that, even apart from *Roe*'s trimester framework which I continue to consider problematic, the *Akron* majority had distorted and misapplied its own standard for evaluating state regulation of abortion which the Court had applied with fair consistency in the past: that, previability, "a regulation imposed on a lawful abortion is not unconstitutional unless it unduly burdens the right to seek an abortion." It is clear to me that requiring the performance of examinations and tests useful to determining whether a fetus is viable, when viability is possible, and when it would not be medically imprudent to do so, does not impose an undue burden on a woman's abortion decision. On this ground alone I would reject the suggestion that § 188.029 as interpreted is unconstitutional. More to the point, however, just as I see no conflict between § 188.029 and *Colautti* or any decision of this Court concerning a State's ability to give effect to its interest in potential life, I see no conflict between § 188.029 and the Court's opinion in *Akron*. The second-trimester hospitalization requirement struck down in *Akron* imposed, in the majority's view, "a heavy, and unnecessary, burden," more than doubling the cost of "women's access to a relatively inexpensive, otherwise accessible, and safe abortion procedure." By contrast, the cost of examinations and tests required by § 188.029 are to be performed when viability is possible. This feature of § 188.029 distinguishes it from the second-trimester hospitalization requirement struck down by the *Akron* majority. [The] State's compelling interest in potential life postviability renders its interest in determining the critical point of viability equally compelling. Under the Court's precedents, the same cannot be said for the *Akron* second-trimester hospitalization requirement. As I understand the Court's opinion in *Akron*, therefore, the plurality's suggestion today that *Akron* casts doubt on the validity of § 188.029, even as the Court has interpreted it, is without foundation and cannot provide a basis for reevaluating *Roe*. Accordingly, because the Court of Appeals misinterpreted § 188.029, and because, properly interpreted, § 188.029 is not inconsistent with any of this Court's prior precedents, I would reverse the decision of the [Court of Appeals].

Justice Scalia, concurring in part and concurring in the judgment.

I join parts I, II-A, II-B, and II-C of the opinion of the Chief Justice. As to Part II-D, I share Justice Blackmun's view that it effectively would overrule *Roe v. Wade*. I think that should be done, but would do it more explicitly. Since today we contrive to avoid doing it, and indeed to avoid almost any decision of national import, I need not set forth my reasons, some of which have been well recited in dissents of my colleagues in other cases. The outcome of today's case will doubtless by heralded as a triumph of judicial statesmanship. It is not that, unless it is statesmanlike needlessly to prolong this Court's self-awarded sovereignty over a field where it has little proper business since the answers to most of the cruel questions posed are political and not juridical—a sovereignty which therefore quite properly, but to the great damage of the Court, makes it the object of the sort of organized public pressure that political institutions in a democracy ought to receive.

Justice O'Connor's assertion that a "'fundamental rule of judicial restraint'" requires us to avoid reconsidering *Roe* cannot be taken seriously. [What] is involved [is] not the rule of avoiding constitutional issues where possible, but the quite separate principle that we will not " 'formulate a rule of constitutional law broader than is required by the precise facts to which it is to be applied.'" The latter is a sound general principle, but one often departed from when good reason exists. [I] have not identified with certainty the first instance of our deciding a case on broader constitutional grounds than absolutely necessary, but it is assuredly no later than [*Marbury v. Madison*], where we held that mandamus could constitutionally issue against the Secretary of State, although that was unnecessary given our holding that the law authorizing issuance of the mandamus by this Court was unconstitutional. [It] would be wrong, in any decision, to ignore the reality that our policy not to "formulate a rule of constitutional law broader than is required by the precise facts" has a frequently applied good-cause exception. But it seems particularly perverse to concert the policy into an absolute in the present case, in order to place beyond reach the inexpressibly "broader-than-was-required-by-the-precise-facts" structure established by *Roe v. Wade*.

The real question, then, is whether there are valid reasons to go beyond the most stingy possible holding today. It seems to me there are not only valid but compelling ones. Ordinarily, speaking no more broadly than is absolutely required avoids throwing settled law into confusion; doing so today preserves a chaos that is evident to anyone who can read and count. Alone sufficient to justify a broad holding is the fact that our retaining control, through *Roe*, of what I believe to be, and many of our citizens recognize to be, a political issue, continuously distorts the public perception of the role of this Court. We can now look forward to at least another Term with carts full of mail from the public, and streets full of demonstrators, urging us—their unelected and life-tenured judges who have been awarded those extraordinary, undemocratic characteristics precisely in order that we might follow the law despite the popular will—to follow the popular will. Indeed, I expect we can look forward to even more of that than before, given our indecisive decision today. And if these reasons for taking the unexceptional course of reaching a broader holding are not enough, then consider the nature of the constitutional question we avoid: In most cases, we do no harm by not speaking more broadly than the decision requires. Anyone affected by the conduct that the avoided holding would have prohibited will be able to challenge himself, and have his day in court to make the argument. Not so with respect to the harm that many

States believed, pre-*Roe*, and many may continue to believe, is caused by largely unrestricted abortion. That will continue to occur if the States have the constitutional power to prohibit it, and would do so, but we skillfully avoid telling them so. Perhaps those abortions cannot constitutionally be proscribed. That is surely an arguable question, the question that reconsideration of *Roe v. Wade* entails. But what is not at all arguable, it seems to me, is that we should decide now and not insist that we be run into a corner before we grudgingly yield up our judgment. The only sound reason for the latter course is to prevent a change in the law—but to think that desirable begs the question to be decided.

It was an arguable question today whether § 188.029 of the Missouri law contravened this Court's understanding of *Roe v. Wade*,[2] and I would have examined *Roe* rather than examining the contravention. Given the Court's newly contracted abstemiousness, what will it take, one must wonder, to permit us to reach that fundamental question? The result of our vote today is that we will not reconsider that prior opinion, even if

---

[2]That question, compared with the question whether we should reconsider and reverse *Roe*, is hardly worth a footnote, but I think Justice O'Connor answers that incorrectly as well. In [*Roe*] we said that "the physician [has the right] to administer medical treatment according to his professional judgment up to the points where important state interests provide compelling justifications for intervention." We have subsequently made clear that it is also a matter of medical judgment when viability (one of those points) is reached. "The time when viability is achieved may vary with each pregnancy, and the determination of whether a particular fetus is viable is, and must be, a matter for the judgment of the responsible attending physician." [*Danforth*.]. Section 188.029 conflicts with the purpose and hence the fair import of this principle because it will sometimes require a physician to perform tests that he would not otherwise have performed to determine whether a fetus is viable. It is therefore a legislative imposition on the judgment of the physician, and one that increases the cost of an abortion. Justice O'Connor would nevertheless uphold the law because it "does not impose an undue burden on a woman's abortion decision." This conclusion is supported by the observation that the required tests impose only a marginal cost on the abortion procedure, far less of an increase than the cost-doubling hospitalization requirement invalidated in [*Akron*]. The fact that the challenged regulation is less costly than what we struck down in *Akron* tells us only that we cannot decide the present case on the basis of that earlier decision. It does not tell us whether the present requirement is an "undue burden," and I know of no basis for determining that this particular burden (or any other for that matter) is "due." One could with equal justification conclude that it is not. To avoid the question of *Roe v. Wade*'s validity, with the attendant costs that this will have for the Court and for the principles of self-governance, on the basis of a standard that offers "no guide but the Court's own discretion," merely adds to the irrationality of what we do today. Similarly irrational is the new concept that Justice O'Connor introduces into the law in order to achieve her result, the notion of a State's "interest in potential life when viability is possible." Since "viability" means the mere *possibility* (not the certainty) of survivability outside the womb, "possible viability" must mean the possibility of a possibility of survivability outside the womb. Perhaps our next opinion will expand the third trimester into the second even further, by approving state action designed to take account of "the chance of possible viability." [Footnote by Justice Scalia.]

most of the Justices think it is wrong, unless we have before us a statute that in fact contradicts it—and even then (under our newly discovered "no-broader-than-necessary" requirement) only minor problematic aspects of *Roe* will be reconsidered, unless one expects State legislatures to adopt provisions whose compliance with *Roe* cannot even be argued with a straight face. It thus appears that the mansion of constitutionalized abortion-law, constructed overnight in *Roe v. Wade*, must be disassembled door-jamb by door-jamb, and never entirely brought down, no matter how wrong it may be. Of the four courses we might have chosen today—to reaffirm *Roe*, to overrule it explicitly, to overrule it sub silentio, or to avoid the question—the last is the least responsible. On the question of the constitutionality of § 188.029, I concur in the judgment of the Court and strongly dissent from the manner in which it has been reached.

Justice Blackmun, with whom Justice Brennan and Justice Marshall join, concurring in part and dissenting in part.

Today, *Roe v. Wade* and the fundamental constitutional right of women to decide whether to terminate a pregnancy, survive but are not secure. Although the Court extricates itself from this case without making a single, even incremental, change in the law of abortion, the plurality and Justice Scalia would overrule *Roe* (the first silently, the other explicitly) and would return to the States virtually unfettered authority to control the quintessentially intimate, personal, and life-directing decision whether to carry a fetus to term. Although today, no less than yesterday, the Constitution and the decisions of this Court prohibit a State from enacting laws that inhibit women from the meaningful exercise of that right, a plurality of this Court implicitly invites every state legislature to enact more and more restrictive abortion regulations in order to provoke more and more test cases, in the hope that sometime down the line the Court will return the law of procreative freedom to the severe limitations that generally prevailed in this country before January 22, 1973. Never in my memory has a plurality announced a judgment of this Court that so foments disregard for the law and for our standing decisions.

Nor in my memory has a plurality gone about its business in such a deceptive fashion. At every level of its review, from its effort to read the real meaning out of the Missouri statute, to its intended evisceration of precedents and its deafening silence about the constitutional protections that it would jettison, the plurality obscures the portent of its analysis. With feigned restraint, the plurality announces that its analysis leaves *Roe* "undisturbed," albeit "modif(ied) and narrow(ed)." But this disclaimer is totally meaningless. The plurality opinion is filled with winks, and nods, and knowing glances to those who would do away with *Roe* explicitly, but turns a stone face to anyone in search of what the plurality conceives as the scope of a women's right [to] terminate pregnancy free from the coercive and brooding influence of the State. The simple truth is that *Roe* would not survive the plurality's analysis, and that the plurality provides no substitute for *Roe*'s protective umbrella. I fear for the future. I fear for the liberty and equality of the millions of women who have lived and come of age in the 16 years since *Roe* was decided. I fear for the integrity of, and public esteem for, this Court. I dissent.

I. The plurality parades through the four challenged sections of the Missouri's statute seriatim. I shall not do this. [Although] I disagree with the [plurality's] misapplication of our past decisions in upholding Missouri's ban on the performance of abortions at "public facilities," the plurality's discussion of these provisions is merely prologue to its consideration of the statute's viability-testing requirement, § 188.029—the only section of the Missouri statute that the plurality construes as implicating *Roe* itself. There, tucked away at the end of its opinion, the plurality suggests a radical reversal of the law of abortion; and there, primarily, I direct my attention. In the plurality's view, the viability-testing provision imposes a burden on second-trimester abortions as a way of furthering the State's interest in protecting the potential life of the fetus. Since under the *Roe* framework, the State may not fully regulate abortion in the interest of potential life (as opposed to maternal health) until the third trimester, the plurality finds it necessary, in order to save the Missouri testing provision, to throw out *Roe*'s trimester framework. In flat contradiction to *Roe*, the plurality concludes that the State's interest in potential life is compelling before viability, and upholds the testing provision because it "permissibly furthers" that state interest.

A. At the outset, I note that in its haste to limit abortion rights, the plurality compounds the errors of its analysis by needlessly reaching out to address constitutional questions that are not actually presented. The conflict between § 188.029 and *Roe*'s trimester framework, which purportedly drives the plurality to reconsider our past decisions, is a contrived conflict: the product of an aggressive misreading of the viability-testing requirement and a needlessly wooden application of the *Roe* framework. The plurality's reading of § 188.029 (also joined by Justice O'Connor) is irreconcilable with the plain language of the statute. [The] statute's plain language requires the physician to undertake whatever tests are necessary to determine gestational age, weight, and lung maturity, regardless of whether these tests are necessary to a finding of viability, and regardless of whether the tests subject the pregnant woman or the fetus to additional health risks or add substantially to the cost of an abortion.

Had the plurality read the statute as written, it would have no cause to reconsider the *Roe* framework. As properly construed, the viability-testing provision does not pass constitutional muster under even a rational-basis standard. [*Lee Optical.*] By mandating tests to determine fetal weight and lung maturity for every fetus thought to be more than 20 weeks gestational age, the statute requires physicians to undertake procedures, such as amniocentesis, that, in the situation presented, have no medical justification, impose significant additional health risks on both the pregnant woman and the fetus, and bear no rational relation to the State's interest in protecting fetal life. As written, § 188.029 is an arbitrary imposition of discomfort, risk, and expense, furthering no discernible interest except to make the procurement of an abortion as arduous and difficult as possible. Thus, were it not for the plurality's tortured effort to avoid the plain import of § 188.029, it could have struck down the testing provision as patently irrational irrespective of the *Roe* framework.

The plurality eschews this straightforward resolution, in the hope of precipitating a constitutional crisis. Far from avoiding constitutional difficulty, the plurality attempts to engineer a dramatic retrenchment in our jurisprudence by exaggerating the conflict between its untenable construction of § 188.029 and the *Roe* trimester framework. No one contests that under the *Roe* framework the State, in order to promote its interest in potential human life, may regulate and even proscribe non-therapeutic abortions once the fetus becomes viable. If, as the plurality appears to hold, the testing provision simply requires a physician to use appropriate and medically sound tests to determine whether the fetus is actually viable when the estimated gestational age is greater than twenty weeks (and therefore within what the District Court found to be the margin of error for viability), then I see little or no conflict with *Roe*. [In] short, the testing provision, as construed by the plurality [could] be upheld effortlessly under current doctrine. [By] distorting the statute, the plurality manages to avoid invalidating the testing provision on what should have been noncontroversial constitutional grounds; having done so, however, the plurality rushes headlong into a much deeper constitutional thicket, brushing past an obvious basis for upholding § 188.029 in search of a pretext for scuttling the trimester [framework].

B. Having set up the conflict between § 188.029 and the Roe trimester framework, the plurality summarily discards Roe's analytic core as "'unsound in principle and unworkable in practice.'" This is so, the plurality claims, because the key elements of the framework more closely resembles a regulatory code than a body of constitutional doctrine, and because under the framework the State's interest in potential human life is considered compelling throughout pregnancy. The plurality does not bother to explain these alleged flaws in *Roe*. Bald assertion masquerades as reasoning. The object, quite clearly, is not to persuade, but to prevail.

1. The plurality opinion is far more remarkable for the arguments that it does not advance than for those that it does. The plurality does not even mention, much less join, the true jurisprudential debate underlying this case: whether the Constitution includes an "unenumerated" general right to privacy as recognized in many of our decisions, most notably, [*Griswold*] and *Roe*, and, more specifically, whether and to what extent such a right to privacy extends to matters of childbearing and family life, including abortion. These are questions of unsurpassed significance in this Court's interpretation of the Constitution, and mark the battleground upon which this case was fought. [On] these grounds, [the] Court should decide this case.

But rather than arguing that the text of the Constitution makes no mention of the right to privacy, the plurality complains that the critical elements of the *Roe* framework—trimesters and viability—do not appear in the Constitution and are, therefore, somehow inconsistent with a Constitution cast in general terms. Were this a true concern, we would have to abandon most of our constitutional jurisprudence. As the plurality well knows, or should know, the "critical elements" of countless constitutional doctrines nowhere appear in the Constitution's text. [E.g.,] the Constitution makes no mention of the rational basis test, or the specific verbal formulations of intermediate and strict scrutiny by which this Court evaluates claims under the Equal Protection Clause. The reason is simple. Like the *Roe* framework, these tests or standards are not, and do not purport to be, rights protected by the Constitution. Rather, they are judge-made methods for evaluating and measuring the strength and scope of constitutional rights or for balancing the constitutional rights of individuals against the competing interests of government.

With respect to the *Roe* framework, [the] fundamental constitutional right [for] which it was developed is the right to privacy, a species of "liberty" [which] under our past decisions safeguards the right of women to exercise some control over their own role in procreation. [The] trimester framework simply defines and limits that right to privacy in the abortion context to accommodate, not destroy, a State's legitimate interest in protecting the health of pregnant women and in preserving potential human life. Fashioning such accommodations between individual rights and the legitimate interests of government, establishing benchmarks and standards with which to evaluate the competing claims of individuals and government, lies at the very heart of constitutional adjudication. To the extent that the trimester framework is useful in this enterprise, it is not only consistent with constitutional interpretation, but necessary to the wise and just exercise of this Court's paramount authority to define the scope of constitutional rights.

2. The plurality next alleges that the result of the trimester framework has "been a web of legal rules that have become increasingly intricate, resembling a code of regulations rather than a body of constitutional doctrine." Again, if this were a true and genuine concern, we would have to abandon vast areas of our constitutional jurisprudence. [That] numerous constitutional doctrines result in narrow differentiations between similar circumstances does not mean that this Court has abandoned adjudication in favor of regulation. Rather, these careful distinctions reflect the process of constitutional adjudication itself, which is often highly fact-specific, requiring such determinations as whether state laws are "unduly burdensome" or "reasonable" or bear a "rational" or "necessary" relation to asserted state interests. [If,] in delicate and complicated areas of constitutional law, our legal judgments "have become increasingly intricate," it is not, as the plurality contends, because we have overstepped our judicial role. Quite the opposite: the rules are intricate because we have remained conscientious in our duty to do justice carefully, especially when fundamental rights rise or fall with our decisions.

3. Finally, the plurality asserts that the trimester framework cannot stand because the State's interest in potential life is compelling throughout pregnancy, not merely after viability. The opinion contains not one word of rationale for its view of the State's interest. This "it-is-so-because-we-say-so" jurisprudence constitutes nothing other than an attempted exercise of brute force; reason, much less persuasion, has no place. In answering the plurality's claim that the State's interest in the fetus is uniform and compelling throughout pregnancy, I cannot improve upon what Justice Stevens [said in *Thornburgh*]: "I should think it obvious that the State's interest in the protection of an embryo—even if that interest is defined as 'protecting those who will be citizens' . . . - increases progressively and dramatically as the organism's capacity to feel pain, to experience pleasure, to survive, and to react to its surroundings increases day by day. The development of a fetus—and pregnancy itself—are not static conditions, and the assertion that the government's interest is static simply ignores this [reality]."

For my own part, I remain convinced [that] the *Roe* framework, and the viability standard in particular, fairly, sensibly, and effectively functions to safeguard the constitutional liberties of pregnant women while recognizing and accommodating the State's interest in potential human life. The viability line reflects the biological facts and truths of fetal development; it marks that threshold moment prior to which a fetus cannot survive separate from the woman and cannot reasonably and objectively be regarded as a subject of rights or interests distinct from, or paramount to, those of the pregnant woman. At the same time, the viability standard takes account of the undeniable fact that as the fetus evolves into its postnatal form, and as it loses its dependence on the uterine environment, the State's interest in the fetus' potential human life, and in fostering a regard for human life in general, becomes compelling. As a practical matter, because viability follows "quickening"—the point at which a woman feels movement in her womb—and because viability occurs no earlier than 23 weeks gestational age, it establishes an easily applicable standard for regulating abortion while providing a pregnant woman ample time to exercise her fundamental right with her responsible physician to terminate her pregnancy. Although I have stated previously for a majority of this Court that "[c]onstitutional rights do not always have easily ascertainable boundaries," to seek and establish those boundaries remains the special responsibility of this Court. [*Thornburgh*.] In *Roe*, we discharged that responsibility as logic and science compelled. The plurality today advances not one reasonable argument as to why our judgment in that case was wrong and should be abandoned.

C. Having contrived an opportunity to reconsider the *Roe* framework, and then having discarded that framework, the plurality finds the testing provision unobjectionable because it "permissibly furthers the State's interest in protecting potential human life." This newly minted standard is circular and totally meaningless. Whether a challenged abortion regulation "permissibly furthers" a legitimate state interest is the *question* that courts must answer in abortion cases, not the standard for courts to apply. [The] plurality makes no attempt to explain or justify its new standard, either in the abstract or as applied in this case. Nor could it. The "permissibly furthers" standard has no independent meaning, and consists of nothing other than what a majority of this Court may believe at any given moment in any given case. The plurality's novel test appears to be nothing more than a dressed-up version of rational-basis review, this Court's most lenient level of scrutiny. One thing is clear, however: were the plurality's "permissibly furthers" standard adopted by the Court, for all practical purposes, *Roe* would be overruled.

The "permissibly furthers" standard completely disregards the irreducible minimum of *Roe*: the Court's recognition that a woman has a limited fundamental constitutional right to decide whether to terminate a pregnancy. [Since,] in the plurality's view, the State's interest in potential life is compelling as of the moment of conception, and is therefore served only if abortion is abolished, every hindrance to a woman's ability to obtain an abortion must be "permissible." Indeed, the more severe the hindrance, the more effectively (and permissibly) the State's interest would be furthered. A tax on abortions or a criminal prohibition would satisfy the plurality's standard. So, for that matter, would a requirement that a pregnant woman memorize and recite today's plurality opinion before seeking an abortion.

The plurality pretends that *Roe* survives, explaining that the facts of this case differ from those in *Roe*: here, Missouri has chosen to assert its interest in potential life only at the point of viability, whereas, in *Roe*, Texas had asserted that interest from the point of conception, criminalizing all abortions, except where the life of the mother was at stake. This, of course, is a distinction without a difference. [The plurality] cannot possibly believe that *Roe* lies "undisturbed" merely because this case does not call upon the Court to reconsider the Texas statute, or one like it. If the Constitution permits a State to enact any statute that reasonably furthers its interest in potential life, and if that interest arises as of conception, why would the Texas statute fail to pass muster? One suspects that the plurality agrees. It is impossible to read the plurality opinion and especially its final paragraph without recognizing its implicit invitation to every State to enact more and more restrictive abortion laws, and to assert their interest in potential life as of the moment of conception. All these laws will satisfy the plurality's non-scrutiny, until sometime, a new regime of old dissenters and new appointees will declare what the plurality intends: that *Roe* is no longer good law.[3]

---

[3] The plurality claims that its treatment of *Roe*, and a woman's right to decide whether to terminate a pregnancy, "hold(s) true the balance between that which the Constitution puts beyond the reach of the democratic process and that which it does not." This is unadulterated nonsense. The plurality's balance matches a lead weight (the State's allegedly compelling interest in fetal life as of the moment of conception) against a feather (a "liberty interest" of the pregnant woman that the plurality barely mentions, much less describes). The plurality's balance—no balance at all—places nothing, or virtually nothing, beyond the reach of the democratic process. Justice Scalia candidly argues that this is all for the best. I cannot agree. [In] a Nation that cherishes liberty, the ability of a woman to control the biological operation of her body and to determine with her responsible physician whether or not to carry a fetus to term must fall within that limited sphere of individual autonomy that lies beyond the will or power of any transient majority. This Court stands as the ultimate guarantor of that zone of privacy, regardless of the bitter disputes to which our decisions may give rise. In *Roe*, and our numerous cases reaffirming *Roe*, we did no more than discharge our constitutional duty. [Footnote by Justice Blackmun.]

The plurality claims that its treatment of *Roe*, and a woman's right to decide whether to terminate a pregnancy, "hold(s) true the balance between that which the Constitution puts beyond the reach of the democratic process and that which it does not." This is unadulterated nonsense. The plurality's balance matches a lead weight (the State's allegedly compelling interest in fetal life as of the moment of conception) against a feather (a "liberty interest" of the pregnant woman that the plurality barely mentions, much less describes). The plurality's balance—no balance at all—places nothing, or virtually nothing, beyond the reach of the democratic process. Justice Scalia candidly argues that this is all for the best. I cannot agree. [In] a Nation that cherishes liberty, the ability of a woman to control the biological operation of her body and to determine with her responsible physician whether or not to carry a fetus to term must fall within that limited sphere of individual autonomy that lies beyond the will or power of any transient majority. This Court stands as the ultimate guarantor of that zone of privacy, regardless of the bitter disputes to which our decisions may give rise. In *Roe*, and our numerous cases reaffirming *Roe*, we did no more than discharge our constitutional duty. [Footnote by Justice Blackmun.]

D. Thus, "not with a bang, but a whimper," the plurality discards a landmark case [and] casts into darkness the hopes and visions of every woman in this country who had come to believe that the Constitution guaranteed her the right to exercise some control over her unique ability to bear children. The plurality does so either oblivious or insensitive to the fact that the millions of women, and their families, have ordered their lives around the right to reproductive choice, and that this right has become vital to the full participation of women in the economic and political walks of American life. The plurality would clear the way once again for government force upon women the physical labor and specific and direct medical and psychological harms that may accompany carrying a fetus to term. The plurality would clear the way again for the State to conscript a woman's body and to force upon her a "distressful life and future." The result, as we know from experience, would be that every year hundreds of thousands of women, in desperation, would defy the law, and place their health and safety in the unclean and unsympathetic hands of back-alley abortionists, or they would attempt to perform abortions upon themselves with disastrous results. Every year, many women, especially poor and minority women, would die or suffer debilitating physical trauma, all in the name of enforced morality or religious dictates or lack of compassion, as it may be.

Of the aspirations and settled understandings of American women, of the inevitable and brutal consequences of what it is doing, the tough-approach plurality utters not a word. This silence is callous. It is also profoundly destructive of this Court as an institution. To overturn a constitutional decision is a rare and grave undertaking. To overturn a constitutional decision that secured a fundamental personal liberty to millions of persons would be unprecedented in our 200 years of constitutional history. Although the doctrine of stare decisis applies with somewhat diminished force in constitutional cases generally, even in ordinary constitutional cases "any departure from stare decisis demands special justification." [This] requirement of justification applies with unique force where, as here, the Court's abrogation of precedent would destroy people's firm belief, based on past decisions of this Court, that they possess an unabridgeable right to undertake certain conduct. [Today's] decision involves the most politically divisive domestic legal issue of our time. By refusing to explain or to justify its proposed revolutionary revision in the law or abortion, and by refusing to abide not only by our precedents, but also by our canons for reconsidering those precedents, the plurality invites charges of cowardice and illegitimacy to our door. I cannot say that these would be undeserved.

II. For today, at least, the law of abortion stands undisturbed. For today, the women of this Nation still retain the liberty to control their destinies.

But signs are evident and very ominous, and a chill wind blows. I dissent.

Justice Stevens, concurring in part and dissenting in part.

[The] reasons why I [would] affirm [the Court of Appeals'] invalidation of § 188.029, the viability testing provision, and § 1.205.1(1) and (2) of the preamble, require separate explanation.

I. [I] am unable to accept Justice O'Connor's construction of the second sentence in § 188.029. [The] meaning of the second sentence [is] too plain to be ignored. The sentence twice uses the mandatory term "shall," and contains no qualifying language. If it is implicitly limited to tests that are useful in determining viability, it adds nothing to the requirement imposed by the preceding sentence. [I] am satisfied that the [courts below] correctly concluded that the Missouri Legislature meant exactly what it said in the second sentence of § 188.029. I am also satisfied, for the reasons stated by Justice Blackmun, that the testing provision is manifestly unconstitutional under [*Lee Optical*], "irrespective of the *Roe* framework."

II. The Missouri statute defines 'conception" as "the fertilization of the ovum of a female by a sperm of a male," even though standard medical texts equate "conception" with implantation in the uterus, occurring about six days after fertilization. Missouri's declaration therefore implies regulation not only of previability abortions, but also of common forms of contraception such as the IUD and the morning-after pill.[4] Because the preamble, read in context, threatens serious encroachments upon the liberty of the pregnant woman and the health professional, I am persuaded that these plaintiffs, appellees before us, have standing to challenge its constitutionality. To the extent that the Missouri statute interferes with contraceptive choices, I have no doubt that it is unconstitutional under the Court's holding in *Griswold, Eisenstadt,* and *Carey.* [One] might argue that the *Griswold* holding applies to devices "preventing conception"—that is, fertilization—but not to those preventing implantation, and therefore, that *Griswold* does not protect a woman's choice to use an IUD or take a morning-after pill. There is unquestionably a theological basis for such an argument, just as there was

[4] An intrauterine device, commonly called an IUD, "works primarily by preventing a fertilized egg from implanting." Other contraceptive methods that may prevent implantation include "morning-after pills," high-dose estrogen pills taken after intercourse, particularly in cases of rape, and the French RU 486, a pill that works "during the indeterminate period between contraception and abortion." Low level estrogen "combined" pills—a version of the ordinarily, daily ingested birth control pill—also may prevent the fertilized egg from reaching the uterine wall and implanting. [Footnote by Justice Stevens.]

unquestionably a theological basis for the Connecticut statute that the Court invalidated in *Griswold.* Our jurisprudence, however, has consistently required a secular basis for valid legislation. Because I am not aware of any secular basis for differentiating between contraceptive procedures that are effective immediately before and those that are effective immediately after fertilization, I believe it inescapably follows that the preamble to the Missouri statute is invalid under *Griswold* and its progeny. Indeed, I am persuaded that the absence of any secular purpose for the legislative declarations that life begins at conception and that conception occurs at fertilization makes the relevant portion of the preamble invalid under the Establishment Clause of the [First Amendment]. This conclusion does not, and could not, rest on the fact that the statement happens to coincide with the tenets of certain religions, or on the fact that the legislatures who voted to enact it may have been motivated by religious considerations. Rather, it rests on the fact that the preamble, an unequivocal endorsement of a religious tenet of some but by no means all Christian faiths, serves no identifiable secular purpose. That fact alone compels a conclusion that the statute violates the [Establishment Clause].

FACING THE FUTURE: THE REALITY OF *WEBSTER*

The public perception of what the justices said—and did not say—was almost as important as the actual opinion. Reaction to *Webster* can best be analyzed by looking at the groups impacted and their immediate response. The media, including polling organizations, sought to find and report public opinion in general; experts called attention to state legislatures and pursued a state-by-state analysis of local elites' responses. Legal actors other than federal courts were suggested as new players in the coming abortion struggle. Finally, probing the possible response of national leaders continued as a hot topic for analysis and prediction.

Polling organizations such as Gallup/*Newsweek* and CBS News/*New York Times* moved immediately to measure the public's reaction to *Webster.* They documented a change from earlier positions: a nineteen-point margin of pro-choice over pro-life attitudes emerged. Public opinion supported leaving reproductive choice legal and available, and more than three-quarters of Americans supported a woman's right to choose an abortion. When the question "Should *Roe* be overturned?" was posed, the answer was clear: 62 percent said no.[216]

Some analysts predicted a new support for abortion in all cases. Moreover, the level of activism of those supporting abortion rights grew dramatically following *Webster*. Pro-choice supporters had always been statistically more numerous than pro-life supporters, but *Webster* galvanized the former group into action, according to the polls. Twice as many donated money to organizations supporting abortion rights; twice as many also wrote letters to elected officials, up from 7 percent in 1979 to 15 percent in 1989. Thus, the Supreme Court's *Webster* decision, apparently giving states increased regulatory power over abortion, made abortion a very hot political issue for the future.[217]

The timing of *Webster*, however, prevented many states from reacting immediately. In many states, the legislative sessions were over before the opinion was handed down in July 1989. However, this did not prevent immediate responses from other state legislatures and political elites across the nation. Within hours of the Supreme Court's ruling, the battle lines began to emerge. From Pennsylvania to Utah, legislatures and state officials were advocating state laws that would match—or go beyond—the Missouri law that the Supreme Court had upheld. "I'm sure that our legislature will rush to enact provisions of the Missouri abortion law," said Louisiana Attorney General William J. Guste Jr. "The Supreme Court has opened the door."[218]

Others also promised to use the Missouri law as a blueprint for restricting abortions in their states. In Michigan, state senator Jack Welborn said he had drafted a measure based mainly on the Missouri law and that he would push for Michigan's legislature to approve the bill. Alabama governor Guy Hunt pledged to "take legal steps to restrict abortion in Alabama" and that he would propose "specific action that the state of Alabama will take" to implement the *Webster* ruling. In Nebraska, State Senator Bernice Labedz said she would draft a law modeled on the Missouri statute "that will go about as far as we can go" to restrict abortion. The state attorney general in Idaho and some legislators in Wyoming predicted that their states would enact tougher abortion laws in response to *Webster*. Pennsylvania state representative Stephen Friend declared, "*Webster* means we can go a hell of a lot further in restricting abortion." Robert Gentzel, a spokesman for Pennsylvania attorney general Ernest D. Preate Jr. said that Pennsylvania laws on fetal viability would, as a result of *Webster*, be upheld in the courts.[219]

In Missouri, Andrew F. Puzder and Samuel Lee, the bill's drafters, rejoiced. "The end for legalized abortion is in sight," Puzder insisted. "In practice, *Webster* will reverse *Roe v. Wade.*" Puzder believed that the Supreme Court was extending an invitation to Missouri to draft a law that outlawed all abortions. Lee suggested, "Maybe what we'll go for is [a law] to prohibit all abortions except to preserve the life or health of the mother." For Louis de Feo, the lobbyist for the Missouri Catholic Conference, only the *life* of the mother was sufficient to allow abortion. His goal was "to get as close to that as we can."[220]

Governor John Ashcroft, agreeing with de Feo, called for even more restrictive regulations and announced that he would call for a special legislative session and appoint "an advisory task force for mothers and unborn children." He promised that he would choose only people who shared his opposition to abortion. "We in Missouri will press on to protect the lives of our future generations and literally, to protect the future of the state," he said. "*Roe v. Wade* is inevitably destined to become a dead letter of American legal history." As he prepared for the special legislative session beginning July 5, Ashcroft promised to consult with members concerning appointment to his panel. His goal, he stated, was to "prohibit abortion like we [did] prior to 1973."[221]

Many of the state legislators in Missouri, however, openly voiced their dismay at the prospect of being the center of abortion policy making. Had Missouri legislators merely played politics when they passed restriction after restriction between 1973 and 1989? Had they believed that they could appease pro-life voters in Missouri, secure in the belief that the Supreme Court would strike down their laws? The shock and dismay that shook many of the state legislators with the announcement of the *Webster* decision and its green light to the state's restrictions seemed to answer these questions in the affirmative.[222]

Beginning with the speaker of the state assembly and moving through the ranks of Missouri state legislators, one after another began to back away from the precipice. On July 10, 1989, only six days after *Webster* hit the press, State Senator Wayne Goode (D-Normandy) commented, "There's a whole bunch of people in the middle [of the abortion controversy] who wish this [*Webster*] had never come along." Representative Robert J. Quinn Jr. (D-Ferguson) noted, "Nobody's going to get any rest." When Governor John Ashcroft promised more abortion regulations—ones that would be "substantial and comprehensive"—more state legislators began to balk. Some who had previously voted for abortion restrictions said they wanted "to go no further." Senator Robert T. Johnson (R-Lee's Summit) said that the current Missouri law was adequate. "I hope we don't bury our heads in the sand and try to outlaw abortion," Johnson said. "If we do, we'll bring back the coat hangers." Senate President Pro Tem James L. Mathewson (D-Sedalia), while terming himself a "hard-core, 100% pro-lifer," said he would "hesitate to further limit abortion." "Based on where Missouri law is, we've kind of done it," Mathewson said, adding, "we don't need any more laws on abortion."[223]

The Missouri Senate had always voted pro-life: only five of the thirty-four senators had opposed abortion restrictions at the time of the *Webster* decisions. These five were all Democrats from the large cities. However, *Webster* raised the specter of the total outlawing of abortion, and according to pro-choice senator, and later lieutenant governor, Roger Wilson (D-Columbia), some antiabortion legislators were ready to switch sides. "You're going to push people beyond what they feel personally comfortable with," he said. Representative Gracia Y. Backer (D-New Bloomfield) predicted that the issue would become "very mean, very nasty." Representative S. Sue Shearer (D-Clayton) agreed, noting that the Supreme Court had deprived state legislatures of their cover. However, some Missouri state legislators still hoped that some other actor would rescue them from their predicament. These legislators urged waiting to see how the Supreme Court would deal with three additional cases in the wake of *Webster.* Senator Richard M. Webster (R-Carthage), father of Attorney General William Webster, urged caution in enacting any more restrictions on abortion. "I haven't thought about where we go next," he said. "I don't think we need to go anywhere."[224]

The inaction of the task force appointed by Governor Ashcroft also signaled that abortion foes faced a very different climate of opinion in post-*Webster* Missouri politics. Appointed in July, the task force met only twice before the end of the year, and one of the meetings was merely a telephone conference call. By December, Ashcroft's appointees admitted they were stalled. The task force's inaction was highlighted when its chairman, Andrew Puzder, resigned on October 4, 1989. Some attributed Puzder's action to the negative publicity resulting from allegations that he had assaulted his ex-wife. In July, following his appointment to the governor's task force, the *St. Louis Post-Dispatch* and other newspapers had printed reports based on court documents in which Puzder's ex-wife, Lisa Heuning, said Puzder had choked, hit, and kicked her. Puzder had responded that his wife had tripped and fallen and that he had not struck her, but he soon resigned.[225]

Without any recommendations from his body, Governor Ashcroft was left without an abortion agenda as the legislature prepared to convene in January 1990. In addition, with both Democratic leaders of the House and Senate now refusing to appoint any legislators to the task force, its legitimacy as a policy-recommending group was destroyed. Mathewson, the senate president pro tem, and House Speaker Bob F. Griffin stated that the governor's decision to include only people active in the antiabortion cause as task force members was unacceptable, and they refused to deal with this group. The state legislative session of late 1989 and 1990 showed, in general, that *Webster* was a Pandora's box and no-win situation for most.

By the time the Missouri legislature met for its regular session, the drive to limit the abortion procedure in Missouri was clearly slowing down. As the legislative session prepared to open in January 1990, four developments cast doubt on the antiabortion movement's chance for continued success in Missouri. Speaker Griffin, who had voted with the antiabortion forces in the past, went on record as now wanting to keep abortion legal. He met with abortion rights supporters and encouraged them to start an initiative petition drive for a state constitutional amendment guaranteeing a woman's right to an abortion. Senate President Pro Tem James Mathewson also made it clear that he now wanted the Missouri legislature to stay away from the abortion issue in 1990. As president pro tem, Mathewson had power to bury a bill in the Missouri Senate by assigning it to an unfriendly committee, and he indicated his willingness to do this. Moreover, even those key legislators who spearheaded the abortion law upheld in *Webster* began to urge caution by the year's end. Representative Jim Barnes and Senator John Schneider said they saw no need to work on the abortion issue. "Missouri doesn't need to be leading the charge in all of this," said Barnes. Representative Judith O'Connor, another legislator who fought for abortion restrictions, declared that she was satisfied with the status quo. "We have some pretty good laws on the books," said O'Connor. "I don't think pro-life is going to do anything real drastic. The consensus is, they're not going to go 'hog-wild.'"[226]

Did *Webster* lead to more abortion restrictions in the states? Was it the victory pro-lifers had acclaimed it to be? Statistics show that only fourteen states actually enacted any abortion laws in the two-year period following *Webster*. Nine states made abortion more difficult, while five states passed laws liberalizing abortion. Connecticut's General Assembly legalized all abortions prior to viability, Maryland enacted the *Roe* guarantees into state law, Nevada liberalized its laws, and Washington State passed a Reproductive Privacy Act guaranteeing choice. State legislators in Florida soundly defeated attempts by their pro-life governor, Bob Martinez, to enact abortion restrictions à la *Webster*. In Louisiana and Utah, however, abortion practically became illegal, as it had been before 1973. The Louisiana legislature, in spite of opinion polls showing that a majority of voters wanted abortion to be kept legal, passed a "life begins at conception" bill outlawing almost all abortions.[227] The Louisiana attorney general openly declared that he would enforce the new law to create a challenge to *Roe v. Wade* yet again. Utah legislators moved to enact Mormon theology into law and in early 1991 criminalized abortion.

Would those voters who wanted abortion to be kept legal at the state level speak decisively about abortion restrictions in the wake of *Webster*? Would they impact state elections for the legislature and for the governor's office? In the six months that remained in 1989 following *Webster*, there were only a few state races where voters could register an impact. In Virginia, a pro-choice African American, Douglas Wilder, was elected governor in a race that clearly drew its lines on the abortion issue. Exit polls showed that Wilder's pro-choice stand had attracted suburban young professionals who disliked the Republican antiabortion position. This was also true in New Jersey, where pro-choice women voters helped elect Jim Florio over the incumbent governor who supported new state laws to restrict abortion. A 1989 state legislative race in California demonstrated that *Webster* had generated negative impact. A pro-choice Catholic woman candidate, Lucy Killea, won an upset victory over her pro-life opponent.

As 1989 gave way to 1990, a number of pro-choice governors were elected to the statehouses: Florida, Texas, and California all shifted from pro-life incumbents to pro-choice candidates. Many governors who had refused to take a stand in the years before *Webster* now declared themselves, so that by the close of the 1990 elections the position of every governor was known. The elections increased the number of governors who favored keeping abortion legal from sixteen to twenty-seven and the number of state legislative bodies from twenty-three to forty-five.[228]

However, by November 1991, many political analysts believed that the public's attention was so focused on other issues that the challenge of *Webster* was being overshadowed. There had been few significant state races in 1991, and thus the impact of *Webster* waited on pending events. These came with the decision of the U.S. Supreme Court to hear a challenge to Pennsylvania's post-*Webster* restrictive abortion law. The case was *Planned Parenthood of Southeastern Pennsylvania v. Casey.*[229] It would be decided on the eve of the 1992 presidential election. *Webster's* impact would finally be assessed.

NOTES

1. David Rohde and Harold Spaeth, *Supreme Court Decision Making* (San Francisco: Freeman, 1976), 155.

2. Charles H. Sheldon, *The American Judicial Process: Models and Approaches* (New York: Dodd, Mead, 1976), 24–29.

3. *Webster v. Reproductive Health Services,* 492 U.S. 490 (1989).

4. *Roe v. Wade,* 410 U.S. 113 (1973).

5. *Planned Parenthood of Central Missouri v. Danforth,* 428 U.S. 52 (1976).

6. *Planned Parenthood Association of Kansas City, Missouri, Inc. v. Ashcroft,* 462 U.S. 476 (1983).

7. Andrew F. Puzder, "Rights of the Unborn Child: Missouri Statute Reaches High Court Because it Declares Life Begins at Conception," *St. Louis Post-Dispatch,* 25 April 1989.

8. Martha Shirk, "Reversal? Many Aimed for Court Test," *St. Louis Post-Dispatch,* 23 April 1989.

9. Ibid.

10. Ibid.

11. *Poelker v. Doe,* 432 U.S. 519 (1977).

12. Shirk, "Reversal?"

13. Ibid.

14. William H. Freivogel, "Justices to Review State Law," *St. Louis Post-Dispatch,* 10 January 1989.

15. Terry Ganey, "Ashcroft Stresses Conservative Roots," *St. Louis Post-Dispatch,* 5 July 1984.

16. William H. Freivogel, "Courtship: State Attorney General Has Successful Agenda," *St. Louis Post-Dispatch,* 2 November 1989.

17. Ibid.

18. Ibid.

19. William H. Freivogel, "Justices to Review State Law."

20. Shirk, "Reversal?"

21. Ibid.

22. Dale Singer, "Webster Sees Hope for Upholding Abortion Curbs," *St. Louis Post-Dispatch*, 20 September 1986.

23. Ibid.

24. Shirk, "Reversal?"

25. William H. Freivogel, "New Attack on Abortion: Administration's Brief Targets Constitutionality," *St. Louis Post-Dispatch*, 24 February 1989.

26. Ibid. See also Craig and O'Brien, *Abortion and American Politics*, chapter 6.

27. "Brief for American Medical Association, et al. as *Amici Curiae*," *Webster v. Reproductive Health Services*, 88–605, 42.

28. "Brief of 281 American Historians as *Amici Curiae* Supporting Appellees," *Webster v. Reproductive Health Services*, 88–605, 31, 30 March 1989.

29. Susan Behuniak-Long, "Friendly Fire: Amicus Curiae and *Webster v. Reproductive Health Systems*," *Judicature* 74 (February–March 1991): 261–270. Among the groups supporting Reproductive Health Services were Americans United for Separation of Church and State, Religious Coalition for Reproductive Choice, the Presbyterian Church (U.S.A.) the General Board of Church and Society of the United Methodist Church, and Judson Memorial Church (American Baptist, New York City). It should be noted that Justice Stevens mainly focused on these briefs filed by religious organizations. His questions in argument and his written dissent indicated their impact on him. See Craig and O'Brien, *Abortion and American Politics*, 214, 218, 226.

30. *Griswold v. Connecticut*, 381 U.S. 479 (1965).

31. *Eisenstadt v. Baird*, 405 U.S. 438 (1972).

32. Kathleen M. Sullivan and Gerald Gunther, *Constitutional Law*, 14th ed. (New York: Foundation Press, 2001), 531–537.

33. *Doe v. Bolton*, 410 U.S. 179 (1973).

34. *Bigelow v. Virginia*, 421 U.S. 809 (1975).

35. *Bellotti v. Baird*, 428 U.S. 132 (1976).

36. *Planned Parenthood of Central Missouri v. Danforth*, 438 U.S. 52 (1976).

37. *Carey v. Population Services International*, 431 U.S. 678 (1977).

38. *Poelker v. Doe*, 432 U.S. 519 (1977); *Beal v. Doe*, 432 U.S. 438 (1977); *Maher v. Roe*, 432 U.S. 464 (1977).

39. *Colautti v. Franklin*, 439 U.S. 379 (1979).

40. *H. L. v. Matheson, Governor of Utah, et al.*, 450 U.S. 398 (1981).

41. *City of Akron v. Abortion Center for Reproductive Health*, 462 U.S. 476 (1983).

42. *Simopoulos v. Virginia*, 462 U.S. 506 (1983).

43. *Thornburgh v. American College of Obstetricians and Gynecologists*, 476 U.S. 747 (1986).

44. Craig and O'Brien, *Abortion and American Politics*, 97–100.

45. *Bellotti v. Baird*, 443 U.S. 622 (1979); *Harris v. McRae*, 448 U.S. 297 (1980); *Williams et al. v. Zbaraz et al.*, 448 U.S. 358 (1980).

46. *H. L. v. Matheson*, 450 U.S. 398 (1981).

47. *City of Akron v. Akron Center for Reproductive Health*, 462 U.S. 476 (1983). *Planned Parenthood Association v. Ashcroft*, 462 U.S. 416 (1983).

48. *Thornburgh v. American College of Obstetricians and Gynecologists*, 476 U.S. 747 (1986).

49. James F. Simon, *The Center Holds: The Power Struggle inside the Rehnquist Court* (New York: Simon & Schuster, 1995), 31.

50. Ibid.

51. William H. Rehnquist, *The Supreme Court: How It Was, How It Is* (New York: Morrow, 1987), 20.

52. *Terry v. Adams*, 345 U.S. 461 (1953). *Brown v. Board of Education*, 347 U.S. 483 (1954).

53. Simon, *The Center Holds*, 36. See also William H. Rehnquist, "Who Writes Decisions of the Supreme Court?" *U.S. News and World Report*, 13 December 1957, 74–75.

54. *Roe v. Wade*, 410 U.S. 171, 172, 174, Rehnquist's dissenting opinion. See also Del Dickson, ed., *The Supreme Court in Conference, 1940–1985: The Private Discussions behind Nearly 300 Supreme Court Decisions* (New York: Oxford University Press, 2001), 806–807.

55. David J. Garrow, *Liberty and Sexuality: The Right to Privacy and the Making of* Roe v. Wade, rev. ed. (Berkeley: University of California Press, 1998), 597.

56. *Poe v. Ullman*, 367 U.S. 497 (1961); *Griswold v. Connecticut*, 381 U.S. 479 (1965).

57. Kim Eisler, *A Justice for All: William J. Brennan, Jr., and the Decisions That Transformed America* (New York: Simon & Schuster, 1993). See also Stephan J. Markman and Alfred S. Regnery, "The Mind of Justice Brennan: A 25-Year Tribute," *National Review* 36, no. 9 (18 May 1984), 30.

58. N. Hentoff, "Profile: The Constitutionalist," *New Yorker*, March 1990. See also E. Joshua Rosenkranz and Bernard Schwartz, *Reason and Passion: Justice Brennan's Enduring Influence* (New York: Norton, 1997).

59. Hentoff, "Profile: The Constitutionalist."

60. Simon, *The Center Holds*, 49.

61. Garrow, *Liberty and Sexuality*, 246–247.

62. Ibid., 193.

63. Dickson, *Supreme Court in Conference*, 800–803.

64. Jeffrey T. Leeds, "A Life on the Court," *New York Times*, 5 October 1986. See also Simon, *The Center Holds*, 50.

65. *Eisenstadt v. Baird*, 405 U.S. 438 (1972), Brennan opinion.

66. Roger Goldman, *Justice William J. Brennan, Jr.: Freedom First*, with David Gallen (New York: Carroll & Graf, 1994).

67. William J. Brennan, speech to the Law Society in London, 10 July 1961.

68. Leeds, "A Life on the Court."

69. "The Making of a Justice," *New York Times*, 8 October 1972.

70. Garrow, *Liberty and Sexuality*, 250–251.

71. "White, Byron R(aymond)," in *Current Biography Yearbook, 1962*, ed. Charles Moritz (New York: H. W. Wilson, 1962), 460. See also the opinion by White in *Robinson v. California*, 370 U.S. 660 (1962).

72. Garrow, *Liberty and Sexuality*, 240.

73. Ibid., 243–244.

74. Stephen Wasby, ed., *"He Shall Not Pass This Way Again": The Legacy of Justice William O. Douglas* (Pittsburgh: University of Pittsburgh Press, 1990), 26n8.

75. White was suggesting the use of *Robinson v. California*, 370 U.S. 660 (1962); see Garrow, *Liberty and Sexuality*, 244.

76. Ibid., 240.

77. Stuart Taylor Jr., "Police May Search People's Trash without a Warrant, Court Rules," *New York Times*, 17 May 1998.

78. *United States v. Vuitch*, 399 U.S. 923 (1970).

79. Wasby, *He Shall Not Pass This Way Again*, 26n8.

80. See Justice White's dissent in *Roe v. Wade*, 410 U.S. 113 (1973) and *Doe v. Bolton*, 410 U.S. 221, 22 (1973).

81. "Transcript of Oral Arguments before Court on Abortion Case," *New York Times*, 27 April 1989.

82. The phrase "policy predilections" is used in *Sinclair v. Atkins*, 370 U.S. 175 (1962), 13. It has a long history dating back to the court fight over the New Deal laws in the 1930s as justices accused each other of voting their "policy predilections."

83. Justice Thurgood Marshall, writing for the Court in *Stanley v. Georgia*, 394 U.S. 557 (1969).

84. Garrow, *Liberty and Sexuality*, 583.

85. Walter F. Murphy, *Elements of Judicial Strategy* (Chicago: University of Chicago Press, 1964), 4.

86. Mark Tushnet, *Making Civil Rights Law: Thurgood Marshall and the Supreme Court, 1961–1991* (New York: Oxford University Press, 1997), 8.

87. "Marshall, Thurgood," in *Current Biography Yearbook, 1989*, ed. Charles Moritz (New York: H. W. Wilson, 1989), 377–381, quote on 378.

88. Linda Greenhouse, "Ex-Justice Thurgood Marshall Dies at 84," *New York Times*, 25 January 1993.

89. Gary A. Hengstler, "Justice Thurgood Marshall: Looking Back, Reflections on a Life Well-Spent," *American Bar Association Journal* 78 (1992): 58.

90. Tushnet, *Making Civil Rights Law*, 186.

91. Hengstler, "Justice Thurgood Marshall," 74.

92. James F. Simon, *In His Own Image: The Supreme Court in Richard Nixon's America* (New York: D. McKay, 1973), 141–148.

93. A decision-making model, the "think tank," uses game strategy to identify options available and possible repercussions. See Andrew Rich, *Think Tanks, Public Policy, and the Politics of Expertise* (Cambridge: Cambridge University Press, 2004). Think tanks are composed of experts in many different areas. They debate policy choices to provide a range of choices for decision makers. According to Rich, they "offer rapidly developing techniques for making assumptions explicit and then testing their validity in terms of value and actualities" (5). President John F. Kennedy set up a think tank in the Oval Office to deal with the Cuban Missile Crisis. This method of decision making is rated as the ideal by most political scientists, and Justice Harry Blackmun used this method to reach his judicial decisions.

94. United States Senate, Committee on the Judiciary, *The Supreme Court of the United States: Hearings and Reports on Successful and Unsuccessful Nominations of Supreme Court Justices by the Senate Judiciary Committee, 1916–1972*, comp. Roy M. Mersky and J. Myron Jacobstein, vol. 8 (Buffalo, NY: W. S. Hein, 1974).

95. Ibid.

96. Ibid.

97. Eloise Snyder, "The Supreme Court as a Small Group," *Social Forces* 36 (March 1958): 232–238.

98. Garrow, *Liberty and Sexuality*, 590–593.

99. "Mr. Justice Blackmun," *In Search of the Constitution* series, video, 59 min. (Alexandria, VA: PBS Video, 1987).

100. Bob Woodward and Scott Armstrong, *The Brethren: Inside the Supreme Court* (New York: Simon & Schuster, 1979), 183, 231–232.

101. Wayne C. Bartee and Alice Fleetwood Bartee, *Litigating Morality: American Legal Thought and Its English Roots* (New York: Praeger, 1993), chap. 1. See also Garrow, *Liberty and Sexuality*, 589.

102. John A. Jenkins, "A Candid Talk with Justice Brennan," *New York Times*, 20 February 1983. For more on Methodist theology, see the United Methodist Church's *Book of Discipline*.

103. Simon, *The Center Holds*, 227. See also David M. O'Brien, "The Politics of Professionalism: President Gerald R. Ford's Appointment of Justice John Paul Stevens," *Presidential Studies Quarterly* 21, no. 1 (Winter 1991): 103–127.

104. Stuart Taylor Jr., "The Last Moderate," *American Lawyers*, June 1990.

105. O'Brien, "The Politics of Professionalism."

106. Simon, *The Center Holds*, 227–229. See also Fowler V. Harper, *Mr. Justice Rutledge and the Bright Constellation* (Indianapolis, IN: Bobbs-Merrill, 1965).

107. H. Leon McBeth, *The Baptist Heritage* (Nashville, TN: Broadman Press, 1987), 64–68. Chief Justice Charles Evans Hughes was also an American (Northern) Baptist and was elected the first president of the American Baptist Convention in 1906. Baptists had split over slavery in the 1840s. See also *Current Biography Yearbook, 1976*, ed. Charles Moritz (New York: H. W. Wilson, 1976), 392, "He [Stevens] is a Baptist and a Republican."

108. Justice Stevens's dissent in *Webster* was the only one that focused on the issue of whether the Missouri statute violated the First Amendment's prohibition against the establishment of religion. His concern for the maintenance of the Baptists' doctrine of separation of church and state can be found in his address "The Bill of Rights: A Century of Progress," delivered at the University of Chicago Law School on October 25, 1991.

109. United States Senate, Committee on the Judiciary, *The Supreme Court of the United States*.

110. O'Brien, "The Politics of Professionalism."

111. "Stevens, John Paul," in *Current Biography Yearbook, 1976*, 391. In a Seventh Circuit Court of Appeals decision, Stevens held that privacy in the home was a preferred freedom.

112. *Groppi v. Wisconsin*, 41 Wis.2d. 312, 164 N.W.2d 266 (1971), 7th.

113. "Stevens, John Paul," 392, references Stevens's view on the Equal Rights Amendment.

114. *Sprogis v. United Airlines*, 44 F.2d. 1194 (1971).

115. *Washington County v. Gunther*, 452 U.S. 161 (1981).

116. McBeth, *The Baptist Heritage*, 202–285.

117. United States Senate, Committee on the Judiciary, *Hearing on the Nomination of Judge Sandra Day O'Connor of Arizona to Serve as an Associate Justice of the Supreme Court of the United States*, 97th Cong., 1st sess., 1981, 57–58.

118. David D. Savage, *Turning Right: The Making of the Rehnquist Supreme Court* (New York: Wiley, 1992), 111–116.

119. The phrase "discrete and insular minority" was created in footnote 4 of *United States v. Carolene Products Co.*, 304 U.S. 144 (1938) and numerous groups have sought protection under it. The footnote contains three paragraphs, the most famous and influential being its third, which calls for Court intervention to protect, "discrete and insular minorities." O'Connor followed that approach in her early years. On the origin of footnote, see Louis Lusky, "Footnote Redux: A *Carolene Products* Reminiscence," *Columbia Law Review* 82 (October 1982): 1093.

120. United States Senate, Committee on the Judiciary, *Hearing on the Nomination of Judge Sandra Day O'Connor*, 57–58.

121. Ibid. The *New York Times* carried eleven articles dealing with Justice O'Connor's formative years and pre-Court career between June and September 1983.

122. Beverly Cook, "Justice Sandra Day O'Connor: Transition to a Republican Court Agenda," in *The Burger Court: Political and Judicial Profiles*, ed. Charles Lamb and Stephen Halpern (Urbana: University of Illinois, 1991), 242, 264–265, 271.

123. United States Senate, Committee on the Judiciary, *Hearing on the Nomination of Judge Sandra Day O'Connor*, 57–58.

124. Ibid.

125. Howard Kohn, "Front and Center on a Changing Supreme Court, Sandra Day O'Connor Has Emerged as a New Power, Especially on the Issue That Will Not Go Away: Abortion," *Los Angeles Times*, 18 April 1993, magazine section.

126. Richard A. Cordray and James T. Vradelis, "The Emerging Jurisprudence of Justice O'Connor," *University of Chicago Law Review* 52 (Spring 1985). 389–459.

127. Garrow, *Liberty and Sexuality*, 640–643.

128. *City of Akron v. Akron Center for Reproductive Health*, 462 U.S. 416 (1983). See Justice O'Connor's dissent with its famous phrases "undue burden" and "collision course with itself."

129. Ibid.

130. *Thornburgh v. American College of Obstetricians and Gynecologists*, 476 U.S. 747 (1986). See Justice O'Connor's dissent.

131. Cordray and Vradelis, "Emerging Jurisprudence," 389–459.

132. Joan Biskupic, "No Shades of Gray for Scalia: Conservative Justice's Biting Opinions, Jabs at Fellow Jurists Add Spice and Tension to the Supreme Court—and Suggest His Frustration Is Increasing," *USA Today*, 18 September 2002.

133. "Scalia, Antonin," in *Current Biography Yearbook, 1986*, ed. Charles Moritz (New York: H. W. Wilson, 1986), 502–505.

134. Antonin Scalia, "Commentary: The Decision as Cure," *Washington Law Quarterly* (1979): 147–157, quote on 153.

135. Ibid., 152.

136. Jeffrey Rosen, "The Leader of the Opposition: The Tortuous Jurisprudence of Antonin Scalia," *New Republic* 208, no. 3 (18 January 2003): 20–25.

137. "Scalia, Antonin," in *Current Biography Yearbook, 1986*, 502–503.

138. Jeffrey Rosen, "Leader of the Opposition," 23.

139. Ibid., 22–23.

140. Ibid., 23.

141. "Scalia, Antonin," in *Current Biography Yearbook, 1986*, 502–503.

142. Scalia, "Decision as Cure," 253.

143. Richard A. Brisbin Jr., "The Conservatism of Antonin Scalia," *Political Science Quarterly* 105, no. 1 (Spring 1990): 1–2.

144. Ibid., 16–17, 27.

145. Ibid., 28–29.

146. Biskupic, "No Shades of Gray for Scalia."

147. "Scalia, Antonin," in *Current Biography Yearbook, 1986*, 504.

148. Ibid.

149. "Justice Kennedy," *U.S. News and World Report*, 17 July 1989.

150. Simon, *The Center Holds*, 67.

151. Ibid.

152. Stuart Taylor Jr., "Speeches Offering Insight Into Judge Kennedy," *New York Times*, 1 December 1987.

153. "Judge Kennedy: In His Own Words," *New York Times*, 1 December 1987.

154. "Kennedy, Anthony M(cLeod)," in *Current Biography Yearbook, 1988*, ed. Charles Moritz (New York: H. W. Wilson, 1988), 289.

155. Ibid.

156. *Beller v. Middendorf*, 632 S.2d. 788 (9th Circuit, 1980). Kennedy's decision was actually a very narrow one, limited to the case facts. Naval regulations and the necessity for order were central to Kennedy's decision. In dicta, he declared that discharge of homosexuals from the Navy was harsh and not necessarily wise. In other places and circumstances, he concluded homosexuals could be entitled to constitutional protection. This was a significant loophole.

157. *AFSCME v. State of Washington*, 770 F.2d. 1401 (9th Circuit, 1985). See George J. Church, "Far More Judicious," *Time*, November 1987.

158. Simon, *The Center Holds*, 69.

159. *AFSCME v. State of Washington*.

160. Linda Greenhouse, "Justice Kennedy Says Rights Are Not Always Spelled Out," *New York Times*, 5 December 1987.

161. Ibid.

162. Unless otherwise stated, all quoted material in this section regarding the oral argument in *Webster* is taken from "Transcript of Oral Arguments Before Court on Abortion Case," *New York Times*, 27 April 1989.

163. Attorney General Webster had delivered just three paragraphs when Justice O'Connor interrupted with, ". . . is that the argument you made below [in the lower courts]?"

164. Andrew Puzder, "Rights of the Unborn Child . . . Missouri Statute Reaches High Court Because It Declares Life Begins at Conception," *St. Louis Post-Dispatch*, 25 April 1989.

165. Ibid.

166. Early in the oral argument, Justice Stevens asked eight questions in rapid-fire succession dealing with the number and types of tests required by the Missouri Senate.

167. Garrow, *Liberty and Sexuality*, 174–175, 190–191.

168. Ibid.

169. Lincoln Caplan, *The Tenth Justice: The Solicitor General and the Rule of Law* (New York: Alfred A. Knopf, 1987). See also Rebecca Mae Salokar, *The Solicitor General: Politics of Law* (Philadelphia: Temple University Press, 1992).

170. Jeffrey Toobin, "Supreme Sacrifice," in *Portraits of American Politics*, ed. Bruce Allen Murphy, 3rd ed. (Boston: Houghton Mifflin, 2000), 420–428. See also Savage, *Turning Right*, 385–399.

171. Philip Shenon, "Profiles of the Three Advocates in the Appeal," *New York Times*, 27 April 1989.

172. Ibid., B12. Justice O'Connor had asked, "Do you say there is no fundamental right to decide whether to have a child or not?" Fried's evasive answer, "I think that that question . . . ," apparently shocked the justice. She interrupted with these queries.

173. Charles Fried used his famous phrase, "pull this one thread," in the fifth sentence of his opening remarks. Frank Susman responded as soon as he took the podium. The laughter in the courtroom, quickly repressed, showed that Susman had scored.

174. Susman named IUDs and low-dose birth control pills as "abortifacients," yet noted that the public perceived them as "contraceptives."

175. O'Connor distinguished her positions in *Thornburgh* and *Akron* on page 531 of *Webster v. Reproductive Health Services*. See also Craig and O'Brien, *Abortion and American Politics*, 226–227.

176. Susman linked Attorney General Webster's tactics in the *Reproductive Health Services* case to those in *Cruzan v. Director, Missouri Department of Health*, 497 U.S. 261 (1990). In both cases, the state attorney general had told the Court that the statutes "do not mean what they say."

177. Garrow, *Liberty and Sexuality*, 675.

178. *Webster v. Reproductive Health Services*, 492 U.S. 490 (1989).

179. Ibid., 522–531.

180. Ibid., 532–537.

181. Ibid., 537–560.

182. Ibid., 560–572.

183. Ibid., 521.

184. Ibid., 511–513.

185. Murphy, *Elements of Judicial Strategy*, 4.

186. Justice Louis Brandeis in *Ashwander v. Tennessee Valley Authority*, 297 U.S. 288, 346 (1936).

187. Ibid.

188. *Webster v. Reproductive Health Services*, 525–526. See also Murphy, *Elements of Judicial Strategy*, 208.

189. *City of Akron v. Akron Center for Reproductive Health*, 462 U.S. 416 (1983).

190. *Webster v. Reproductive Health Services*, 531. See also Craig and O'Brien, *Abortion and American Politics*, 226–227.

191. *Webster v. Reproductive Health Services*, 533.

192. Murphy, *Elements of Judicial Strategy*, 55.

193. Simon, *The Center Holds*, 141.

194. Garrow, *Liberty and Sexuality*, 677–679.

195. Murphy, *Elements of Judicial Strategy*, 29. See also Stephen L. Wasby, *The Supreme Court in the Federal Judicial System*, 4th ed. (Chicago: Nelson-Hall, 1993), 33.

196. Alexander Bickel, *The Least Dangerous Branch: The Supreme Court at the Bar of Politics* (Indianapolis, IN: Bobbs-Merrill, 1962), 88.

197. Richard Posner, *The Federal Courts: Crisis and Reform* (Cambridge, MA: Harvard University Press, 1985), 205.

198. *Ashwander v. Tennessee Valley Authority*, 346.

199. *Webster v. Reproductive Health Services*, 537–560.

200. "Judicial activism" refers to the belief that the Court has a special obligation to use its powers to protect rights, including individual rights. Footnote 4 of *U.S. v. Carolene Products* lists some of the areas calling for this special protection.

201. For judicial tests, see Dickson, *Supreme Court in Conference*, 822–823. See also van Geel, *Understanding Supreme Court Opinions*, 153, for the definition of "standards of review."

202. Justice O'Connor's "unduly burdensome" test owes its origin to the phrase used by Justice Blackmun in *Bellotti v. Baird*, 428 U.S. 132 (1976) (*Baird I*). It has been compared to Justice Felix Frankfurter's "shock of conscience" test from *Rochin v. California* and is open to judicial idiosyncratic interpretations.

203. Statutory analysis is the procedure used by justices to give meaning to the laws passed by Congress. It involves a focus on the meaning of words to explain the law on its face or as written.

204. *Webster v. Reproductive Health Services*, 529–543.

205. "Framers' intent" is another name for originalism. It interprets the Constitution by focusing on the debates at the Constitutional Convention and the meaning of the words or consequences of the text in 1789. See van Geel, *Understanding Supreme Court Opinions*, 45.

206. *West Virginia State Board of Education v. Barnette*, 319 U.S. 624 (1943). Justice Jackson's prose is still regarded as a masterpiece of judicial thought.

207. Van Geel, *Understanding Supreme Court Opinions*, 57.

208. *Brown v. Board of Education*, 347 U.S. 483 (1954). See Chief Justice Earl Warren's footnote 7 in which he lists articles based on sociological and psychological data, particularly K. B. Clark, "Effect of Prejudice and Discrimination on Personality Development" (Washington, DC: Midcentury White House Conference on Children and Youth, 1950).

209. *Webster v. Reproductive Health Services*, 543. Blackmun cited statistics from Willard Cates Jr. and Robert W. Rochat, "Illegal Abortions in the United States, 1972–1974," *Family Planning Perspectives* 8, no. 2 (March–April 1976): 86–92.

210. *Webster v. Reproductive Health Services*, 543. See also the American Medical Association's amicus curiae brief for *Webster*.

211. Justice O'Connor's citation and reliance on the American Medical Association's brief in *Webster* occupied an entire paragraph on page 531 of the decision.

212. Murphy, *Elements of Judicial Strategy*, 43–45. According to Murphy, persuasion on the merits involves intellectual factors, arguments, and "massing legal precedents and history to bolster an intellectually and morally defensible policy" (45).

213. *Webster v. Reproductive Health Services*, 543–545.

214. The Reverend Doctor George W. Truett, in his "Speech from the Capital Steps" (1929), claimed "a free church in a free state" as the unique Baptist contribution to American democracy. See Everett C. Goodwin, ed., *Baptists in the Balance: The Tension between Freedom and Responsibility* (Valley Forge, PA: Judson Press, 1997), 219–221.

215. *Webster v. Reproductive Health Services*, 560–572.

216. Craig and O'Brien, *Abortion and American Politics*, 264.

217. Lynn D. Wardle, "The Road to Moderation: The Significance of *Webster* for Legislation Restricting Abortion," *Journal of Law, Medicine, and Health Care* 17, no. 4 (1989): 376–383. The polling data are recorded in Craig and O'Brien, *Abortion and American Politics*, 264.

218. Robert L. Koenig, "States Draw Up Battle Lines on Restricting Abortion," *St. Louis Post-Dispatch*, 4 July 1989.

219. Bill Smith, "Abortion Foes See Inevitable Victory," *St. Louis Post-Dispatch*, 4 July 1989.

220. Virginia Young, "Ashcroft Will Press for Tighter Rules," *St. Louis Post-Dispatch*, 4 July 1989.

221. Ibid.

222. Tim Mosley and Virginia Young, "Abortion Issue Spawns Three Sides: Pros, Cons, and Those Who Wish It Would Go Away," *St. Louis Post-Dispatch*, 10 July 1989.

223. Ibid.

224. Virginia Young, "Abortion Foes Hit Brakes . . . Legislators Caught in No-Win Situation," *St. Louis Post-Dispatch*, 31 December 1989.

225. Virginia Young, "Puzder Quits Abortion Panel," *St. Louis Post-Dispatch*, 5 October 1989.

226. Ibid.

227. Craig and O'Brien, *Abortion and American Politics*, 280–283.

228. Ibid., 296–303.

229. *Planned Parenthood of Southeastern Pennsylvania et al. v. Casey*, 505 U.S. 833 (1992).

4

Living to Lose, Dying to Win!

When does life begin? When is a person dead? Modern technology makes seemingly simple questions like these difficult, defying a straightforward answer. Who should give the answer? Who should have authority and power to make such decisions for individuals and for society? Americans particularly look to the Supreme Court and its justices and the entire spectrum of the judicial process for answers. The judicial process provides legitimacy; the vote of five Supreme Court justices stamps life and death definitions as legitimate or illegitimate. Some will lose as a result of the Supreme Court's definition, while others will win. The impact of a decision differs for each individual. Yet hope remains. Winners hope for increased gains, losers for a chance to try again. As justices write opinions, as they define life and death, they choose words which by their very nature are susceptible to manipulation. Loopholes in the opinions come into sight and, as the litigation process begins again, the Court's initial impact on the critical issues of life and death changes.

The impact of a Supreme Court decision involves a number of factors. Was the case decided by the justices unified and speaking in a clear voice? Was the language so plain and unequivocal that no doubt could exist about the decision? Was the public prepared to accept the decision and comply with it? Would state decision makers agree to enforce the ruling? Unless most of the questions can be answered affirmatively, Supreme Court decisions will fail to have a definitive impact on public policy. Whenever the Court itself is ambivalent and the public divided, the decision will lead to new cases that raise corollary questions, forcing additional decisions.[1]

This was the situation that resulted when the Supreme Court accepted the nation's first "right to die" case: *Cruzan v. Missouri.*[2] The impact of the Supreme Court's decision in this emotional and groundbreaking case would be far from conclusive. The Supreme Court's holding was at odds with its own dicta, and an invitation to the loser to "try again" was seemingly extended. Shaken by very personal empathetic fears, the Supreme Court sent mixed signals to a society equally uncertain. The right of an individual to refuse unwanted medical treatment was the issue posed in *Cruzan v. Missouri.* It was a life-or-death issue that created intense feeling. It seemed to many to be a moral issue about which there could be no compromise. The impact of this judicial decision would be tested as the litigants, the state elite, and the public reacted.

CREATING A CASE: A TRAGIC ACCIDENT

At 12:50 A.M. on Tuesday, January 22, 1983, on her way home, twenty-five-year-old Nancy Beth Cruzan drove her old Rambler auto down an icy highway southeast of Carthage, Missouri, in Jasper County. Nancy Cruzan was probably tired; she had worked a late shift at Schreiber Foods. Certainly she was anxious to get home to her husband of one year, Paul Davis. Evidently, she was in a hurry. Such factors often lead to accidents, and such was the case this time. Yet this accident, which left Nancy Cruzan lying face down in a ditch, was to have an impact on American law that would continue into the twenty-first century.

What happened that night had to be reconstructed from the physical evidence at the scene after the wreck. The car had run off the pavement. It had struck some small trees and a mailbox, swerved back across the pavement, crashed into a fence, and overturned several times. Cruzan was not wearing a seatbelt and was thrown out of the car. She was found by the Missouri State Highway Patrol. They received a call within five minutes of the crash and were on the scene by 1:00 A.M. Paramedics accompanying the police assessed the condition of the victim: she had no pulse rate and she was not breathing. They went to work immediately using all techniques available, beginning with CPR and then employing other life-support procedures. Finally, at 1:13 A.M. Nancy Cruzan began to breathe spontaneously and showed a pulse rate. Yet, for fifteen minutes, her body had been deprived of oxygen. What had happened to her during that time? Medical science's answer was clear: even six minutes without oxygen would produce brain damage. Yet Nancy Cruzan was alive—or was she?[3]

The case of *Cruzan v. Missouri* would become the nation's first major right-to-die case. It would pit advocates of public policy to preserve life in all situations by the use of the most advanced medical techniques and devices against the individual's claim of personal privacy. Unlike abortion or homosexuality, death is universal; however, it is not as simple as it once was. Is it the "stoppage of both heart and lungs"? Is it the "irreversible loss of consciousness"? Moreover, if the individual needs artificially delivered food, water, or oxygen, can the state require its use? This debate over death and dying and a personal privacy right to refuse unwanted treatment would be played out in the experiences of the Cruzan family. The unfolding of those events created a case that continues to impact the entire country.

MISSOURI LAW AND THE CRUZAN DILEMMA

It would take four years for Nancy Beth Cruzan's family to realize that she was not going to recover. Immediately following the accident, paramedics had taken her to the emergency room of a small, nearby hospital. Lacking facilities to cope with the problem, the hospital sent her to a larger facility, Freeman Hospital in Joplin, Missouri. Surgery was performed. However, consciousness did not return. Intravenous feeding could not be used indefinitely and Nancy Beth seemed unable to swallow either food or water orally. Doctors sought consent from her husband and also from her father to surgically implant a feeding tube.[4]

As that first January gave way to February, the days passed with no response from Nancy Cruzan. Her husband, Paul Davis, moved her from the hospital to his grandmother's home and brought in professional nursing care. Once again, a major attempt was made to wean Cruzan from her feeding tube as nurse after nurse patiently sought to get soft foods and liquids down her throat. She did swallow some of it, but the results were immediately catastrophic. Cruzan's lungs, not her stomach, filled with the food and water she swallowed. With the food and water sucked into the lungs, known medically as "aspiration," pneumonia followed immediately. Once again, Cruzan had to be hospitalized.

A cycle was set in motion: antibiotics cured the disease; she was released from the hospital and returned to nursing home care; attempts at oral feeding followed, only to result in new infections and rehospitalization. The months continued to pass. Winter gave way to spring, then summer. By October 1983, the Cruzan family was "economically strapped." The personal finances of Cruzan and Davis had been depleted, and he decided to dissolve the marriage. What would happen to Nancy Cruzan now? The answer brought another actor, the state of Missouri, into the slowly unfolding tragedy.[5]

THE RIGHT OF PRIVACY AS A RIGHT TO DIE:
THE MISSOURI DEBATE

It has been said that Missouri is unique among states. Politically, the state is referred to as a "bellwether" state, one whose vote for president demonstrates the mood of the country at large. "As Missouri goes, so goes the nation" is a slogan often used by political analysts. However, in the 1980s, Missouri's image took on a different hue. Three major cases set Missouri outside mainstream America. The *Webster* case (1989) showed that the state was determined to require that "once conceived, one must be born."[6] Once born, however, could one have a "good time" in Missouri? Not if one lived in a town like Purdy, Missouri, and attended the local high school there; not if one defined a "good time" as dancing at a junior-senior prom. The "Purdy dance ban" forbade dancing in school facilities.[7] It was justified as a valid exercise of state police power to preserve good morals and to protect students' health from drugs and alcohol that might be found at a school dance. Some people in the town suggested that the ban represented the religious views of the fundamentalist Southern Baptists who dominated that area. Nonetheless, it was clear that the state of Missouri could both require birth and prevent frivolity. It could also prevent dying.

MISSOURI LAW AND PRIVACY RIGHTS: COURTS AND STATUTES

Missouri's state constitution, like the federal one, does not contain the word "privacy." However, the 1875 version had included a "general welfare" clause asserting that the purpose of government was to insure individuals' "natural rights to life, liberty, and the enjoyment of gain from their own industry." In the revised constitution of 1945, this passage remained verbatim, with an added provision defining all persons as created equal and entitled to equal rights and opportunities. Using these rather vague phrases, Missouri had read a "privacy right" guarantee into the law.

As early as 1942, in the landmark case *Barber v. Time*, the Missouri Supreme Court had declared that a right of privacy in Missouri law and practice was grounded in the state constitution. Specifically in that case, privacy was defined to include the right to be free from publicity about one's medical treatment. The court declared that the basis of this right of privacy was the "right to be let alone," and it found privacy rights in the rights of liberty and happiness in the state constitution. This right of privacy was an "inalienable" right, which could not be "lawfully denied so long as individuals behav[ed] properly." The constitutional right of privacy included a ban on "unreasonable publicity."[8]

Forty years later, a new Missouri Supreme Court reaffirmed this right and defined an individual's right of privacy as a "legally protected, constitutional right." In *Sofka v. Thal* (1983), the court admitted that all the issues protected under this right were not "completely clear." However, any "unreasonable intrusion upon one's seclusion" struck at a protected right.[9]

Missouri courts also found a right of privacy in the common law traditions of the state. The "right of informed consent" was a judge-made concept that had been articulated in old precedents. Missouri defined this in three parts: the right to be "let alone," the right to be "free of unwanted medical treatment," and the right to determine what should be done with one's own body. However, the extent of this common-law or judge-made right was not clear. It did not always apply in the cases of minors or convicted criminals, for example. In the case of incompetent individuals, its scope and applicability were open to question. Certainly an "informed consent" right was not an "absolute" right. As with all civil liberties and rights, it could be limited when a state presented a "compelling reason" for a restriction.[10]

Like Missouri judges, Missouri lawmakers had also been involved over time with the question of the scope and limits of a right to privacy. They had reached very different conclusions, however. Lawmakers consistently asserted the state's right to prevent "suicide, homicide, and injury to innocent parties," and this was codified into law. The "informed consent" doctrine had never been clearly codified. In fact, Missouri statute law in 1983 was in actual conflict with the common-law doctrine of informed consent: Missouri statute law denied citizens a right to refuse "any medicine or procedure that would provide comfort, care or alleviate pain." In 1985, Missouri law stated that individuals could not refuse "any procedure to provide nutrition or hydration." Competent people, even though they were terminally ill, were thus prevented by state law from exercising this common-law right as recognized by Missouri courts. Guardians of incompetent patients were also denied the right to refuse these medical treatments for their wards.[11]

Thus the privacy right inherent in the refusal to consent to treatment, the "right to die," was put to the test as the *Cruzan* case asked the judiciary to decide. As they did so, Missouri courts would have to deal with the specific words of the Missouri statutes; however, they also could focus on their own judicial precedents and the practices of sister states.

By 1987, a number of precedents and actions of other states were available to Missouri decision makers. The majority of the state courts had found a way to allow individuals to refuse life-sustaining treatment. Thirteen states— Arizona, California, Colorado, Connecticut, Delaware, Florida, Massachusetts, Minnesota, New Jersey, New York, Ohio, Pennsylvania, and Washington— allowed the removal of "death-prolonging devices." Some of these state courts asserted a common-law right to forgo medical treatment; others identified either a "fundamental" or a "liberty" interest found in their particular state constitution. Some states asserted natural-law rights, with others invoking federal constitutional law. Overall, they had uniformly found a right of privacy to refuse or withdraw medical treatment.[12]

States, of course, required some standard of proof to make certain of the patient's desires. Where written documents such as living wills were absent, a "clear and convincing" evidence test might be used. Some states accepted a "preponderance of evidence" standard. Where state statutes prohibited withdrawal of food and water, as in Missouri and Maine, most supreme courts had ruled that the common-law tradition superseded state law if nourishment was being supplied artificially.[13]

Few of these legal precedents or laws were known by the Cruzan family in 1987. Their attention for four years had been focused on the unresponsive body of their daughter, who now lay on her bed in the state hospital in Mt. Vernon, Missouri. Her parents were her guardians, but the taxpayers of the state of Missouri were paying her yearly bill in excess of $100,000. Why not let this state of affairs continue? It was the sight of a "rigid body, knees and arms locked into a fetal position, hands so tightly bent that her fingernails cut into her wrists"[14] that finally spurred Nancy's family to action. Day after day, they had watched her seizures and her vomiting; they had seen her eyes open and stare at them with no sign of recognition. For them, their daughter was dead. It was not their decision to make, however, as they soon learned. The state of Missouri would fight to continue Nancy's treatment. The contest had begun.

IN PROBATE COURT:
MISSOURI OPPOSES A PRIVACY RIGHT TO DIE

Although it became the first right-to-die case to ultimately reach the U.S. Supreme Court and raise complex questions, the *Cruzan* case began with a relatively simple proceeding. The place was the Circuit Court of Jasper County, Probate Division, in Carthage, Missouri; the parties were the co-guardians, Lester ("Joe") and Joyce Cruzan, versus Robert Harmon of the Missouri Rehabilitation Center. The proceeding itself was a petition for a declaratory judgment giving the family the power to ask the center to discontinue the tubal feeding of Nancy Cruzan. The date was May 12, 1987.

Representing the parents' request was William H. Colby of the law firm of Shook, Hardy, and Bacon of Kansas City, Missouri; representing the state was Attorney General William L. Webster and Assistant Attorney General Robert Presson. In addition, on October 26, 1987, the court appointed two other attorneys, Thad C. McCanse and David B. Mouton, to act as Nancy Cruzan's guardians *ad litem.* Their job was to ensure that the parents' request was actually in the best interest of their daughter.[15]

On November 25, 1987, the state filed a motion to dismiss in response to the declaratory judgment petition. The Missouri officials thus entered their opposition to the Cruzan family's request. The state cited a St. Louis County circuit court decision of June 3, 1987, that interpreted Missouri's "living will" statute as denying guardians the right to withdraw nutrition and hydration.

State officials demanded that Judge Charles E. Teel Jr. apply this precedent in Jasper County and dismiss the Cruzan's petition.[16]

Briefs, arguments, and evidence in the Cruzan case were presented during a three-day bench trial in Judge Teel's court. Medical testimony was central to this first hearing. Was Nancy Cruzan in a persistent vegetative state (PVS)? Seven doctors testified at the hearing. Two, Dr. Anita Isaacs and Dr. James Dexter, were witnesses for the state's position. Both argued that Cruzan was not a "classic" PVS patient. Dr. Isaacs, however, had so diagnosed Cruzan two years earlier. Dr. Dexter, chair of Department of Neurology at the University of Missouri–Columbia, also changed his testimony between giving his deposition and the actual hearing. Moreover, he admitted that he had never done a complete neurological exam on Cruzan. Five other doctors testified at the trial: Drs. H. S. Majzout, Saad Al-Shatir, James Davis, George Wong, and Ronald Cranford. Two of these five were board-certified neurology specialists. All five had examined Cruzan repeatedly, and all agreed that Cruzan was in a persistent vegetative state.[17]

The hearing also sought to elicit information about the wishes and desires of Nancy Cruzan. Would she, if competent, refuse the tubal feeding? Nancy's sister, Christy White, testified about two specific conversations she had had with Nancy concerning quality of life and the preferability of death. They had discussed the case of their terminally ill grandmother and the death of their sister's brain-damaged, abnormal child. Nancy's parents then testified about their daughter's personality and character. Describing their daughter as independent, assertive, and fastidious about her appearance, they believed she would be "horrified by her state and the inability of her family to help her." Finally, Athena Comer, a one-time roommate of Nancy Cruzan's, also testified. She described a specific conversation with Nancy in which Cruzan called the death of Comer's vegetative sister "a blessing." Comer declared that Cruzan had specifically repudiated life "as a vegetable."[18]

Extensive pre- and posttrial briefs were filed before the Missouri Supreme Court. Their purpose was to debate a number of legal questions based on interpretations of law, on precedents, and on the specific issues which the court should decide. These included the question about a right of privacy in the Missouri Constitution as interpreted by Missouri courts. Did Nancy Cruzan have a state constitutional right to privacy and common-law rights to sovereignty over her own body? Did Missouri law permit guardians of incapacitated and incompetent persons to withdraw nutrition and hydration from their wards? What was the correct interpretation of Missouri's 1985 "living will statute"? Should courts use the law retroactively? Should Missouri disregard the right-to-die precedents of its sister states?

Interpretation of the state constitution to secure expanded privacy rights was contested by Missouri's attorney general, William Webster, who denied that Missouri courts had ever articulated a concept of privacy that was as comprehensive as the federal one. For Webster, Missouri did not recognize a right to die. Evaluating the state cases that involved privacy, he dismissed them as inapplicable to *Cruzan* because they centered on the rights of individuals to be protected from the publication of private facts. It was true that the Missouri Supreme Court had specifically held in 1986 that the reach or extent of a right to privacy had not been defined in Missouri. State courts, including Missouri's, are assumed to be the best interpreters of their own state constitutions. Missouri courts, while asserting this power, have often assured the public that they define their powers of judicial review narrowly and defer to the legislature unless the legislature enacts laws that "palpably violate the fundamental law of the [state] constitution." This judicial approach to the state constitution is significant, because in the last analysis any constitutional provision will mean what the judges interpret it to mean. This claim for an individual right of privacy growing out of the Missouri Constitution was dependent on the attitude of the court that, absent clear constitutional privacy statements, might be a narrow and limiting or a broad and expansive ruling defining individual liberties in Missouri.[19]

In all, it took seven briefs to argue the numerous issues raised at the probate court hearing. Numerous groups also filed amicus curiae briefs. Judge Teel was not overstating the amount of information he had received when he later wrote that the court had been "fully advised."[20] All of the central and supplementary questions that would ultimately be raised as this case moved forward were identified and argued at the probate hearing. In addition to the central question concerning a federal or state right to privacy that could be extended to the right to refuse tubal feeding, there were four related questions: Could state statute law override state common-law decisions? Were those privacy rights that grew out of reproductive choice decisions limited to personal, informed choices, and thus not exercisable by surrogate decision makers? Did the state of Missouri's interest in life outweigh the individual's privacy right in this case? What standard should be used to decide who won and who lost?[21]

Judge Teel ruled in favor of the individual's privacy right to die and against the state's interest in life. In doing so, he answered each of the arguments that had been raised. With respect to the individual liberty involved here, the judge identified it as a "fundamental natural right" to refuse medical treatment. He anchored this right in both the state and federal constitutions within the concept of a "right to liberty." Defining nutrition and hydration supplied through an invasive gastrostomy tube as medical treatment, and asserting an individual's common-law right to refuse, Judge Teel declared that Missouri's living will prohibition on withdrawal was unconstitutional.[22] The judge accepted the family as appropriate and traditional surrogate decision makers, empowered to make choices of this nature. He found no state interest in preserving life, preventing suicide or harm to third parties, or regulating medical ethics to be sufficiently compelling to override the individual right claimed here. Convinced that *Cruzan* was a PVS case, the judge did agree that the state had a right to insist upon proof that her intent would have been to forgo tubal feeding, but declared that this could be appropriately established through the "clear and convincing" evidence requirement. Teel believed that the testimony of family and friends met this standard. He granted the Cruzan family the authority to "exercise [Nancy Cruzan's] constitutionally guaranteed liberty to request the [Missouri Rehabilitation Center] to withhold nutrition and hydration." The court also directed Missouri officials to carry out the request of the family under a subtle threat of a civil liability suit if they refused. It was July 27, 1988.[23]

THE MISSOURI STATE SUPREME COURT: LIMITING PRIVACY RIGHTS

The constitutional question involving privacy rights had been raised in the initial *Cruzan* action, and attorneys had repeated it throughout subsequent proceedings. The way was open for an appeal to the Missouri Supreme Court. Attorney General William Webster filed this appeal in September 1988; the case would be decided on November 16, 1988.[24]

The state supreme court at that time consisted of only six "duly appointed regular judges." These were Chief Justice Billings and judges Robertson, Rendlen, Blackmar, Higgins, and Welliver. A temporary special judge, Judge Reinhard, was assigned to participate in this specific case since the court membership was incomplete. When the case was finally decided, the six regular judges were evenly divided; it was thus Judge Reinhard's vote that was decisive. Should the case have been reargued before an entire court of regular judges? There were procedural state law requirements which several of the judges claimed demanded this action. Nevertheless, once decided, the case was not reheard. The decision of this panel of seven stood, and by a 4–3 vote the Missouri Supreme Court handed down a landmark decision seriously limiting civil liberties claims of privacy for Missouri citizens.

Cruzan v. Harmon denied a right of privacy encompassing refusal of medical treatment. The decision clearly defined the Missouri Constitution. There was no constitutional "unfettered right of privacy" that could support the right of a person to refuse medical treatment in every circumstance, said the court. In addition, the court limited the common-law right to refuse medical treatment by insisting that, since no right was "absolute," this right also could be limited and infringed by the state. The state could force even terminally ill competent patients to accept nutrition and hydration. The court also limited the federal privacy right claim that depended on the reproductive choice precedents of *Griswold* and *Roe* by distinguishing their facts from those in *Cruzan* and insisting that privacy rights required a personal, informed choice.[25]

For the four majority judges on the state supreme court in 1988, individual rights and liberties had to give way to the interests of the state of Missouri. The court majority interpreted the state laws on abortion and the living will statute to mean that ensuring development of conceived life and prolongation of life itself were both essential and necessary state objectives. For these judges, Missouri's interest in the life of its citizens at all stages was absolute; it was superior to individual rights and liberties.

The three dissenting judges disputed each point. Judge Blackmar focused on the traditional and historical right of families, rather than states, to be decision makers for family members. Judge Higgins argued that appellate courts had no power to ignore the evidentiary findings of the trial court and that the earlier hearing had found clear and convincing evidence of Cruzan's intent to refuse treatment. Judge Welliver argued that the Missouri Living Will Act perpetuated a "fraud on Missourians, making them believe that they had a right to execute a living will" while actually denying them the right to refuse treatment. The dissenting justices all noted that the majority's opinion was in direct conflict with the decisions of other state supreme courts. The stage was sct for an appeal to the U.S. Supreme Court.[26]

THE UNITED STATES SUPREME COURT: A NEW CONSTITUTIONAL RIGHT CHALLENGES MISSOURI

For a case to be taken from a state supreme court to the U.S. Supreme Court, it must pass several hurdles. Among these is the question of whether there is a federal right involved in the case. *Cruzan* had involved a mixture of state common law, statutes, and constitutional provisions; however, it had also raised the question of the federal right to privacy. Moreover, the Missouri decision had interpreted the U.S. Supreme Court's federal privacy decisions differently from other states where the right to die was accepted as a right of privacy. Nevertheless, the Supreme Court did not rush to accept *Cruzan*. The Court accepted it reluctantly on writ of certiorari and docketed it for oral argument.[27]

When the decision was announced on June 25, 1990, the public was mystified. Newspaper headlines sent confusing signals and legal experts scrambled to explain who had won and who had lost in the first right-to-die case. Headlines proclaiming "Court Recognizes Right to Die" were correct—but so were headlines proclaiming "Cruzan Loses Right to Die." The Supreme Court's holding and dicta in the case created this confusing situation as they handed Missouri both a yes and a no.[28]

The U.S. Supreme Court in 1990 contained two blocs. Five justices were committed to state's rights: Chief Justice Rehnquist and justices White, Scalia, Kennedy, and O'Connor. The other four justices—Brennan, Marshall, Blackmun and Stevens—had long-standing records of commitment to individual liberties. As these two blocs approached *Cruzan*, they found unexpected agreement. Most of the justices seemed to acknowledge or assume a constitutional right to die under certain circumstances. Writing for the majority, the chief justice stated, "We assume that the [Constitution] would grant a competent person a constitutionally protected right to refuse lifesaving hydration and nutrition."[29] Justice O'Connor's separate concurrence added that "a protected liberty interest in refusing unwanted medical treatment may be inferred from our prior decisions and that the refusal of artificially delivered food and water is encompassed within that liberty interest."[30] Justices Brennan, Marshall, Blackmun, and Stevens moved even beyond this to assert the right was a "fundamental" one—not just a constitutionally protected liberty interest. Of the nine Supreme Court justice deciding *Cruzan,* only Justice Scalia seemed totally unwilling to recognize the right to die as a constitutional right of privacy.

Why then did Nancy Cruzan's family lose its case and the right to remove her feeding tube? The answer lies in the narrow question on which the five majority justices chose to focus, namely, "[Does] the [U.S.] Constitution prohibit Missouri from . . . apply[ing] a clear and convincing evidence standard in proceedings where a guardian seeks to discontinue nutrition and hydration of a person diagnosed to be in a persistent vegetative state?" Focusing on this question, Rehnquist, White, Kennedy, and O'Connor reached *four* conclusions.

First, they held that the Court's "prior decisions" based on the Fourteenth Amendment established the principle "that a competent person has a constitutionally protected liberty interest in refusing unwanted medical treatment" and that this included "hydration and nutrition." Second, this constitutional value was a "liberty interest," not a fundamental right; it could be limited by a judicial balancing test. The relevant state interests would be weighed against the individual's civil liberty claim. Third, the Court read its own meaning into the Missouri's Living Will Act, interpreting it to say that "Missouri . . . recognize[s] that under certain circumstances a surrogate may act for the patient in electing to have hydration and nutrition withdrawn in such a way as to cause death." This had not been the interpretation advanced by Attorney General Webster or by the Missouri Supreme Court. Fourth, the Court upheld the procedural safeguard that Missouri courts asserted as appropriate in "assur[ing] that the action of the surrogate conforms as best it may to the wishes expressed by the patient while competent . . . [namely, a] clear and convincing evidence [test]."

Based on these four conclusions, Rehnquist, White, Kennedy, and O'Connor decided that there was nothing in the U.S. Constitution to "forbid the establishment of this procedural requirement by the State." The state supreme court had held that this test had not been met, and to this extent the state decision was upheld.[31] Justice Scalia, believing that the case did not involve a federal right, voted with Rehnquist, White, and Kennedy. O'Connor's separate concurrence, however, maintained that the right to refuse medical treatment was a constitutional liberty protected from state invasion. It was a right that included freedom from the artificial delivery of food and water. She suggested that there might also be a "constitutional command to states to implement the decision of a patient's duly appointed surrogate."[32]

Justices Brennan, Marshall, and Blackman insisted that Nancy Cruzan had a "fundamental right to be free of unwanted artificial nutrition and hydration," and that this right was "not outweighed by any interests of the state." These three justices wanted to evaluate Missouri's evidentiary rule under a strict or heightened judicial scrutiny test. They maintained that Missouri was significantly interfering with the exercise of a fundamental right and should be required to prove that the state interests were "compelling" and "essential" ones and that the rule was "closely tailored" to secure only those interests. Justice Stevens's separate dissent agreed and added the point that the Constitution did not give a state the "power to define life."[33]

REINVENTING MISSOURI'S LAW

Evaluation of the five opinions written in *Cruzan* reveals the different questions and standards used by the justices. A careful comparison of these opinions demonstrates what was won and what was lost in this case.

Cruzan did score some victories for individual rights. Eight justices had agreed that a competent person had a federally protected right to refuse medical treatment, including hydration and nutrition. This was a loss for Missouri, which had maintained that hydration and nutrition could never be refused. At least five justices believed that surrogates or guardians were proper decision makers for incompetent persons even when the issue was classified as that of a personal choice within a privacy right. Thus a surrogate could order removal of a feeding tube.

However, the state also won in *Cruzan*. The right to refuse treatment was not accorded the status of a fundamental right under privacy; it was listed as merely one individual "liberty," which the state could easily regulate. The position taken by five of the justices said that the state could balance its interests against that of the individual and, upon showing a rational relationship between the state law and the right being limited, could prevail. Missouri could also require a high standard of proof that Nancy Cruzan desired withdrawal of food and hydration before agreeing to comply. The "clear and convincing" evidence standard that Missouri courts had articulated allowed the state to impose significant barriers for anyone seeking to avoid death-prolonging devices. Thus the Supreme Court's decision on June 25, 1990, upheld Missouri's right to continue the gastrostomy tube feeding of Nancy Cruzan. The Court, however, left open the door for "the discovery of new evidence regarding the patient's intent," which could allow a lower court in a new trial to rule in favor of Cruzan's "right to die."[34]

PERSONAL IMPACT: THE ROAD TO *CRUZAN II*

The six months that followed the announcement of the Court's opinion were fraught with conflicting and confusing events. At first, the public simply could not understand what the Supreme Court had said and what it had not said. The media were partly to blame. Television coverage, newspaper reports, and magazine hype all conveyed different messages. Since the state of Missouri was allowed to continue the gastrostomy feeding of Cruzan, many assumed there was no right to die. Some parts of the media made this approach their primary focus. However, others noted that eight of the nine Supreme Court justices had implied that such a right did exist. The public response varied according to the perception of the decision. Public attention had been intensely engaged by this life-and-death struggle as news coverage reached into "nooks and crannies" of the populace. What impact would this decision have? How would it be understood? How would it be applied? How would voters react? How would the elite decision makers—state governors, state legislatures, and state courts—respond?

The Court's decision had a major impact on the Cruzan family as well as the national public at large. While the public in general was confused and even mystified by the Supreme Court's decision, the Cruzan family was not. As William Colby commented, "I was frankly amazed to watch what the press calls 'spin control,' as groups on both sides of the case came out immediately and pronounced the decision a victory for their side. But, from my point of view, it was not a victory in anyway [for the right to die], but a devastating loss [for the Cruzans]. The court did, for the first time, recognize that there is a constitutional right for conscious, competent people to refuse unwanted medical treatment [including, artificial feeding]. [T]he court, however . . . did not overrule the evidentiary barriers that Missouri had erected."[35]

What this meant for Nancy Cruzan was continued existence in a persistent vegetative state for perhaps thirty or even fifty more years. Doctors had made this clear to the family: Nancy's conditions had not changed during the seven years since the accident and hers was a young body. Missouri law had been upheld by five of the justices on the Court. This law required the highest level of evidence. Chief Justice Rehnquist, writing for the majority, had confirmed a state's right to define tightly the circumstances under which the right to die could be asserted. The state's interest in protecting life, he said was primary. The Court (at least five of the justices) wanted the state in control. Courts could also demand an irrefutable document showing a patient's wishes. However, a so-called living will might be considered insufficient if not accompanied by both a "medical directive" and a durable power of attorney.

Remarks made to friends and family did not constitute "clear and convincing evidence" of a person's intent. Nancy Cruzan's "evidence" was thus insufficient under Missouri's standard. While the trial judge, Charles Teel, had ruled the testimony of friends and family sufficient, he had been reversed by the Missouri State Supreme Court. That court's test worked so that in Missouri the state "virtually would always win."[36] The state court had described the state interest in Nancy Cruzan's life as an "unqualified" interest in life. It could be overcome only if medical treatment caused pain. If "compelling evidence" (a living will, etc.) was perfectly clear, a competent person *might* be allowed to refuse treatment.[37] But Nancy Cruzan's family could not provide this evidence. Confronting the loss in both state and federal courts, the Cruzans saw no way out of their predicament. The state legislature resisted demands to write a new law and courts were known to be reluctant to overturn their earlier decisions.

Yet judges and justices do function in a political environment. Courts have seldom held out against the popular will, and most people reject a persistent vegetative state existence for themselves. Poll after poll has confirmed this, and the Missouri Supreme Court was not unaware of this. The state judges also had to accept the Supreme Court's requirement that Missouri define artificial feeding as medical treatment, which citizens could refuse. Could the state court redefine the evidence produced in *Cruzan* so as to yet find it "clear and convincing"? Would additional conversations and examples satisfy the court or would it continue to demand a living will?

NEW EVIDENCE, NEW CASE

The two central players were now veterans of this battle: Missouri Attorney General William Webster and the Cruzan's attorney, William Colby. As early as January 1990, Webster had suggested to the state legislature that Missouri's living will statute be modified to establish an evidentiary standard Nancy Cruzan could meet. His proposal was stopped by John Schneider (D-Florissant), a strong antiabortion, pro-life state senator. Schneider had the support of Catholic legislators as well as Protestant fundamentalists, including the Southern Baptists. They defined Webster's plan as a "harbinger of euthanasia."[38] Webster needed support from these powerful groups for his up-coming gubernatorial campaign and so he "sat silent while Senator Schnei-der stopped [his proposed standard] cold."[39] Webster and his family mem-bers, including his father, state senator Richard Webster, had detailed living wills for themselves, however.

William Colby also was aware of the political currents that were sweeping through the state. The climate of public opinion gave him renewed hope. While conversations did not equate with a written directive, Colby believed that additional examples might sway a state court, a state attorney general, and ultimately a state legislature. Could Colby find this new evidence and so reopen the case? The answer was not long in coming, and the story behind it shows once again the power of the press to generate or inhibit response to court decisions and thus impact public and personal policy making.

As the Supreme Court decision made headlines, pictures of Nancy Beth Cruzan flashed across the country. News magazines such as *Time* and *Newsweek* carried her photo; television put a face with a name. People saw her and a number of them, heretofore unknown to the Cruzan family, rec-ognized her. A part of Nancy Cruzan's life reemerged and took center stage to give new hope to those defending her right to die.

The legal authorities dealing with her case had never sought a biographi-cal sketch of Nancy Beth Cruzan. It would have been a simple matter to trace her life: place of birth, parents, siblings, education, friends, jobs, places of residence, and companions. It simply had not seemed important. Early in her life, Nancy Cruzan had married her childhood sweetheart, and as Nancy Hayes she had become a teacher's aide at the Stapleton School in Joplin, Mis-souri, in 1978. That marriage did not last long, and shortly after it ended in 1981, Nancy moved to Oklahoma City and took a clerical job in an office supply company. Subsequently she quit that job to go to Texas with Paul Davis, whom she later married.[40] Had Nancy communicated her life and death views to her associates and friends during this earlier period of her life? Indeed she had.

At the Stapleton School, Debi Havner and Marianne Smith would have de-nied knowing a "Nancy Cruzan." But *Time's* picture showed them the per-son they had known as Nancy Hayes, the teacher's aide they had known and worked with daily for seven months. They had had a difficult job. The school catered to severely handicapped children, many of them blind and deaf; some were both mentally retarded and disabled. In this environment, it was natural that the three teachers would have occasions to consider the plight of these unfortunate children. Nancy Beth (Cruzan) Hayes had done so, and Debi Havner and Marianne Smith were in a position to testify to her remarks. Nancy had been in charge of a severely retarded and disabled three-year-old girl who had to be forcibly fed. It was almost too much for Nancy Beth Hayes. "I don't ever want to end up like this," she had told her coworkers.

Havner and Smith rushed to identify Nancy Hayes as Nancy Cruzan, and new "clear and convincing evidence" entered the record.[41]

From Oklahoma City came another call. Tom Turner had employed Nancy Hayes when she had moved to Oklahoma. He remembered how concerned she had been about the case of Karen Quinlan, the nationally publicized young woman who had existed in a coma, kept alive by a respirator. Quinlan's family had sought to have the respirator removed, only to meet with refusal from the doctors. The New Jersey Supreme Court had supported the parents and had articulated a "right to privacy broad enough to allow a patient to decline medical treatment under certain circumstances."[42] Moreover, the state court had given the parents the right to decide for their comatose daughter. "The only practical way to prevent the destruction of the right to privacy is to permit the guardian and family of Karen to render their best judgment as to whether she would exercise it in those circumstances," the state court had declared.[43] Thus in 1974, this New Jersey family had proceeded to remove Karen Quinlan's respirator. Quinlan lived on without the respirator for some time, however, with her feeding tube still in place. Public interest in the case revived when she finally died. Tom Turner and Nancy Hayes had discussed this case, Turner said. Nancy Beth's earlier experiences had made her a vocal exponent that "death that was preferable to life." She had convinced Turner that "life as a vegetable" would not be life for her. When Turner saw the face of Nancy Cruzan, he saw Nancy Hayes and he had evidence to add to the record. Turner contacted William Colby; his story was credible, confirmed, and thus definitive.[44]

With these three new witnesses—along with the earlier testimony of Athena Comer, Nancy's roommate, and Christy White, Nancy's sister—Colby was ready to defy the courts to require any greater evidence that Nancy Cruzan would choose not to be "kept alive on a machine, force fed, or exist in a vegetative state."[45] On August 30, 1990, Colby, acting for the Cruzan family, filed a new petition in Jasper County, Missouri, asking the trial court to "authorize removal of medical treatment."

The state of Missouri wavered for two weeks. Finally, on September 14, 1990, the Office of the Attorney General withdrew from the case, noting that the "State of Missouri had nothing further to add to the proceedings as a party of an active participant." Attorney General William Webster knew when to quit; his "win" in the U.S. Supreme Court had sent negative shock waves through the state. Candidate Webster's eye was on his upcoming gubernatorial bid.[46]

Judge Charles E. Teel Jr. once again presided over the proceedings in Jasper County, which became known as *Cruzan II*.[47] He reviewed the testimony, the new evidence, and the briefs presented by Attorney William H. Colby for the Cruzans and by the court-appointed guardian *ad litem*, attorney Thad C. McCanse. Both attorneys assured Judge Teel that the U.S.

Supreme Court decision allowed the Cruzan family to act as surrogate and "have hydration and nutrition withdrawn in such a way as to cause death." The procedural safeguards created by the state of Missouri were satisfied; there existed clear and convincing evidence that this was Nancy Cruzan's choice. Judge Teel, for a second time, ruled in favor of the individual's right to die: he issued the order to remove Nancy's gastrostomy tube on December 14. She died on December 26, 1990.

TWELVE CRUCIAL DAYS

Between the time of Judge Teel's order and the death of Nancy Cruzan, six separate lawsuits or appeals were filed in different courts throughout Missouri related to this case, beginning on December 18. The first, *State ex rel Tebbets v. Tell*, No. 17306-2, was an appeal filed in the Missouri Court of Appeals. The next day, December 19, that same court received a second appeal: *State ex rel. Williams v. Bagby*, No. 17312-1, which was also filed as *State ex rel. Williams v. Bagby*, No. 73324 (MO). On the twentieth, *Mahoney v. Missouri Rehab. Center*, No. 90-5055-CV-SWI (W.D. MO.), was filed and then appealed on December 22 as *Mahoney v. Missouri Rehab. Center*, No. 903085 WM (9th Cir.). In the Cole County Circuit Court, the state court in Missouri's capital, Jefferson City, Yvette Williams filed a lawsuit, which Judge Byron Kinder dismissed.[48]

The parties to these suits were individuals who wanted to force the state of Missouri to act. Some, like Gary Tebbets, also took part in direct action protests. Angry with Attorney General Webster for his withdrawal, the litigants in these appeals sought to be appointed as Nancy's guardians to protect her from her parents and the state. Their legal protests were fueled by organized religious groups, Baptists and Catholics in particular, who had lobbied for Missouri's restrictive law. The Missouri Citizens for Life petitioned Governor John Ashcroft to seek a court ruling prohibiting the removal of the feeding tube. Letters to the editor inundated all the newspapers throughout the state, some in support of Cruzan's right to die, but many in violent opposition to the court order.

The intensity of the opposition was dramatized by the actions of protestors who mobilized and surrounded the Missouri Rehabilitation Center in Mount Vernon, Missouri. Calling themselves "rescuers," they tried to burst into Cruzan's hospital room. Their plan was to reconnect her feeding tube. Some eleven men and women, including Wanda Frye, a Kansas City nurse equipped with medical tubing, planned to enter the room and perform this "rescue" mission. When they were stopped by police, they knelt outside the door and began praying. Other protestors lined a stairway and a lower level hallway and began reading from the Bible and singing hymns. When they were arrested, each one gave "Nancy Cruzan" as his or her name. Many other protestors remained outside, encircling the center. They carried signs and banners. Some marched around and around. A number of the protestors belonged to an antiabortion organization called Operation Rescue that often engaged in blockades and demonstrations at abortion clinics. Others represented a group called Prisoners of Christ. They came from Kansas, Missouri, Nebraska, and Georgia—to name only a few states. At night, candles were lighted and the candlelight vigils provided tremendous "sight bites" for the television cameras covering the event. Cameras recorded their sobs and prayers, "Lord, change Joe Cruzan's mind about this, Lord . . . Oh Lord we're in a huge mess. Our judges can't tell right from wrong. Help us get back on the right track." A private death thus became a national spectacle as pictures and interviews with the protestors flashed around the country.[49]

Sam Lee, a lobbyist for Missouri Citizens for Life and one of the author's of Missouri's antiabortion statute, held a press conference to announce a proposed hunger strike. "I will refuse to eat," he said, "until I can persuade the Cruzan family to reconnect Nancy's feeding tube, or until she dies." He was joined in his fast by some nineteen protestors, who were arrested for trespass and unlawful assembly. Some members of the Mt. Vernon nursing staff joined in the protest. They gave press interviews, claiming that Cruzan was only disabled and thus adding to the mounting tension and anger engulfing the center.[50]

Courts quickly dismissed all the lawsuits, law officials moved to curb violence, and the days passed. It was the day after Christmas in 1990 when Nancy Cruzan died. However, the personal and public impact of the case remained. It was only the beginning for the claim of a right to die as a right of personal privacy.

POSTMORTEM: THE CRUZAN FAMILY SIX YEARS LATER

Joe and Joyce Cruzan from the beginning had both supporters and critics. However, those who opposed the family's decision were much more vocal. Vicious letters labeled the Cruzans "murderers" and warned them of "God's judgment" on their actions. Few people really understood the toll the *Cruzan* case had taken on the family. The battle to win a right to die left Nancy's father a "wounded man." His enemies claimed that he was "tortured by guilt" and personally "despondent." Nevertheless, for six years after Nancy's physical death, Joe Cruzan worked to make the political-legal system more responsive to the right-to-die issue.

He first took his appeals to the Missouri legislature. As early as 1990, Joe Cruzan testified before a Missouri Senate committee about the need to let a family, not the state, make these private decisions. The *Cruzan* litigation and Joe Cruzan's personal crusade finally prompted Senator John Danforth (R-Mo.) to push the Patient Self-Determination Act through Congress. This measure, which took effect in 1991, required hospitals, nursing homes, and health care providers who received federal Medicaid or Medicare money to respect a patient's right to refuse treatment. The law also ordered these entities to inform patients of their rights and to secure a written document laying out the patients' wishes should they become incapacitated. Danforth praised Joe Cruzan in a 1992 ceremony held at Freeman Hospital in Joplin, Missouri. "With his family, he has done more to prevent human misery than anyone else in our state," Danforth said as he presented Cruzan with a Quality in Medicine Award.[51]

Some change in Missouri law came about because of Joe and Joyce Cruzan. In 1991, the state legislature agreed that citizens had a right to designate someone other than the state to make health care decisions for them, including authorizing the removal of artificially supplied food and water. One Missouri state senator summed up the Cruzans' crusade: "It's Nancy Cruzan's legacy, but it's the fact that her father was willing to share those experiences of the family with Missouri and the nation [that helped get the bills passed]."[52]

However, even six years after *Cruzan*, the Missouri state legislature still refused to pass a bill automatically allowing families to make health care decisions for incapacitated patients who left no advance directive. The Missouri Health Care Act also still required competent adults to name, in writing, the person who would act as surrogate for them in the event they became incapacitated. Furthermore, it required certification by at least one physician that a patient was incapacitated before a proxy could act and prevented the proxy from withholding artificially supplied food and water unless specifically granted that power in the patient's advance declaration. The act also required doctors to give patients a chance to revoke their living will provisions or proxy decision.[53]

The right to die would not be easily implemented in Missouri. Religious groups never gave up their own crusade to return state law to its original status, where no patient could *ever* refuse food and water, however supplied.

The Cruzans' fight had helped bring living will laws into existence in some forty states. Joe Cruzan himself had spoken at seminars across the nation and put a human face on the right-to-die issue. His willingness to go public with his family's pain in order to secure change only increased the attacks of his critics. This finally broke him. In August 1996, Joe Cruzan hanged himself in the carport of his home in Carterville, Missouri. He was sixty-two. The note he left for his wife was private.[54] The battle for a right to die had indeed been a costly one.

CRUZAN'S IMPACT: MISSOURI AND BEYOND

During the months of June through December 1990, public opinion in Missouri expressed itself through articles and letters to the editor in newspapers and "living will seminars." Organized groups, from Missouri Citizens for Life at one extreme to the Hemlock Society—which advocates physician-assisted suicide—at the other, experienced membership growth. Hospitals, doctors, and lawyers found themselves submerged under a barrage of questions from a concerned public seeking clarification of both law and practice. The most conservative part of Missouri is the southwestern part of the state, the very area where Nancy Cruzan resided. The largest city in that area, Springfield, is the world headquarters of the Assemblies of God and also home to the fundamentalists of the Baptist Bible Fellowship; John Ashcroft and Jerry Falwell are the products of these groups, respectively. Springfield is a center for other ultraright-wing groups, such as the "Covenant, Sword, Arm of the Lord," and religious fundamentalists and political extremists exercise significant influence in the area. The city is also a major regional health care center, with St. John's (Catholic) and Cox hospitals providing services to a wide area.

The major newspaper of this area, the *Springfield News-Leader*, provided an interesting record of the local public response to the *Cruzan* case during the summer and fall of 1990. Letters to the editor poured into the paper, the majority overwhelmingly supporting the Cruzan family. The Reverend Dick Viney of Branson wrote:

> My heart is heavy for you Joe and Joyce Cruzan in your depressing struggle to free your daughter and ease your unwelcome suffering. Once again the laws of the land and man supersede the laws, the compassion and the mercy our loving father in heaven.[55]

Ray and Nancy Steinhoff's opinion mirrored that of the Branson minister, and they spoke for many of the residents of this Ozark Mountains region in an interview with the staff of the *Springfield News-Leader*. "I don't want to be a burden to anybody," Ray Steinhoff declared. "If there's no use in living, there's no use in living. That's the point right there," he continued. His wife elaborated, "If I should become ill and I have no chance of getting better, I don't want to be on a machine. Just let me die. We see the Cruzans and say, 'Gosh, that could happen to anyone.'"[56]

Local legislators, recognizing the pro-Cruzan sentiment of the area, promised action. State senator Dennis Smith (R-Springfield) promised to introduce legislation that would give courts "a clear path to take when someone has not indicated what they would want if they wound up like Cruzan." He continued, "The courts have not yet given us a guide, they've just said what you can and can't do based on existing law." Smith wanted reform of the Missouri Living Will Act so that it would become an "aid" in dying, not a hindrance.[57] Most Missourians, before *Cruzan*, had assumed that the statute actually gave them a choice concerning life support devices; *Cruzan* proved the opposite. Smith drafted a provision to expand surrogate law to increase the power of those given authorities to make a choice. Under this bill, Joe and Joyce Cruzan's right to decide for their daughter would override the state's power to intervene. Absent a living will, and without officially named surrogates, Nancy Cruzan under this proposal would have been in the hands of family. Smith explained, "[The] greater majority of people don't take time to designate a surrogate [or make a living will] until they're older and start thinking about those kinds of things."[58]

Attorneys in southwestern Missouri also supported the local demands for change, registering the impact of *Cruzan* on even this conservative area. Empathetic fear had generated action. Attorney Vincent Tyndall of Springfield advocated a "super living will," which the Kansas City Metropolitan Bar Association had proposed. Tyndall praised this document. "A Super Living Will is more detailed and has space for people to write in instructions and medical information," he explained. "This not only allows a person to express a desire not to have life prolonged under terminal conditions, but also when medical treatment does not relieve pain, provide comfort, or provide a 'reasonable expectation' that the person will regain a 'meaningful quality of life,'" Tyndall added. Under the existing Missouri Living Will Act, such a choice was not possible. Tyndall explained, "Living Wills [in Missouri] do not do what the patient expects. Even if Nancy Cruzan had had a living will, it would not have made a whit of difference as Missouri law currently exists. But if you are very clear about what you desire, it might just make a difference despite what Missouri law says." Therefore, he supported the idea of the "super" living will.[59] Attorneys like Tyndall, however, understood the pressures that could prevent the state legislature from changing the law. The powerful interest groups representing Catholics and fundamentalist Baptists were ever present in the halls of the legislature, and they opposed any relaxation of state restrictions. Most attorneys did not expect legislative change.

Area hospitals and doctors found patients demanding information about their policies. According to Springfield health practitioners, the Supreme Court's ruling of June 1990 inspired an increased interest in living wills. Springfield gerontologist Cheryl Bluestein said that in the days following the ruling she had received between thirty and forty phone calls from people interested in writing a living will. "The thing I hear most often is, 'I don't want to be put on a machine,'" Bluestein said. "The thing they say is, 'I want to die in peace.'" She concluded, "Older people are afraid of being powerless; a [true] living will would give them some control over what may happen to them."[60]

Cox South Medical Center in Springfield, Missouri, also recorded a sharp increase in living wills. Tom Brewer, Cox's manager of Senior Advantages, a senior citizen support group, distributed living will forms to clients. Brewer explained: "People are concerned. They don't want to live in an unnatural state and don't want to be kept alive by heroic means."[61] Cox Hospital's assistant administrator and attorney, Lee Peninger, noted that living wills were not a perfect solution. "[They] provide limited protection under state law since they only apply to people who have terminal illnesses. It really comes right down to what we decide is 'artificial means,'" she said. Peninger, expanding on her analysis, pointed out that "it is really tough to specify every possible situation that comes up. The state says someone in a persistent vegetative state is alive. If you withdrew hydration and nutrition, then you've committed murder."[62]

The *Cruzan* decisions generated more questions than answers, and the answers differed among doctors, hospitals, and attorneys. In St. Louis, one geriatrician, Dr. Douglas Miller of St. Louis University (Catholic), saw the decision as one which "reinstated the family and other loved ones as the party helping physicians make decisions."[63] Miller's coworker at St. John's Mercy Medical Center in Creve Coeur predicted that the decision would give families and doctors the freedom to try life sustaining technology in hard-to-predict cases, knowing that the treatment could be stopped. Other health care professionals, however, worried that doctors would still allow their fear of being sued to move them into more conservative medical diagnosis. Moreover, the decision also lent itself to "misinterpretation" according to several hospital administrators. "People think it means you can't ever withhold nutrition and hydration without a specific living will," said Joan Killion of Midwest Bio-ethics Center in Kansas City, Missouri.[64]

The three major newspapers of the state, the *St. Louis Post-Dispatch* , the *Kansas City Star*, and the *Springfield News-Leader*, all agreed that public opinion was divided over the right-to-die issue. Reaction seemed to differ according to the intensity of religious views, age, economic status, and race.[65] Personal experiences naturally played a role, as letters to the editor in the papers showed. Those who wrote in often told stories of people they had known. Fears about a right to die were expressed by some disabled adults and by health care professionals who attended disabled infants. Polling data confirmed the mixed response generated when specific factors were introduced. Issues such as pain, no hope of recovery, and types of medical devices involved all affected the opinions Missourians had about the *Cruzan* decisions. Linkage of a right to die with suicide caused ultraconservative religious Missourians to oppose the decisions vehemently. Yet some religious leaders, even Catholics and Baptists, stepped forward to propose a "balanced" response and not an automatic no.[66]

Missourians' responses were not so different from these found in other states. The *Dallas* (Texas) *Morning News* of October 24, 1992, gave support as the editors decried a "technology-driven agenda" that had tried to keep Nancy Cruzan alive.[67] The *San Francisco Chronicle* and the *Los Angeles Times* agreed.[68] However, the *St. Petersburg* (Florida) *Times* focused on the need not to condone euthanasia or suicide, and the *Orlando Sentinel Tribune* noted that "denying treatment to a patient should be a rare circumstance."[69] The *Chicago Tribune*, on the other hand, showed support for the *Cruzan* decisions, as did numerous papers on the East Coast, including the *New York Times*, *Boston Globe*, *Buffalo News*, and *Washington Post*.[70] National polling data was consistent with that in Missouri in showing how responses differed as questions were changed to reflect differing factors. It was clear that the *Cruzan* decisions had not settled the right-to-die issue. New cases were waiting to challenge courts and citizens.

CRUZAN REDUX: THE CASE OF CHRISTINE BUSALACCHI

An organized, vocal, and powerful minority in Missouri had responded negatively to the right-to-die principle seemingly won in *Cruzan*. Their influence was evident in the narrowness of the legal changes made in Missouri's living will laws. Their power was also exerted through state leaders and institutions. Governor John Ashcroft, a Republican and religious advocate (member of the Assemblies of God), had never retreated from his pro-life agenda as it touched both birth and death. His daily prayer meetings with his staff gave evidence of his commitment. At the same time, Attorney General William Webster had lost supporters when he withdrew the state from the *Cruzan II* litigation and was anxious to recover his followers. State officials who supported the state Republican Party platform were ready to use their positions to avoid or evade implementation of a right-to-die principle.

The failure of the changes hoped for after *Cruzan II* soon became evident. The case that documented this—*In Re: The Matter of Christine Busalacchi*, No. 73677, Circuit Court of St. Louis County, Probate Division—was filed on January 7, 1991, entering the Missouri legal system just twelve days after the death of Nancy Cruzan. Christine Busalacchi, like Nancy, had already spent years in a vegetative state. Unlike Nancy, though, Christine had been a minor when her automobile accident occurred; she was seventeen at the time of the accident, legally still a child. She was twenty-two when Nancy Cruzan was finally allowed to die in December 1990.

Like Cruzan, Christine Busalacchi had been consigned to the Missouri Rehabilitation Center in Mt. Vernon, Missouri; she had been there from 1987 to 1990. Extensive brain surgery had failed to help her, and she existed only with the assistance of a feeding tube. In 1988 the center had recommended to Christine's father that she be moved to a skilled nursing facility. They did not specifically tell him that in a private facility he would have greater power to make decisions about his daughter, but this was implied. Their recommendation did not reflect any belief that Christine might recover. It was not until 1990, two years later, and exactly two days after Nancy Cruzan's death, that Peter J. Busalacchi, Christine's father and guardian, decided to act upon this suggestion. His decision created a new battlefront for opponents of a right to die.[71]

Peter Busalacchi understood the problems the Cruzans had faced. He also understood the difficulties that still remained in Missouri law and practice even in the wake of *Cruzan II*. However, he assumed that he would be allowed to follow the state-run center's recommendation: to send Christine elsewhere. He was mistaken. When Busalacchi tried to move his daughter to Riverside Medical Center in Minneapolis, Minnesota, Missouri state officials stopped him. Attorney General William L. Webster and his staff were determined to halt right-to-die changes. Webster's own decision probably reflected his concern over the criticism he was getting due to the *Cruzan* decision. His staff, composed of pro-life advocates such as attorney Patrick King, was anxious to return state policy to its ultraconservative pre-*Cruzan* position. Once again, the state of Missouri claimed its right to decide issues of life and death rather than to permit a family to make this decision.

Missouri's attorney general accused Peter Busalacchi of "intending to have Christine's gastrostomy tube removed," thus allowing her to die. "Peter Busalacchi wants to take his daughter to Minnesota because he knows that the laws there don't have Missouri's 'clear and convincing evidence standard,'" the attorney general's staff complained. "He intends to kill her." Peter Busalacchi had talked to the press, he had given news interviews, and his criticism of Missouri practice was well known. Publicity mounted as the state asserted its claim over Christine. Confrontation occurred first in the courtroom of Judge Louis M. Kohn in St. Louis Probate Court.[72]

The legal issue before this trial court did not specifically involve Christine Busalacchi's right to die. The question at first focused on the civil right to travel.[73] Peter Busalacchi asserted this as both a national and a state fundamental right guaranteed by the Constitution. It was a right of citizenship, Busalacchi's attorney argued. Judge Kohn agreed. The judge cited the "full faith and credit" clause of the federal Constitution and noted that Missouri was required to recognize the validity of the laws of Minnesota. Judge Kohn also stated that he could find no provisions in Missouri law that prohibited Busalacchi from moving his daughter to another state. Who should make decisions about appropriate medical treatment for children? The judge's answer was clear. "[Under Missouri law] these decisions have always been made by the doctor and family," he said. "The *Cruzan* decision does not affect that right."[74]

Attorney General Webster disagreed. The state appealed Judge Kohn's decision to the Missouri Court of Appeals, Eastern District. As the three-judge panel considered the question, tensions increased across the state. Was Christine Busalacchi in a persistent vegetative state? Or was she only "disabled"? Did her father want to kill her? Could the state stop him? The three judges on the court of appeals took the easy way out; they sent the case back to the probate court, demanding "additional evidentiary hearings on Christine's condition." The judges asked the state to expand on its case and the "motives of [Christine's] guardian." This 2–1 decision showed the divisions within the state. Judge Gerald Smith had agreed totally with Judge Kohn, and he dissented from returning the case for more hearings. "Minnesota is not a medical or ethical wasteland," Smith wrote, and he urged his brethren to affirm Kohn's decision. However, the 2–1 vote returned the Busalacchi case to the probate court.[75]

In the meantime Peter Busalacchi, through his attorney, William H. Colby of the *Cruzan* litigation, sought a transfer of the case from the court of appeals to the Missouri Supreme Court. This was granted on April 15, 1991. In reaction, Department of Health officials acted quickly. Within three days, they had moved Christine to St. Louis and placed her in the Midtown Habilitation Center. They reclassified Christine as "developmentally disabled" and began attempts to feed her orally. Additionally, some replacement surgery was also performed at a nearby hospital. These proceedings were resisted by Christine's father, who secured a court order requiring the state to cease its attempts.[76]

This new determination on the part of the state to keep Christine Busalacchi alive was evident when oral argument opened before the state supreme court on October 7. This court, too, responded cautiously. The justices remanded the case back to the Probate Division of the Circuit Court of St. Louis County, with orders to hear additional evidence and make findings about Christine Busalacchi's medical condition.[77] Unhappy with the prospect of returning to Judge Kohn's court, Attorney General Webster's staff filed motions to secure a different judge. This was denied on November 6 and again on November 12, and the case returned to familiar surroundings. Attorneys for Peter Busalacchi filed motions on November 19 to have Christine classified as a PVS patient and to grant her father and guardian the right to order removal of her feeding tube while she resided in Missouri. The legal proceedings continued.[78]

The probate judge heard testimony from eighteen witnesses and received sworn depositions from another two. The judge examined fifty-nine exhibits, including medical reports from eleven physicians. In all, some twenty-two hours of court time were absorbed by these proceedings. By the end of it, the judge was unpersuaded by the state's arguments and evidence. In his December 20, 1991, ruling, Judge Kohn held that Christine Busalacchi was indeed in a persistent vegetative state and that under the new 1991 Missouri Health Care Act, her father, acting as her guardian, could withdraw her artificial feeding treatment, thus terminating her life.

Once again the state of Missouri appealed. Briefs were filed before the Missouri Supreme Court during June and July 1992, with the state arguing that Judge Kohn had exceeded his instructions. The state also contended that the case had now become a right-to-die case and was thus controlled by *Cruzan's* evidentiary standard of clear and convincing proof of intent. The state also insisted that no guardian had power to withdraw a feeding tube without a living will declaration or other clear and convincing evidence of the ward's wishes.[79]

The judges on the state supreme court faced tough choices. The medical evidence, even after a second hearing in the St. Louis probate court, was not clear. The state's doctor had testified that Christine Busalacchi was "alert to her name and tracked with her eyes"; a nurse had testified to Busalacchi's "responsive laughter." However, other doctors and nurses testified that Busalacchi was in a persistent vegetative state. It was true that she had taken some food orally between January and July 1991, but this did not equate with the medical and legal definition of "eating normally." In fact, swallowing small amounts of food might be a reflexive action, and the amount ingested had not been sufficient to nourish her apart from the gastrostomy tube. A second issue facing the judges in the Missouri Supreme Court dealt with the fact that Christine had been a minor when the accident occurred and had never had power to legally express her wishes. Now that she was an adult, could her parents still decide for her?[80]

As the attorneys argued, Missouri's citizens divided. Some opponents of a right to die, like the Sabine family, made their position known in dramatic fashions. During the oral argument before the Missouri Supreme Court, the Sabines sat in the courtroom with their daughter Erin in a wheelchair next to them. A victim of Rett's syndrome, Erin at seventeen functioned at the level of a five- to six-month-old baby. Her parents told reporters that they were there to send a message to the state that "it must value and protect all life, even if it is life in a persistent vegetative state."[81]

On the other hand, support for Peter Busalacchi came even from prominent ministers. The Reverend Patrick Norris of the St. Louis Medical Center in an "open letter" urged the court to consider carefully whether courts should usurp "ethical decision making prerogative from patient and parent."[82] Norris was joined by other experts such as Sandra D. Scott, a law professor at the University of Missouri, who urged the court to avoid the narrow focus on PVS status and clear and convincing evidence. Instead, she urged, people might want to forgo treatment that was "overly burdensome, offered no benefit, and was ineffective for securing one's goals."[83]

Thus Missourians continued to be divided. Some believed that removing life support from persons who would not recover cognitive function was morally acceptable; others believed that this was murder. There was no consensus and no true dialogue; thus there could be no compromise. It would be either a legal or a political decision in the end.

The legal process seemed to be at a standstill as the Missouri Supreme Court, for a second time, evaluated the Busalacchi briefs and arguments. The political process, however, was moving forward as the 1992 presidential election drew closer. Throughout August, September, and October the political momentum overtook the legal process, and by November 1992, it was clear that the right-to-die decision would be made at the polls.

Election Day's Democratic landslide in Missouri swept into office, among others, a new attorney general with a very different ideology from that of William Webster. Former state senator and newly elected attorney general Jay Nixon was committed by his campaign pledge to "withdraw the state from the Busalacchi case."[84] Indeed, all of the new leadership of the state was in agreement on the right-to-die question. Governor Mel Carnahan and Lieutenant Governor Roger Wilson had both made their positions clear. During a 1990 debate in the Missouri Senate, Wilson and Nixon had both gone on record opposing attempts by the state's Mental Health Department to refuse to implement patients' advance directives. "This [action] . . . contravenes [our new] state law," said Wilson. "It is wrong." Nixon, in the same debate added, "This is a part of a Republican Administration's continuing agenda, its moral crusade to involve themselves in the personal lives of patients who have rights [to privacy]."[85] Carnahan, as lieutenant governor, had called the 1990 Mental Health Directive an "extremist interference with the rights of individuals and families to make decisions for themselves."[86]

The voters of Missouri had had a clear choice as they went to the polls that November day in 1992. If they had selected their former attorney general, William Webster, to be governor, the right to die, partially gained in *Cruzan*, would have been lost in a welter of new state-imposed regulations and administrative directions. Votes for Carnahan, Wilson, and Nixon would insure *Cruzan*'s gains and open the door for greater protection for privacy rights in general. The electorate made its choice clear: Webster lost the election, Carnahan won. What did this mean for Christine Busalacchi?

Webster, now a lame-duck attorney general, refused to withdraw the state from the Busalacchi litigation. As Peter Busalacchi was seeking a circuit court order to allow him to move Christine, Webster was before the state supreme court asking for a reversal of any such order. This was the stalemate that existed on December 9, 1992, as the *St. Louis Post-Dispatch* went to press with its editorial entitled "Keep Politics Out of Life-Support Cases."[87] Would the Missouri Supreme Court intervene before the state administration changed in January?

Two months remained before Inauguration Day, and the court could have decided the *Busalacchi* case at any day during that time. Peter Busalacchi had reason to worry. The state supreme court had not been friendly to Nancy Cruzan nor was it friendly to Christine Busalacchi. However, the political change had impacted the judges, and they hesitated, looking for a way to maintain their power and protect their position. Busalacchi's attorney, William Colby, offered them this option: a moot case. "The [Missouri State Supreme Court] should declare this case moot because there will not be a plaintiff when the new administration for Missouri takes office," Colby declared in his motion.[88]

As the Missouri Supreme Court pondered and procrastinated, the days passed, until finally in January 1993 it dismissed the case. On February 19, 1993, Peter Busalacchi moved his daughter. However, he did not try to move her to Minnesota as originally planned. Instead Busalacchi took his daughter to Barnes Hospital, a nationally known medical facility in St. Louis. Once again a team of neurologists were called upon to evaluate Christine. Their verdict was firm: Christine Busalacchi was in a persistent vegetative state. They advised the removal of the feeding tube.[89]

Again, legal action began at once as petitions were filed throughout the state to prevent Christine's father from acting. None of the individuals filing these petitions knew the Busalacchi family personally. Nevertheless, people like Elizabeth McDonald, an anti–right-to-die activist, insisted that courts should grant them the "natural right of a parent." McDonald argued that Peter Busalacchi was not a "fit" father and that she herself would better represent Christine's interests. She asked the St. Louis Probate Court to appoint her guardian. McDonald's petition was not dismissed summarily. Instead, attorneys were required to defend Peter Busalacchi's right to remain guardian. Even though the state had removed itself from this position, another person could still challenge Christine's father concerning her medical treatment. This petition also went to the Missouri Supreme Court, where it was rejected on February 23, 1993. Peter Busalacchi and the doctors of Barnes Hospital were finally free to remove Christine's feeding tube.[90]

The intensity of the Busalacchi battle, however, showed that a clear right-to-die principle had not been won in *Cruzan* nor in *Busalacchi*. Peter Busalacchi was never granted the right to move his daughter out of state. Missouri retained the right to issue extensive rules, regulations, and directives that could severely curtail decisions concerning refusal of medical treatment. A political upheaval had served to halt the most restrictive limitations, but the powerful pro-life groups in Missouri remained undeterred. They would continue their campaign for state control that could deny patients a right to refuse nutrition or hydration. What would it take to insure a privacy right to die in Missouri? Political events during the next eight years would give hope to those who had defended Cruzan's and Busalacchi's right to die.

Attorney General William Webster would never again pose a threat to the supporters of privacy rights. He went to jail. Charged with and convicted for embezzlement and conspiracy during his tenure as attorney general, Webster began serving a two-year jail sentence on January 20, 1994. He was also fined $100,000 and lost his license to practice law. Webster, the judge said, "had violated the public trust."[91] Governor John Ashcroft was able to distance himself from the attorney general by the simple device of "remaining silent." Two years later in 1994, Ashcroft won a seat in the U.S. Senate only to lose it in 2000 to his deceased rival, Mel Carnahan.[92] His appointment to the post of U.S. attorney general by President George W. Bush drew intense and bitter criticism as did his subsequent job performance. He had to abort all attempts to run for president.

Did these events indicate that Missouri had turned its back on those seeking to limit the right of privacy, particularly as it involved the "right to die?" The response would be an incremental one.

Other states would be involved in *Cruzan*-like dilemmas and would seek answers from the Missouri experience.[93] The scope and limit of the living will and the power of a guardian to deny food and water to a ward without a medical directive was not settled. This issue actually took specific form almost at the very moment of Cruzan's death, and fifteen years later it would embroil the country in a national debate of epic proportions. The states involved were different: Florida replaced Missouri. The PVS litigants were different: Terri Schiavo replaced Nancy Cruzan. Courts came under attack by state and national political actors. The privacy right to die would be tested once again as America sought a definitive answer concerning the role of courts and judges in making this, the most final of all privacy decisions.

NOTES

1. Stephen L. Wasby, "Toward a Theory of Impact," in *The Impact of Supreme Court Decisions*, ed. Theodore L. Becker and Malcolm M. Feeley, 2nd ed. (New York: Oxford University Press, 1973), 100, 216. See also Stephen L. Wasby, *The Impact of the United States Supreme Court* (Homewood, IL: Dorsey Press, 1970), 246–248; and Bradley C. Canon and Charles A. Johnson, *Judicial Policies: Implementation and Impact*, 2nd ed. (Washington, DC: CQ Press, 1999).

2. *Cruzan v. Director, Missouri Department of Health*, 497 U.S. 261 (1990).

3. For more details on this case, see Alice Fleetwood Bartee, "Reinventing Privacy Rights in Missouri: The Right to Die Case," in *Reinventing Missouri Government: Case Studies in State Experiments at Work*, ed. Denny Pilant (Fort Worth, TX: Harcourt Brace, 1994), 97–145.

4. Ibid., 97. See also William H. Colby, *Long Goodbye: The Deaths of Nancy Cruzan* (Carlsbad, CA: Hay House, 2002), 21–33.

5. Bartee, "Reinventing Privacy Rights," 98; Colby, *Long Goodbye*, 27–29.

6. *Webster v. Reproductive Health Services*, 92 U.S. 490 (1989).

7. *Clayton v. Place*, 494 U.S. 1081 (1990), *cert. denied* ("The Purdy Dance Ban Case").

8. *Barber v. Time, Inc.*, 159 S.W. 2d 291 (Mo. 1942).

9. *Sofka v. Thal*, 662 S.W. 2d 502 (Mo. 1983).

10. Bartee, "Reinventing Privacy Rights," 98–99. See also trial brief of Guardians *ad litem* Thad C. McCanse and David B. Mouton (LF 66–70), and posttrial brief (LF 94–95).

11. The Uniform Rights of the Terminally Ill Act, § 495.015.1, 495.010 (3) (RS Mo. 1986).

12. See "Plaintiffs—Respondents' Brief, William H. Colby," *Cruzan v. Harmon*, 760 S.W. 2d 408 (Mo. 1988), *on appeal* (Sup. Ct. Mo. 1988) (No. 70813), 13–14.

13. Ibid. See also "The Right to Die Question," editorial, *Kansas City Star*, 27 June 1990.

14. *Cruzan v. Harmon and Lampkins* (Jasper Cir. Ct. Prob. Div. Mo. 1987) *Petition for Declaratory Judgment* (No. CV 384–9P). See also Colby, *Long Goodbye*, 84–86; and William H. Colby, "The Lessons of the Cruzan Case," *University of Kansas Law Review* 39 (1991): 523.

15. *Cruzan v. Harmon and Lampkins, Petition for Declaratory Judgment*. See also Colby, *Long Goodbye*, 84–86; Colby, "Lessons of the Cruzan Case," 523.

16. *John L. Sullivan, Guardian of the Person of Lucy K. Stoppe v. St. John's Mercy Medical Center* (St. Louis Cir. Ct. Mo. 1987) (No. 561631).

17. Bartee, "Reinventing Privacy Rights," 102. See also Colby, *Long Goodbye*, 129–133, 197–207, 209–218, 347.

18. *Cruzan v. Harmon and Lampkins, Petition for Declaratory Judgment* and plaintiff's posttrial brief (1988).

19. Bartee, "Reinventing Privacy Rights," 99. See also "Appellant's Brief, William L. Webster, Attorney General," *Cruzan v. Harmon*. See also *State v. Walsh*, 713 S.W. 2d 568 (1986).

20. Bartee, "Reinventing Privacy Rights, 103. See also *Cruzan v. Harmon*, 5.

21. *Cruzan v. Harmon*, 5.

22. Ibid.

23. Ibid.

24. Bartee, "Reinventing Privacy Rights," 104.

25. *Cruzan v. Harmon*.

26. Bartee, "Reinventing Privacy Rights," 104–105. See also Colby, *Long Goodbye*, 257–258.

27. Colby, *Long Goodbye*, chap. 31.

28. Bartee, "Reinventing Privacy Rights," 105–107. See also Colby, *Long Goodbye*, 321–323.

29. *Cruzan v. Director, Missouri Department of Health*, 497 U.S. 261 (1990), 276–277, 279.

30. Ibid., 287.

31. Ibid., 265–287, 287–291.

32. Ibid., 287–291.

33. Ibid., 330–357.

34. Ibid., 283. See also Colby, *Long Goodbye*, 321–323.

35. Colby, "Lessons of the Cruzan Case," 525. See also Bartee, "Reinventing Privacy Rights," 105–106.

36. Colby, "Lessons of the Cruzan Case," 524.

37. *Cruzan v. Harmon*, 760 S.W. 2d 408, 416–417, 419–420 (Mo. 1988).

38. "A Time for Mercy," editorial, *St. Louis Post-Dispatch*, 26 June 1990.

39. Ibid.

40. Bartee, "Reinventing Privacy Rights," 107–108. See Colby, *Long Goodbye*, Chapter 37, 333–336, 344–347.

41. Ibid.

42. *In re: Quinlan*, 70 N.J. 10, 335 A.2d 647 (1976). See also 70 N.J. 38–42; 335 A.2d 662–664.

43. 70 N.J. 41; 335 A.2d 664. See also Laurence Tribe, *American Constitutional Law*, 2nd ed. (Mineola, NY: Foundation Press, 1988), 1365.

44. Colby, *Long Goodbye*, 322, 347, 351. See also Bartee, "Reinventing Privacy Rights," 107–108.

45. Colby, *Long Goodbye*, 323, 329–333, 336, 338.

46. William L. Webster, Attorney General of the State of Missouri, "Suggestions in Support of Motion to Dismiss," 14 September 1990, from court record. See also Colby, "Lessons of the Cruzan Case," 519–528.

47. *Cruzan v. Director, Missouri Department of Health, and Administrator of the Missouri Rehabilitation Center at Mt. Vernon* (Jasper Cir. Ct. Mo. 1990) (No. CV 384–9P).

48. Colby, "Lessons of the Cruzan Case," 520.

49. Lane Beauchamp, "Police Stop Effort to Reach Cruzan," *Kansas City Star*, 19 December 1990. See also Colby, *Long Goodbye*, 369, 371–373.

50. "A Time to Die," editorial, *St. Louis Post-Dispatch*, 19 December 1990.

51. Terri Gleich, "Court Battle Clarified Issues on Withholding Treatment," *Springfield News-Leader*, 20 August 1996.

52. Linda Eardly, "Proposal to Ban Option for Death Is Protested," *St. Louis Post-Dispatch*, 22 August 1992.

53. Terri Gleich, "The Missouri Durable Power of Attorney for Health Care Act," *Springfield News-Leader*, 20 August 1996. Among other provisions, the law allows competent adults to name, in writing, a health care proxy; however, no one can be required by a health care provider or insurance company to do so. The power to withhold food and water must be listed specifically in the document, and the doctor must give the patient a chance to revoke it. The Act also prohibits the withholding of food and water from a patient who can eat normally. The Missouri living will has a significant statement that differs from a durable power of attorney. There are several significant limitations of the living will as defined by Missouri statutes. The living will may apply only where death will occur within a short period of time whether or not certain treatment is provided. The statute prohibits a living will from withholding or withdrawing artificially supplied nutrition and hydration. An "advance directive" *can* secure that right, however. The "advance directive" which exceeds the limitations of the living will statute, must be "clear and convincing" about withholding or withdrawing food and water artificially supplied.

54. Tamlya Kailaos, "Those Cruzan Left Recall Tortured Soul," *Springfield News-Leader*, 20 August 1996.

55. Dick Viney, "Minister Wears Heavy Heart Over Cruzan Family Suffering," letter to the editor, *Springfield News-Leader*, 2 July 1990.

56. J. Lee Howard, "I Don't Want to be a Burden to Anybody," *Springfield News-Leader*, 1 July 1990.

57. J. Lee Howard, "More Want Living Wills After Cruzan," *Springfield News-Leader*, 1 July 1990.

58. Ibid.

59. Ibid.

60. Ibid. See also "Nancy Cruzan's Accomplishment," editorial, *New York Times*, 6 March 1991.

61. Howard, "More Want Living Wills."

62. Ibid.

63. Theresa Tighe, "Opinions Divided on Right-to-Die Case," *St. Louis Post-Dispatch*, 15 December 1990.

64. Ibid.

65. Ibid.

66. "Sensitive Decisions," editorial, *Christian Science Monitor*, 29 June 1990. See also Nancy Gibbs, "Love and Let Die," *Time*, 19 March 1990.

67. Robert Lowes, "Ethics by Committee," *Dallas Morning News*, 2 February 1994.

68. "The Cruzan Case," letter to the editor, *San Francisco Chronicle*, 3 July 1990; Robin Abarian, "When the State Makes a Family Tragedy Worse," *Los Angeles Times*, 11 March 1992.

69. Dan Allison, "Euthanasia, Abortion, Suicide Should Not Be Condoned," *St. Petersburg* (Florida) *Times*, 12 December 1990; Myriam Marquez, "Court's Decision Prolongs the Pain of Medical-Ethics Nightmare," editorial, *Orlando Sentinel Tribune*, 16 February 1994.

70. Philip Schwimmer, "Voices of the People: Dying Instructions," *Chicago Tribune*, 12 November 1990; "Doctors Today Learn Greater Awareness," *New York Times*, 25 December 1992; "Supreme Court's Latest Sacrifice is the Re-emergence of States' Rights," editorial, *Boston Globe*, 27 June 1990; "Spelling Out the Right to Die," editorial, *Boston Globe*, 27 June 1990; James J. Kilpatrick, "Right to Die Is a Touchy Legal Issue," *Buffalo News*, 25 October 1993; "Supreme Blunders," editorial, *Washington Post*, 2 July 1990; editorial, *Buffalo News*, 27 October 1990.

71. Sandra Davidson-Scott, "In the Matter of Christine Busalacchi," editorial, *St. Louis Post-Dispatch*, 6 September 1992.

72. Bartee, "Reinventing Privacy Rights," 108–111.

73. *In re: The Matter of Christine Busalacchi* (St. Louis Cir. Ct. Prob. Div. Mo. 1991), No. 737677.

74. Ibid.

75. *In re: The Matter of Christine Busalacchi* (Mo. Ct. App., E.D. 1991).

76. Bartee, "Reinventing Privacy Rights," 109.

77. *In re: The Matter of Christine Busalacchi* (*on transfer*, Mo. Sup. Ct. 1991).

78. Bartee, "Reinventing Privacy Rights," 109.

79. *In re: The Matter of Christine Busalacchi* (Mo. Ct. App., E.D. 1991).

80. *In re: The Matter of Christine Busalacchi* (*on transfer*, Mo. Sup. Ct. 1991).

81. Davidson-Scott, "In the Matter of Christine Busalacchi."

82. Margaret Bittman, "Deciding It's Time to Die," editorial, *St. Louis Post-Dispatch*, 16 September 1992.

83. Davidson-Scott, "In the Matter of Christine Busalacchi."

84. Bartee, "Reinventing Privacy Rights," 110.

85. Eardly, "Proposal to Ban Option."

86. Ibid.

87. Kevin P. O'Rourke, "Keep Politics Out of Life-Support Cases," commentary column, *St. Louis Post-Dispatch*, 9 December 1992.

88. Terry Ganey, "Court Dismisses Busalacchi Case: Stricken Woman's Failure in Father's Hands," *St. Louis Post-Dispatch*, 27 January 1993.

89. "Comatose Woman, Focus of Court Battles, Dies," *New York Times*, 8 March 1993.

90. William C. Lhotka, "Busalacchi Family Wins Ruling Over Guardianship," *St. Louis Post-Dispatch*, 6 February 1993.

91. Terry Ganey and Tim Poor, "Webster Gets Maximum 2-Year Prison Term: Defendant Ducked Responsibility, Judge Says," *St. Louis Post-Dispatch* 22 September 1993, 1A.

92. Jo Mannies, "U.S. Senate: Late Governor Carnahan Edges Ashcroft in Emotionally Charged Contest," *St. Louis Post-Dispatch*, 8 November 2000.

93. Louis Markam, "Cruzan Decision Shifts Debate to State Battlegrounds," *St. Louis Post-Dispatch*, 1 July 1990.

5

All Is Not Lost

Privacy Causes Won

The controversial questions of privacy rights were not settled by the cases of *Poe*, *Bowers*, *Webster*, and *Cruzan*. Even before the announcement of the Supreme Court's decisions, the losers began to plan new strategies. Each of the cases lost generated its own unique issues and required different tactics to keep the cause of privacy rights alive. Everyone, however, anticipated another attempt to secure judicial legitimization. Judicial approval of a policy goal seems to confer greater legitimacy on that policy than the approval of the legislative or executive branch. The American public has a penchant for judicial resolution of critical issues.[1] This acceptance of judicial authority has been generated by the judicial myth that stamps the Court as the appropriate protector of the Constitution. Winning, therefore, is not enough unless the Supreme Court places its imprimatur, its stamp of approval, on the policy.

This would seem to create a paradox. On the one hand the Court's decision is seen as final; on the other hand, modification or even reversal of that decision becomes the new goal. Although losers may turn to the legislature or to the executive for help in securing these goals, they continue to focus on the judicial branch. In fact, judicial opinions are accepted because the judicial process is open to continuing the debate over policy issues and the Court allows losers to "try again."

In attempts to secure judicial legitimization of the various issues in the privacy rights cause, litigants and their attorneys pored over the Court's opinions, searching for any loophole. Groups affected by each decision pondered its implication and assessed their options. Elected decision makers evaluated their choices under the decision and weighed the value of compliance against that of noncompliance. Could they avoid, evade, or delay the implementation of the decision while awaiting another opportunity for a judicial rematch?[2] The media coverage of each case decision served to mobilize the public into new groups, while polling organizations prepared data analyzing public opinion. The communication of the Court's decision was particularly significant in the highly charged emotional atmosphere of the privacy rights cases. On these cases, the Court most definitely heard from the public.

The Court expects this type of response. It expects "feedback."[3] The Court expects issues, presumably settled in a definitive decision, to reappear. The only question is when and in what form the issues will arise. While justices routinely deny that public opinion influences their decisions, experts assert that most often the Court follows, rather than leads, public opinion.[4] Yet activist Courts have served to push forward social, moral, and economic policies; they have also served to hold back innovative changes. In every respect, the Supreme Court is a political body, functioning as a "continuing constitutional convention" to relate the Constitution to the critical questions of the day.[5] The judicial process culminating in feedback always generates new questions which courts may use to confirm, modify, or alter earlier case decisions. This is what happened with the privacy rights cases that ran the gauntlet of emotional moral issues from those of birth to those of death.

Poe v. Ullman's 1961 decision denying a constitutional right to possess and use birth control would be challenged just four years later. Anti-*Poe* feedback generated the new case of *Griswold v. Connecticut* (1965) and the Court would at last see the birth control ban as it was actually applied. The loss of the right to abortion almost occurred in 1989's *Webster v. Reproductive Health Services.* Yet four years later the feedback from that decision brought still another case in *Planned Parenthood of Southeastern Pennsylvania v. Casey* (1992) with an unexpected win for pro-choice groups. Gay rights activists, unwilling to accept their loss in *Bowers v. Hardwick* (1986), would have to wait seventeen years before the Supreme Court would squarely face an identical case, *Lawrence v. Texas* (2003), and revisit and retract its earlier decision. Finally, the Court found itself facing a growing number of "right-to-die" cases, and the issues raised in *Cruzan v. Missouri* would generate new cases of ever increasing complexity. Foremost among these was *Schiavo v. Bush* (2005), which pitted the legislative and executive branches of both state and national government against the power of the courts to determine the scope and limit of the right to die. These new cases showed the feedback process at work in judicial decision making. They demonstrated the validity of the axiom "We only win by losing."[6]

CONTRACEPTION: CONSTITUTIONAL PROTECTION WON

Poe v. Ullman was not a complete loss for the advocates of birth control. Within the decision itself lay seeds that would generate its destruction. *Poe* was anything but a unanimous decision. A 5–4 opinion with a separate concurrence and dissents, *Poe* offered a weak precedent. Justice Felix Frankfurter had only a plurality, and the fifth vote, Justice William Brennan's concurrence, was narrowly worded. Citing the "skimpy record," Brennan had refused to believe that Connecticut would really apply the law against married couples. The four dissenters, however, made a powerful case to contradict this assumption. In particular, Justice William O. Douglas's magnificent prose was memorable. Describing the real threat to privacy inherent in Connecticut's statute, Douglas wrote, "If we imagine a regime of full enforcement of the law in the manner of an Anthony Comstock, we would reach the point where search warrants issued and officers appeared in bedrooms to find out what went on."[7] This graphic portrayal would impact all those who read the opinion, and newspapers were quick to focus on it.

It was, however, the dissent of Justice John Marshall Harlan II that shook the foundations of the Frankfurter majority opinion. Thirty-three pages in length, Harlan's dissent meticulously attacked the plurality's argument on two major grounds: justiciability and constitutionality. Massing precedent, analyzing judicial barriers such as ripeness, and defending the standing to sue of the appellants, Harlan made points that impressed the academic legal profession. He also focused on actual prosecution that had occurred in Connecticut as early as the 1940 *Nelson* case and accused his brethren of "indulg[ing] in a bit of sleight of hand to be rid of this case."[8] Harlan, too, reached a high level of impressive descriptive prose when he wrote:

> Precisely what is involved here is this: the state is asserting the right to enforce its moral judgment by intruding upon the most intimate details of the marital relation with the full power of the criminal law. Potentially, this could allow the deployment of all the incidental machinery of the criminal law, arrests, searches, and seizures; inevitably, it must mean at the very least the lodging of criminal charges, a public trial, and testimony . . . as to the mode and manner of the married couples' sexual relations. In sum, the statute allows the states to enquire into, prove, and punish married people for the private use of their marital intimacy.[9]

The arguments advanced by Justice Harlan also highlighted that most revered of English common-law precepts, the right to privacy of the home. These dissents, as well as the weak plurality opinion in *Poe*, clearly pointed birth control advocates to the paths they needed to follow in creating a new case: They should open clinics, offer birth control information and advice, and accept arrest and imprisonment.[10] Thus was the landmark case *Griswold v. Connecticut* born. It was 1965 and finally the time was ripe for judicial legitimation of a constitutional right of privacy for the distribution and use of birth control.

Griswold v. Connecticut began with the opening of a birth control clinic in New Haven only five months after the *Poe* decision. The Planned Parenthood

League of Connecticut, under the leadership of a new director, Estelle Griswold, organized the clinic's opening so as to secure maximum publicity. More than forty "media representatives" were present. Accompanied by attorney Fowler Harper and Dr. Lee Buxton, both veterans of the *Poe* litigation, Griswold held what amounted to a press conference. She explained the services the clinic would offer, detailed the qualifications of its staff, and outlined its hours of operation. It was a high-profile event, and its purpose was clear: to invite attack. The clinic personnel hoped that someone would step forward, invoke the Connecticut statute, and demand prosecution.

Unlike the earlier cases of *Tileston v. Ullman* (1943) and *Poe v. Ullman* (1961), both Dr. Buxton and clinic director Griswold were openly breaking the law in order to test the legality of Connecticut's birth control statute. Attorney Harper would have a real, as opposed to hypothetical, case. Similar to civil disobedience cases, the final birth control action had as its champions people ready to lose their liberty and their profession. Dr. Buxton's license to practice medicine was at risk. Thus the loophole that had allowed Justice Frankfurter and his colleagues to dismiss *Poe* using a procedural technicality was closed. This would be a concrete case where harm and damage awaited the violators of the law. The elements of case and controversy and standing to sue clearly existed. All that was needed was a complaining party who would push the state to begin a criminal prosecution. This action was not long coming.

It was an ordinary citizen, a Mr. James G. Morris, who lodged the complaint. Outraged by the open violation of Connecticut law, Morris began his attack. He called the mayor; he called the chief of police; he called the local prosecuting attorney. The state acted. Police were sent to investigate the clinic, where, to their surprise, staff and patients were eagerly awaiting them. Estelle Griswold delivered a ninety-minute lecture, during which she demonstrated to the police all the various devices of birth control available at the clinic. All of these violated the Connecticut law, she asserted, calling upon Dr. Buxton to confirm her statements. Buxton, assuming responsibility for all of the action of the clinic, invited arrest, as did Griswold. The police detectives, bemused, hurriedly departed.

Several days would pass before the state would respond to this unexpected set of events. Continually harassed by Citizen Morris, the circuit court prosecutor, Julius Maretz, ordered the police back to the clinic with new instructions. Would the clinic provide the names of at least two women who had received birth control advice and supplies at the clinic and who were engaged in using them? Buxton and Griswold found two birth control advocates who were ready to step forward: Joan Bates Forberg had received and was consuming birth control pills; Rosemary Stevens had obtained contraceptive jelly. The case was clear: open, deliberate violations of every part of the Connecticut statute had occurred. Maretz issued arrest warrants for Estelle Griswold and Dr. Lee Buxton, and a new birth control case was born.[11]

Starting in November 1962, the various court actions that would move *Griswold v. Connecticut* forward on its way to the U.S. Supreme Court began to unfold. The hearing and plea stage in December brought the case to its first court trial on January 2, 1963. The judge, J. Robert Lacey, immediately found both Griswold and Buxton guilty. Attorney Catherine Roraback duly filed her appeal and waited for the case to be considered by an intermediate court of appeals consisting of a three-judge panel. The process then halted. It would be July before Judge Lacey would complete the necessary paperwork to allow the appeal to go to this appellate division of the state circuit court. Summer gave way to fall, and finally in mid-October, *State of Connecticut v. Griswold and Buxton* was on the court's docket for oral arguments.[12] The litigants again were told to wait. The expected defeat came on January 17, 1963, with all three appellate judges unanimously affirming the convictions of Dr. Buxton and Griswold.

The Connecticut Supreme Court was the next stage and those justices agreed to hear the appeal. Spring again gave way to summer and then to fall. It was November 12, 1963, before the state supreme court heard the oral argument in the case. The final state court decision was handed down on May 12, 1964. *State of Connecticut v. Griswold et al.* was, like the lower court opinions, unanimous in its decision against Griswold and Buxton.

In all of the actions at the various state levels, the Connecticut judges adhered to the same arguments used in *Tileston* and *Poe*. The overriding issue for them involved the "proper role of the court." This point was clearly stated by Connecticut Supreme Court justice John M. Cornly:

Courts may not interfere with the exercise by a state of the police power to conserve public safety and welfare, including health and morals, if the law has real and substantial relation to the accomplishment of those objects.[13]

No federal constitutional argument based on the First or Fourteenth Amendments, no sociological data or references to contemporary morality, and certainly no analysis of liberty interests—much less privacy rights—was considered by the Connecticut courts. It was, for them, simply a question of the proper role or job of a justice as they saw it.

Nevertheless, the attorneys for Estelle Griswold and Lee Buxton remained confident of their ultimate victory. Fowler Harper once again reassured birth control advocates that he and attorney Catherine Roraback had expected to lose at every stage in the Connecticut judicial process. Harper's confidence stemmed in part from the fact that he believed *Griswold* was a procedurally air-tight scenario. All of the judicially created elements of standing to sue, harm and damage, concreteness of the issues, and so forth, had been satisfied. Harper did not believe that the Supreme Court would be able to find any procedural flaw.

There were other reasons for Harper's optimism. The Roman Catholic leadership had altered its stance against birth control. Archbishop Richard Cardinal Cushing had openly declared, "Catholics do not need the support of civil law to be faithful to their own religious convictions and they do not seek to impose by law their moral values on other members of society."[14] Another Catholic leader stated, "No one group may impose its . . . moral viewpoint through the clenched fist of legislative fiat."[15] The news media's coverage of the events and participants in *Griswold v. Connecticut* was all sympathetic to Dr. Buxton and Mrs. Griswold. This coverage included a CBS program and articles in the *Saturday Evening Post, Time, Newsweek,* and national newspapers as well as the local Connecticut ones. Legal scholars appeared to support *Poe's* dissenters, Harlan and Douglas. The *New York University Law Review* published an impressive legal and constitutional analysis supportive of the constitutional rights involved in the birth control cases. It was particularly laudatory in its references to Justice Harlan's dissent in *Poe v. Ullman.* Public opinion appeared to be highly in favor of privacy rights, and polls found even Catholics agreeing with the birth control advocates.[16]

Nevertheless, *Griswold* was not without problems. The assassination of President John F. Kennedy had involved the Supreme Court in the investigation. The Warren Commission's work would tax the chief justice, his law clerks, and staff, as well as other court personnel. Moreover, now that procedural loopholes were closed, the Court would need to address the birth control case on its merits. The constitutional basis for finding this right of privacy would become paramount. Attorneys had never faced questions of this type, and the justices themselves were moving into unfamiliar territory. Finally, attorney Fowler Harper was facing death from prostate cancer: he would not live to argue *Griswold* before the Court. Could Professor Tom Emerson, the new attorney for the defendants, be prepared in time? Did Emerson possess that unique ability necessary to persuade at least five very different and independent judicial minds? The Supreme Court that was to evaluate the issues in the case of *Griswold v. Connecticut* was composed of just such personnel. In 1964 it consisted of Chief Justice Earl Warren and justices Hugo Black, William O. Douglas, Tom Clark, John Marshall Harlan, William J. Brennan, Byron R. White, and Arthur J. Goldberg.

Oral argument in *Griswold* was actually a question-and-answer session: the justices' concerns, prejudices, and desire to foresee the possible outcome of a decision overshadowed all else. Attorney Tom Emerson later complained, "They never let me give my argument, but kept up a running barrage of questions. . . . I felt rather frustrated."[17] The questions jumped from one issue to another with great rapidity. What was the proper constitutional foundation for the right asserted, the justices queried? Was it equal protection? Was it due process? Was there a First Amendment argument to be made? Did "privacy" reside in a combination of Amendments—Third, Fourth, Fifth?

Was it a "reserved to the people" right, according to the historical background of the Ninth Amendment?

The state legislature's purpose in passing and retaining the birth control ban also became a point of argument. Had religion been the basis for the statute? Some justices wondered aloud if there was a difference between the use of birth control devices and abortion. Both Justice Black and Justice White raised this issue. Professor Emerson's response would later reappear to haunt supporters of reproductive choice. Emerson noted that abortion, unlike contraception, was not "conduct . . . occur[ring] in the privacy of the home."[18] The point at which birth control and abortion could come together as one issue was left unanswered, as was the question, When does life begin? *Griswold's* oral argument, therefore, was flawed on at least two major points: first, it was primarily confined to the privacy rights of married couples only; second, it failed to address creatively the abortion issue. Nevertheless, it was a winning argument.

Are cases or causes won because one attorney has a better argument, a better command of data, or greater proficiency in responding to questions? One justice at least has said no. Justice Antonin Scalia remarked that many times a case would be won in spite of the attorney.[19] In *Griswold*, Emerson seemed to be only tangential to the results. So why did the Court finally decide, on this third try, to overturn the Connecticut statute and to create a fundamental right to reproductive privacy?

An analysis of the *Griswold* conference sheds some light on this question. Justices Douglas and Harlan voted as they had voted in *Poe*: the Connecticut statute was unconstitutional. However, Douglas focused on the First Amendment as a constitutional foundation, while Harlan held to the Fourteenth's "due process liberty." Two justices in *Poe's* majority, Clark and Brennan, changed their minds. For both of these justices, the constitutional basis was to be found in "the right to be let alone," namely, the right of privacy.

Two other justices also changed their position from the *Poe* vote. Justice Potter Stewart, who had dissented in *Poe*, now reversed himself, saying the Constitution offered no protection for this right of privacy. Chief Justice Earl Warren, searching now for a proper basis to reverse his vote in *Poe*, found himself isolated. The only constitutional basis acceptable to Warren was a narrow Fourteenth Amendment position focusing on the discriminatory application of the statute, which had been used to close clinics. The chief justice rejected every other argument. He refused to accept a First Amendment argument, rejected equal protection and due process as constitutional bases, and disliked the privacy argument. Yet Chief Justice Warren was ready to void the Connecticut statute![20]

The two new justices who had not participated in *Poe* were White and Goldberg. White did not identify a constitutional basis for his vote. "I reverse," he declared, and the conference discussion moved to Justice Goldberg.

In agreement with Douglas, Goldberg focused on the First Amendment as his constitutional basis for voting to reverse the Connecticut Supreme Court as well as overturn *Poe*.

It was a 7–2 win for birth control advocates. However, closer analysis showed that the victory lacked a firm foundation.[21]

Chief Justice Warren assigned the opinion to Justice Douglas. Apparently Warren thought Douglas's position represented a larger coalition of justices than did that of Justice Harlan. Warren was wrong. The problems surrounding the drafting of the opinion demonstrated the fragile basis on which this new right was grounded. *Griswold v. Connecticut's* final form was produced only after intense negotiation among the justices. Justice Douglas found that it was a most difficult task to accommodate all the divergent positions taken in the conference. He needed, if possible, to draw the six other favorable votes together with his into a coherent whole, agreeing on a proper constitutional provision that would uphold a right to reproductive privacy.

The records of the justices' law clerks reveal the major difficulties. Douglas's clerk, James Campbell, suggested the inclusion of "privacy" in the justice's opinion, and in this he was supported by Justice Brennan's clerk, Paul Posner. The privacy argument also appealed to Justice Goldberg's clerk, Stephen Breyer. Thus three justices and their clerks had found at least one clear constitutional point on which they agreed. However, the privacy argument alarmed Chief Justice Warren's clerk, John Hart Ely, whose influence on the chief justice seemed pervasive. Opinions circulated, were revised, and recirculated. Clerks criticized and expressed "scorn," according to one source. Douglas's draft came under increasing attack by the "would-be justices"— the law clerks.

Douglas himself began to believe that he could not put together an opinion that would solidify the seven votes voiding the Connecticut statute. Justice White drafted a separate concurrence—six pages in length—in which he specifically avoided recognizing a right to privacy. His concurrence rested on the Fourteenth Amendment's due process, which protected liberty. Justice Harlan's concurrence simply restated his *Poe* dissent and also stood on a Fourteenth Amendment due-process clause protecting liberty.

Negotiations continued with Justice Goldberg's attempts to unite the majority around a Ninth Amendment "reserved to the people" argument. Unexpectedly, this approach suddenly attracted the chief justice in spite of his earlier statements. The number of opinions now stood at six. The final decision in *Griswold v. Connecticut* is cited by some experts as a 3–4–2 decision. Other experts describe it as a (2+3+1+1)–2 decision. Justice Douglas delivered "the opinion of the Court." His six-and-a-half-page opinion was joined by Justice Clark. Justice Goldberg, joined by Chief Justice Warren and Justice Brennan, "concurred in the Court's opinion." Goldberg's concurrence covered more than twelve pages. Justice Harlan "concurred in the judgment"; his was a three-page opinion and referenced his *Poe* dissent. Justice White also concurred in the judgment in a separate six-page opinion. Justice Black's twenty-page dissent was joined by Justice Stewart, and Stewart's dissent of three pages was joined by Black.[22]

The reactions created by the *Griswold* decision were interesting. Public opinion was generally favorable. Southern newspapers were critical, while Northeastern ones were more positive. The Catholic Church issued "muffled" responses—low key and ambiguous. Academics and law school professors, however, sent very negative signals. It soon became clear that the right to privacy asserted in *Griswold* might well be a hollow victory.[23]

The significance of law school critics who attack Supreme Court decisions and undermine them escapes the average American. For the public, law in many ways is like a football game. Who won? The answer should be either team A or team B. Few are concerned for very long with the score. However, even in this type of game analysis, strategists are looking at the mistakes made and the possible corrections that could turn a losing team into a winning one. In this respect at least, legal cases are similar to games played on the athletic battlefield. The legal strategists' intense and ongoing criticism of the *Griswold* decision would begin to undermine that victory for the cause of reproductive privacy.

A review of Justice William O. Douglas's opinion for the Court helps in understanding the basis for the attacks. Douglas's choice of words became the focus of critics. He explained the right to privacy thus:

> The First Amendment has a penumbra where privacy is protected from governmental intrusion. . . . Specific guarantees in the Bill of Rights have penumbras, formed by emanations from the guarantees that help give them life and substance. . . . Various guarantees create zones of privacy. The right of association contained in the penumbra of the First Amendment is one. . . . The Third Amendment in its prohibition against the quartering of soldiers "in any house" in any time of peace without consent of the owner is another facet of that privacy. The Fourth Amendment explicitly affirms the "right of the people to be secure in their persons, houses, papers, and effects against unreasonable searches and seizures." The Fifth Amendment in its Self-Incrimination Clause enables the citizen to create a zone of privacy which government may not force him to surrender to his detriment. The Ninth Amendment provides: "The enumeration in the Constitution of certain rights, shall not be construed to deny or disparage others retained by the people."[24]

Law school critics attacked this language and reasoning using such terms as "nebulous language," "a curious, puzzling mixture of reasoning," "muddled," and "opaque." The particular words that irritated academicians were "penumbra" and "emanations."[25] Yet these terms were not new to the legal vocabulary, having appeared at least twenty times in various opinions.

Justice Oliver Wendell Holmes had been particularly fond of using "penumbra" in his opinions. In fact, Holmes had actually spoken of the "penumbra" of the Fourth and Fifth Amendments. Other famous justices such as Benjamin Cardozo and Felix Frankfurter had also used the term. However, in the context of the highly emotional issue of birth control, Douglas's use of the term was counterproductive. Critics focused on it and announced that it did not clarify the source of this "new" right and served only to "obfusticate."[26]

The extent to which the cause of reproductive privacy was actually won in *Griswold* would unfold over the next twenty-two years. The Court took the first step toward this in 1972 in the case of *Eisenstadt v. Baird*. This case, like *Griswold*, involved a law banning the distribution of contraception. In addition, it raised the question of the right of unmarried persons to possess and use birth control devices. In finding the law unconstitutional, Justice William J. Brennan wrote: "If the right of privacy means anything, it is the right of the individual, married or single, to be free from unwarranted governmental intrusion into matters so fundamentally affecting a person as the decision whether to bear or beget a child."[27] It was 1987 when the final test of this constitutional right occurred. The circumstances were unusual, as was the event that tested the question, Is the right to possess and use birth control a cause that has finally been won?

The actors involved in the final drama that would settle this question included the president of the United States, Ronald Reagan; the Judiciary Committee of the U.S. Senate; and a judicial nominee for a Supreme Court vacancy, Judge Robert H. Bork. Surrounding these central players were numerous pro-life and pro-choice interest groups, movie stars such as Gregory Peck, and constitutional lawyers such as Laurence Tribe. The controversy centered on Judge Bork's attitude toward privacy rights, particularly the one identified in *Griswold v. Connecticut*.

Bork, like Fowler Harper and Tom Emerson, was a Yale Law School professor. At first Professor Bork had praised the decision reached by the Court in *Griswold*. At that time he even approved the concepts of penumbras and emanations, stating that the idea of deriving new rights (such as privacy) from old sources (e.g., the Bill of Rights) was "valid and valuable." Bork even went so far as to tout the Ninth Amendment as the source for judge-made "new natural rights."[28]

Then he changed his mind, completely reversing his earlier position and beginning an intense attack on *Griswold*. What happened between 1965 and 1971 to create this reversal is not clear. Whatever it was became critical to Bork's future. His opening attack appeared in the *Indiana Law Journal* and was entitled "Neutral Principles and Some First Amendment Problems."[29] He had converted to a new judicial philosophy, that of originalism, in which literal text and history alone determine the meaning of the Constitution. The 1789 Constitution, for Bork, remained fixed at that date. Between 1971 and

1987 Bork expanded his attack on *Griswold* in lectures, articles, and symposiums. Within his constitutional and philosophical arguments, however, there emerged a personal reason. The acclaim given law professors Harper and Emerson may have been the catalyst. At any rate Bork insisted that the *Griswold* case had been an "academic exercise" created by Yale Law School professors to demonstrate their cleverness and in a sense play a litigation game they enjoyed. While Bork claimed to believe in privacy, he agreed with Justice Black that a "silly" or "outrageous" law was not necessarily unconstitutional.

As more and more critiques of *Griswold* flowed from Bork's pen, his level of harsh rhetoric increased. Now Bork rejected "emanations" and "penumbras," rejected the case facts of the litigants who had claimed damage to their health in *Poe*, and rejected the reality of enforcement of the Connecticut statute. Bork at this point defined *Griswold* as an exercise of raw judicial power. Issues of sexual morality, he announced, were questions for state legislators, not justices attempting to interpret the Constitution.

At this juncture, Justice Lewis Powell retired and President Reagan nominated Professor Bork to replace him on the U.S. Supreme Court. At the Senate hearings on his nomination, Bork went on the offensive to convince senators and the public that *Griswold* was without a basis in "legal reason" and that it had been incorrectly decided. The right to privacy and birth control "remains a live controversy," he told the senators.[30] The American public reacted. Would Bork, as an associate justice on the Supreme Court, work to overturn *Griswold* and the right to possess and use birth control devices? The public thought so. Bork's restricted vision of privacy defeated his bid for the Supreme Court. The Senate rejected him 58–42.[31]

What did this mean for the cause so long fought for in *Tileston, Poe,* and *Griswold?* Would the case win in *Griswold* finally receive judicial and academic legitimation? Experts answered in the affirmative. One legal analyst declared, "Allegiance to *Griswold* [became] a litmus test for membership in the 'mainstream of constitutional thought.'" Another expert asserted that the rejection of the Bork nomination "enshrinc[d] *Griswold v. Connecticut* as a 'fixed star in our constitutional firmament.'" It was so. Judge Anthony Kennedy had to pass this litmus test to gain the seat denied to Bork. Kennedy confirmed that the cause of privacy was indeed won when he stated, "*Griswold* is settled law."[32]

CLOSING THE BEDROOM DOOR: *BOWERS* REVERSED

The seventeen-year reign of the antigay decision *Bowers v. Hardwick* ended abruptly and dramatically on June 26, 2003. In a voice that trembled slightly with emotion, Justice Anthony Kennedy intoned *Bowers's* death warrant in these words: "*Bowers* was not correct when it was decided, and it is not correct today. It ought not to remain binding precedent. *Bowers v. Hardwick* should be and now is overruled."[33]

For Laurence Tribe, seated in the courtroom, it was a cause won. With tears in his eyes, he spoke of the effects of his loss in 1986 and gratification for the victory now awarded his argument in *Bowers*.[34]

Although victory seemed long in coming, a number of events had signaled the erosion of the *Bowers* position. Notable among these were judicial pronouncements, state and federal court cases, scholarly critiques, and revisions of laws. Even before the ink was dry on the *Bowers* opinion, the story of that "confused conference" and Justice Lewis Powell's "switch" had shaken the credibility of the case decision. When Powell followed up by admitting that his "switch" was a mistake—that the dissent had the better argument—he raised the hopes of gay rights advocates.

Powell's retirement brought Justice Kennedy to the bench of the high court with a commitment to privacy rights as articulated in the birth control case *Griswold v. Connecticut*. Would Kennedy be affected by the knowledge that his predecessor regretted his role in *Bowers* and, had he remained on the court, would have reversed it? Powell's judicial pronouncement on *Bowers* was unusual: it commanded attention. The stage was set for renewed challenges.

Gay rights advocates in the wake of *Bowers* turned their attention to the states: state constitutions, state judges and courts, and state laws. Would state constitutions provide protection for greater privacy rights than those recognized in the federal constitution? Five states in particular said yes. Kentucky, Tennessee, Montana, Georgia, and Arkansas were leaders in this process.

A Georgia Supreme Court ruling was particularly notable because *Bowers v. Hardwick* itself was a Georgia case involving a state antisodomy law. While Michael Hardwick had lost in federal court in the 1980s, his counterpart would win in the 1990s in the Georgia Supreme Court. It was a landmark victory for privacy rights for gays. Georgia's antisodomy statute, said that Georgia court, was unconstitutional under the Georgia Constitution. The U.S. Constitution was not relevant: the state statute violated the state constitution. As the judges of Georgia's supreme court interpreted their own constitution, they found valid reasons for such a pronouncement, reasons which lawmakers had ignored. Thus the very statute under which Michael Hardwick had been prosecuted and which the U.S. Supreme Court had upheld in *Bowers* now became null and void. Only an amendment to the Georgia constitution could restore it.[35]

Federal law did not apply here, according to the constitutional law doctrines that govern relations between the states and the national government. The doctrine that specifically controlled was known as the "adequate and independent state grounds" barrier to Supreme Court review.[36] Under this doctrine, state judges were recognized as those best qualified to interpret the various state constitutions. Unless a citizen had been deprived of a federal right, federal courts, judges, and the Constitution would not be involved.

Thus, while "privacy rights" protection for gays was not a federal constitutional right, according to *Bowers v. Hardwick*, it was a Georgia state constitutional right according to the ruling in *Powell v. State*. Georgia's Constitution was broader than its national counterpart. *Commonwealth v. Wasson* did the same for Kentucky in 1992. The Tennessee Supreme Court ignored *Bowers* and announced state constitutional privacy rights in *Campbell v. Sunquist* in 1996. Montana's supreme court followed suit in *Gryczan v. State* in 1997. In 2002 the Arkansas Supreme Court joined this group of states with its decision in *Jegley v. Picado*.[37]

There were also federal court cases that struck at the roots of the *Bowers* doctrine. From the outset, *Bowers* had been at odds with the line of privacy decisions established by the Supreme Court. These included all the birth control cases—*Griswold v. Connecticut* (1965), *Eisenstadt v. Baird* (1972), and *Carey v. Population Services Int'l* (1977). These three cases had established the right of married persons, single persons, and minors, respectively, to secure birth control devices and information. The privacy right to sexual activity for pleasure, not procreation, became settled law. The succession of reproductive privacy cases moved to encompass abortion rights as well as those of birth control. *Roe v. Wade* (1973) as reaffirmed in *Planned Parenthood of Southeastern Pennsylvania v. Casey* (1992) established this right, even though state regulations were numerous and onerous. The Court had dismissed all these cases as not applicable to *Bowers*. It was a disingenuous position.

In 1996, just ten years after *Bowers*, the Supreme Court had the opportunity to establish new precedent dealing specifically with the issue of gay rights. The case, from Colorado, involved a direct attack on homosexuals as a class. *Romer v. Evans* centered on an amendment passed by the Colorado electorate on November 3, 1992, to repeal previously adopted gay rights ordinances passed by the cities of Denver, Boulder, and Aspen. Amendment 2 to the Colorado constitution forbade governmental entities from "enact[ing], adopt[ing], or enforc[ing] any statute, regulation, ordinance, or policy whereby homosexuals, lesbians, bisexual by orientation, conduct, practice or relationship [may] claim . . . protected status or discrimination." Supported by Governor Roy Romer and opposed by the cities of Boulder, Denver, and Aspen, in conjunction with a coalition of individual gay and lesbian plaintiffs, the issue was presented to the Colorado courts in the case that became known as *Romer v. Evans*. In both the district court and the state supreme court, the state lost: the amendment "affected a fundamental right of an identifiable class."[38] It was unconstitutional.

Oral argument before the U.S. Supreme Court on October 10, 1995, pitted the solicitor general of Colorado, Timothy Tymkovich, against Jean E.

Dubofsky of Denver, Colorado. Argument began at 10:02 A.M. Within less than two minutes, Justice Kennedy irritably interrupted the Colorado solicitor general with the first and most significant question. He expostulated, "I've never seen a case like this. Is there any precedent that you can cite to the Court where we've upheld a law such as this?"[39]

Kennedy went on to signal the basis of his antipathy toward the amendment: it adopted a classification—homosexual, lesbian, or bisexual—for "its own sake." He queried whether "orientation mean[t] something more than conduct." The source of Kennedy's questions was a brief submitted by Professor Laurence Tribe and cosigned by a few other distinguished law professors, including Gerald Gunther and Kathleen Sullivan of Stanford Law School and Philip Kurland of the University of Chicago Law School. It was a unique "individual brief," and it had a "major impact," according to attorney Jean Dubofsky.[40]

Justice Kennedy's opening question focusing on the "unusual" nature of Colorado's law came from Tribe's brief. Moreover Professor Tribe had steadily pursued a campaign to win Kennedy's vote for liberal causes. A number of his outstanding students had served as law clerks to Justice Kennedy. In memos and conversation with the justice, these bright young lawyers articulated the arguments and legal reasoning that had resulted in Tribe's designation as "the foremost constitutional thinker of our time," or even the "tenth justice" in some cases.[41]

The disposition of *Romer v. Evans* showed that Tribe had planned his strategy well. In a 6–3 vote, with Justice Anthony Kennedy writing for the majority, the Supreme Court struck down Colorado's Amendment 2. Justice Kennedy's language paralleled that of Tribe's brief. He wrote:

> We cannot accept the view that Amendment 2's prohibition on specific legal protections does no more than deprive homosexuals of special rights. To the contrary, the amendment imposes a special disability upon those persons alone. [This was Tribe's rationale.] Homosexuals are forbidden the safeguards that others enjoy or may see without constraint. . . . A state cannot so deem a class of persons a stranger to its laws.[42]

In conclusion, the Court majority found that Colorado's amendment "was born of animosity toward the class of persons affected." It lacked a "rational relation" to a legitimate governmental purpose and failed that Supreme Court test. Significantly, *Romer v. Evans* did not cite or use *Bowers v. Hardwick*. It was as though *Bowers* did not exist. Thus, with *Romer*, it became abundantly clear that state courts and federal courts were uncomfortable using *Bowers v. Hardwick*.

Other attacks from very different sources also began to erode the foundation of *Bowers*. Scholarly articles by leading constitutional lawyers appeared in prestigious legal journals. They attacked, in particular, the historical arguments used by the *Bowers* majority, denying that "there is a long-standing history in this country of laws directed at homosexual conduct as a distinct matter."[43] Instead, a number of professors of history insisted that the Colonial American prohibition on sodomy had been inherited from English *criminal* laws. While American authorities read these to criminalize deviant sexual relations, these experts noted that the concept of homosexual as a "distinct category of person" did not emerge until the late nineteenth century. These laws were in fact motivated by the same principle that produced anti–birth control laws: that sexual relations existed only for procreation, not enjoyment.

Scholars were prolific in their writings and in their in-depth historical analyses. By 1995 most of these themes had been compiled into a significant reader by John D'Emilio and Estelle Freedman entitled *Intimate Matters: A History of Sexuality in America.*[44] The overriding thesis was that laws prohibiting sodomy were aimed to protect people who could not really "consent" to the relationship, such as minors and victims of assaults and threats. Consensual relations were seldom prosecuted. A second thesis noted that American laws targeting same-sex couples did not develop until the latter part of the twentieth century, and their purpose was directed against conduct in public places.

The recent scholarship also focused on the changing attitude of Americans as documented in the removal of same-sex prohibitions in law. Adopting the American Law Institute's Model Penal Code recommendations of 1955, Illinois led the way in decriminalizing private consensual relations. Other states followed suit. Moreover the antisodomy laws that existed even at the time of the *Bowers* decision were often ignored and unenforced. While twenty states had laws criminalizing this conduct in 1986 when *Bowers* was decided, this number began to decrease, and by 2003 there were only thirteen, plus Puerto Rico. Nine of these retained the old-fashioned antisodomy statutes that ostensibly applied to "gays and straights" alike; these states were Alabama, Florida, Idaho, Louisiana, Mississippi, North Carolina, South Carolina, Utah, and Virginia. Four other states applied their criminal penalties only to same-sex conduct: Kansas, Missouri, Oklahoma, and Texas.[45]

One way to test the effectiveness of a Court decision is to count the number of times it is used as precedent. Did lower courts cite *Bowers?* Did it govern the way courts decided current issues before them? Six federal courts of appeals had cited *Bowers* in a total of eleven cases. The Fourth Circuit Court of Appeals used *Bowers* to reject challenges to a police department's questionnaire that asked prospective employees about homosexual activity.[46] The Sixth Circuit Court of Appeals used *Bowers* in three cases. In one case, the court cited *Bowers* to reject a claimed fundamental right to commit adultery.[47] Neither did a job promotion satisfy the fundamental rights test of *Bowers.*[48] In the third case, the Sixth Circuit used *Bowers* to reject a prisoner's claimed fundamental right to HIV testing.[49] The Seventh Circuit used *Bowers* to underscore the right of legislative bodies to pass laws dealing with moral issues.[50] *Bowers* was cited in an Eighth Circuit Court of Appeals ruling that refused to extend fundamental rights protection to the naming of children; a state could restrict surnames that can be given at birth.[51] Four cases that relied on *Bowers* occurred within the jurisdiction of the Ninth Circuit Court of Appeals. *Bowers* was the precedent cited to uphold bans against homosexual conduct in the military.[52] It was used to uphold a bisexual's discharge from the armed forces.[53] Grandparents lacked a "fundamental liberty interest" in the adoption of grandchildren under the *Bowers* definition of fundamental rights, said the Ninth Circuit.[54] The Defense Department's policy of intense background checks of gay and lesbian applicants for secret and top secret security clearances was also upheld under *Bowers*.[55] Finally, the Eleventh Circuit Courts of Appeals used *Bowers* to uphold a prohibition on the sale of sex toys.[56]

Such examples indicate that *Bowers*, during its seventeen-year reign, had had limited usefulness. The cases dealing with the armed services involved military law and statutes, and *Bowers* was not crucial to the outcome of such cases. Many of the other citations of *Bowers* were incidental to the Court's statement of precedent defining fundamental rights. *Bowers*, therefore, had not been followed to such an extent as to establish it as settled law. It remained open to challenge.

Bowers Redux: The Case of John Lawrence and Tyron Garner

The date was September 17, 1998; the time, night; the place, Houston, Texas. The parties involved were police officers, an anonymous tipster, and two men engaged in a sex act. The police officers had received a report of a "weapons disturbance" and were directed to the apartment of John Geddes Lawrence. No weapons were involved, however, but the police found a valid cause for making an arrest. The Texas Penal Code made "deviant sexual intercourse" a criminal offense. John Lawrence and Tyron Garner had, like Michael Hardwick, been "caught in the act" by police acting on false information.[57] In Hardwick's case it had been a lapsed warrant that led police to his bedroom door;[58] in Lawrence's, it was a fabricated "disturbance" phone call for assistance. The scenarios of the two cases were almost identical.

Like Hardwick, Lawrence and Garner spent the night in jail. Unlike Hardwick, however, Lawrence and Garner were convicted before a justice of the peace of violating the Texas statute, in spite of the false report that had sent police there; the right of the police to enter was not questioned, unlike Hardwick's situation. Lawrence and Garner were fined two hundred dollars each. The major damage suffered, however, was that the two men were now defined as sex offenders. In the four states of Kansas, Missouri, Oklahoma, and

Texas, they were required to register with state law enforcement agencies. Securing employment would become a major problem with this record.[59] There was "real harm and damage," and it gave them a concrete case with standing to sue.

It constituted a case worthy of appeal. Citing invasion of privacy and the equal protection clause of the Fourteenth Amendment, attorneys for Lawrence and Garner challenged the constitutionality of the Texas statute. A three-judge panel of the Texas Court of Criminal Appeals agreed with the appellees, but it was later reversed when all nine judges of the Texas Supreme Court met and declared the Texas law constitutionally valid. The court majority went beyond this narrow point, as well, holding that gays and lesbians did not constitute a protected class because the statute served the "compelling state interest" in preserving "public morality and family values." *Bowers v. Hardwick* was the central precedent cited.

The next step was to the U.S. Supreme Court. Some expected the Court to deny certiorari, but on December 2, 2002, the Court accepted the case for briefs and oral arguments. Could the court be signaling that *Bowers v. Hardwick* was not, in fact, settled law?[60]

The legal team that would represent Lawrence and Garner consisted of six attorneys, with Ruth Harlow and Paul Smith playing the leading roles. In their brief, they first distinguished the Texas law from that of Georgia, which Michael Hardwick had attacked in *Bowers*. They then advanced an extensive sociological or contemporary morality argument, accompanied by statistical and quantifiable data to bolster their position. Harlow's brief attempted to educate the justices as to the true nature of the homosexual relationship and to portray its similarity with the very best of heterosexual relations. She described her clients, bringing to life their feelings and emotions, their anguish and sense of humiliation, and their fear.

A third major point in the brief focused on favorable federal and state court precedents that demonstrated the tenuous position of *Bowers*. Prominent among these cases, of course, was *Romer v. Evans* with its condemnation of majority attempts to impose traditional moral standard on a minority, solely on the basis of sexual preference.[61] The lawyers met directly the question, Should *Bowers v. Hardwick* be overturned? Their answer quoted the Georgia Supreme Court's opinion in 1998 invalidating the very law that had set *Bowers* in motion and had been upheld by the U.S. Supreme Court. Striking down that law, the Georgia court had declared, "We cannot think of any other activity that reasonable persons would rank as more private and more deserving of protection from governmental interference than unforced, private, adult sexual activity."[62]

The legal team representing Lawrence and Garner recognized the need to challenge the historical argument basis of *Bowers*. Harlow's brief addressed this argument using a quote from Justice Anthony Kennedy, who had written in *County of Sacramento v. Lewis,* "History and tradition are the starting point, but not in all cases the ending point of substantive due process."[63] Harlow wanted to persuade the Supreme Court that this was one of those cases where they were not the ending point. The brief also noted other case precedents where history and tradition had to give way to progressive egalitarian principles that ensure the "living," evolving nature of the Constitution's promise of "equal protection." For example, in 1967 the Supreme Court had determined that history and tradition could not justify bans on interracial marriage; *Loving v. Virginia* was a landmark case, demonstrating the need to move beyond the historic mores of past generations.[64]

The American Civil Liberties Union also took up the task of dealing with the historical data that had governed *Bowers.* In an impressive brief, the ACLU attorney analyzed and evaluated the history of sodomy laws: their origin, purpose, and the scope and limits of their actual application. The ACLU brief summarized this study of historical traditions in the following conclusion:

> People have long been aware that their neighbors, friends, and family engaged in consensual sexual intimacies in private, in undoubted violation of various sodomy, fornication, and/or adultery laws. And [homosexuals] have hardly been invisible, in either 19th or 20th century, or contemporary America. . . . [But] people do not report the sexual activities of their neighbor's and acquaintances.[65]

Other amicus briefs that supported Lawrence and Garner and brought another perspective were filed by Amnesty International and the Human Rights Watch.[66] Noting that American courts were beginning to consider international and foreign law in their opinions, these two organizations urged the Supreme Court to do so in this case. In a very clever move, these briefs used quotes from Justice Sandra Day O'Connor, Justice Antonin Scalia, and Chief Justice William Rehnquist. O'Connor had noted that "conclusions reached by other countries should at times constitute persuasive authority in American courts."[67] The chief justice had once suggested that the time had come for "United States courts . . . to begin looking to the decision of other constitutional courts to aid in [decision making]."[68] The amicus briefs of Amnesty International and Human Rights Watch[69] were replete with citations of international and foreign cases that had protected sexual conduct between same-sex partners. *Bowers* had been rejected by the international community using the concept of privacy. Sexual relations, they had noted, should be considered a "fundamental liberty" implicit in the very concept of "ordered liberty." These terms, used by Justice Benjamin Cardozo in the landmark case of *Palko v. Connecticut* (1937) were the touchstone for all tests for fundamental rights in American law.[70] The foreign court citations included a Colombian court ruling that sexual privacy was a "fundamental aspect of one's personhood." Canadian, Israeli, and British courts had justified pro-gay decisions using the concept of relational or associational privacy.

The Supreme Court justices thus had before them the current and best arguments of the gay rights community. These would be presented to the Court on March 26, 2003, by Paul Smith, a talented, articulate, experienced advocate. As a former Supreme Court law clerk, Smith understood the personalities and predilections of the nine justices who sat there—those that would support his position, those who would be adamantly opposed, and those who might be "persuadable." He could anticipate the types of questions that would dominate the proceedings.

It was 11:00 A.M. when Chief Justice Rehnquist called for *Lawrence v. Texas.* It was the climax in the battle for sexual privacy rights. The courtroom audience itself was testimony that this date and time, Wednesday, March 2, 2003, 11:09 A.M., was a momentous one, "constitutionally and culturally." Filling the seats in the center of the courtroom's section for members of the Supreme Court Bar were "gay men and women from among the core of elite Washington lawyers." Professionally and elegantly attired, they made an impressive sight. They were people of status, fame, prestige, wealth, and position. They were intellectual elites. Their quiet presence made its own statement.[71]

With oral argument limited to thirty minutes for each side, Paul Smith averaged nearly one question per minute. He answered thirty-five questions. All of the justices except John Paul Stevens and Clarence Thomas asked Smith at least one question. Justice Scalia dominated the scene, however, asking twenty-three of the thirty-five questions.[72]

The first question came within a minute of Smith's opening argument, and it came from the chief justice himself. In essence, it was not a question but a pronouncement. Rehnquist spoke categorically and forcefully, declaring that "the kind of conduct we are talking about here had been banned for a long time. . . . A right that is going to be sustained . . . has to have been recognized for a long time. And that simply isn't so." It was a strong statement identifying the chief justice's view of the historical argument as made in Smith's brief, but Smith was prepared. "If you look at history as a whole," he responded, "you find a much more complicated picture. . . . Sodomy [regulations] didn't focus on same-sex couples."

As Smith demonstrated the need to understand historical trends, Justice David Souter, the expert in historical constitutional arguments, asked, "Do you think you should win this case on the history argument?" Smith's reply was immediate: "Yes," he answered. Quickly summarizing the "state of law" on the books in the nineteenth century and earlier, Smith analyzed the historical roots of sexual privacy. "[We] really have a tradition of respect for the privacy of couples in their home, going back to the founding," he concluded. As an example of this, Smith pointed to the fact that three-quarters of the states had repealed their criminal sodomy laws for everyone. "[Americans] recognize that [these laws] are not consistent with our basic American values about the relationship between the individual and the state," he declared.

Smith also used historical data to demonstrate the recent, as opposed to an ancient, basis for laws singling out only same-sex sodomy. In response to a question from Justice Scalia, Smith stated, "First of all, the first laws that appeared on the books in the states of this country which singled out only same-sex sodomy appeared in the 1960s and the 1970s and it did not—and does not—go way back, this kind of discrimination." In addition, Smith cleverly worked in historical arguments when answering other questions and comments to the advantage of his own position. For example, Justice Scalia denied that courts could find fundamental rights based on an "evolution in the laws" as opposed to something deeply rooted in tradition. Smith seized this opportunity to cite history and to appeal to Justice Kennedy's position in *County of Sacramento v. Lewis*. His voice, smooth and assured, Smith declared, "[The] court's decisions don't just look at history, they look at the function that a particular claimed freedom plays in the lives of real people." He gave contraception and abortion as prime examples and mentioned the changing attitudes toward both death penalty cases (Eighth Amendment) and right-to-die cases (Ninth Amendment).

Smith's confidence that "he should [and would] win on the history argument" was manifest not only to all the justices, but also to the courtroom audience. "Are you asking the Court to overrule *Hardwick*?" The question came from Justice Ruth Bader Ginsburg.

When attorney Smith answered yes, Scalia and Rehnquist pounced. Their questions were designed to project a "parade of horribles," predicting disaster upon disaster that would result were *Bowers v. Hardwick* reversed. Adultery, bigamy, and homosexual kindergarten teachers were the issues around which their questions centered—all designed to create fear. The chief justice asked, "Do you think . . . a state could not prefer heterosexuals to homosexuals to teach kindergarten?" "Are laws against adultery unconstitutional?" Justice Scalia queried sarcastically, continuing, "and what about prohibitions on bigamy? Aren't these laws bigoted against bigamists?"

Smith quickly and efficiently distinguished adultery and bigamy laws from those involved in the Lawrence and Garner relationship. "[Laws against] bigamy protect an institution that the state creat[ed] for its own purposes— the institution of marriage," Smith explained. As Laurence Tribe had noted in *Bowers v. Hardwick*, the violation of a contract was the appropriate purpose behind laws against adultery: "Adultery is a violation of a contract." Both Tribe and Smith had so distinguished these laws. Smith also reminded the Court that bans on interracial marriage had been struck down precisely because they did not threaten the institution of marriage as bigamy did, nor did they create a violation of a contract. Laws against interracial marriage were similar to the Texas law criminalizing (in the case of Lawrence and Garner) "deviate [*sic*] sexual intercourse, namely anal sex, with a member of the same sex (man)."

Court watchers had predicted the central focus of *Lawrence v. Texas* would address the question of "whether a decision [focusing on the question] of equal protection would sidestep the more fundamental question of the Constitutional status of gay rights."[73] Linda Greenhouse, writing for the *New York Times*, suggested that the Court might do this, delivering a narrow and limited decision by answering the question, "Does petitioners' criminal conviction under the Texas 'Homosexual Conduct' law—which criminalized sexual intimacy by same sex couples, but *not* identical behavior by different-sex couples—violate the Fourteenth Amendment guarantee of equal protection of laws?"[74]

Paul Smith and Ruth Harlow were naturally prepared for the equal protection argument, even though they hoped to win on the bigger issue, the reversal of *Bowers v. Hardwick*. Their job was to persuade at least five justices that "equal protection" as a basis for a ruling in *Lawrence* would be insufficient. It might signal states to continue passing laws supportive of discrimination. Abortion had been limited by narrowly drawn state regulations. Could a Court decision based on equal protection effectively deal with the problem created by the discriminatory Texas law? The attorneys for Lawrence and Garner thought not. This could be accomplished only by the overturning of a flawed precedent. Equal protection as a basis for the Court decision in *Lawrence* would not effectively secure that standard itself, and Smith and Harlow wanted to avoid this outcome. Overturning *Bowers v. Hardwick* was therefore the main goal to pursue, and the equal protection arguments must be used for that purpose.

"There's no legitimate and rational justification under the Equal Protection Clause for a law that regulates forms of sexual intimacy that are permitted in the state only for same-sex couples, thereby creating a kind of second-class citizenship to the group of people," attorney Smith had argued early during his opening remarks to the Court. He then moved immediately to link this with another issue that had governed the *Bowers* holding, namely, history.

Justice Scalia rushed to halt this unexpected approach. "Let's separate these two arguments," he insisted. "[A] fundamental rights argument [based on history] has nothing to do with [an] equal protection [argument]," Scalia asserted.

Smith disagreed. What followed was a subtle attack on the principles undergirding *Bowers v. Hardwick*. One central principle Smith raised involved the precise nature of ancient sodomy laws. Textual analysis of the statutes showed that sodomy had been regulated for everyone, not just same-sex couples in particular. "Equal protection" was thus made to serve the historical and traditional standard used in *Bowers*. Smith carved out of the equal protection question a far more powerful basis for declaring the Texas law unconstitutional: the *Bowers* Court had failed to understand the complete history of sodomy statutes.[75]

When it came to his turn, Charles Rosenthal, the district attorney for Harris County, Texas, which contains Houston, could not compete with Smith's presentation. Reporters concluded that the "argument proved to be a mismatch of advocates to a degree rarely seen at the court."[76] Unlike Smith, Rosenthal was not adept in responding to the quickly changing focus of the justices' questions. "Rosenthal was making his first Supreme Court argument," reporter Greenhouse explained, "and he made first-timer's mistakes. He appeared surprised by questions that more experienced lawyers would easily have anticipated and unable to recognize the helping hand that Justice Scalia regularly offered. The justices ended up talking over Mr. Rosenthal, sparring with one another."[77]

In retrospect, Rosenthal committed three faux pas. First, Rosenthal claimed that "it's not known whether Lawrence and Garner are gay." Three of the justices openly noted that this was irrelevant. Even Justice Scalia, Rosenthal's main defender, could not "buy it" as a valid argument. Second, "I don't know" is an answer few attorneys want to give to a judicial question, and Rosenthal found himself having to make this response several times. "How does Texas law define a family?" asked Justice Ginsburg. "Does Texas allow same sex couples to adopt or be foster parents?" Rosenthal had to admit that he did not know. He had not done his homework.

Third, the Texas attorney was also ill prepared for questions involving the judicial "rational basis" test. This was essential to his position, claiming that "there is a rational basis for [Texas's] statute sufficient to withstand equal protection scrutiny." However, Rosenthal could not articulate the rational basis for the Texas law. The beleaguered attorney fell back on discredited and disingenuous arguments. Texas "wants to discourage harmful experimentation and drugs," he suggested at one point. Other responses included "threats to health" and "immorality." "Why then does the law exempt straight couples who perform these very same acts?" the justices inquired. "If the basis for the law is 'health' and 'immorality,' it should apply to everyone," Justice Breyer pointed out. Rosenthal's attempts to defend sodomy among heterosexual couples because it could ultimately lead to "marriage and procreation" were unpersuasive given the very definition of sodomy. Admitting, without defense, that Texas did not criminalize sex between unmarried straight couples and did not criminalize adultery either, Rosenthal's equal protection argument appeared fatally flawed.

With these three false steps, the oral argument in *Lawrence v. Texas* ended. Rosenthal's defense of the Texas law appeared to have been insufficient to persuade the justices. He had left the law open to the charges that it targeted gays, that it treated similar acts dissimilarly when performed by heterosexual and homosexual couples, and that the law had no rational basis for justifying state control. The Texas attorney had failed to show that the law was part of a "long and historic tradition," admitting that it had singled out gays in 1973, not 1793.[78]

With the closing of oral argument, the reporters departed. They were in a rare state of agreement: Texas had lost. One journalist reported that the "Court appears ready to reverse a sodomy law."[79] Another observer expressed his impression thus:

> I am notoriously poor at reading the Supreme Court's tea leaves, but my gut reaction is that while [there may not be] the votes to overturn *Bowers v. Hardwick* outright, I don't think Texas' law will survive the equal protection challenge.[80]

Bowers Overturned: The Supreme Court Recognizes Gay Rights

On June 26, 2003, exactly three months following oral argument in *Lawrence*, the Supreme Court justices gathered in the courtroom to render a landmark decision affecting a controversial "cause"—gay rights. The decision would establish the reputation of Justice Anthony Kennedy for all time. It was an unusual decision in that it directly reversed a precedent of seventeen years. It was a surprising opinion because of the breadth of legal justifications used. It was a harsh opinion that castigated an earlier Court majority, even singling out two justices by name. And it was an unexpected decision: the Supreme Court justices refused to decide the case on the easy and narrow grounds of equal protection, choosing instead to link their holding to reproductive choice cases that had asserted privacy as a right.

The senior associate justice in the *Lawrence* majority, Justice John Paul Stevens, had the responsibility for the assignment of the opinion. His choice of Justice Kennedy surprised no one. Kennedy's experiences from the days of his nomination to the Supreme Court through his fifteen-year career on that body had placed him in the center of privacy rights cases. His confirmation to the Supreme Court had been won when he assured senators that *Griswold v. Connecticut*—a birth control case whose legal basis was privacy—was "settled law." The Court had found this fundamental privacy right in the "penumbra and emanation" of the Bill of Rights, particularly First, Third, Fourth, Fifth, and Ninth Amendments. Kennedy's confirmation experiences inexorably linked him to a continued affirmation of this right. His legal thought had been influenced by his "model justice," Justice John Marshall Harlan II and that justice's articulation of the right at stake in *Griswold v. Connecticut* had impacted Kennedy. Furthermore, Justice Kennedy's selection of law clerks trained by Harvard law professor Laurence Tribe may have predisposed him to approach gay rights cases sympathetically. Finally, Kennedy knew that his predecessor, Justice Lewis Powell, openly regretted the vote that had established *Bowers* as precedent. *Lawrence v. Texas* and Anthony Kennedy seemed, therefore, to be "made for each other," and for history.

Justice Kennedy's opinion opened with a definition of *liberty*, which, after reviewing the facts of the case and the three questions the Court had agreed to consider, he linked to his holding. "We conclude," he wrote,

> the case should be resolved by determining whether the petitioners were *free* as adults to engage in the private conduct in the exercise of their *liberty under the Due Process Clause of the Fourteenth Amendment to the Constitution*. For this inquiry we deem it necessary to reconsider the Court's holding in *Bowers*.[81]

Due process liberty is a precise term in constitutional law with unique and different characteristics from equal protection. Justice Harlan had given the best definition of this concept in his famous dissent in *Poe v. Ullman*. He explained that it

> represent[s] the balance . . . of respect for the liberty of the individual and the demands of organized society. The balance . . . is . . . struck by having regard to what history teaches are the traditions from which [the country] developed as well as the traditions from which it broke. That tradition is a living thing. The full scope of the liberty guarantee by the Due Process Clause cannot be found in or limited by the precise terms of the specific guarantees elsewhere provided in the Constitution. This "liberty" is not a series of isolated points pricked out in terms of [such specific guarantees as speech and religion]. It is a rational continuum which . . . includes a freedom from all substantial arbitrary impositions and purposeless restraints [such as the "intolerable and unjustified invasion of privacy in the conduct of the most intimate concerns of an individual's personal life," that is, the use of birth control devices]. . . . The state [here] is asserting the right to enforce its moral judgment by intruding upon . . . intimate details . . . [which are] a fundamental aspect of "liberty," . . . embrac[ing] the concept of the privacy of the home. . . . [The protection of privacy of the home] protects the privacies of the life within.[82]

This "due process liberty" is part of the second clause of the Fourteenth Amendment's prohibition on states. "No state shall abridge the privileges or immunities of citizens" constitutes the Amendment's first clause, while the third clause forbids states "to deny any person equal protection of the laws." The second clause of the Fourteenth Amendment repeats part of the Fifth Amendment and states, "[No] state shall deprive any person of life, *liberty*, or property, without *due process* of law" [emphasis added]. It was this clause with its reference to "liberty" through "due process" that underlay Justice Harlan's thesis concerning what is commonly referred to as "privacy rights." It would be the constitutional clause on which Justice Kennedy would base the Court's holding in *Lawrence v. Texas*.

In order to reach this conclusion, Kennedy organized his opinion into distinct segments. His initial focus began with an analysis of the precedents that addressed "the substantive reach of liberty under the Due Process Clause." "The most pertinent beginning point," he continued, "is our decision in *Griswold v. Connecticut.*" The protected interest in that case had been described by the Court as a "right to privacy." Kennedy appealed to *Griswold's* progeny—*Eisenstadt v. Baird* (1972), *Roe v. Wade* (1973), and *Carey v. Population Services* (1977). He described these as decisions which "protect[ed] liberty under the Due Process Clause" and which recognized that the clause had "a *substantive* dimension of *fundamental* significance" (emphasis added). The impact of these precedents as defined and cited here was noteworthy. Analysts immediately seized upon this as a deliberate reaffirmation of abortion, observing that Justice Kennedy had asserted that there was "real and substantial protection" for the right to elect to have an abortion and that this abortion right was "an exercise of [the woman's] liberty under the Due Process Clause."[83]

Justice Kennedy then moved to the second segment of his opinion—the relationship between these precedents and the 1986 Court's opinion in *Bowers v. Hardwick. Bowers* was out of step with the reproductive choice precedents, he said firmly. Kennedy was ruthless in his analysis as he declared, "[The] Court . . . fail[ed] to appreciate the extent of the liberty at stake [in *Bowers*]." Moreover, he concluded, "this liberty protected by the Constitution allows homosexual persons the right to make this choice [concerning a sexual relationship]."[84]

Kennedy then began his rebuttal of the arguments used by the *Bowers* Court with a concentration on the historical underpinning used by that Court. It was truly a case of *Bowers* redux. Citing the brief submitted by a group of professors of history and those from the ACLU and the Cato Institute, Kennedy particularly took note of this historical information. He asserted an axiom which, he said, had been missed by the *Bowers* majority. "There is no longstanding history in this country of laws directed at homosexual conduct as a distinct matter," he declared.[85] English precedent, English common law, and English criminal law had never singled out homosexuals but had applied the law neutrally against both heterosexual and homosexual conduct. Homosexuals qua homosexuals was a late nineteenth-century concept, certainly not a tradition with ancient roots. The purpose of the law was identical to that of anti–birth control laws: "sex of a non-procreative form was forbidden."[86] The impact of attorney Paul Smith's oral argument and of the ACLU's historical brief was obvious. Kennedy's opinion cited data, used phrases, and adopted the conclusion from those sources.

In the course of tearing down the historical argument upon which *Bowers* had been based, Justice Kennedy, in a forthright manner, placed the blame for the seventeen-year-old precedent squarely on the shoulders of Chief

Justice Warren E. Burger and Justice Byron R. White. While he generally used the term "the Court in *Bowers*," he named names in several places. For example, after repeating the chief justice's historical assumption in *Bowers*, Kennedy stated categorically, "As with Justice White's assumptions about history, scholarship casts some doubt on the sweeping nature of the statement by Chief Justice Burger."[87] He noted that Burger's reference to "the history of Western Civilization and to Judeo-Christian moral and ethical standards did not take account of other authorities pointing in an opposite direction."[88] Kennedy himself then cited those authorities. On seven of the eighteen pages of his opinion, Kennedy's harsh statements concerning the *Bowers* Court majority demonstrated a near-contempt for those who wrote the opinion.

The surprising breadth and the unexpected nature of the *Lawrence* opinion was demonstrated in its refusal to ground the holding in the equal protection clause, its avoidance of the traditional approach of defining "fundamental rights," and its disregard for articulating the judicial test usually applied by the Court. This allowed Justice Kennedy to pen a "more forceful opinion that could have broader implications"[89]—"one that could [have a] profound impact" and might even become "constitutionally revolutionary."[90]

Kennedy did not expressly use the term "fundamental rights" to identify the "protected liberty interests," but his description did as much. Thus, Kennedy noted that adults have the right to "choose to enter upon [a] relationship in the confines of their own homes and their own private lives and still retain their dignity as free persons." Homosexuals, the Court continued, share in this "liberty protected by the Constitution." States cannot "control a personal relationship that . . . is within the liberty of persons to choose without being punished." A fundamental right by another name is still a fundamental right.

The Court gained flexibility for itself by refraining from employing any particular judicial test. The fact that the Court could "tether the constitutional right of privacy to the Due Process Clause of the Fourteenth Amendment—and specifically to the liberty interest it protects"[91] without defining its "test" leaves the door open for future gains for privacy rights. Whether a "rational basis" test or a "strict scrutiny" test should be used in privacy cases in the future may not be relevant to the inquiry. Indeed the Court may have implied this by emphasizing the "role of autonomy and personhood in assessing what rights are too important to be toyed with."[92] Thus the fact that the Court did not specifically use the terminology of "fundamental rights," with its tests of rational basis and strict scrutiny, could be seen as suggesting a new approach to privacy rights cases. Privacy rights resting on a general right to liberty (due process liberty) are perhaps more secure than ever before.

In the future, if an action is deemed to be a proper exercise of liberty, the government would have to justify its restriction on liberty. Citizens would not have to prove a fundamental right requiring a heightened level of scrutiny from the Court. The landscape of privacy rights litigation has thus been changed.

In evaluating the strength of any majority opinion, there are a number of questions which need to be addressed. How many justices wrote separate opinions? On what grounds were they based? Did they serve to weaken or to strengthen the majority opinion? Similarly, when evaluating the role of dissenting opinions, several aspects need to be analyzed. How many dissenting opinions were filed? Did the dissenters come together and pen one powerful argument? Was it written and presented in a powerfully orchestrated performance? Did the dissenters reach out to a separate concurrence, suggesting similarities in reasoning and laying the groundwork for future cooperation? To what types of groups was the dissent directed? How was it received? In summary, Is the strength and vitality of a majority opinion placed in jeopardy by separate concurrents and dissents? Neither the concurrence nor the dissent in *Lawrence* weakened the majority opinion.

Justice Sandra Day O'Connor's concurrence did nothing to undermine the court majority: she agreed with the other justices, but simply focused on a more narrow ground.[93] Basing her concurrence on the Fourteenth Amendment's equal protection clause, Justice O'Connor found the Texas statute unconstitutional under a rational basis test. Moreover, her sympathetic portrayal of the plight of gays and lesbians under this statute clearly set her apart from the dissent. "The consequences of conviction [under the Texas law] . . . would disqualify them . . . [from] professions . . . and require them to register as sex offenders," she noted.[94] O'Connor refused to accept "moral disapproval" as a legitimate state interest justifying discriminatory statutes. In this she was totally out of step with the dissenters—Justice Scalia, Justice Thomas, and Chief Justice Rehnquist. The tone of Justice O'Connor's opinion as she dissected the Texas law conveyed the revulsion she felt. Finally, O'Connor, while not voting to overrule *Bowers v. Hardwick*—which she had joined in 1986—nevertheless did not undertake a defense of that opinion. Instead, she adhered to one of her long-standing strategies for deciding difficult cases, namely, "Do not decide a constitutional issue in advance of the necessity for doing so." Under her philosophy of judicial restraint, *Lawrence v. Texas* could be decided without addressing the issue of overturning *Bowers v. Hardwick*. She preferred to decide cases on the narrowest grounds and use statutory rather than constitutional analysis. A separate concurrence of this scope did not undercut the majority opinion, but neither did it lend support to the dissent.

Dissenting opinions can serve a number of different functions, some noble, others ignoble. A dissent may be an "appeal to the bar of history," in the words of Chief Justice Charles Evans Hughes.[95] A dissent may carry a message to future litigants by highlighting the weak points in a majority opinion, suggesting different ways to interpret data and precedents, pointing out loopholes and inconsistencies, and offering advice on alternate strategies; these dissents encourage the losing side to continue working within the system and not to give up hope, and they may actually provide the weapons for another battle. Dissents may also attempt to minimize the majority opinion's holding, thus narrowing its interpretation and lessening its impact.

Dissents are at their worst, however, when they simply register violent, emotional outbursts on the part of angry, frustrated justices. Unable to persuade their colleagues through rational discourse, these dissenters strike out blindly, venting their spleen on those who dared to oppose them. This has become a pattern particularly in cases of abortion and sodomy rights, which trigger strongly held religious views. Some political analysts consider this a "massive retaliation attack."[96] Certainly forming future alliances with justices attacked so violently will not be easy. It is not a productive strategy for a member of a collegial court.

The dissent written by Justice Antonin Scalia in *Lawrence v. Texas* did, in some respects, follow the "noble" standard. However, it so quickly degenerated into personal and professional attacks as to cast a pall over the future reputation of this controversial justice. By consistently and regularly violating the norms of professional judicial behavior and failing to demonstrate the standards of correct "judicial temperament," Justice Scalia may have irreversibly damaged his reputation.

Scalia began his tenure on the Court with a high reputation for intellectual prowess, intelligence, cleverness, and charisma. His forceful personality, combined with legal brilliance, cast him as a possible "star" on the Court. That reputation soon began to erode. *Lawrence v. Texas* is one of a long list of cases demonstrating Justice Scalia's problems in dealing with defeat.

Scalia's first attack strategy was a traditional one and could have been presented in a credible fashion.[97] The point to be made was, Why is the Court abandoning stare decisis (that is, reliance on precedence)? As late as 1992 the Court had praised the role of stare decisis in American law and had counseled against abandoning it lightly. Justice Scalia began by attempting to address this change and point out reasons to uphold precedent, but he almost immediately degenerated into a caustic, sarcastic, personal rebuke addressed to justices Kennedy, O'Connor, and Souter. "What's happened to the Court's 'sententious' adherence to stare decisis," he taunted. "Why uphold abortion on stare decisis grounds but not sodomy?" Scalia suggested impure motives: biased pro-choice Court members "manipulated" stare decisis to justify their policy goals. He continued in this vein by claiming that the Court—particularly in *Planned Parenthood of Southeastern Pennsylvania v. Casey*—had pretended to sound a "paean to stare decisis" only to use it to justify its "judicially invented abortion rights." In fact, Scalia concluded, his colleagues' "extraordinary deference to precedent was a cover for a 'result-orientated expedient.'"[98]

Claiming that *Bowers* should be preserved under the doctrine of stare decisis, Justice Scalia cited every case he could unearth to lend verisimilitude to his position. In all, he found only thirteen cases that had cited *Bowers* as part of their holdings. Several could have been decided without using that case precedent, however, and did little to support Scalia's argument. Nevertheless, he railed, "What a massive disruption of the current social order the overruling of *Bowers* entails!"[99]

A final point raised in Justice Scalia's attack on Justice Kennedy's abandonment of stare decisis focused on two data sources used in the majority opinion. Kennedy had cited Charles Fried's *Order and Law: Arguing the Reagan Resolution*, and Richard Posner's *Sex and Reason*.[100] Scalia implied that Kennedy did not understand the policy position of Fried and Posner. In this he was wrong: Kennedy knew that both of these experts opposed sexual privacy rights. He recognized, as did the academic and legal communities, that both men were ultraright-wing conservatives who used their prestigious positions—that of professor and of judge—to publicize their pro-*Bowers*, anti-*Roe* views. Their books nevertheless contained significant material about the negative attitudes generated by *Bowers*. Did Kennedy choose to cite them precisely because even the supporters of *Bowers* had to admit that "criticism of *Bowers* has been substantial and [there is] continuing disapproval of its reasoning in all respects"?[101] An avid admirer of Justice Harlan, Kennedy also knew that Harlan's Fourteenth Amendment "due process liberty" argument was the exact argument penned by Charles Fried, working as law clerk for Harlan at the time of the *Poe* decision. Fried, having flip-flopped on privacy rights, lived to see his abandoned argument become the centerpiece of a pro–privacy rights decision. He saw his old privacy rights argument and his own treatise used to provide data supporting the very position he had now abandoned.

Justice Scalia's attempt to confine the birth control decision—from *Griswold v. Connecticut* and *Eisenstadt v. Baird*—to the basis of "penumbra rights" as opposed to "substantive due process" or "due process liberty" was flawed from beginning to end. Had Scalia himself forgotten that the concurrence of Justice Harlan in *Griswold* put forward an eloquent basis for Fourteenth Amendment due process liberty rights? Scalia made another slip when he noted, "The *Roe* court . . . made no attempt to establish that this right was deeply rooted in this Nation's history and tradition."[102] The *Roe* court had done precisely that. Justice Harry Blackmun had specifically grounded the right to abortion in the history of English and early American common law. Thirteen pages of his opinion are replete with citations from English authorities and with historical evidence for a "fundamental right to abortion" grounded in the "received common law" of early state constitutions. Abortion was, according to Justice Blackmun, part of this nation's tradition and history, inherited from English common law, which had apparently granted women the right to abort even a "quickened" fetus.[103]

After denigrating Kennedy's opinion because it failed to follow the expected procedure used in privacy rights cases—namely, establishing a fundamental right and its appropriate test—Justice Scalia then addressed the Fourteenth Amendment equal protection argument used in Justice O'Connor's concurrence. Scalia has a history of attacking this particular justice. His words and terms have often bordered on being sexist in their phraseology; this was certainly the case in *Webster v. Reproductive Health Services*. In *Lawrence v. Texas*, Scalia simply dismissed one of O'Connor's arguments: "[What O'Connor is saying] could be said of any law." Continuing his attempt to minimize her legal talents, he charged that, "[She] simply decrees application of a more searching form of rational basis review to the Texas Statute . . . [and] the cases she cites do not recognize such a standard." He charged that "Justice O'Connor [cannot] explain precisely what her [standard] consist[s] of."[104]

The very personal nature of this attack on O'Connor's concurrence is demonstrated in Justice Scalia's final condemnatory paragraph:

> In the jurisprudence Justice O'Connor has seemingly created, justices can violate laws by characterizing them as "preserving the tradition of society" (good); or invalidate them by characterizing as "expressing moral disapproval" (bad).[105]

Justice Scalia had abandoned persuasion as a method of interaction with others on the Court. Given the history of statements such as these, one might wonder if Justice Scalia will ever again negotiate or bargain with O'Connor in future cases.

The attack on O'Connor led Justice Scalia into his final tirade against the Court majority as a group. He assessed his colleagues in the harsh and sarcastic rhetoric that has become his trademark:

> Today's opinion is the product of a court, which is the product of a law profession culture, that has largely signed on to the so-called homosexual agenda . . . [to eliminate] the moral approach that has traditionally attacked homosexual conduct. . . . It is clear that the court has taken sides in the culture war.[106]

Continuing this line of attack, he wrote, "So imbued is the Court with the law profession's anti-anti-homosexual culture, that it is seemingly unaware that the attitudes of that culture are not obviously 'mainstream.'" The Court, he declared, seemed unaware that "many Americans do not want persons who openly engage in homosexual conduct as partners in their business, as scout masters for their children, as teachers in their children's schools, or as boarders in their home."[107] Turning from his colleagues who had ignored him, he appealed to public opinion. He offered a worst-case scenario of a post-*Lawrence* society. His "parade of horribles" reached its peak with the threat of same-sex marriage unions.

A short addendum offered by Justice Clarence Thomas, who, along with Chief Justice Rehnquist joined Justice Scalia's dissenting opinion, added little. He tied his short opinion to the dissent of Justice Potter Stewart in *Griswold v. Connecticut*, noting that he thought the Texas law "uncommonly silly," but not unconstitutional. Justice Thomas chose not to find in the Constitution either a "general right of privacy" or the "liberty [right] of the person both in its spatial and more transcendent dimensions."

To what extent did *Lawrence v. Texas* represent a "cause won" for gay rights activists? Legal scholars across the academic community poured forth their analyses, polling organizations created questionnaires and compiled data, op-ed commentary dominated the newspapers, and talk show hosts organized panel debates. The bottom line, however, was, Would the *Lawrence* decision make a difference for homosexuals? The answer is clearly yes.

Joanna Grossman, professor of family law and sex discrimination at Hofstra University, wrote: "*Lawrence* is a strong . . . embrace of rights, and a proclamation of freedom for gays and lesbians. . . . [It] is a monumental development in constitutional law."[108] Professor Sherry F. Colb of Rutgers Law School noted that "one need only read [Scalia's] dissent to know what a monumental event *Lawrence v. Texas* really is."[109]

Legal historians such as the University of Oklahoma's Paul Finkelman have compared both the tone and content of Justice Scalia's dissent with the infamous opinion of Chief Justice Roger B. Taney in *Dred Scott*. Taney had declared that historical disdain for "Negroes" was "deeply rooted" in the nation's legal history and the Constitution's founders believed that blacks "had no right which the white man was bound to respect."[110] Likewise, Scalia had asserted that the history of morality laws and laws against gay sex were "deeply rooted" in the nation's history and traditions and that the Constitution allowed gays to be denied rights that others enjoyed. University of Iowa law professor Lea Vandervelde noted that both Taney and Scalia had employed legal history to freeze morality to a point in time. This literal interpretation of the Constitution—known as "originalism"—refuses to allow any expansion of liberties. Thus the cause won in *Lawrence v. Texas* truly is "a very big deal": it is "the road to freedom."[111]

George Washington University Law School's Professor Jonathan Turley declared:

[*Lawrence*] is more about *privacy* than homosexuality. The result should be encouraging not just for gay rights advocates and libertarians but abortion rights advocates as well. . . . Now the court has adopted a more consistent approach to privacy linking the right to choose to a right to intimate sexual relations and greatly strengthened all privacy interests as a result. *Privacy* now dominates this line of decisions.[112]

"What does this all mean? It means that as of today, all sodomy laws are unconstitutional," proclaimed Georgetown University law professor Chai Feldblum.[113] "The decision's rationale would seem also to disdain laws that allow discrimination in employment, parenting, and marriage," added Professor Vincent J. Samar of the University of Chicago's School of Law.[114]

The academic world debated the nature of the "cause won" in the *Lawrence v. Texas* decision. Some law professors insisted that it was a pro-libertarian decision,[115] others declared that it was a "return to substantive due process considerations of the past,"[116] while still others found a new "moral argument" that recognized a right that could not be "overridden by particular social mores, even the social mores of a majority."[117] Nevertheless, in spite of the disagreement concerning the implications of rights grounded in "due process liberty" as announced in Lawrence, there was agreement that those rights, often declared to be "privacy rights," had advanced significantly.

"TRUMPING *WEBSTER*, REAFFIRMING *ROE*"

The challenge of *Webster* had not accomplished its purpose: *Roe v. Wade* still stood. Opponents of *Roe* zealously sought another case centering on a state law with increased innovative restrictions in order to push the Court to abandon *Roe* and allow states to resume their legislative prohibitions of abortion. Among these, Pennsylvania moved to the forefront with a law designed to test the scope of *Webster*. Of the thirteen major abortion cases that had confronted the Supreme Court between *Roe* and *Webster*, two had come from Pennsylvania. In 1979 a Pennsylvania fetal protection statute had been voided by the Court in *Colautti v. Franklin*.[118] Only three years before *Webster*, Pennsylvania had once again worked its way into Court in the case of *Thornburgh v. America College of Obstetricians and Gynecologists*.[119] With five major restrictions and regulations—including counseling, reporting, and attempts to keep the aborted fetus alive—this law had been struck down by the Court in 1986. In 1989, however, *Webster's* victory opened the door once again, and Pennsylvania was ready with yet another law.[120]

Pennsylvania's legislature moved quickly to add new abortion restrictions to existing state law. The new restrictions were carefully written with the express goal of forcing the Court to reverse *Roe*. Several restrictions that the Court had earlier struck down were revived and inserted into the new law. Known as the Abortion Control Act, Pennsylvania's statute included five major requirements: counseling, a waiting period, parental consent, spousal notification, and public disclosure of the entire proceeding. The passage of these restrictions immediately generated a legal challenge, as Planned Parenthood of Southeastern Pennsylvania, asserting that the restrictions were unconstitutional under the due process clause of the Fourteenth Amendment, took the state to federal district court. Thus began the litigation battle that would answer the question left by *Webster.* Is there a constitutional right to abortion?

The first round of *Planned Parenthood of Southeastern Pennsylvania v. Casey*[121] was a win for the pro-choice litigants. Federal district court Judge Daniel Huyett struck down most of the restrictions. On appeal to a three-judge panel of the Third Circuit in November 1991, however, this ruling was reversed; only the spousal notification provision was voided. Thus four out of the five restrictions had been declared constitutional under the *Webster* guidelines. In January 1992, the Supreme Court announced that it would accept *Casey* and by March the date of oral argument had been set for April 22. Once again the President George H. W. Bush administration, as it had in *Webster,* joined forces with the state to press for the reversal of *Roe v. Wade.*[122]

The three years that had elapsed between *Webster* and *Casey* had brought a number of changes. To whose advantage would they work? For example, the retirement of Justice William Brennan and his replacement by the unknown Justice David Souter left abortion rights supporters nervous and anxious. The retirement of Justice Thurgood Marshall and the confusion surrounding his successor, Justice Clarence Thomas, added to their apprehension. The abortion cases the Court had decided following *Webster* also had deepened the alarm of pro-choice groups. *Hodgson v. Minnesota* and *Ohio v. Akron Center for Reproductive Health* had been decided by the Supreme Court on June 25, 1990.[123] These cases, limited to minors, had upheld parental consent requirements, but only with a judicial bypass option. However, a minor did not have to notify *both* parents—only one.

In spite of the loss of *Rust v. Sullivan,*[124] several positive aspects of the Court's internal decision-making process in that case offered some encouragement to pro-choice groups. It was a narrow 5–4 opinion that upheld federal restrictions on abortion counseling in programs funded by the Public Health Service Act of 1970. Without the support of newly appointed Justice Souter, Chief Justice William Rehnquist's bare majority would have collapsed. Souter's support had indicated his concern about the language of the decision, and he had delayed until the last moment before agreeing to endorse Rehnquist's opinion. In oral argument, Justice Souter had expressed skepticism of Solicitor General Kenneth W. Starr's arguments and defense of the gag rule that prevented doctors from discussing an abortion option when engaged in family planning counseling. Was this not a First Amendment issue? he asked. What about a doctor's right under that amendment to counsel his patients to the best of his medical ability? Souter was clearly concerned. Another signal in *Rust* came from Justice Sandra Day O'Connor when she dissented. While O'Connor focused on technical grounds of statutory construction, she had, in fact, continued to follow the independent approach she had carved out for herself in *Webster*.[125]

Legal analysts for the pro-choice advocates were also encouraged as they reanalyzed and rethought O'Connor's record. "Justice O'Connor's opinions have never abandoned *Roe* in holding that at least in some situations a woman has a fundamental right to an abortion," commented one authority.[126] Unlike Chief Justice Rehnquist and Justice Byron White, the two dissenters in *Roe v. Wade*, Justice O'Connor refused to use the lowest level of court review when evaluating state regulations. Instead, "O'Connor has held that a woman's liberty interest in abortion can outweigh the state's interest in protecting future life: the regulations cannot prohibit that choice completely," asserted another analyst.[127] These points came into focus following *Webster*, and O'Connor's subsequent record confirmed them. *Webster* did not undo the right to privacy. All of the justices (except Justice Antonin Scalia) seemed willing to preserve that right particularly when it involved birth control devices and the right to refuse medical treatment, including food and water, artificially delivered.[128] Was there a move to recognize a right to abortion—as a liberty interest protected by the due process clause of the Fourteenth Amendment? The crucial question became, What level of state interest can justify an infringement of this right? This question set the stage for *Planned Parenthood of Southeastern Pennsylvania v. Casey*.

The three years between *Webster* and *Casey* had been marked by changes in public opinion and among state governmental elites. The political climate of the nation itself had changed. *Webster* generated a negative response from the public, with 58 percent opposing it. A majority of Americans clearly wanted to keep abortion legal and available. However, there was also approval for regulations, particularly those that prevented abortion for economic or career reasons.

For their part, opponents of reproductive choice never wavered in their determination to ban all abortions. Questions about birth control that involved the use of abortifacients were evaded as pro-life groups continued to push for ever-increasing restrictions.

Webster also generated a mixed response from states and their leaders—governors, legislators, and judges. More restrictions were placed on abortion rights in Michigan, North Dakota, and Ohio. Other states merely clarified their laws concerning parental notification, waiting periods, and counseling. Louisiana and Utah restricted abortions to situations involving rape or incest, grave infant defects, or major threats to the woman's life.[129] Some governors, like Missouri's John Ashcroft, pushed for restrictions sufficient to prohibit all abortions. On the other hand, some states moved to codify *Roe v. Wade's* guarantees: The state of Washington passed a Reproductive Privacy Act, and Massachusetts adopted an equal rights amendment. Connecticut wrote *Roe* into its state law, as did Maryland and Nevada. Idaho's Governor Cecil Andrus vetoed restrictive laws, claiming that groups outside Idaho had written the legislation.

Across the nation, there was the sense that a bitter fifty-state battle was about to erupt, and no state decision maker could avoid taking a stand. The Supreme Court's *Webster* decision had opened the door to restrictions, and state legislatures and governors were under intense pressure now from their pro-choice constituencies, which had heretofore felt protected. Moreover, disingenuous state restrictive laws might actually stand: the Supreme Court could not be counted on to rescue state elites from the consequences of their own decisions. Thus the abortion issue became a critical election campaign issue.

The election of 1989 was the first test, and it demonstrated that those seeking elective office were wise to study the polls. With majorities demanding that abortion remain legal and available, pro-life candidates began to "soft-pedal" their rigid antiabortion positions. Some did this by asserting their personal opposition to abortion but denying the "appropriateness of imposing one's personal views on others." One analyst summed it up thus: "This way a politician could vote pro-choice while mouthing pro-life."[130] Other candidates merely cut back on their rigid stance on regulations, now supporting only those which polls showed were the most widely accepted. The election results of 1989–1990 showed an increase in the number of pro-choice governors, but by 1991 the right to reproductive choice had moved from center stage as other issues clamored for attention.

The political climate nationwide in 1991–1992 mirrored this shifting attention of the country. The opening guns of the first Gulf War sounded in January 1991, and public attention focused on issues of the nation's self-interest. This was quickly replaced, however, by the economic recession that continued to grow. Foreign policy versus domestic policy became the central issue for debate at the national level. Pro-life forces, however, refused to be sidetracked, and groups like Operation Rescue staged numerous incidents at abortion clinics, particularly during 1991. These tactics involved "blockades and rescues" at the clinics and were often accompanied by violence. In Missouri, the birthplace of *Webster,* antiabortion harassment in Springfield, the home of Governor Ashcroft, resulted in an attack that wounded two people at the city's only clinic. The gunman fled the scene and escaped, and the incident made national news.[131]

The Bush administration's support for Operation Rescue during the summer of 1991 and the early months of 1992 alarmed pro-choice groups. The president's veto of an appropriations bill that would have allowed federal funding for abortion and his determination to uphold regulations banning abortion counseling in any clinic receiving federal funds helped push the abortion issue into the spotlight once again. The confrontation assumed major proportions as the administration entered the case of *Planned Parenthood of Southeastern Pennsylvania v. Casey* as an amicus curiae. Solicitor General Kenneth Starr, fresh from his victory in *Rust v. Sullivan*, was elated at this final opportunity to overturn *Roe v. Wade.*

The Court he would argue before, unlike the one Solicitor General Charles Fried had faced in *Webster*, appeared to be a pro-lifer's dream. Justice O'Connor no longer held the balance of power. With the new justices, Souter and Thomas, it would be possible to overturn *Roe* without O'Connor's vote. Justice Thomas had insisted he had no position on *Roe*, but Starr as well as others knew that Thomas's evasion cloaked a determination to overturn *Roe*. A protégé of Missouri senator John Danforth, Thomas once had worked for Danforth in the office of Missouri attorney general. Danforth's litigation of *Planned Parenthood v. Missouri* had been the first major challenge to *Roe*, and Thomas followed the tactics and ideology of his mentor as the case developed. Thus Starr could feel very confident about Thomas's position in *Casey*.[132] Justice Souter also appeared to be a safe vote. He had voted with the majority in *Rust v. Sullivan*, and his supporters had assured President Bush that Souter would be a "home-run"[133] appointment for abortion opponents. Justice Kennedy, too, appeared to be firmly in the anti-*Roe* category. Starr predicted a solid win in *Casey* with Rehnquist, White, Scalia, Kennedy, Souter, and Thomas. O'Connor might even concur and, if so, there would be a 7–2 decision to reverse the 7–2 decision that had created abortion rights in the first place in 1973's *Roe v. Wade.*

Predictions about the future of reproductive choice were therefore primarily pessimistic. It was expected that the Court would do what it had failed to do in *Webster*. This pessimism was the driving force behind the litigation strategy adopted by the attorneys representing Planned Parenthood of Southeastern Pennsylvania. Like Starr, these veteran attorneys could also count the votes. They prepared for the worst-case scenario, a defeat in *Casey*, and therefore decided to pursue a unique strategy: a warning to the Court and an appeal to the American voters. A Court that abolished reproductive rights could trigger a backlash in the 1992 elections, they warned the Court. A pro-choice presidential candidate could campaign on the issue and use the negative Court decision to win. New judicial appointments could then begin the process of re-creating privacy rights. This litigation strategy focused on the public, not just the judges. Pro-choice strategists proposed an eloquent appeal to be broadcast nationwide: reproductive rights would be lost if the Republicans won. Kathryn Kolbert, a veteran attorney of the abortion battle, and Roger K. Evans, director of litigation for the Planned Parenthood Federation of America, described their strategy thus:

> *Casey* is a vehicle for addressing a wider public beyond an unreceptive Court. The Court is not so much an audience as a foil, an instrument through which the public will be galvanized into protesting at the polls the right that is withering in the courtroom. . . . The audience for [our] arguments is the 10th Justice, the American people.[134]

As Kathryn Kolbert took the podium that morning of April 22, 1992, her voice, her stance, and her words dominated the courtroom, which was filled beyond its usual capacity; Court officials, in a most unusual step, had pulled back the red velvet curtains at the rear of the chamber to accommodate several dozen extra seats for the public.[135] Kolbert did not disappoint her audience. In an "all-or-nothing" challenge to the justices, she electrified the listeners as she defined the issue as "the most important event in abortion litigation since January 1973." It was an "impressively articulate opening" that kept the justices silent for a remarkable seven minutes. This is an unusually long time for a lawyer to receive no questions from the bench; one reporter described the prolonged silence from the justices as "almost eerie." "Most of the justices cast their eyes downward, appearing to examine stacks of papers in front of them,"[136] reported Linda Greenhouse, an expert analyst for the *New York Times*. Another reporter noted that Justice David Souter alone "stared intently at Ms. Kolbert."[137]

What had Kolbert said to produce this extraordinary response? Some commented on the "fervency" with which she described the history of *Roe v. Wade* and the threat that "women might again be forced to the back alleys for their medical care." Others suggested that the unique way she posed the question facing the Court shook some of the justices. Finally, Kolbert brought the justices face to face with the impact a reversal of *Roe* would have on the lives of American women who had come of age believing that they possessed the right of reproductive choice. "Never before has this Court bestowed and [then] taken back a fundamental right that has been a part of the settled rights and expectations of literally millions of Americans for nearly two decades," Kolbert chided the justices.[138] This opening accusation that the justices had decided to do precisely that was effective in its "shock" value: it was unexpected, and it brought justices face to face with political reality.

Justice Sandra Day O'Connor posed the first question, finally interrupting Kolbert. That question would prove to contain the two holdings that the Court majority would ultimately reach in *Casey*. Acknowledging that the issue of stare decisis was certainly a question the Court must answer as it considered overturning *Roe*, O'Connor also wanted to know if Kolbert planned to address the specifics of the Pennsylvania Abortion Control Act.[139]

Kolbert responded by posing her own question that put the justices on notice of the enormity of the problems they were facing:

> Your Honor, I do [plan to address the constitutionality of the specific limitations of the Pennsylvania law]. However, the central question in this case is, what is the standard that this Court [will] use to evaluate the restrictions?[140]

It was a bold move and a disconcerting one to the justices who generally expect an attorney to merely attempt to persuade them to adopt one standard over another. Kolbert did not do that. Instead, her choice of words implied a warning. It was not a deferential tactic of persuasion.

Kolbert began to address Pennsylvania's restrictions, starting with what was to prove the most intrusive: spousal notification. Kolbert's focus on the dangers facing a Court that overturned a precedent of *Roe v. Wade*'s magnitude, and her challenge to justices who might hope to apply a judicial test of less scrutiny to state laws, was not the typical argument heard in the Court. It was not so much a dialogue between counsel and court as it was a message from the attorney to the justices. Its power was reflected throughout the thirty minutes of Kathryn Kolbert's allotted time as very few questions were interjected—three from O'Connor, one each from justices Antonin Scalia and Anthony Kennedy, and two from Chief Justice William Rehnquist. Kolbert had succeeded in following her planned strategy. Would it be effective?

As Pennsylvania's attorney general Ernest D. Preate Jr. took the podium, the behavior of the justices shifted dramatically. The justices, so passive when Kathryn Kolbert was at the podium, suddenly became active participants. They ignored the briefs filed by Attorney General Preate and U.S. Solicitor General Kenneth Starr, and both attorneys found themselves responding to unexpected questions. Kolbert had been able to remain focused and to stick to her game plan, but Preate and Starr became reactors following the lead of the different justices.

Pennsylvania's attorney general had spelled out his original strategy and game plan in his brief. He expected to build on what Missouri's attorney general, Bill Webster, had won in *Webster v. Reproductive Health Services*. He first planned to challenge the validity of *Roe* as a precedent: "Overrule *Roe*" was his demand. Preate had also decided to ask the Court to accept the lowest standard or test to apply to state laws governing reproductive choice. The plurality in *Webster* had recommended a "rational basis" test, and now Preate was going to ask a new majority to adopt it.[141] Preate was prepared to argue grand principles of constitutional law by turning *Roe* against itself. A focus on such phrases in *Roe* as "no absolute right to abortion on demand" and "a limited right subject to . . . state regulation"[142] could be used to rewrite *Roe*'s basic holding that had recognized a privacy right for reproductive choice decisions. Attacking *Roe* from within could lessen the concern of justices about stare decisis and the overruling of long-standing precedent.

Solicitor General Kenneth Starr also expected to engage in this type of constitutional debate with the justices. He wanted to remove *Roe* from the protection of the "liberty provisions" of the Fourteenth Amendment and classify it as a "due process" precedent and not one involving fundamental rights. This argument, like Preate's, would diminish *Roe* as precedent. Justices then would not need to be too concerned about allegiance to stare decisis.[143]

As it happened, neither attorney was able to pursue his strategy. The oral argument was marked by questions about other points. Dismissing Preate's attempt to redefine *Roe*, Justice Harry Blackmun, *Roe*'s author, suggested that Preate had not even read *Roe*.[144] Blackmun's interruption early in Preate's presentation and his flat contradiction of Preate's thesis opened the door for a judicial onslaught. Justice O'Connor peppered Preate with a series of skeptical questions.[145] She quizzed him specifically about the spousal notification provision of the Pennsylvania statute. Ignoring Preate's argument for a rational basis test for state restrictions, O'Connor demanded that Preate apply her "undue burden" standard to the Pennsylvania provision. Surely, the attorney general insisted, it was no "undue burden" for a woman to notify her husband about her proposed abortion. O'Connor was not pleased. This surprised the Pennsylvania attorney general; it was an unexpected position for Justice O'Connor to take. The influence of the various sociological briefs that had been submitted by amici curiae was obvious as O'Connor expressed concern for women with abusive husbands. The law would clearly be an undue burden in those cases, she maintained. O'Connor was first joined by Justice John Paul Stevens, who was a firm supporter of *Roe*, and then by Justice Kennedy, who had always voted against *Roe*. With Attorney General Preate under attack, Justice Scalia came to his aid with informative arguments thinly disguised as questions, which only served to confirm the inadequacy of Preate's own arguments.[146]

Pennsylvania's attorney general nevertheless hoped to salvage his case by summing up in his conclusion the initial points he had planned to make. He was denied even that privilege as Justice Souter suddenly asked a probing question about the spousal notification provision of the Pennsylvania law: "How would the statute affect women who were separated or estranged from their husbands?"[147] Similar to Justices O'Connor's questions about this same point, Souter's participation at the last moment was evidence of another unexpected problem for the state's attorney. Preate's argument had served to bring justices O'Connor, Souter, and Kennedy together on common ground, focusing on the practical effect of the statute on ordinary people. This approach moved *Casey* from the abstract realm of constitutional law to that of the real world, where the restrictions would have enormous impact.

It was not an auspicious ending for Attorney General Ernest Preate—nor an auspicious beginning point for Solicitor General Starr. Starr's game plan was upset almost immediately by Justice Stevens, with help from Justice O'Connor and Justice Souter. Stevens broke into the solicitor general's opening remarks with what, at first, appeared to be a trivial question. The mild manner of the question belied the perilous nature of the issue. "May I ask you one rather basic question?" the justice inquired. "What is the position of the Department of Justice on the question whether a fetus is a person within the meaning of the Fourteenth Amendment?"[148]

The exchange that followed was described as "tense."[149] The solicitor general sought to evade the question, but O'Connor would allow no escape. "Well, the court decided that [the fetus is not a person under the Fourteenth Amendment] in *Roe*, did it not?"[150] she asked. Kenneth Starr clearly did not welcome this question; he had not expected it. His weak response, "We do not have a position on that question,"[151] satisfied neither O'Connor nor Souter, much less Stevens. Starr, like Preate, had to be rescued from this predicament by Justice Scalia, who used his question to suggest an answer to the beleaguered Starr.

As he attempted to refocus his argument in his concluding remarks, Starr was once again caught off-guard by Justice Stevens, who had the final question. Insisting that Starr's call for the rational basis test would actually leave no exceptions even when a woman's life was at stake, Stevens immediately enlisted the support of Justice Souter. Starr ended by protesting, "The common law would never deprive an individual of her right to life. . . . The state cannot proceed in an arbitrary and capricious fashion."[152] This was not the valedictory ending Starr had envisioned for his argument.

Observers and expert analysts leaving the courtroom agreed that Kathryn Kolbert had "vastly outperformed" her rivals.[153] Would this save *Roe*? Would it make a difference? Few thought so. Justice Scalia had stated the issue succinctly when he asserted, "Often the attorney who delivers the poorest argument will, nevertheless, win the case."[154] If personal judicial ideology rules, then debate is ineffective. The voting patterns of Chief Justice Rehnquist and justices Scalia, White, Kennedy, and O'Connor were on record. Justice Clarence Thomas, the newest justice on the court, had not asked a single question during oral argument, but his friendship with Justice Scalia, combined with his misleading remarks about his knowledge of *Roe*, suggested he would vote to overrule. Justice Souter's position was still an enigma; it was also possible that O'Connor might decide to follow her *Webster* strategy. Nevertheless with only justices Stevens and Blackmun firmly committed to *Roe*, the chances of securing the other three votes necessary to win appeared to be a lost cause.

Oral argument had taken place on Wednesday, April 22, 1992. The justices would have Thursday for a "study day" before meeting for their conference discussion and vote on Friday morning, April 24. "That Thursday would go down in legal history as one of the more momentous days" in Supreme Court history.[155]

In the various judicial chambers, nothing of great significance occurred until one came to the suite on the far southeastern corner of the main floor. These chambers were occupied by Justice David H. Souter, who at that time was the second newest justice on the Court. They were sparsely furnished rooms, with no computer terminals and no electric desk lamps: Justice Souter disliked such modern equipment. The focal point of the main room was a large portrait of Harlan Fiske Stone. Like Souter, Stone had been born and reared in New Hampshire, and his official portrait at the time he became chief justice likened Stone to a "hunk of New Hampshire granite."[156] Stone was a legend in the legal history of the Court. Meticulous in his research, slow and deliberate in his writing, Stone authored some of the major doctrines that define the role of the Court even today. Did David Souter remember Stone's challenge to the Court to "restrain itself?"[157] Did Stone's concern for real people caught in difficult moral dilemmas—like the World War I pacifists Stone had judged—communicate itself to Souter?[158]

For Justice Souter, Thursday was a day of quiet, internal contemplation, a period of reflection on the oral argument he had listened to so intently the day before. During his confirmation hearings two years earlier, he had told the senators, "When an existing case is attacked any reconsideration [must] involve not only the correctness of the earlier decision but also the extremely significant issues of precedent."[159] Kathryn Kolbert's masterful argument for the reaffirmation of *Roe* as precedent offering security to women for their child-bearing decisions had struck a responsive chord in Souter; he believed in seeing the real, nonhypothetical people, in a case. Souter also acknowledged his respect for precedent and the doctrine of judicial self-restraint. It was evening when Justice Souter reached his final conclusion: *Roe* was workable precedent and must be affirmed.[160]

The next day was Friday, the day of the judicial conference, the day *Roe*'s fate was to be decided. The vote appeared to be clear, certain, and precise. A majority of five voted to uphold the Pennsylvania antiabortion statute in its entirety. There were also five votes to overrule two important pro-*Roe* Supreme Court decisions of the 1980s: *City of Akron v. Akron Center for Reproductive Health, Inc.* and *Thornburgh v. American College of Obstetricians and Gynecologists*. The chief justice had triumphed, and he and Justice Byron White, the two dissenters in *Roe*, had finally won, though Rehnquist "graciously" declared that it would "not be necessary" to state that *Roe* was overruled. Rehnquist and White were joined in the majority by justices Antonin Scalia, Clarence Thomas, and Anthony Kennedy. Justice Souter's heart-searching ordeal of the day before had convinced him to reaffirm *Roe*, but he was not able to convince the others. Justice Sandra Day O'Connor also cast her vote to reaffirm *Roe*, but it was too late—she was no longer the swing vote and *Roe* could be overturned without her support.[161]

As leader of the majority, Chief Justice William Rehnquist had the privilege of assigning the opinion in *Planned Parenthood of Southeastern Pennsylvania v. Casey*, and he chose to write it himself. It was his, this ultimate victory, and he immediately set to work on the opinion. In his zeal, however, he forgot a vital fact about conference votes: they are not binding. Conference history and tradition documents justices who, even at a later date, shift position. That this could happen to his emerging majority opinion in this case was unthinkable to the chief justice.

Without Rehnquist's knowledge, Justice Kennedy was reconsidering his vote. Kennedy had been "anguish[ing]" for some time over *Casey*. Justice Souter and Justice O'Connor had been "working on him."[162] While Rehnquist was drafting the opinion to nullify *Roe*, Kennedy, O'Connor, and Souter were meeting secretly, holding what is known as a "rump conference," a well-known device in judicial decision-making history.[163] A secret meeting of a bloc or small group of like-minded justices to develop a strategy, the rump conference in *Casey* included justices Kennedy, O'Connor, and Souter only. The place chosen for meeting was the chamber of Justice Souter. Sitting together on Souter's sofa, these three justices planned a new majority opinion for *Casey*, essentially a new life for *Roe*. "They agreed to join their efforts to write an opinion carving out middle ground that would still clearly uphold a woman's right to an abortion and to be free from burdensome state regulations."[164] Secrecy and privacy surrounded these meetings. Clerks and secretaries remained silent. Justice Blackmun had exhausted his talents and those of his clerks from the beginning as he attempted to influence *Casey's* justices. He would never know which, if any, of his arguments affected Kennedy.

By all appearances, the case seemed settled. Chief Justice Rehnquist circulated his first draft on May 27. But then came May 29 and a note that would alter everything. "I need to see you as soon as you have a few moments," Justice Kennedy wrote to Justice Blackmun. "I want to tell you about a new development in *Planned Parenthood v. Casey*. It should come as welcome news."[165] The two justices, Blackmun and Kennedy, met in the library the next day, May 30. Although Blackmun had already read hope into Kennedy's note—"*Roe* sound," he had written on a pink memo pad[166]—he became worried during the face-to-face meeting. As Blackmun recounted, Kennedy "was concerned about being saddled with this issue for the rest of his career. He was especially worried about the attention he would get as a Roman Catholic reaffirming *Roe*." Kennedy was also concerned about the death threats Blackmun had endured as well as an assassination attempt. Would he also experience this? Blackmun wondered, even then, if Kennedy would "stick."[167]

Blackmun's record of the events that followed in the days and weeks before *Casey* was announced is found in his papers and oral interviews, which were finally revealed in March 2004, five years after his death. In oral interviews with National Public Radio's Nina Totenberg, and in his notes and papers, Blackmun's discussion of these events is terse and dramatic. "Justice Kennedy informed the Chief Justice [as to his shift]," Justice Blackmun noted. "The Chief Justice . . . then spent some time in walks with Justice Kennedy to persuade him to change his mind, but Rehnquist was unable to move Kennedy."

On June 3, the rump conference members, now designated the "Troika," circulated their bombshell. Totenberg, using Blackmun's papers, described the unfolding events:

> Four days after [Kennedy's] meeting with Blackmun, the group that came to be known as the Troika inside the Court . . . circulated their first draft reaffirming what they called the core holding of Roe. The Chief Justice, however, was not giving up. Two weeks later he circulated a second draft, still styled as a majority opinion. It attacked the reasoning in the Troika Opinion, still contending that his approach was not overruling *Roe*. The Troika didn't budge though. Indeed, some clever editing by Justice John Paul Stevens that moved a half-dozen paragraphs around, allowed the first three sections of the Troika Opinion to win two more votes. Two weeks later, on June 26th, Rehnquist circulated a third draft, this time styled as a dissent and conceding that in the dissenters' view *Roe* was wrongly decided and should be overruled.[168]

There are many different ways of winning but in the last analysis, it is not the size of the victory or the scope of the victory that really matters. It is the simple fact of winning that counts. *Planned Parenthood of Southeastern Pennsylvania v. Casey* was such a win: women do have a right to choose abortion. It was an unexpected win, a surprising win.

Courtroom spectators that June morning in 1992 sat spellbound as the drama unfolded. It was, without question, an "unprecedented event."[169] It was, in essence, the "most important statement by the Court in more than twenty-eight years."[170] The decision was driven by three very different justices acting as one, and justices Kennedy, O'Connor, and Souter knew that they could pay a political price for this act of "personal courage and constitutional principles."[171] O'Connor and Souter had both enjoyed popularity with First Lady Barbara Bush. She and Justice O'Connor were tennis partners; Justice Souter was her favorite "eligible bachelor" to invite to White House dinners. Justice Kennedy had reason to see himself following Rehnquist in the role of chief justice. But now, all of these relationships would change, and if President Bush won reelection in 1992, the "three centrist justices could pay a price for disagreeing with the White House's view on abortion," wrote Justice Blackmun's clerk.[172]

So a unique event occurred the morning of June 29, 1992. This was brought home to the spectators when Chief Justice Rehnquist recognized justices O'Connor, Kennedy, and Souter as coauthors of the majority opinion in *Casey* and each in turn "read [aloud] successive sections of their joint opinion."[173] Seldom do justices read their opinions aloud, and seldom is an opinion signed by more than the principal author. Those who had studied legal and political history were the only ones who could recall that in *Cooper v. Aaron*, all nine justices had signed the one opinion.[174] With its power and prestige threatened by Arkansas governor Orval Faubus's refusal to obey the Court decision of *Brown v. Board of Education*,[175] the Court had then come together as one. Justice O'Connor, Kennedy, and Souter did the same in *Casey*. Furthermore, the Court had abandoned reading case decisions aloud from the bench as an unproductive use of time. Yet the emotion of the human voice finds no substitute in the written word, and its impact is lost in the silence. As O'Connor, Kennedy, and Souter each read aloud, the public could hear their anger, feel their frustration, and sense their joy in a unified purpose, driven by principle. It was a bonding experience for these justices—a Three Musketeers' "all for one and one for all." Those who heard them that day would not soon forget the experience. The justices themselves were changed by their very act of reading aloud an opinion that brought "out of many, one."[176]

Casey's record tells the story. O'Connor, Kennedy, and Souter announced the judgment of the Court. They also delivered *the* opinion of the Court, which included parts I, II, III, V-A, V-C, and VI. They delivered *an* opinion with respect to parts IV, V-B, V-D, and V-E, with Justice Stevens joining the opinion on part V-E. Like many of the modern case decisions, *Casey* was complicated, as the six remaining justices joined parts of the judgment and parts of the opinion and dissented from other parts.[177] *Casey*'s judgment and opinion, however, left no room for doubt. The cause—the right to abortion— was won.

The three justices made this clear in inspired words and phrases. "Liberty finds no refuge in a jurisprudence of doubt," they wrote. Those doubts that had plagued *Roe* for nineteen years needed to be removed, the justices continued, and they then proceeded to do so:

> The essential holding of [*Roe v. Wade*] should be retained and once again reaffirmed. [*Roe*'s] central holding, the holding we reaffirm, has three parts. First is recognition of the right of the woman to choose to have an abortion before viability and to obtain it without undue interference from the State. Before viability, the State's interests are not strong enough to support a prohibition of or the imposition of a substantial obstacle to the woman's effective right to elect the procedure. Second, is a confirmation of the State's power to restrict abortions after fetal viability, if the law contains exceptions for pregnancies which endanger a woman's life or health. And third, is the principle that the State has legitimate interests from the outset of the pregnancy in protecting the health of the woman and . . . the fetus.[178]

Part II of the opinion justified reaffirming *Roe v. Wade*.[179] It identified the constitutional basis for the individual right recognized in *Roe*, anchored *Roe* in precedent, and asserted the judicial test appropriate for a court to use. Justice Anthony Kennedy, delivering most of this section orally, reached impassioned heights as he described the "real woman"—her feelings, emotions, pain. The judicial sensitivity shown to women in this part of *Casey* would place it among the great passages of judicial prose.

The Fourteenth Amendment's "due process liberty" clause was identified by the justices as the anchor or birthplace of the right of reproductive choice. Justice Kennedy explained: "Due process liberty," he noted, identified a "promise of the Constitution." Personal liberty had been recognized by both the framers of the Constitution and the justices who interpreted it as "a realm . . . which government may not enter"—a realm of "basic" decision-making power. Personal liberty decisions included three basic rights: the "right to define one's own concept of existence, of meaning"; the right to define the "universe" for oneself; and the right to define the "mystery of human life." The individual alone had the right to choose how to interpret these theological and philosophical questions. Government could not impose on anyone its beliefs about these "attributes of personhood." The Constitution recognized this right in the Fourteenth Amendment's "due process liberty" clause.

Justice Kennedy next called attention to Court precedents that had recognized this liberty. He cited *Loving v. Virginia*, which outlawed prohibitions on interracial marriage. He also cited *Griswold v. Connecticut, Eisenstadt v. Baird*, and *Carey v. Population Services* as examples of the personal liberty involved in birth control decisions.[180] This latter right—to possess and use contraceptive devices—was settled law, Kennedy asserted, and the abortion decision in *Roe* was based on their reasoning. The Constitution, as interpreted by Court precedents, protected this liberty. Those case decisions also identified how justices should behave in the process of making the decision. The Court traditionally applied the test of "reasoned judgment."[181] Justices were not free to impose their own moral principles, to "mandate [their] own moral code."[182] What justices should do—and what they were going to do in *Casey*—was to "balance interests."[183] The individual liberty involved outweighed the government's right to control and limit. This was the bottom line.

Why? The answer is found by looking at a "real woman" contemplating abortion. Justice Kennedy had done just that when he penned the following:

> The liberty of the woman is at stake in a sense unique to the human condition and so unique to the law. The mother who carries a child to full term is subject to anxiety, to physical constraints, to pain that only she must bear. . . . Her suffering is too intimate and personal for the State [to insist that she make this sacrifice].[184]

The depth of emotion, of insight into another's pain and agony, expressed in this section of *Casey* significantly impacted those in the courtroom that day. The vivid picture it painted made *Casey* a classic. It gave to the decision a sense of reality that is so often lost in the game of constitutional litigation.

Part III of the opinion was delivered by Justice David H. Souter. Sixteen pages of closely reasoned analysis flowed from the justice's pen. A true scholar at heart, Souter was in his element as he defended the principle of stare decisis, reliance on precedents. His argument, however, was not theoretical but practical. A sociological or contemporary morality analysis demonstrated the degree of reliance upon *Roe* and with it the need to preserve that decision. "The ability of women to participate equally in the economic and social life of the nation has been facilitated by their ability to control their reproductive lives," he declared.[185] A historical analysis of the Court's record of overturning cases showed that *Roe* was completely different. Unlike *Plessy v. Ferguson* and *Lochner v. New York*,[186] *Roe* did not rest on "fundamentally flawed" assumptions.[187] In fact, *Roe*'s factual underpinnings had *not* been shown to be incorrect.

Dictates of prudence, concern for the power and image of the Court, and views about the proper role of the Court coalesced to explain the need for retaining *Roe v. Wade*. "To overrule under fire . . . would subvert the Court's legitimacy," Justice Souter wrote.[188] It would also weaken people's respect for the rule of law, the "constancy" that they expected from their legal system. If the Court "surrendered to political pressure," it would lose its authority.[189]

The Court concluded its holding with the introduction of a new judicial test for evaluating the constitutionality of state law. The "undue burden" test had been mentioned by Justice Harry Blackmun in 1976 in *Bellotti v. Baird*.[190] Usually linked to Justice O'Connor, this test is defined as the best means for balancing a woman's liberty against the state's interest in protecting fetal life. A state regulation would be struck down by this test if the regulation "plac[ed] a substantial burden in the path of a woman seeking an abortion of a non-viable fetus."[191] The test also continued to use *Roe*'s "viability standard" as the dividing line.

Casey's record documents the reaction of the other six justices involved in the decision. The two liberal justices, Blackmun and Stevens, were overjoyed and signed on to an opinion that breathed new life in *Roe*. They were not happy with the "undue burden" test, but were hopeful that in practice a number of state restrictions would be found to violate its principle. This was true even in *Casey*. The section of Pennsylvania's law requiring "spousal notification" was struck down by the majority.

On the other hand, Chief Justice William Rehnquist and justices Byron White, Antonin Scalia, and Clarence Thomas were not only frustrated but also angry. Rehnquist's dissent was marked by sarcasm and personal attacks against justices O'Connor, Kennedy, and Souter. Calling the opinion a "façade" and a "judicial Potemkin Village,"[192] the chief justice penned a diatribe that lacked legal justification. History would take note of that. Likewise, the "harsh" and "mocking" dissent written by Justice Scalia would mark the beginning of the end of his claim to judicial leadership of the Court.[193]

That an opinion could generate such an outpouring of anger and bitterness only showed how powerful it was. *Casey*, in one sense, ended the debate over a constitutional right to abortion. The extent to which that right could be circumscribed remained, but the justices had settled the issue of outlawing abortion. Missouri's attorney general, Bill Webster, had remarked earlier, "Abortion is here to stay."[194] It was so; it was a cause won.

Casey was a unique win in the cause of reproductive rights. It was certainly the "last thing one would have expected" from a Court dominated by justices who had been appointed to overrule *Roe v. Wade*.[195] Were the justices—particularly O'Connor, Kennedy, and Souter—angry at the White House for "repeatedly bringing the abortion issue to the Court"?[196] The "judicial abortion wars" had caused personal wounds that could not heal if cases were constantly pushed into the Court. Did the justices resent the Reagan and Bush administrations' "aggressive advocacy" of the antiabortion cause? Did they long for the middle ground? The majority of justices in the *Casey* opinion suggested this when they wrote, "The United States, as it has in five other cases in the last decade, again asks us to overrule *Roe*."[197]

The departure of justices William Brenner and Thurgood Marshall had left the conservative ideology of Chief Justice Rehnquist, Justice Scalia, and Justice Thomas seemingly unchecked. Did justices O'Connor, Kennedy, and Souter feel the need to restore the balance? Linda Greenhouse, court reporter for the *New York Times*, suggested that these justices were "responding to forces within [the Court] . . . and to the personal animosity and internal tension they had experienced."[198] Justice O'Connor had been mocked and ridiculed by Justice Scalia in the *Webster* case. This only increased with the announcement of the *Casey* opinion as Rehnquist joined the attack and expanded it to include Kennedy and Souter as well as O'Connor.

As a result, these three justices of "personal moral courage"[199] could take grim satisfaction in breathing new life into *Roe*. *Casey* did more. It "placed the constitutional right to abortion on a coherent and plausible theoretical basis."[200] *Casey* was "clearer and stronger than the precedent [*Roe*] itself." Focusing on the "status of women," *Casey* "placed the question of women's ability to control their reproductive lives in the context of the modern doctrine of equality." As Professor Laurence Tribe of Harvard Law concluded, "This opinion makes sense and puts the right to abortion on a firmer jurisprudential foundation than ever before."[201]

THE CASE OF TERRI SCHIAVO:
NANCY CRUZAN DID NOT DIE IN VAIN

The U.S. Supreme Court had not explicitly ruled in June 1990 that Nancy Cruzan had a right to die. Nevertheless, using the loopholes provided by the Court opinion and clear statements about the right to refuse artificially delivered food and water, Nancy Cruzan's guardians had finally won that right for their daughter. Missouri had to recognize the right of competent individuals and that of appropriate surrogates to forgo unwanted medical treatment that included food and water, as well as medicine. Even though death would be the result, the process could not be criminalized. *Cruzan v. Missouri* had won a victory on this narrow but significant point. On balance, the Court had indeed announced some kind of a constitutional right to die. Supporters of privacy rights were now ready to challenge the ability of the states to regulate the process of dying with overly restrictive laws. To what extent should states be allowed to regulate and restrict the gains made in *Cruzan?*

Nancy Cruzan's ordeal had attracted national attention when her family members appeared on television talk shows and gave recorded interviews that were shown on such television networks as PBS and ABC. Ted Koppel's *Nightline* show carried the personal as well as the legal story into homes across America.[202] Technical, medical, and legal terms became topics of everyday conversations. What is a persistent vegetative state (PVS) condition? How does one recognize it? What is a living will? Is it sufficient? Should everyone have one? A living will, combined with a medical directive and durable power of attorney, is the means for exercising one's right to die. For the individual who lacks these documents and has failed to make these choices about treatment, dying may become a living death. No one can be forced to exercise this right: to list treatments they wish to forgo or to name a decision maker to act in their place. The *Cruzan* case forced the American public to face issues of death and dying as changed by modern technology.

As a result of this, states passed laws to allow people to govern their end-of-life choices. Problems arose when, because of the absence of documents such as the living will, the medical directive, or the durable power of attorney, there were questions about the true intent of the patient in a persistent or permanent vegetative condition. What standards should be employed and what role should the state play in creating and administering these standards? What should be the role of lawmakers, executives, courts, and judges in determining the constraints placed upon and the freedom granted to the patient seeking a right to die? Who should be primary decision maker for the patient—the state itself or someone else? Is the state better positioned to look after the interests of patients on life support than a family, particularly if the family is dysfunctional or divided in its opinions? Such is one sequel of the Nancy Cruzan case. It represented the first truly national response to these questions and the right of an individual to govern end-of-life decision making. Did it elevate the *Cruzan* holding into a "cause won" for right-to-die advocates?

Terri Schiavo's "First Death"

It was February 1990, a tragic month for a twenty-seven-year-old Florida woman, Terri Schindler-Schiavo. Nancy Cruzan would be allowed to die in December of that year after an ordeal that had lasted seven years. Nancy Cruzan's brain, deprived of oxygen for twelve minutes, had never regained normal function following a car accident. Terri Schiavo suffered similar brain damage that February; her heart had stopped, thus depriving her brain of oxygen.[203]

Nancy Cruzan's brain had been deprived of oxygen because her nostrils were buried in icy mud when she was tossed from her car. But what had caused Terri Schiavo's heart to stop beating? Experts could not agree. Some suggested a chemical imbalance brought on by an eating disorder. Certainly her heart had stopped around 6:00 A.M. when she fell as she got out of bed. Her husband Michael Schiavo had called the paramedics, who "performed aggressive resuscitation" and "seven defibrillations en route [to the hospital]." She was rushed to the emergency room, where testing began to ascertain what was wrong. Was it a heart attack? Not according to blood chemistries and serial EKGs—normal blood gases and chest X-ray ruled out a pulmonary or lung cause for the disorder. Could it have been septic toxic shock syndrome? The answer was not clear. In other words, "the diagnosis of the cause of her condition was unknown."

Among the symptoms that were known were the following: a low potassium level, a markedly elevated glucose (sugar) level, a urinary tract infection, and a low blood pressure. Terri Schiavo experienced "seizures" and at first went into a prolonged coma, requiring, for a time, ventilator support. In November 1990, the hospital decided to send her to an intensive rehabilitation center because she had "a difficult hospital course." However, at the Mediplex in Brandon, Florida, Schiavo was described as "poorly responsive" to treatment.

In December, Michael Schiavo took his wife to California for an experimental implant and the use of a brain stimulator. A return to home care was unsuccessful and Terri was moved from one rehabilitation center to another and finally to a nursing home. Nothing succeeded in altering her state and like Nancy Cruzan, Terri Schiavo was regularly hospitalized with infection. Terri, like Nancy, was classified as being in a persistent vegetative state with no hope for recovery. In Schiavo's case, this certification was made first in 1990 and then again in 1998.

The *Cruzan* ruling was well known in Florida: its impact on that state had produced "one of the most explicit right-to-die laws" in the country. The

Florida Supreme Court had affirmed that law, saying, "[Florida residents] have the constitutional right to choose or refuse medical treatment." *Cruzan v. Missouri* had made it clear that medical treatment included food and water, particularly when it was artificially delivered. Terri Schindler-Schiavo, like Nancy Cruzan, had not made end-of-life choices: there was no living will, no medical directive, and no durable power of attorney. However, Florida had specified in its law that in such cases a surrogate could make these choices and that the appropriate surrogate for a married person was the spouse. In Terri's case, it was her husband, Michael Schiavo. Terri's parents, Bob and Mary Schindler, agreed and signed a document making Michael Schiavo their daughter's legal guardian. This was in conformity with Florida law.[204]

Nancy Cruzan's guardians had been her parents; her husband had secured a divorce and relinquished responsibility to them. There was no money in that family situation and no disagreement about Nancy's wishes. The Schindler-Schiavo situation was very different. In the first place, there was a sizable financial settlement from medical malpractice suits based on doctors' failure to detect the low potassium levels that could have triggered a heart attack. Sources disagree about the amounts of the settlements: estimates range from $1.2 million to $1.9 million. There were separate suits and separate awards: a personal award for Michael Schiavo based on "loss of consort" and awards for Terri Schiavo for "misdiagnosing her condition" and for her care. As guardian, Michael Schiavo was in charge of these funds. However, Terri's parents became suspicious of their son-in-law and a "venomous" relationship developed.

In a letter dated July 16, 1993, the Schindlers detailed their concerns. Bob Schindler reminded Michael Schiavo about agreements they had reached privately during various malpractice trials in 1991–1992. Apparently, Terri's parents thought that Michael would use some of the award money to purchase a house where they could live with Terri and bring in nursing help to take care of her. However, when Michael returned with Terri following her treatment in California, he had changed his mind. The doctors in California had dashed hope for any sort of recovery for Terri. Therefore, Michael Schiavo had come to accept that Terri was truly in a persistent vegetative state and would not want to live.

A few days after sending the letter protesting Michael's change of view, the Schindlers filed a court petition to remove Michael as guardian. They accused him of attempted murder (strangulation) and blamed Terri's heart stoppage on this. They charged him with financial greed and adultery. The petition was rejected by the court.

In March 1994, Michael's care of Terri was praised by the first guardian *ad litem*, John H. Pecarek. Between 1994 and 1998, Michael Schiavo and Schindlers fought each other over Terri's treatment. Michael refused additional treatment, describing it as repetitive. The Schindlers continually asked to see details of Terri's medical record and a list of all the current treatments. Having succeeded in this, they then could charge Michael Schiavo with neglect for his failure to repeat tests and continue therapy.[205]

Dueling in State Courts: A Family Divided

Privacy issues became public in 1998 when Michael Schiavo sought to have his wife's feeding tube removed after eight years of unsuccessful rehabilitation. "My wife had always focused on her appearance—body, make-up, clothes," Schiavo declared. He believed that Terri Schiavo, like Nancy Cruzan, would have been "horrified at the sight of herself."

Schiavo won a series of legal battles as court after court in Florida agreed with his request to remove life support. The legal struggle revolved around the issue of guardianship, with the Schindlers filing various motions to have Michael Schiavo removed. The first trial began on January 24, 2000, in the circuit court of Pinellas-Pasco County with Judge George Greer presiding. It would be the first in a long series of legal maneuvers in Greer's courtroom.

Judge Greer ruled that Terri Schiavo would have chosen to have her feeding tube removed and issued an order to that effect. This decision was based on the evidence submitted by Michael Schiavo and that of friends. It was upheld on January 24, 2001, by the Second District Court of Appeals for the state of Florida. On March 29, Greer set a date for removal of the tube: April 20, 2001.

The Schindlers' appeal to the Florida Supreme Court on April 18, 2001, was refused. However, on April 20, a federal district court granted the Schindlers a stay to exhaust appeals. On April 23, the U.S. Supreme Court refused to intervene. The next day, the feeding tube was removed—only to be reinserted on April 26. The Schindlers had filed a new civil suit, claiming Michael Schiavo had committed perjury.

Some fourteen legal actions occurred from that date until June 6, 2003. In October 2001, new doctors evaluated Terri. New charges were levied against Michael Schiavo in November 2002. Additional legal actions that occurred included repeated debates over the Schindlers' visitation rights, petitions for rehearings, and routine filings for stays of court orders. The Schindlers also petitioned Judge Greer for an extraordinary writ of *quo warranto* directed to Michael Schiavo to show cause as to why he should not be dismissed as guardian. The petition included every infraction the Schindlers had previously named against Terri's husband. The Schindlers wanted Terri to have more swallowing tests and to have therapy to learn how to eat without the tube. These requests were rejected summarily on the basis of Terri's history of aspiration of food, similar to Nancy Cruzan's.

The Schindlers attacked Judge Greer's objectivity throughout the proceedings, demanding that Greer recuse himself or be subjected to removal by a higher court. Nevertheless, Judge Greer, acting on another request from Michael Schiavo to remove Terri's feeding tube, granted that permission for the second time. The removal of Terri's tube was to take place on October 15, 2003. Immediately the Schindlers appealed the ruling to the Florida Supreme Court, which once again refused to hear the case. Like the state supreme court, the U.S. Supreme Court also rejected review of the case for a second time.[206] Blocked by the Florida right-to-die law as interpreted by the courts, Terri's parents finally turned from the judicial process to the political process.

Governors and Legislators versus Courts: Who Decides?

On October 15, 2003, Bob and Mary Schindler reacted to the court order allowing removal of the feeding tube by approaching Florida governor Jeb Bush and asking him to reverse the courts. Governor Bush "went on record with us that he would . . . use every resource he has to save Terri's life," Bob Schindler reported, and Governor Bush did. In a spirited legislative session, the governor requested a specific law ("Terri's Law") that would give the governor "control of cases where a feeding tube is removed from a person in a persistent vegetative state and a family member contests the decision." The Florida Senate hastily voted 23–15 for the legislation, and the House passed the final version 73–24 only minutes later. Governor Bush signed the bill into law and issued an order to reinstate Terri Schindler-Schiavo's feeding tube an hour later. Some supporters of the legislative intervention, however, expressed concern about their actions, according to news reports. Senate president Jim King, a Republican, agonized, "I keep thinking, 'What if Terri didn't really want this done at all?' May God have mercy on all of us."[207]

Was this new Florida law, "Terri's Law," constitutional? George Felos, the attorney for Michael Schiavo, stated the issue succinctly: Was Terri's constitutional right to refuse medical treatment cast aside by a statute that allows the governor to do that under any whim and without any standards and without any review? Thus began a series of legal and political moves that would pit the power of the executive and the legislature against the power of the judiciary.

Governor Bush defended his actions. He pointed to the videos of Terri Schiavo, which her parents had secured and publicized over the Internet in violation of a court order. These videos had generated support for the Schindlers from all over the country. Within Florida, more than forty thousand people had urged the governor to defy the courts, which Bush proceeded to do. After seeking to have one judge disqualified, the governor then requested a jury trial where he could present evidence vindicating his actions. Insisting that the videos showed movement and responses suggesting that Terri was only disabled, Bush ignored the overwhelming medical testimony about PVS patients. Similar videos exist of Nancy Cruzan. However, the public responded emotionally to the tapes and supported Governor Bush. In addition, he had the support of all antiabortion and anti-right-to-die groups nationwide.

The governor's brother, President George W. Bush, hastened to affirm the law. The president himself, as governor of Texas, had favored a law that would guarantee PVS patients the right to be sent to a public-supported institution that would keep them on life support in spite of medical advice concerning recovery. With statistics indicating that there were between 16,000 and 35,000 PVS patients in the state, and life support estimated at $500,000 per patient per year, the bill did not pass in Texas. Governor George Bush had then vetoed a living will statute for Texans because it lacked this provision. Although he later signed one that appeared to recognize the right to die, Bush maintained that it did not represent his position.[208]

The refusal of such powerful politicians as the president and the Florida governor to recognize a "privacy right to die" jeopardized that right. Their power to reverse the right secured in *Cruzan* was increased when the Catholic Church weighed in. On April 2, 2004, Pope John Paul II declared that "feeding tubes are a moral obligation." The pope insisted that Catholic hospitals should refuse to honor both living wills and medical directives and should continue hydration and nutrition, artificially administered and in spite of an individual's wish to the contrary. The church thus took sides in the legal and political battles dividing the country on the right-to-die issues.[209]

Yet in spite of political opposition, the judicial process continued to function methodically. The Florida Supreme Court held oral argument on Terri's Law on August 30, 2004, and the court decision came on September 23. It was a unanimous ruling in favor of Michael Schiavo and seemed to settle the issue. The seven justices on Florida's highest court made their disapprobation of the hastily passed law clear. Terri's Law was "an unconstitutional encroachment on the power that has been reserved for the independent judiciary," Chief Justice Barbara J. Pariente wrote. The law letting the governor order the feeding tube reinserted violated the separation of powers guaranteed by the state's constitution, according to the Florida judges.[210]

A ruling based on the state constitution and state laws, it did not appear to raise any substantial federal question and made review by the U.S. Supreme Court unlikely. In such cases, the Supreme Court has generally followed the procedure known as the "adequate and independent state grounds barrier" to Court review. Federalism is thus protected and a balance is maintained. State judges are acknowledged as the best interpreters of their state's constitution and laws, and the Supreme Court moves cautiously, always careful to show great deference to the state courts. Only a "substantial federal question" claim can overcome this barrier.

At first, the legal and political response to the Florida Supreme Court's decision seemed to indicate that Governor Bush would not continue to fight.

"I'm disappointed for the moral reasons . . . but I'm respectful of the Supreme Court's decision," the governor said. He continued, "We will review what the ruling says. We will make a determination if there are any additional steps that can be taken. . . . If not, we will let the actions of the Supreme Court stand." It was clear that the Court's reminder that "we are a nation of laws, and we must govern our decisions by the rule of law and not our emotion," had been a sobering reminder to Governor Bush of the Watergate debacle.[211]

Terri Schiavo's parents, however, did continue to fight. Charging Michael Schiavo with moral depravity and with being unfit to act as his wife's guardian, the Schindlers included a new argument. They argued that Pope John Paul II's April 2, 2004, directive to all Catholic agencies and hospitals had set church law over constitutional law. The pope had ordered that living wills be disregarded and that all people classified as PVS "must receive food and water," even if artificially administered. Otherwise, the pope declared, it would be a sin, a violation of Christian principle. Like Governor Bush, the Schindlers were Roman Catholics, and their argument focused on the fact that freedom of religion is a constitutional guarantee. However, their assertion of the superiority of "God's law" over "Man's law" challenged the very nature of the secular American political system.

Governor Bush, encouraged by the elections of November 2, 2004, reversed his earlier plan and appealed to the U.S. Supreme Court. An election influenced decisively by religious and moral issues required recognition. Both the governor of Florida and the president of the United States were ready to see how the Supreme Court would respond. The governor's brief alleged that the Florida Supreme Court had "misapplied the separation-of-powers principle . . . and the due process clause of the Fourteenth Amendment."[212]

The nation awaited the Supreme Court's response. On January 24, 2005, the Court without comment refused to grant to a writ of certiorari, declining to hear Governor Bush's challenge to the Florida Supreme Court's decision.[213] As George Felos, Michael Schiavo's attorney put it, "This means the decision by the Florida Supreme Court declaring Terri's Law unconstitutional stands." It certainly meant that the executive and legislative branches could not override judicial rulings in this case. Nevertheless, the debate continued as the Schindlers vowed to continue their legal and political campaign.

Into the National Political Process: President Bush and Congress Act

Why would political actors at the national level get involved in the issue of Terri Schiavo's right to die? The answers were numerous and complex. Republicans had a core group of supporters from right-to-life organizations who pressured them to override the state courts. Those opponents of a right to die had deluged their congressional delegates with e-mails, faxes, and telephone messages. The pressure was intense. Some Republican leaders also saw a chance to expand their power base. Others genuinely feared a move toward euthanasia and physician-assisted suicide.

The political environment was also right for an attack on the judicial branch. Although President Bush had been highly successful in his nomination and confirmation of conservative judges, he had failed with his ten most controversial nominees. Democrats had invoked the filibuster threat, and President Bush had been thwarted in his attempt to "pack the courts." Moreover, at the appellate level, the Republican Party was extremely disappointed with some of the earlier appointments. Supreme Court justices John Paul Stevens and David Souter, both nominal Republicans, had voted for abortion rights and for gay rights. Republican justices Sandra Day O'Conner and Anthony Kennedy had also moved in this direction, often voting with the two Democrats on the Court: Ruth Bader Ginsberg and Stephen Breyer. Republicans were disappointed and angry.[214]

In Florida, Republicans also had reason to be disappointed in many of their own judicial appointments. The Florida courts had consistently sided with Michael Schiavo and against the Schindlers, the Florida legislature, and Governor Jeb Bush. The Schindlers knew that President George W. Bush was in agreement with his brother, who had already exhausted his own resources seeking to keep Terri alive. They also knew that several powerful national lawmakers were on their side. The Schindlers had been successful in developing a close relationship with Representative Dave Weldon (R-Fla.) and Senator Mel Martinez (R-Fla.). In addition, one of the Schindlers' attorneys had a personal relationship with House Majority Leader Tom DeLay of Texas. DeLay was also eager to lead a battle to keep Terri Schiavo alive. He believed this would resonate to his personal advantage at a critical time when he was under attack on charges of ethics violations. These events set the stage for federal legislation to override state law and state judicial opinions.[215]

In the House of Representatives, DeLay spearheaded the offensive. He was joined by the Senate majority leader, Bill Frist, a medical doctor by profession. Frist had gone on record to call the diagnosis of Schiavo's condition "mistaken." "Terri Schiavo is not in a persistent vegetative state," he insisted after seeing videos of Terri, although he had never actually seen Terri or examined her. Both DeLay and Frist knew that they had only a very short time to get a bill drafted, passed by both the House and Senate, and signed by the president. Moreover, the two leaders had different ideas about the content of the bill. DeLay supported a broad bill that would give federal courts power to intervene in any situation comparable to Schiavo's. Frist supported a more narrow version that would apply only to Terri Schiavo.

Moving at breakneck speed, the House, on March 16, 2005, passed the Protection of Incapacitated Persons Act, which provided for the removal of cases like Schiavo's from state to federal court. The next day, the Senate passed a "private bill" applying to the Schiavo case alone and thus differing from House Resolution 1332. Private bills apply to specified individuals, in this case the parents of Terri Schiavo. Identified as U.S. Senate 653 ES, this bill accorded "Relief of the Parents of Theresa Marie Schiavo." It allowed federal courts to have jurisdiction in the Schiavo case, naming the U.S. District Court for the Middle District of Florida in particular. Granting the Schindlers "standing to bring suit" relating to the "withholding or withdrawal of food, fluids, or medical treatment necessary to sustain the life of Theresa Marie Schiavo," the Senate bill was more narrow than that passed by the House. The House bill, as noted above, gave federal courts power to reach into cases of any "disabled person" in a condition similar to Schiavo's.

When the Senate and the House produce different versions of a bill, it usually takes time for a conference committee to meet and settle the differences. Time was exactly what Congress did not have in March 2005. The Easter recess was imminent. The House had already adjourned before the Senate bill was completed. Nevertheless, House Republican leaders "scrambled" to bring enough representatives back to Washington for an emergency vote. They first agreed to accept the Senate version and then prepared to vote. It was a politically contentious vote, which ironically would be referred to as the "Palm Sunday Compromise." The House was forced to debate for three hours before passing the new version by a 203–5 vote shortly after midnight on March 21, 2005. Democrats had demanded a roll call vote in the House. They opposed the bill, which they called a political exploitation of tragic family matters, a disregard for the principle of federalism, and an attack on state's rights. In the Senate, however, there was no debate. Only a few senators were present to approve the session. It was a voice vote and quickly over.

Newspapers would call it an "extraordinary congressional maneuver." Republican congressional leaders had kept President Bush appraised of every move, and the White House had made arrangements for the president to sign the measure at any hour. In fact, President Bush interrupted his Easter vacation in Texas. He rushed into the nearby waiting Air Force One, reportedly pulling his clothes on over his pajamas for the flight back to Washington. After landing, Bush signed the bill at 1:11 A.M. immediately after receiving it from Congress. He then returned at once to his ranch near Crawford, Texas.

The federal district court in Florida had been told to be ready to act as soon as it received the call from Washington. Most expected the judge to sign an order to replace Terri Schiavo's feeding tube, which had been removed on March 19. An ambulance was on standby outside the Woodside Hospice Center, and state officials had orders to take custody of Terri and move her to a public institution where the governor's power to act as guardian could be enforced. However, this did not happen. The hours ticked by with no action by the federal district judge.[216] Legal and constitutional experts had predicted that the intervention of Congress and President Bush in the Schiavo case would not convince federal courts to act. Why?

Failure of the National "Terri's Law": An Attorney's Mistake

The national "Terri's Law" had carried several unique provisions. First, as already noted, it had given federal courts an unusual jurisdiction that was "under-inclusive" on its face since it singled out one person. Second, it raised the issues of federalism, that is, state versus national power, and of separation of powers among the legislative, executive, and judicial branches. Third, the bill had instructed the federal district court in Florida to "determine *de novo*" the violation of Terri Schiavo's rights. Congress and the president wanted and expected the federal district court to ignore the records of seven years of legal proceedings in state courts—records that already filled some forty-five volumes. Congress had made its intention clear in the words of the new law. Federal courts were ordered to proceed "notwithstanding any prior state court rulings." It was to be an entirely new case.

Why did this not happen? Why did the U.S. District Court, Middle District of Florida, Tampa Division, argue and decide the case on the data of state court records? The attorney for the Schindlers, David Gibbs III, and his associates made mistakes.

Gibbs filed a "motion for temporary restraining order" in response, he claimed, "to an order of Pinellas County Probate Judge George W. Greer to discontinue [Schiavo's] nutrition and hydration." In his motion, Gibbs noted the basis for the motion for a restraining order. He charged Judge Greer with violation of Terri Schiavo's due process rights and her First Amendment rights to free exercise of religion. This motion changed the issue before the court to one of "whether temporary injunctive relief is warranted." In a sense, the attorneys for the Schindlers had turned the case into an appeal instead of a *de novo* review.[217] They were asking the federal court to review the state court's actions and procedures. The federal district court had to act in accordance with what the attorneys had asked, and this meant a review of Judge Greer's actions. It was not a new case, not a *de novo* action.

The claim in the motion that Judge Greer had violated Terri Schiavo's constitutional rights of religion and due process produced the following response from U.S. District Court judge James Whittemore:

> This court has carefully considered the Act and is mindful of Congress' intent that Plaintiffs have an opportunity to litigate any deprivation of Terri Schiavo's federal rights. The Court is likewise mindful of Congress' directive that a de novo determination be made "not withstanding any prior state court determination." In resolving Plaintiffs' motion for Temporary Restraining Order, however, the court is limited to a consideration of the constitutional and

statutory deprivation alleged by Plaintiffs in their Complaint and motion. Because Plaintiffs urge due process violations and premised primarily on the procedures followed and orders entered by Judge Greer in his official capacity as the presiding judge in the dispute between Michael Schiavo and Plaintiffs, their Complaint necessarily requires a consideration of the procedural history of the State Court case to determine whether there is a showing of any due process violation. On the face of these pleadings, Plaintiffs have asserted five constitutional and statutory claims. To obtain temporary injunction relief, they must show a substantial likelihood of success on at least one claim.[218]

Judge Whittemore could not conduct a *de novo* hearing since the Schindlers had based their case on the procedure in state courts. Whittemore had to examine, analyze, and decide on this basis. Attorney Gibbs had filed a request at odds with the law signed by President Bush directing the federal courts to consider the case *de novo* without taking into account the state court findings.

Gibbs and his associates also faced other difficulties. The Supreme Court precedent in the 1990 *Cruzan* case made it clear that a person in a persistent vegetative state had a constitutional right to be removed from a feeding tube. In a 1997 ruling, Chief Justice William Rehnquist had affirmed that the *Cruzan* case assumed that "the due process clause protected the traditional right to refuse unwanted lifesaving medical treatment." Even Justice Antonin Scalia had written a similar opinion in a 1995 case, *Plaut*, striking down a congressional law that had directed courts to reopen final judicial judgment. Constitutional lawyers had noted that "it [was] not clear that Congress could dictate guardianship rules to states."

Judge Whittemore's opinion in the present case was a model of judicial logic. After discussing jurisdiction and standing, Whittemore turned to the four "applicable standards" necessary to secure injunctive relief. The Schindlers had listed three claims: violation of the Fourteenth Amendment due process right to a fair and impartial trial; violation of the Fourteenth Amendment's equal protection of the law; and violation of the First Amendment's free exercise of religion clause. Judge Whittemore carefully analyzed each claim and dismissed each in turn as being "without merit."

Whittemore's study of the past history of the case found "no violation of Fourteenth Amendment Due Process Rights to a Fair and Impartial Trial." He found no Fourteenth Amendment violations at all: Terri Schiavo had had two independent attorneys to represent her interests and Judge Whittemore noted that the court had applied the traditional balancing test well. Her case had been "exhaustively litigated." There had been extensive hearings, expert testimony asserting that "no meaningful treatment was available," and six appeals. "Few, if any, similar cases have ever been afforded this heightened level of process," Whittemore asserted, quoting the statement of Florida's Second District Court of Appeals.

Judge Whittemore's opinion was tightly reasoned and well documented. It infuriated the Republican leaders in Congress, who immediately focused their hopes on the U.S. Court of Appeals for the Eleventh Circuit.

A panel of three judges from the Eleventh Circuit Court of Appeals in Atlanta was the first to hear the Schindlers' appeal from Judge Whittemore's district court. In a *per curiam* opinion, the panel sided with the district court. It was actually a 2–1 ruling with appellate judges Ed Carnes and Frank M. Hull siding with Whittemore. Judge Charles R. Wilson, a Clinton appointee, dissented. As a result, the entire Eleventh Circuit of judges decided to hear the appeal. The vote was not officially revealed but was probably 10–2 in support of the district court opinion: Terri's feeding tube should not be reinserted and the injunctive relief sought by her parents' attorneys was denied.

The court of appeals reviewed the district court's denial of temporary injunctive relief to see if Judge Whittemore had abused his discretionary powers. He had not. Instead, the appeals court agreed with Whittemore's findings that the Schindlers had "failed to demonstrate a substantial case on the merits of any of the claims," noting that Judge Whittemore's decision had been "carefully thought-out."

"Any further action by our court or the district court would be improper," wrote Judge Stanly F. Birch Jr., an appointee of President George H. W. Bush. Birch also "scolded" President George W. Bush and Congress for their attempts to intervene in the judicial process and attempts to "rob federal courts of the discretion they had been given in the Constitution." Judge Birch concluded, "President Bush and the Congressional Republicans have acted in a manner demonstrably at odds with our Founding Fathers' blueprint for governance of a free people—our Constitution."[219]

With their options dwindling, the Schindlers sought relief at several levels. They appealed to the U.S. Supreme Court, appealed to the Florida legislature and Governor Jeb Bush for another Terri's Law, and requested for the second time for Congress to "do something quickly." Congress acted first. The Republican leadership issued a subpoena for Terri Schiavo to be brought before a congressional committee to allow her presence to speak for her. Michael Schiavo was also subpoenaed to appear. The Senate Health Committee and the House Government Reform Committee joined forces and lodged an "emergency request" with the U.S. Supreme Court asking the justices to reinstate Schiavo's feeding tube while the committee filed appeals to have its subpoenas recognized. However, the Court denied this request without comment.

Attempts by the Florida Department of Children and Family Services, along with U.S. marshals, to remove Terri Schiavo from the Woodside Hospice in Pinellas Park, Florida, were halted by the local law enforcement officials of Pinellas Park. The local officials were acting under the orders of the state circuit judge George Greer, who as probate judge had issued the order removing her feeding tube in the first place.[220]

Meanwhile, the Schindlers' attorneys filed their own appeals of the Eleventh Circuit Court of Appeals' ruling. Again, the U.S. Supreme Court refused to overturn the lower court's ruling. In all, the Supreme Court had refused on six separate occasions to enter the case.[221]

The Florida legislature and Governor Jeb Bush were meanwhile trying to draft a new bill that could be general enough to be approved by the Florida Supreme Court yet sufficiently specific to target Terri Schiavo. The Florida House of Representatives drafted a bill that would block doctors from denying food and water to someone in a persistent vegetative state, making exceptions for patients who left specific instructions. The Senate version proposed blocking the denial of food and water only in cases where "family members disagreed on whether to maintain the feeding"; then the patient would be kept alive "unless he or she had expressed different wishes in writing." The House passed its version by a vote of 78–37, while the Senate bill was defeated on a 21–16 vote. Leaders in the Florida Senate then concluded that they lacked support for any version of a new "Terri's law."

The Schindlers had hoped that public pressure would force the reinsertion of Terri's feeding tube. The Florida Department of Children and Family Services cited numerous phone calls charging Michael Schiavo with "abuse," but this did not persuade the judge to act. The Schindlers had also urged the legislature to pass a law allowing Terri to divorce her husband on grounds of adultery since he was living with another woman and had fathered two children by her. Florida judges, however, had refused to count this as evidence of an abusive or neglectful guardian and would not remove Michael Schiavo from his position as husband and guardian. Options and time finally ran out. Some twelve hours after the U.S. Supreme Court rejected the Schindlers' last appeal, Terri Schindler-Schiavo died. It was March 31, 2005, thirteen days after doctors, acting under orders of State Circuit Judge George Greer, had ordered Terri's feeding tube removed on March 19.

The constitutional right to liberty had outweighed the constitutional right to life, and in the fifteen-year contest, Terri Schiavo's ordeal had confirmed the right tenuously granted in the case of Nancy Cruzan. It truly represented a "cause won" for the right to die. The Supreme Court stood by its *Cruzan* ruling and the country at large agreed. Over the years, the *Cruzan* decision had been largely forgotten after many states passed some type of living will law. The Schiavo case played before a national audience with around-the-clock television, Internet, and newspaper documentation of every detail. The public response was intense and clear. Americans did not want government involved in their end-of-life decision. The public disapproved of the actions of the president, Congress, governor, and legislature. Nancy Cruzan's ordeal to establish a right to refuse medical treatment, including food and water artificially delivered, had been confirmed in the Schiavo case by court after court's decisions and by public opinion polls.

The release of Terri Schiavo's autopsy report overwhelmingly confirmed the reasons for allowing a guardian to withdraw food and nutrition in a case such as hers. The autopsy confirmed that Terri was truly in a persistent vegetative state. It showed massive and irreversible brain damage that no amount of therapy could have regenerated; it also showed that she was blind.

The American public's support for the right to die with dignity, in peace and quiet, without governmental intervention increased. Those who had living wills wanted to revisit them. Did their documents include "removal of food and water" in a medical directive? Did they leave a durable power of attorney for a decision maker of their choice to choose death for them, trumping governmental intervention? Thus, a narrow limited win for Nancy Cruzan had become a major victory for "right to privacy as a right to die" in the Terri Schiavo case.

NOTES

1. Jethro K. Lieberman, *The Litigious Society* (New York: Basic Books, 1981), 15.

2. Albert P. Blaustein and Clarence C. Ferguson Jr., "Avoidance, Evasion, and Delay," in *The Impact of Supreme Court Decisions*, ed. Theodore L. Becker and Malcolm M. Feeley, 2nd ed. (New York: Oxford University Press, 1973), 100–109.

3. David Easton, *A Framework for Political Analysis* (Englewood Cliffs, NJ: Prentice-Hall, 1965), 110–117.

4. Robert G. McCloskey, *The American Supreme Court* (Chicago: University of Chicago Press, 1960), 224.

5. See Louis Lusky, *Our Nine Tribunes: The Supreme Court in Modern America* (New York: Praeger, 1993), 14.

6. Dr. Michael Fuhrman, "An Analysis of the Book of Revelation," address given at University Heights American Baptist Church, Springfield, MO, October 2003.

7. *Poe v. Ullman*, 367 U.S. 497 (1961), 519–521.

8. Ibid., 522–525, quote on 533. The *Nelson* case was *State v. Nelson*, 126 Conn. 412 11A. 2d 856 (1940).

9. *Poe v. Ullman*, 548.

10. Ibid., 533, 534.

11. *Griswold v. Connecticut*, 381 U.S. 479 (1965), 48.

12. *State of Connecticut v. Griswold et al.*, 151 Conn. 544, 546, 200 A. 2d 479 (1964).

13. Ibid., 545.

14. Richard [Cardinal] Cushing, foreword to *Catholics and Birth Control*, by Dorothy B. Bromley (New York: Devins-Adair, 1965), xi.

15. Joseph L. Dorsey, "Changing Attitudes toward the Massachusetts Birth Control Law," *New England Journal of Medicine* 271 (October 1964): 823–827.

16. Ibid.

17. David J. Garrow, *Liberty and Sexuality: The Right to Privacy and the Making of Roe v. Wade*, rev. ed. (Berkeley: University of California Press, 1998), 237–239.

18. Philip B. Kurland and Gerhard Casper, eds., *Landmark Briefs and Arguments of the Supreme Court of the United States: Constitutional Law*, vol. 61, *Griswold v. Connecticut* ([Washington, DC]: University Publications of America, 1975), 1–453, esp. 452.

19. Justice Antonin Scalia, interview by Paul Duke, "Inside the Marble Temple," program 2 of *This Honorable Court*, video, 58 min. (Alexandria, VA: PBS Video, 1988).

20. Garrow, *Liberty and Sexuality*, 241.

21. Robert G. Dixon, "The *Griswold* Penumbra: Constitutional Charter for Expanded Right of Privacy?" *Michigan Law Review* 64 (December 1965): 197–218, esp. 213, 214, 217.

22. Marjorie Hunter, "High Court Hears Birth-Curb Case; Told Devices are Sold 'Under Counter' in Connecticut," *New York Times*, 30 March 1965.

23. Paul G. Kauper, "Penumbras, Peripheries, Emanations, Things Fundamental and Things Forgotten: The *Griswold* Case," *Michigan Law Review* 64 (December 1965): 235–258, especially 242, 244.

24. *Griswold v. Connecticut*, 483, 484.

25. Kauper, "Penumbras, Peripheries, Emanations," 235–258.

26. Burr Henly, "Penumbra: The Roots of a Legal Metaphor," *Hastings Constitutional Law Quarterly* 15 (Fall 1987): 81–100.

27. *Eisenstadt v. Baird*, 405 U.S. 438 (1972), 453.

28. Robert Bork, "The Supreme Court Needs a New Philosophy," *Fortune*, December 1968, esp. 170.

29. Robert Bork, "Neutral Principles and Some First Amendment Problems," *Indiana Law Journal* 47 (Fall 1971): 416–421.

30. Patrick B. McGuigan and Dawn M. Weyrick, *Ninth Justice: The Fight for Bork* (Washington, DC: Free Congress Research and Education Foundation, 1990), 285–303.

31. Robert H. Bork, *The Tempting of America* (New York: Free Press, 1989), 95–96, 169, 234, 263.

32. Garrow, *Liberty and Sexuality*, 672.

33. *Lawrence v. Texas*, 539 U.S. 558 (2003), 578.

34. Laurence Tribe, interview by Nina Totenberg, "Analysis: Final Day of the Supreme Court Term, 2002–2003," *Morning Edition*, National Public Radio, 27 June 2003.

35. *Powell v. State*, 270 Ga. 327, 510 S.E. 2d 18, 24 (1998).

36. An "independent state grounds" barrier to Supreme Court review is one of the doctrines that the Supreme Court uses to determine which cases to review. Applying the doctrine, the Court declines jurisdiction over cases that do not contain a federal issue and that have been decided in a state court on the basis of state law that is sufficient to dispose of the cases. See Alice Fleetwood Bartee, *Cases Lost, Causes Won: The Supreme Court and the Judicial Process* (New York: St. Martin's, 1984), 82–83.

37. *Commonwealth v. Wasson*, 842 S.W. 2d 487 (Ky. 1992); *Campbell v. Sunquist*, 926 S.W. 2d 250 (Tenn. app. 1996): *Gryczan v. State*, 283 Mont. 433, 142 P. 2d 112 (1997); *Jegley v. Picado*, 349 Ark. 600, 80 S.W. 3d 332 (2002).

38. *Romer v. Evans*, 517 U.S. 620 (1996), 635.

39. Marouf A. Hasian Jr. and Trevor Parry-Giles, "A Stranger to Its Laws: Freedom, Civil Rights, and the Legal Ambiguity of *Romer v. Evans*," *Argumentation and Advocacy* 34, no. 1 (1997): 27–43.

40. Jeffrey Toobin, "Supreme Sacrifice," in *Portraits of American Politics*, ed. Bruce Allen Murphy, 3rd ed. (Boston: Houghton Mifflin, 200), 422, 424.

41. Rowland Evans and Robert Novak, "Justice Kennedy's Flip," *Washington Post*, 4 September 1992.

42. *Romer v. Evans*, 635.

43. Quote is from the opinion of Justice Kennedy in *Lawrence v. Texas*, which originally came from the historians' brief in that case.

44. John D'Emilio and Estelle B. Freedman, *Intimate Matters: A History of Sexuality in America*, 2nd ed. (Chicago: University of Chicago Press, 1997).

45. David J. Garrow, "Sodomy and the Supremes," *Advocate*, 4 March 2003, 52–53.

46. *Walls v. Petersburg*, 895 F. 2d 188, 193 (Cal.4 1990).

47. *Marcum v. McWhorter*, 308 F. 3d 638, 640–642 (Cal.6 2002).

48. *Charles v. Baesler*, 910 F. 2d 1349, 1353 (Cal.6 1990).

49. *Doe v. Wigginton*, 21 F. 3d 733, 739–740 (Cal.6 1994).

50. *Milner v. Apfel*, 148 F. 3d 812, 814 (Cal.7 1998).

51. *Henne v. Wright*, 904 F. 2d 1208, 1214–1215 (Cal.8 1990).

52. *Holmes v. California Army National Guard*, 124 F. 3d 1126, 1136 (Cal.9 1997).

53. *Schowengerdt v. United States*, 944 F. 2d 483, 490 (Cal.9 1991).

54. *Mullins v. Oregon*, 57 F. 3d 789, 793–794 (Cal.9 1995).

55. *High Tech Gays v. Defense Industrial Security Clearance Office*, 895 F. 2d 563, 570–571 (Cal.9 1988).

56. *Williams v. Pryor*, 240 F. 3d 944, 949 (Cal.11 2001).

57. *Lawrence v. Texas*, 563.

58. Peter Irons, *The Courage of Their Convictions* (New York: Free Press, 1988), 381–391.

59. Garrow, "Sodomy and the Supremes," 52–53.

60. "Supreme Court Grants Review of Texas Sodomy Case; Will Confront Question of Overruling *Bowers v. Hardwick*," *Lesbian/Gay Law Notes*, January 2003, www.qrd.org/qrd/www/usa/legal/lgln/01.2003.pdf.

61. *Romer v. Evans*, 624.

62. *Powell v. State*, 24.

63. *County of Sacramento v. Lewis*, 523 U.S. 833, 857 (1998).

64. *Loving v. Virginia*, 388 U.S. 1 (1967).

65. Brief Amicus Curiae: George Chauncey et al., *Lawrence v. Texas* ("The Historians' Case against Gay Discrimination," 2002).

66. Brief Amici Curiae: Mary Robinson, Amnesty International, Human Rights Watch, Interights, The Lawyers Committee for Human Rights, and Minnesota Advocates for Human Rights in Support of Petitioners, *Lawrence v. Texas*, No. 02-102.

67. *Lawrence v. Texas*, 573.

68. See *Washington v. Glucksburg*, 521 U.S. 701, 710, 718n6. Rehnquist's list of courts of other countries included Canada, New Zealand, Australia, and Colombia.

69. Brief Amici Curiae Mary Robinson, Amnesty International, Human Rights Watch, Interights, The Lawyers Committee for Human Rights, and Minnesota Advocates for Human Rights in Support of Petitioners, *Lawrence v. Texas*, No. 02-102.

70. *Palko v. Connecticut*, 302 U.S. 319 (1937).

71. Linda Greenhouse, "The Supreme Court: Texas Law; Court appears ready to reverse a sodomy law," *New York Times*, 27 March 2003.

72. Ibid. Unless otherwise stated, the quoted material in the following description of the oral argument is taken from "*Lawrence v. Texas*, transcript of oral argument, March 26, 2003" (Washington, DC: Alderson Reporting, 2003).

73. Greenhouse, "The Supreme Court: Texas Law."

74. Ibid.

75. See also Barrett Brick, "Today at the Supremes," *Sodomy Laws*, www .sodomylaws.org/lawrence/lwnews025.htm, 26 March 2003.

76. Greenhouse, "The Supreme Court: Texas Law."

77. Ibid.

78. Ibid.

79. Ibid.

80. Brick, "Today at the Supremes."

81. *Lawrence v. Texas*, 564 (emphasis added).

82. *Poe v. Ullman*, 522–553 (1961). Justice Harlan's dissent in *Poe* won enormous praise from scholars.

83. *Lawrence v. Texas*, 565.

84. Ibid., 567.

85. Ibid., 568.

86. Ibid., 569.

87. Ibid., 571.

88. Ibid., 572.

89. Tony Mauro, "Justices, 6–3, Strike Texas Sodomy Law," *New York Law Journal* 229 (27 June 2003): 1.

90. Vincent J. Samar, "The Supremes and Gay Rights: A Closer Look at *Lawrence v. Texas*," *In These Times*, 1 July 2003, www.inthesetimes.com/site/main/article/596.

91. Joanna L. Grossman, "Assessing the Legal Fallout after the *Lawrence v. Texas* Ruling," *CNN.com Law Center*, www.cnn.com/2003/LAW/07/08/findlaw.analysis .grossman.lawrence, 8 July 2003.

92. Samar, "Supremes and Gay Rights."

93. Justice O'Connor's concurrence, *Lawrence v. Texas*, 579–585.

94. Ibid., 581.

95. Charles Evans Hughes, *The Supreme Court of the United States* (New York: Columbia University Press, 1928) 68.

96. Walter F. Murphy, *Elements of Judicial Strategy* (Chicago: University of Chicago Press, 1964), 55. Massive retaliation is a "nuke 'em" strategy and is effective only if it is never actually used. A justice who resorts to open, vicious attacks alienates future allies. Massive retaliation, or "washing dirty linen in public," is usually a sign that the justice is aware that he or she has lost the argument and that persuasion will never succeed.

97. Justice Scalia's dissent, *Lawrence v. Texas*, 586–605.

98. *Lawrence v. Texas*, 586–605, quotes on 587.

99. Ibid., 591.

100. Ibid., 576. See Charles Fried, *Order and Law: Arguing the Reagan Revolution; A Firsthand Account* (New York: Simon & Schuster, 1991); Richard A. Posner, *Sex and Reason* (Cambridge, MA: Harvard University Press, 1992).

101. *Lawrence v. Texas*, 576.

102. Ibid., 588, 595; quote on 595.

103. *Roe v. Wade*, 410 U.S. 117 (1973). See also Wayne C. Bartee and Alice Fleetwood Bartee, *Litigating Morality: American Legal Thought and Its English Roots* (New York: Praeger, 1993), 4–6.

104. *Lawrence v. Texas*, 601, 602.

105. Ibid., 602.

106. Ibid.

107. Ibid.

108. Grossman, "Assessing the Legal Fallout," 8 July 2003.

109. Sherry F. Colb, "The Supreme Court Welcomes Gays and Lesbians into the Fold," *CNN.com Law Center*, www.cnn.com/2003/LAW/06/30/findlaw.analysis.colb .bowers, 30 June 2003.

110. Stephen Henderson, "Anti-Sodomy Dissent Mirrors Justification of Slavery, Scholars Say," Knight Ridder, 18 July 2003, available at www.sodomylaws.org/ lawrence/lwnews/6335998.htm.

111. Ibid.

112. Jonathan Turley, "Not as Radical as All That," *National Law Journal* 25, no. 96 (2003): 31; available at www.jonathanturley.com/Articles/Not_as_radical.htm.

113. Mauro, "Justices, 6–3," 1.

114. Samar, "Supremes and Gay Rights."

115. Randy E. Barnett, "Kennedy's Libertarian Revolution," *National Review*, 10 July 2003, available at www.nationalreview.com/comment/comment-barnett 071003.asp.

116. Samar, "Supremes and Gay Rights."

117. Ibid.

118. *Colautti v. Franklin*, 439 U.S. 379 (1979).

119. *Thornburgh v. American College of Obstetricians and Gynecologists*, 476 U.S. 747 (1986).

120. Barbara Hinkson Craig and David O'Brien, *Abortion and American Politics* (Chatham, NJ: Chatham House, 1993): 32.

121. *Planned Parenthood of Southeastern Pennsylvania v. Casey*, 505 U.S. 833 (1992).

122. Brief Amicus Curiae: United States supporting respondents, *Planned Parenthood of Southeastern Pennsylvania v. Casey*, reprinted in Kurland and Casper, *Landmark Briefs and Arguments*, vol. 91, 363–399.

123. *Hodgson v. Minnesota*, 497 U.S. 417 (1990). *Ohio v. Akron Center for Reproductive Health*, (*Akron II*), 497 U.S. 502 (1990).

124. *Rust v. Sullivan*, 500 U.S. 173 (1991).

125. Ibid., 224.

126. James F. Simon, *The Center Holds: The Power Struggle inside the Rehnquist Court* (New York: Simon & Schuster, 1995), 156–157.

127. Charles H. Baron, "Abortion and Legal Process in the United States: An Overview of Post-*Webster* Legal Landscape," *Law, Medicine, and Healthcare* 17, no. 4 (1989): 370.

128. Ibid., 369.

129. Craig and O'Brien, *Abortion and American Politics*, 279–303.

130. Ibid., 27.

131. "Two Wounded in Abortion Clinic Shooting" and "Protesters on Hand to Witness Shooting at Springfield Clinic," *Springfield News-Leader*, 29 December 1991. See also Garrow, *Liberty and Sexuality*, 689.

132. David A. Kaplan, "Judging Thomas: The Life and Contradictions of the Supreme Court Nominee," *Newsweek*, 16 September 1991. Thomas had shared an office with John Ashcroft.

133. Paul M. Barrett, "Independent Justice: David Souter Emerges as Reflective Moderate on the Supreme Court," *Wall Street Journal*, 2 February 1993.

134. Linda Greenhouse, "Both Sides in Abortion Argument Look Past Court to Political Battle," *New York Times*, 20 April 1992.

135. Linda Greenhouse, "Both Sides Stress Broad Effect of Any Ruling; Abortion and the Law: Constitutional Questions and Political Agendas Intersect," *New York Times*, 23 April 1992.

136. Ibid.

137. David J. Garrow, "Justice Souter: A Surprising Kind of Conservative," *New York Times Magazine*, 25 September 1994.

138. Philip B. Kurland and Gerhard Casper, eds., "1991 Supplement: *Planned Parenthood of Southeastern Pennsylvania v. Casey*," vol. 91 of *Landmark Briefs and Arguments* (Arlington, VA: University Publications of America, 1993).

139. Ibid., 1196.

140. Ibid.

141. Ibid., 1204, 1210–1211.

142. Ibid.

143. Ibid., 1214.

144. Ibid., 1204.

145. Ibid., 1204–1214.

146. Ibid., 1208–1209.

147. Ibid., 1206–1213.

148. Ibid., 1214.

149. Greenhouse, "Both Sides Stress Broad Effect."

150. Kurland and Casper, "1991 Supplement," 1215–1216.

151. Ibid.

152. Ibid., 1219.

153. Greenhouse, "Both Sides Stress Broad Effect." See also Garrow, *Liberty and Sexuality*, 692.

154. Scalia, interview, "Inside the Marble Temple."

155. Garrow, "Justice Souter," 36.

156. Alpheus T. Mason, *Harlan Fiske Stone: Pillar of the Law* (New York: Viking, 1956), 11, 20, 106.

157. Ibid., 410.

158. Ibid., 106–107.

159. Garrow, "Justice Souter," 36.

160. Ibid.

161. Ibid., 38.

162. Ibid.

163. A rump conference is a judicial strategy first devised by Chief Justice William Howard Taft—"a small group meeting, in secret, to thrash over difficult cases in order to present a unified front to the rest of the Court" (Murphy, *Elements of Judicial Strategy*, 79).

164. Garrow, "Justice Souter," 38.

165. "Papers Reveal *Roe v. Wade* Almost Overturned," *CNN.com*,www.cnn.com/2004/LAW/03/04/scotus.blackmun.papers/index.html, 4 March 2004.

166. Fred Barbash, "Blackmun's Papers Shine Light Into Court; Justice's Trove Opened by Library of Congress," *Washington Post*, 5 March 2004.

167. Justice Harry A. Blackmun, interview by Nina Totenberg, *National Public Radio News*, 4 March 2004, available at www.npr.org/templates/story/story.php?storyId=2101289. Totenberg was given first access to Justice Blackmun's papers, and he also recorded oral interviews with her. The coverage of the *Casey* appeal is extensive.

168. Ibid.

169. Linda Greenhouse, "A Telling Opinion about Abortion and the Court," *New York Times*, 30 June 1992.

170. David J. Garrow, "A Landmark Decision," *Dissent* 39 (Fall 1992): 427–729.

171. *Planned Parenthood of Southeastern Pennsylvania v. Casey*.

172. Totenberg, *National Public Radio News*, 4 March 2004.

173. Garrow, *Liberty and Sexuality*, 692.

174. *Cooper v. Aaron*, 358 U.S. 1 (1958). See Kathleen M. Sullivan and Gerald Gunther, *Constitutional Law*, 14th ed. (New York: Foundation Press, 2001), 24–25.

175. *Brown v. Board of Education*, (*Brown I*), 347 U.S. 483 (1954).

176. *E pluribus unum*, the Latin phrase meaning "out of many, one," is the motto of the United States of America.

177. *Planned Parenthood of Southeastern Pennsylvania v. Casey*, 844–845.

178. Ibid., 846.

179. Ibid., 846–853.

180. *Loving v. Virginia*, 388 U.S. 1 (1967); *Griswold v. Connecticut*, 381 U.S. 479 (1965); *Eisenstadt v. Baird*, 405 U.S. 438 (1972); *Carey v. Population Services International*, 431 U.S. 678 (1977).

181. *Planned Parenthood of Southeastern Pennsylvania v. Casey*, 848–849.

182. Ibid., 850.

183. Ibid., 853.

184. Ibid., 852.

185. Ibid., 854.

186. *Plessy v. Ferguson*, 163 U.S. 537 (1896); *Lochner v. New York*, 198 U.S. 45 (1905).

187. *Planned Parenthood of Southeastern Pennsylvania v. Casey*, 855–857, 860.

188. Ibid., 867.

189. Ibid.

190. *Bellotti v. Baird* (*Bellotti I*), 428 U.S. 132 (1976).

191. Ibid., 145, 147–148.

192. R. Alta Charo, "Life after *Casey*: The View from Rehnquist's Potemkin Village," *Journal of Law, Medicine, and Ethics* 21, no. 1 (1993): 59–66. The "Potemkin Village"

reference is to sham villages supposedly created by Catherine the Great's favorite, Grigori Alexandrovich Potemkin, to make her think her subjects were prosperous and happy.

193. David Broder, "The Scalia Model," *Washington Post*, 29 June 2004.

194. Dale Singer, "Webster Sees Hope for Upholding Abortion Curbs," *St. Louis Post-Dispatch*, 20 September 1986.

195. Greenhouse, "A Telling Opinion."

196. Ibid.

197. *Planned Parenthood of Southeastern Pennsylvania v. Casey*, 844.

198. Greenhouse, "A Telling Opinion."

199. *Planned Parenthood of Southeastern Pennsylvania v. Casey*, 923.

200. Greenhouse, "A Telling Opinion."

201. Ibid.

202. William Colby, *Long Goodbye: The Deaths of Nancy Cruzan* (Carlsbad, CA: Hay House, 2002), 181–186.

203. Unless otherwise noted, the quoted material and descriptions of the facts of the Schiavo case are taken from Kathy Cermin and Kenneth Goodman, "Key Events in the Case of Theresa Marie Schiavo," Joint Project of University of Miami Ethics Program and Shepard Brood Law Center, 6 April 2005, available at www.miami .edu/ethics2/schiavo/timeline.htm.

204. Adult children, if any, would have been the appropriate guardians in the absence of a spouse. Parents' rights as guardians were thus superseded.

205. Letter of Bob Schindler to Michael Schiavo, 29 November 2004, available at http://journals.aol.com/shjusticeforall/SavingTerriSchiavo/entries/844.

206. "U.S. S. Ct. Refuses on Oct. 15, 2003 to Hear Schiavo Case." See *In re: Guardianship of Schiavo*, 855 So. 2d. 621 (Fla. 2003).

207. Steven Ertelt, "Florida Senate Passes 'Terri's Bill,' Gov. Bush Will Sign Legislation," *LifeNews.com*, www.lifenews.com/bio102.html, 21 October 2003.

208. David E. Sanger, "Bush Backs His Brother's Decision in Feeding Tube Case," *New York Times*, 29 October 2003.

209. "Vatican Appeals for Terri Schiavo's Life," 14 March 2005, available at www.apfn.net/messageboard/03-14-05/discussion.cgi.11.html. See also Kathleen O'Dell, "Pope Declares Feeding Tube is a Moral Obligation," *Springfield* (Missouri) *News-Leader*, 2 April 2004.

210. *Bush v. Schiavo*, 885 So. 2. 321 (Fla. 2004).

211. Abby Goodnough, "Feed-Tube Law Is Struck Down in Florida Case," *New York Times*, 24 September 2004. See also *Bush v. Schiavo*, 885 So. 2. 321 (Fla. 2004).

212. "Gov. Bush Appeals to Supreme Court on Schiavo Case," *CNN.com Law Center*, www.cnn.com/2004/LAW/12/01/schiavo.supreme.court/index.html, 1 December 2004. See also "U.S. Supreme Court Turns Down Appeal," *Bush v. Schiavo*, 125 S. Ct. 1086 (January 24, 2005).

213. *Bush v. Schiavo*, 125 S. Court 1086 (January 24, 2005).

214. Elaine C. Cassel, "The Terri Schiavo Case: Congress Rushes in Where Only Courts Should Tread," *FindLaw*, http://writ.news.findlaw.com/cassel/20050324.html, 24 March 2005. See also David Kirkpatrick and Sheryl Gay Stolberg, "How Family's Cause Reached the Halls of Congress," *New York Times*, 22 March 2005.

215. Kirkpatrick and Stolberg, "How Family's Cause."

216. Hope Yen, "Supreme Court Won't Hear Schiavo Case," March 25, 2005, http://sfgate.com/cgi-bin/article.cgi?file=/n/a/2005/03/24/national/w072914S58 .DTL.

217. Jerald Hill (former president, Landmark Legal Foundation), interview by the author, 15 June 2005. See also Dana Milbank, "Legal Experts Say Parents are Unlikely to Prevail," *Washington Post*, 22 March 2005.

218. *Theresa Marie Schindler Schiavo, incapacitated ex rel. Robert Schindler and Mary Schindler, her parents and next friends v. Michael Schiavo, Judge George Greer and The Hospice of the Florida Suncoast, Inc.*, 357 F. Supp 2d 1378 (M.D. Fla. 2005)

219. *Schiavo ex rel. Schindler v. Schiavo*, 403 F. 3d 129, 2005 U.S. App (11 Cir Fla., March 25 2005). See also 403 F 3d 1223; 2005 U.S. App (11 Cir Fla., March 25, 2005)

220. See "Five Members of the U.S. House of Representatives Ask the U.S. Supreme Court to File a 'Friend of the Court' Brief on March 28, 2005," U.S. Supreme Court Docket, Case No. 04A825, www.supremecourtus.gov/docket/04a825.htm.

221. The first time the U.S. Supreme Court turned down the Schindlers' appeal was April 20, 2001, when Justice Anthony Kennedy refused to send the appeal to the whole Court. Kennedy was the justice assigned responsibility for this part of the country. The following citations trace the subsequent refusals of the Supreme Court to hear appeals:

- *Bush v. Schiavo*, 125 S. Ct. 1086 (January 24, 2005)
- *Schindler v. Schiavo*, 125 S. Ct. 1622 (March 17, 2005)
- On March 18, 2005, the Court refused the House of Representatives requests for subpoena for Terri Schiavo and Michael Schiavo.
- *Schiavo ex rel. Schindler v. Schiavo*, 125 S. Ct. 1692 (March 4, 2005)
- *Schiavo ex rel. Schindler v. Schiavo*, 125 S. Ct. 1722 (March 30, 2005)

Epilogue

The twentieth century closed with apparent victories for privacy rights causes: a right to have and use birth control drugs and devices, a right to a choice of sexual intimacies that create a family and home, a right to end a pregnancy, and a right to die.[1] The twenty-first century, however, opened with new and intensified challenges to the scope of privacy rights. In each area, new questions and issues arose to challenge these privacy victories.

Do American women have an effective constitutional right to possess and use birth control drugs and devices? *Griswold v. Connecticut* had said so, but *Griswold* had not laid out a list of appropriate and legal drugs and devices for preventing contraception. Each new drug, pill, or contraceptive device was therefore a potential target for a constitutional attack either as a health risk or as a mislabeled abortifacient. The "morning after" pill was one such issue.

Ordinary birth control pills, when taken in two heavy doses, may interfere with ovulation or prevent implantation of a fertilized egg. Used for this purpose, the doses may be taken up to seventy-two hours after sexual intercourse and still have a high degree of success. "Emergency contraception kits" also became increasingly popular. So packaged, the drug, Preven, had been recommended by an independent review board of the Food and Drug Administration (FDA) for over-the-counter sales, no prescription required. But in May 2004, the FDA denied approval. Usually the FDA follows the recommendation of its advisory panels, but in this case it gave way to pressure from the Bush administration and refused approval. Raising restrictive barriers such as age, maturity, and education of the user, the FDA in this instance had limited a woman's right to birth control.[2] What effect will aggressive marketing of RU-486, a nonsurgical abortifacient, have on the already blurred line between contraception and abortion?[3]

"What issue will define the work of the Supreme Court in the twenty-first century?" This question was directed to Justice Sandra Day O'Connor during a month-long educational series televised by C-SPAN in May 2003. Her answer was clear and unequivocal: "Cases . . . relating to how homosexuals are treated legally."[4] Clearly the cause won for gay rights in *Lawrence v. Texas* would not go unchallenged.

Even before the Supreme Court announced the reversal of *Bowers* and the establishment of constitutional protection for homosexual couples on June 26, 2003, various state legislatures were acting to impose limits and regulate the exercise of these rights. While many state courts had established protection for those pursuing a homosexual lifestyle,[5] state legislatures expressed their hostility to the Supreme Court's insistence on "respect for the private lives and private sexual conduct of adults engaged in a homosexual lifestyle." Three-quarters of states had soon enacted laws to define marriage as the "union between a man and a woman."[6] Congress had already entered the fray with the passage of the Defense of Marriage Act in 1996. Proposals for both federal and state constitutional amendments to reinforce this restriction on marriage gained momentum.[7]

The win for protection for gays in *Lawrence* had a negative impact on public opinion. Polls showed support for gay rights on the issues of Social Security benefits, joint-tax filings, inheritance, estate, and property decisions. However, gay marriage with its possible component of adoption and child rearing generated a negative response. The Court's specific assurance that the *Lawrence* decision "does not involve whether the government must give formal recognition to any relationship that homosexual persons seek to enter" fell on deaf ears.

What impact would state refusals to allow same-sex marriages or to recognize those which other states might allow have on the guarantee of the Constitution's Article IV, the "full faith and credit" clause? Courts would most certainly have to face this question. The Founders had insisted that each state must grant full faith and recognition to the public acts, records, and judicial proceedings of every other state. Would this essential part of American federalism become a victim in the battle for privacy rights for gays? It could, as Justice O'Connor stated, be a major focus for the nation's courts in the twenty-first century and a defining issue for the Supreme Court.

The right to abortion came under a different type of attack in the years following *Casey*. Abortion opponents decided to attack the methods used in performing abortions, and suddenly state and national legislators became experts in discussing the medical techniques available for surgical abortions. The focus was on a particular method denigrated by abortion opponents as "partial birth abortion," the proper medical term being "intact dilation and extraction" or "D and X." It differs from the older procedure known as "dilation and evacuation" or "D and E" in that the "D and X" procedure removes the fetus as a whole, while in the "D and E" procedure parts of the fetus are removed separately. This type of attack on abortion techniques permitted a detailed description of a gruesome surgery. Medical and individual privacy rights were pushed aside as graphic illustrations of a bloody and invasive surgery made daily headlines. On the floors of state legislative houses, in television specials and news interviews, the language in and of itself generated revulsion.[8]

It was 1995 and the pro-choice gains made during the first two years of the Clinton administration had been halted by the 1994 midyear election. A Republican-controlled House and Senate were prepared to confront the reproductive choice issue. They focused on the so-called partial birth techniques and introduced legislation to criminalize the procedure. States then followed suit. One state, in particular, Nebraska, made legal history with litigation of its law banning partial birth abortion. A Nebraska physician, Dr. LeRoy Carhart, challenged the law, and the case soon made its way to the U.S. Supreme Court.

The constitutional question in *Stenberg v. Carhart* was clear: Did an absolute ban on one form of abortion technique constitute an "undue" burden on a woman's right to choose as guaranteed by *Casey*?[9] Had the Nebraska legislature been willing to include an exception in the ban—allowing a doctor to use it not only if life were endangered but also if health were at risk— the Court might have upheld the law. But Nebraska's legislature had refused to provide for a "health"-related exception to the ban; Missouri's legislature and those of a number of other states had likewise adopted this language. The Supreme Court by a vote of 5–4 struck down the "partial birth abortion ban" as an unconstitutional burden on the right to exercise reproductive choice. It was Justice O'Connor's concurrence that stressed the major reason: the lack of an exception for health.[10]

Yet Congress refused to take notice of the Court's ruling and its advice. A bill almost exactly like that of Nebraska's passed both houses of Congress and was signed into law by President George W. Bush in 2004. The legislature and the executive had "thrown down the gauntlet" in a direct challenge to the judiciary. The bill declared, "Congress is far better equipped than the judiciary to amass and evaluate" evidence about using the "D and X" technique; the method is "never medically indicated to preserve the health of the mother," the bill continued. Ignoring the Court's holding and reasoning in *Stenberg v. Carhart*, the legislative and executive branches disregarded the Court. Once again the judicial process would be called upon to either overturn or legitimize a restrictive regulation on reproductive choice rights.

Since the older "D and E" method and the "D and X" method both involved common elements, the attack was far broader than most Americans realized. Moreover, the law certainly required intense scrutiny of doctors performing abortions. Political ideology had overridden medical concerns. The effect of the law and questions about it coalesced into legal challenges in federal courts in San Francisco, New York, and once again Nebraska.

The first ruling came on June 2, 2004. Federal district judge Phyllis J. Hamilton in San Francisco struck down the Partial Birth Abortion Ban Act, giving three reasons: the law placed an undue burden on women seeking abortion; the language in the statute was "dangerously vague"; and the law "lacked a required exception for medical actions needed to preserve the woman's health." As Judge Hamilton noted, the procedure is "a variant of and in some ways safer than the most common form of abortion used in the second trimester of pregnancy," and it could apply to ban the "D and E" abortions as well as those designated "D and X."[11]

A second ruling followed suit: U.S. district judge Richard C. Casey dealt another blow to the Partial Birth Abortion Ban Act on August 26, 2004. The New York judge "faulted the ban for not containing an exception to protect a woman's health, something the Supreme Court had made clear is required in a law prohibiting a particular type of abortion."[12] The third ruling on September 9, 2004, confirmed the former two. U.S. District Judge Richard Kopf of Lincoln, Nebraska, agreed with his colleagues, saying Congress had ignored the "most experienced doctors" when it determined that the banned procedure would never be necessary to protect the health of the mother.[13]

Will the Supreme Court hear the question? Generally, the Court acts only when lower federal courts disagree. Such is not the case here; nevertheless, the issue remains.

The last of all privacy rights, the right to die, still generates controversy as intense and enduring as the right-to-life issue. The Schiavo case had confirmed a privacy right to die. However, the controversy took on another dimension. Did this right belong only to those who had executed end-of-life choices in a medical directive and a durable power of attorney? Otherwise, should the state have powers to decide? These disputes continued after Terri Schiavo's death.

At both a private family level and at the public level, attempts to sway public opinion continued and intensified. At the private level, questions focused around Terri's husband, Michael. Had Michael Schiavo been a loving husband or was he a "prince of darkness"? Should he have been allowed to refuse Terri's parents the right to be at her bedside when she died? Should Michael Schiavo have prevailed in his plan to cremate Terri's body when her parents wanted her embalmed? The family had argued over the place of burial: Michael's family plot in Pennsylvania or the Schindlers' in Florida. Michael had agreed to a burial in Florida. Yet there was no peace. The family split, once again, on the autopsy report. The report had confirmed that Terri was in a persistent vegetative state with a "withered brain" and unable to be helped by therapy. Moreover, she was blind. The Schindlers refused to accept these findings.[14]

At the public level, lawmakers also argued. Senate Majority Leader Bill Frist wanted to forget that he had diagnosed Terri Schiavo from afar and had said she was not a persistent vegetative state (PVS) case, but he was confronted by his own words to the contrary on video. House Majority Leader Tom DeLay, while apologizing for some of his inflammatory rhetoric, nevertheless continued to call for judicial impeachments, beginning with Justice Anthony Kennedy, who had first received the Schindlers' appeals. "The legal system did not protect the people who needed protection most, and this will change," DeLay promised. Calling the judges "arrogant and out of control," DeLay threatened investigations of "a judiciary that dares to thumb its nose at Congress and the President."[15]

In Florida, Governor Jeb Bush attempted to launch another inquiry into the Schiavo case. The governor asked the state prosecutor to investigate "the possible gap between the time when Ms. Schiavo fell unconscious and the time when her husband called the paramedics."[16] However, on July 8, 2005, Governor Bush retreated from his position. When Florida's state attorney informed the governor that "there is no evidence that criminal activity was involved [in the collapse of Terri Schiavo]," Bush stopped the investigation. In a terse two-sentence letter he wrote, "I follow the recommendation that the inquiry by the state be closed." The state, to the dismay of the Schindlers, did not consult them and, moreover, ended the investigation's report citing "an eating disorder" as the cause of Terri's collapse.[17]

Some states considered making changes in their post-*Cruzan* laws concerning the right to die. The new laws targeted those without a medical directive or a durable power of attorney document expressing end-of-life intent. Some states discussed requiring doctors to provide and maintain feeding tubes for all PVS patients without these documents. Even though the American Medical Association had gone on record opposing such laws, some conservatives pushed for their enactment.[18]

The Republican Party began to divide on this issue. John Danforth, Missouri's former senator and an ex-ambassador to the United Nations, also opposed governmental intervention in end-of-life decisions. A Yale Law School graduate and an Episcopal priest, Danforth had spearheaded the Republicans' takeover of Missouri's political system. He was a highly regarded GOP leader. Nevertheless, Danforth launched a personal crusade against the "Religious Right," which, he warned, had come to dominate the Republican Party. Danforth publicly supported Terri Schiavo's right to die and also praised the actions of the Cruzan family in their struggle to gain Nancy Cruzan's right to die. Danforth feared that if moral and religious views about the right to die and other privacy issues controlled the political process, "they would turn the country into a theocracy."[19] He urged his party and all Americans to remember that the country's founders had embraced separation of church and state precisely because of the discord created when government was controlled by religious ideologies with a social and political agenda.

Other political leaders agreed that the Schiavo case and the right-to-die issue would impact future elections. Some thought that the Republican Party would suffer as a result; others believed that the party's uncompromising commitment to a "culture of life" would only increase Republican dominance.

Only one thing was clear. The issue of a right to die was still not settled. In fact, it had expanded into a bigger issue: Is there a right to physician-assisted suicide? Americans fear death. They want "palliative care" necessary to alleviate pain. Some even want a doctor to help them to avoid pain even though it might hasten their death. Most states, however, had laws prohibiting physician-assisted suicide, and the Supreme Court has upheld such laws.[20] Nevertheless, Oregon voters have twice enacted laws allowing physician-assisted suicide. It was Attorney General John Ashcroft's challenge of these laws that the Supreme Court agreed to hear. Under pressure because it refused to intervene in the *Schiavo* case, the U.S. Supreme Court would continue to face a tide of expectations concerning the scope and power of the judicial branch to settle issues of life and death.

The divisions in American society are mirrored in these new questions about privacy issues as they work their way through the ins and outs of the judicial process. What kind of differences will this debate make? Will it perhaps reinforce the belief in the rule of law? Will it create a calm, balanced, open political system where respect for rights creates civility and respect even for the "thoughts and actions" we hate? The privacy issues litigation of the twenty-first century will ultimately answer this question, for better or worse. A polarized society may yet relearn the art of compromise.

NOTES

1. Guaranteed, respectively, by *Griswold v. Connecticut,* 381 U.S. 479 (1965); *Lawrence v. Texas,* 539 U.S. 558 (2003); *Planned Parenthood of Southeastern Pennsylvania v. Casey,* 505 U.S. 833; and *Schiavo ex rel. Schindler v. Schiavo,* 125 S. Ct. 1722 (March 30, 2005).

2. Gardiner Harris, "U.S. Rules Morning-After Pill Can't Be Sold Over-the-Counter," *New York Times,* 7 May 2004.

3. RU-486 has long been used in Europe. According to David Garrow, "The drug, Mifepristone, impedes a fertilized egg from attaching to the uterine wall. However it can only be used effectively during the first eight or nine weeks of pregnancy. The first dose has to be followed by oral or vaginal application of a second drug, Misoprostol, to trigger uterine contraction" (*Liberty and Sexuality: The Right to Privacy*

and the Making of Roe v. Wade, rev. ed. [Berkeley: University of California Press, 1998], 709). Classified as a "medical miscarriage," it seems to many to be more natural than surgical abortion, but is still an involved procedure. Contract disputes over the manufacture of RU-486 have slowed down the production and distribution of the drug.

4. "Supreme Court Justice: Gay Rights Cases on the Increase," *USA Today*, 1 May 2003.

5. For example, *Commonwealth v. Wasson*, 842 S.W. 2d 487 (Ky. 1992).

6. "States Firmly Behind Traditional Marriage," *Lancaster* (Pennsylvania) *New Era*, 13 November 2004.

7. "Reproductive Rights Assaulted," *New York Times*, 5 April 2004.

8. "Rep. Roscoe Bartlett Praises End to Hideous Partial Birth Abortion," *Congressional Record Online*, 2 October 2003, H9135–9155; available at http://frwebgate5.access.gpo.gov/cgi-bin/waisgate.cgi?. See also "Pelosi Democrats Wrong on Partial-Birth Abortion," RNC Research Briefing, 6 November 2003, available at www.freerepublic.com/focus/f-news/1016109/posts; this article quotes from a debate of January 2003 and describes the procedure in its most gruesome details.

9. *Stenberg v. Carhart*, 530 U.S. 914 (2000).

10. Ibid., 950.

11. Adam Liptak, "Judge Rejects Ban on Abortion Procedure," *St. Louis Post-Dispatch*, 2 June 2004.

12. "Second Federal Judge Finds 'Partial Birth Abortion' Ban Unconstitutional," *St. Louis Post-Dispatch*, 27 August 2004.

13. "Third Judge Rules Against Abortion Ban," *Springfield* (Missouri) *News-Leader*, 9 September 2004.

14. Abby Goodnough, "Schiavo Autopsy Says Brain, Withered, Was Untreatable," *New York Times*, 16 June 2005.

15. Jennifer Loven, "DeLay Targets Legal System in Schiavo Case," *ABCNews.com*, http://abcnews.go.com/Politics/print?id=630508, 31 March 2005.

16. Abby Goodnough, "Gov. Bush Seeks Another Inquiry in Schiavo Case," *New York Times*, 18 June 2005.

17. David Royse, "Gov. Bush Ends Inquiry Into Schiavo's Collapse," Associated Press, 8 July 2003, available at www.hcraldtribune.com/apps/pbcs.dll/article?AID=/20050708/BREAKING/50708009.

18. Peggy Peck, "AMA Faces Issues of Schiavo Replays," *MedPage Today*, www.medpagetoday.com/tbprint.cfm?tbid=1216, 20 June 2005.

19. John C. Danforth, "Onward Moderate Christian Soldiers," *New York Times*, 17 June 2005.

20 *Washington v. Glucksberg*, 512 U.S. 702 (1997).

Bibliography

Alderman, Ellen, and Caroline Kennedy. *The Right to Privacy*. New York: Alfred A. Knopf, 1995; Vintage Press, 1997.

Baron, Charles H. "Abortion and Legal Process in the United States: An Overview of Post-*Webster* Legal Landscape." *Law, Medicine, and Healthcare* 17, no. 4 (1989): 368–375.

Bartee, Alice Fleetwood. *Cases Lost, Causes Won: The Supreme Court and the Judicial Process*. New York: St. Martin's, 1984.

———. "Reinventing Privacy Rights in Missouri: The Right to Die Case." In *Reinventing Missouri Government: Case Studies in State Experiments at Work,* ed. Denny Pilant, 97–145. Fort Worth, TX: Harcourt Brace, 1994.

Bartee, Wayne C., and Alice Fleetwood Bartee. *Litigating Morality: American Legal Thought and Its English Roots*. New York: Praeger, 1993.

Becker, Theodore L., and Malcolm M. Feeley, eds. *The Impact of Supreme Court Decisions*. 2nd ed. New York: Oxford University Press, 1973.

Behuniak-Long, Susan. "Friendly Fire: Amicus Curiae and *Webster v. Reproductive Health Systems*." *Judicature* 74 (February–March 1991): 261–270.

Bickel, Alexander. *The Least Dangerous Branch: The Supreme Court at the Bar of Politics*. Indianapolis, IN: Bobbs-Merrill, 1962.

Binion, Rudolph. *Defeated Leaders: The Political Fate of Caillaux, Jouvenel, and Tardieu*. Morningside Heights, NY: Columbia University Press, 1960.

Bork, Robert. "Neutral Principles and Some First Amendment Problems." *Indiana Law Journal* 47 (Fall 1971): 416–421.

———. *The Tempting of America*. New York: Free Press, 1989.

Brisbin, Richard A., Jr. "The Conservatism of Antonin Scalia." *Political Science Quarterly* 105, no. 1 (Spring 1990): 1–29.

Brown, Cynthia, ed. *Lost Liberties: Ashcroft and the Assault on Personal Freedom*. New York: New Press, 2003.

Canon, Bradley C., and Charles A. Johnson. *Judicial Policies: Implementation and Impact.* 2nd ed. Washington, DC: CQ Press, 1999.

Caplan, Lincoln. *The Tenth Justice: The Solicitor General and the Rule of Law.* New York: Alfred A. Knopf, 1987.

Charo, R. Alta. "Life after *Casey*: The View from Rehnquist's Potemkin Village." *Journal of Law, Medicine, and Ethics* 21, no. 1 (1993): 59–66.

Colby, William H. "The Lessons of the *Cruzan* Case." *University of Kansas Law Review* 39 (Spring 1991): 519–529.

———. *Long Goodbye: The Deaths of Nancy Cruzan.* Carlsbad, CA: Hay House, 2002.

Cook, Beverly B., "Justice Sandra Day O'Connor: Transition to a Republican Court Agenda." In *The Burger Court: Political and Judicial Profiles,* ed. Charles Lamb and Stephen Halpern, 242–271. Urbana: University of Illinois, 1991.

Cordray, Richard A., and James T. Vradelis. "The Emerging Jurisprudence of Justice O'Connor." *University of Chicago Law Review* 52 (Spring 1985): 389–459.

Craig, Barbara Hinkson, and David O'Brien. *Abortion and American Politics.* Chatham, NJ: Chatham House, 1993.

D'Emilio, John, and Estelle B. Freedman. *Intimate Matters: A History of Sexuality in America.* 2nd ed. Chicago: University of Chicago Press, 1997.

Dickson, Del, ed. *The Supreme Court in Conference, 1940–1985: The Private Discussions behind Nearly 300 Supreme Court Decisions.* New York: Oxford University Press, 2001.

Dixon, Robert G. "The *Griswold* Penumbra: Constitutional Charter for Expanded Right of Privacy?" *Michigan Law Review* 64 (1965): 197–218.

Douglas, William O. *The Court Years, 1939–1975: The Autobiography of William O. Douglas.* New York: Random House, 1980.

Dripps, Donald A. "*Bowers v. Hardwick* and the Law of Standing: Non Cases Make Bad Law," *Emory Law Journal* 44 (Fall 1995): 1417.

Dudziak, Mary. "Just Say No: Birth Control in the Connecticut Supreme Court before *Griswold v. Connecticut.*" *Iowa Law Review* 75 (May 1990): 915–939.

Dugan, Thomas S. *The Catholic Church in Connecticut.* New York: States History, 1930.

Easton, David. *A Framework for Political Analysis.* Englewood Cliffs, NJ: Prentice-Hall, 1965.

———. *The Political System.* New York: Alfred A. Knopf, 1953.

———. *A Systems Analysis of Political Life.* New York: Wiley & Sons, 1965.

Eisler, Kim. *A Justice for All: William J. Brennan, Jr., and the Decisions That Transformed America.* New York: Simon & Schuster, 1993.

Ely, James W., Jr. *The Chief Justiceship of Melville W. Fuller, 1888–1910.* Columbia: University of South Carolina Press, 1995.

Epstein, Lee, and Jack Knight. *The Choices Justices Make.* Washington, DC: CQ Press, 1998.

Ernst, Morris. "How We Nullify." *Nation* 134 (27 January 1932): 113–114.

Fried, Charles. *Order and Law: Arguing the Reagan Revolution; A Firsthand Account.* New York: Simon & Schuster, 1991.

Garrow, David J. "Justice Souter: A Surprising Kind of Conservative," *New York Times Magazine,* 25 September 1994.

———. "A Landmark Decision." *Dissent* 39 (Fall 1992): 427–729.

———. *Liberty and Sexuality: The Right to Privacy and the Making of* Roe v. Wade. Rev. ed. Berkeley: University of California Press, 1998.

Goldman, Roger. *Justice William J. Brennan, Jr.: Freedom First.* With David Gallen. New York: Carroll & Graf, 1994.

Gunther, Gerald, and Gerhard Casper, eds. *Landmark Briefs and Arguments of the Supreme Court of the United States: Constitutional Law.* Vol. 68, *Bowers v. Hardwick.* [Washington, DC]: University Publications of America, 1975.

Harlan, John M. "The Role of Oral Argument." In *The Supreme Court: Views from Inside,* ed. Alan F. Westin, 57–65. New York: W. W. Norton, 1961.

Harper, Fowler V. *Mr. Justice Rutledge and the Bright Constellation.* Indianapolis, IN: Bobbs-Merrill, 1965.

Hasian, Marouf A., Jr., and Trevor Parry-Giles. "A Stranger to Its Laws: Freedom, Civil Rights, and the Legal Ambiguity of *Romer v. Evans.*" *Argumentation and Advocacy* 34, no. 1 (1997): 27–43.

Henly, Burr. "Penumbra: The Roots of a Legal Metaphor." *Hastings Constitutional Law Quarterly* 15 (Fall 1987): 81–100.

Hentoff, N. "Profile: The Constitutionalist," *New Yorker,* March 1990.

Howard, J. Woodford. *Mr. Justice Murphy: A Political Biography.* Princeton, NJ: Princeton University Press, 1968.

Irons, Peter. *The Courage of Their Convictions.* New York: Free Press, 1988.

Jefferies, John C., Jr. *Justice Lewis F. Powell, Jr.* New York: C. Scribner's Sons, 1994.

Kauper, Paul G. "Penumbras, Peripheries, Emanations, Things Fundamental and Things Forgotten: The *Griswold* Case." *Michigan Law Review* 64 (December 1965): 235–258.

Kurland, Philip B., and Gerhard Casper, eds. *Landmark Briefs and Arguments of the Supreme Court of the United States: Constitutional Law.* Vol. 61, *Griswold v. Connecticut.* Washington, DC: University Publications of America, 1975.

Lerner, Max. *Nine Scorpions in a Bottle: Great Justices and Cases of the Supreme Court,* ed. Richard Cummings. New York: Arcade, 1994.

Lieberman, Jethro K. *The Litigious Society.* New York: Basic Books, 1981.

Lunardini, Christine A. *From Equal Suffrage to Equal Rights.* New York: New York University Press, 1986.

Lusky, Louis. *Our Nine Tribunes: The Supreme Court in Modern America.* New York: Praeger, 1993.

Mason, Alpheus T. *Harlan Fiske Stone: Pillar of the Law.* New York: Viking Press, 1956.

———. *William Howard Taft, Chief Justice.* New York: Simon & Schuster, 1965.

Mauro, Tony. "Justices, 6–3, Strike Texas Sodomy Law." *New York Law Journal* 229 (27 June 2003): 1.

McBeth, H. Leon. *The Baptist Heritage.* Nashville, TN: Broadman Press, 1987.

McCloskey, Robert G. *The American Supreme Court.* Chicago: University of Chicago Press, 1960.

McElwain, Edwin. "The Business of the Supreme Court as Conducted by Chief Justice Hughes." *Harvard Law Review* 63 (1949): 5.

McGuigan, Patrick B., and Dawn M. Weyrick. *Ninth Justice: The Fight for Bork.* Washington, DC: Free Congress Research and Education Foundation, 1990.

Murphy, Walter F. *Elements of Judicial Strategy.* Chicago: University of Chicago Press, 1964.

Murphy, Walter F., and C. Herman Pritchett, eds. *Courts, Judges, and Politics: An Introduction to the Judicial Process*. New York: Random House, 1961.

O'Brien, David M. "The Politics of Professionalism: President Gerald R. Ford's Appointment of Justice John Paul Stevens." *Presidential Studies Quarterly* 21, no. 1 (Winter 1991): 103–127.

Pollack, Harriet. "An Uncommonly Silly Law: The Connecticut Birth Control Cases in the U.S. Supreme Court." Ph.D. diss., Columbia University, 1967.

Posner, Richard. *The Federal Courts: Crisis and Reform*. Cambridge, MA: Harvard University Press, 1985.

———. *Sex and Reason*. Cambridge, MA: Harvard University Press, 1992.

Powell, Lewis F., Jr. "What Really Goes On at the Supreme Court." *New York State Bar Journal* 52 (1980): 454–459.

Pursey, Merlo J. *Charles Evans Hughes*. New York: Macmillan, 1951.

Rehnquist, William H. *The Supreme Court: How It Was, How It Is*. New York: Morrow, 1987.

———. "Who Writes Decisions of the Supreme Court?" *U.S. News and World Report*, 13 December 1957.

Rohde, David, and Harold Spaeth. *Supreme Court Decision Making*. San Francisco: Freeman, 1976.

Rosen, Jeffrey. "The Leader of the Opposition: The Tortuous Jurisprudence of Antonin Scalia." *New Republic* 208, no. 3 (18 January 2003): 20–25.

Rosenkranz, E. Joshua, and Bernard Schwartz. *Reason and Passion: Justice Brennan's Enduring Influence*. New York: Norton, 1997.

Salokar, Rebecca Mae. *The Solicitor General: Politics of Law*. Philadelphia: Temple University Press, 1992.

Samar, Vincent J. "The Supremes and Gay Rights: A Closer Look at *Lawrence v. Texas*." *In These Times*, 1 July 2003, www.inthesetimes.com/site/archivesmain/article/596.

Savage, David D. *Turning Right: The Making of the Rehnquist Supreme Court*. New York: Wiley, 1992.

Scalia, Antonin. "Commentary: The Decision as Cure." *Washington Law Quarterly* (1979): 147–157.

Schubert, Glendon. *Constitutional Politics: The Political Behavior of Supreme Court Justices and the Constitutional Policies They Make*. New York: Holt, Rinehart, & Winston, 1960.

Schwartz, Bernard. *Super Chief: Earl Warren and His Supreme Court*. New York: New York University Press, 1983.

Sheldon, Charles H. *The American Judicial Process: Models and Approaches*. New York: Dodd, Mead, 1976.

Simon, James F. *The Center Holds: The Power Struggle inside the Rehnquist Court*. New York: Simon & Schuster, 1995.

———. *In His Own Image: The Supreme Court in Richard Nixon's America*. New York: D. McKay, 1973.

Sine, Tom. *Cease Fire: Searching for Sanity in America's Culture Wars*. Grand Rapids, MI: Eerdmans, 1995.

Snyder, Eloise. "The Supreme Court as a Small Group." *Social Forces* 36 (March 1958): 232–238.

Sullivan, Kathleen M., and Gerald Gunther. *Constitutional Law.* 14th ed. New York: Foundation Press, 2001.

Toobin, Jeffrey. "Supreme Sacrifice." In *Portraits of American Politics,* ed. Bruce Allen Murphy, 420–428. 3rd ed. Boston: Houghton Mifflin, 2000.

Tribe, Laurence. *American Constitutional Law.* 2nd ed. Mineola, NY: Foundation Press, 1988.

Tushnet, Mark. *Making Civil Rights Law: Thurgood Marshall and the Supreme Court, 1961–1991.* New York: Oxford University Press, 1997.

United States Senate, Committee on the Judiciary. *The Supreme Court of the United States: Hearings and Reports on Successful and Unsuccessful Nominations of Supreme Court Justices by the Senate Judiciary Committee, 1916–1972,* comp. Roy M. Mersky and J. Myron Jacobstein, vol. 8. Buffalo, NY: W. S. Hein, 1974.

Van Geel, T. R. *Understanding Supreme Court Opinions.* 3rd ed. New York: Longman, 2002.

Wardle, Lynn D. "The Road to Moderation: The Significance of *Webster* for Legislation Restricting Abortion." *Journal of Law, Medicine, and Health Care* 17, no. 4 (Winter 1989): 376–383.

Warren, Samuel, and Louis D. Brandeis. "The Right to Privacy." *Harvard Law Review* 4 (1890): 193.

Wasby, Stephen L, ed. *"He Shall Not Pass This Way Again": The Legacy of Justice William O. Douglas.* Pittsburgh: University of Pittsburgh Press, 1990.

———. *The Impact of the United States Supreme Court.* Homewood, IL: Dorsey Press, 1970.

———. *The Supreme Court in the Federal Judicial System.* 4th ed. Chicago: Nelson-Hall, 1993.

———. "Toward a Theory of Impact." In *The Impact of Supreme Court Decisions,* ed. Theodore L. Becker and Malcolm M. Feeley, 2nd ed., 214–217. New York: Oxford University Press, 1973.

Westin, Alan F. *Privacy and Freedom.* New York: Atheneum Press, 1967.

Woodward, Bob, and Scott Armstrong. *The Brethren: Inside the Supreme Court.* New York: Simon & Schuster, 1979.

Index

About the Author

Alice Fleetwood Bartee is professor of political science at Missouri State University. Professor Bartee's research and teaching interests include constitutional law, civil liberties, and the judicial process. She has authored two books, *Cases Lost, Causes Won* (1984) and *Litigating Morality: American Legal Thought and Its English Roots* (1992), and has contributed a chapter in *Reinventing Missouri Government*. She has also written two articles for the *Yale Biographical Dictionary of American Law* (forthcoming) and three articles for the *Oxford Companion to the Supreme Court of the United States* (2005).